A SHORT HISTORY OF THE MIDDLE AGES

A SHORT HISTORY OF THE MIDDLE AGES

VOLUME I: FROM *c.*300 TO *c.*1150

BARBARA H. ROSENWEIN

FIFTH EDITION

UNIVERSITY OF TORONTO PRESS

Toronto Buffalo London

utorontopress.com

Library and Archives Canada Cataloguing in Publication

Rosenwein, Barbara H., author
A short history of the Middle Ages / Barbara H. Rosenwein. — Fifth edition.

Also published together in one complete volume.
Includes bibliographical references and indexes.
Contents: v. 1. From c.300 to c.1150.
Issued in print and electronic formats.
ISBN 978-1-4426-3626-2 (v. 1: softcover).—ISBN 978-1-4426-3627-9 (v. 1: PDF).—
ISBN 978-1-4426-3628-6 (v. 1: HTML)

1. Middle Ages. 2. Europe—History—476-1492. I. Title.

D117.R67 2018b 940.1 C2018-901197-1
C2018-901198-X

We welcome comments and suggestions regarding any aspect of our publications—please feel free to contact us at news@utphighereducation.com or visit our Internet site at www.utorontopress.com.

North America
5201 Dufferin Street
North York, Ontario, Canada, M3H 5T8

2250 Military Road
Tonawanda, New York, USA, 14150

ORDERS PHONE: 1–800–565–9523
ORDERS FAX: 1–800–221–9985
ORDERS E-MAIL: utpbooks@utpress.utoronto.ca

UK, Ireland, and continental Europe
NBN International
Estover Road, Plymouth, PL6 7PY, UK

ORDERS PHONE: 44 (0) 1752 202301
ORDERS FAX: 44 (0) 1752 202333
ORDERS E-MAIL: enquiries@nbninternational.com

The University of Toronto Press acknowledges the financial support for its publishing activities of the Government of Canada through the Canada Book Fund.

Printed in Canada.

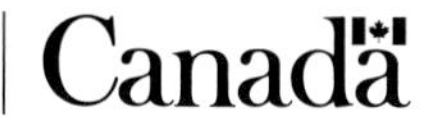

For Sophie and Natalie

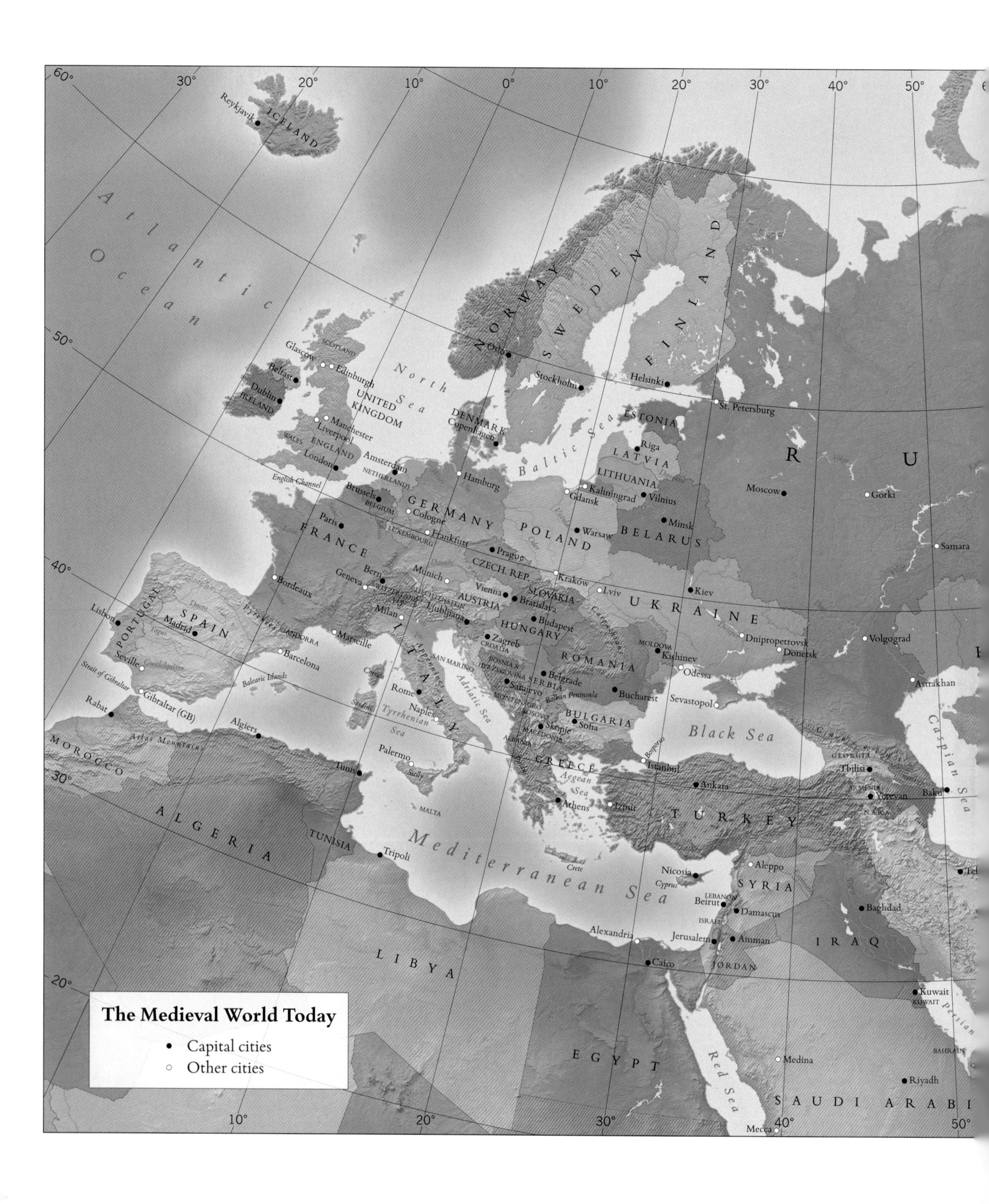

The Medieval World Today
Capital cities
Other cities
Atlantic Ocean
North Sea
Baltic Sea
Black Sea
Mediterranean Sea
Caspian Sea
Red Sea
Adriatic Sea
Tyrrhenian Sea
Aegean Sea
ICELAND
Reykjavik
NORWAY
Oslo
SWEDEN
Stockholm
FINLAND
Helsinki
ESTONIA
LATVIA
Riga
LITHUANIA
Vilnius
Kaliningrad
BELARUS
Minsk
UNITED KINGDOM
SCOTLAND
Glasgow
Edinburgh
Belfast
IRELAND
Dublin
WALES
ENGLAND
Manchester
Liverpool
London
English Channel
DENMARK
Copenhagen
NETHERLANDS
Amsterdam
BELGIUM
Brussels
LUXEMBOURG
GERMANY
Hamburg
Cologne
Frankfurt
POLAND
Gdansk
Warsaw
Kraków
CZECH. REP.
Prague
FRANCE
Paris
Bordeaux
Marseille
SWITZERLAND
Bern
Geneva
Munich
LIECHTENSTEIN
AUSTRIA
Vienna
SLOVAKIA
Bratislava
HUNGARY
Budapest
Ljubljana
Zagreb
CROATIA
BOSNIA & HERZEGOVINA
Sarajevo
SERBIA
Belgrade
MONTENEGRO
KOSOVO
MACEDONIA
Skopje
ALBANIA
Balkan Peninsula
ROMANIA
Bucharest
MOLDOVA
Kishinev
BULGARIA
Sofia
GREECE
Athens
UKRAINE
Lviv
Kiev
Dnipropetrovsk
Donetsk
Odessa
Sevastopol
R U
Moscow
St. Petersburg
Gorki
Samara
Volgograd
Astrakhan
PORTUGAL
Lisbon
SPAIN
Madrid
Seville
Barcelona
ANDORRA
Pyrenees
Balearic Islands
Strait of Gibraltar
Gibraltar (GB)
ITALY
Milan
Rome
Naples
Palermo
SAN MARINO
Corsica
Sardinia
Sicily
MALTA
MOROCCO
Rabat
Atlas Mountains
ALGERIA
Algiers
TUNISIA
Tunis
LIBYA
Tripoli
EGYPT
Alexandria
Cairo
TURKEY
Istanbul
Bosporus
Ankara
Izmir
Crete
Cyprus
Nicosia
SYRIA
Aleppo
Damascus
LEBANON
Beirut
ISRAEL
Jerusalem
Amman
JORDAN
IRAQ
Baghdad
GEORGIA
Tbilisi
ARMENIA
Yerevan
Baku
KUWAIT
Kuwait
BAHRAIN
SAUDI ARABI
Medina
Mecca
Riyadh
Danube
Dnieper

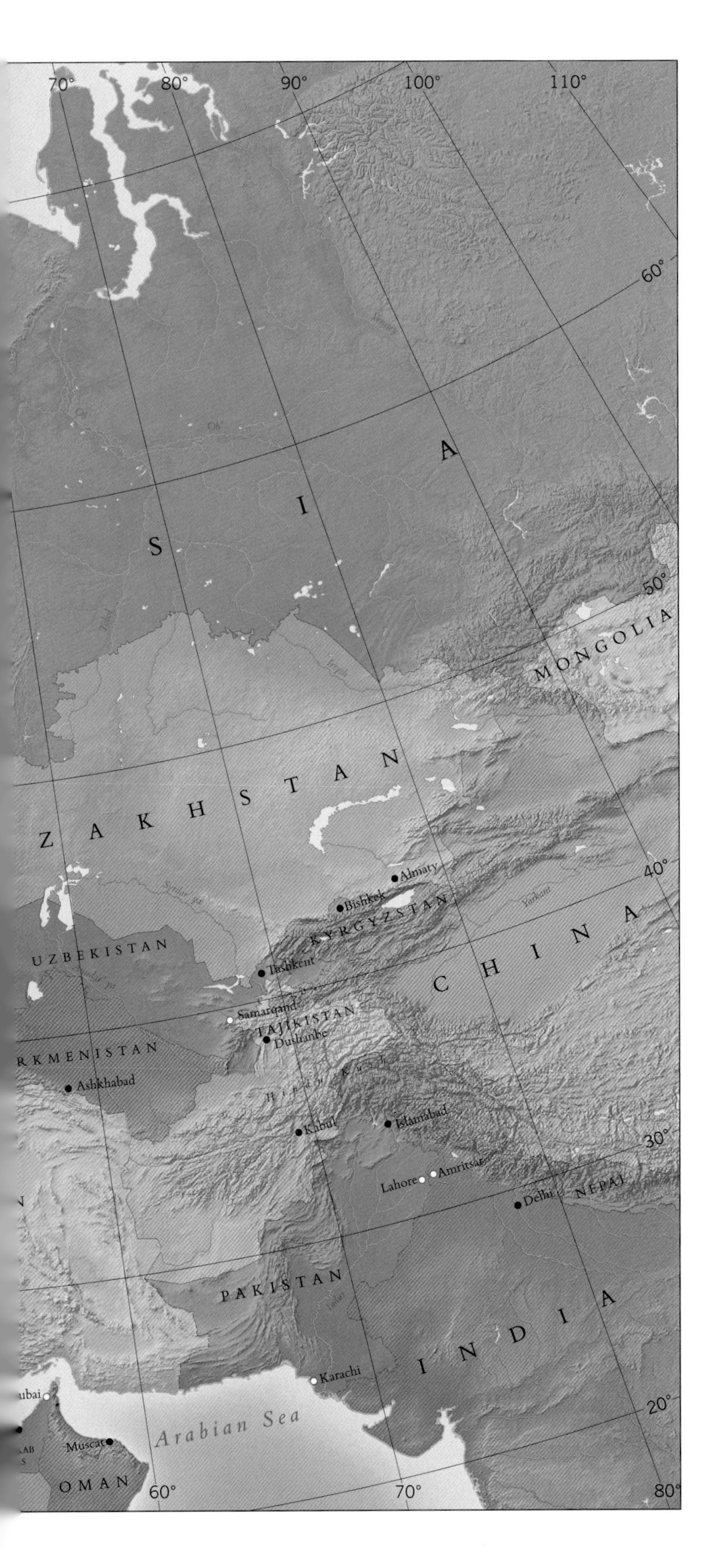

The union of the Roman empire was dissolved; its genius was humbled in the dust; and armies of unknown barbarians, issuing from the frozen regions of the North, had established their victorious reign over the fairest provinces of Europe and Africa.

Edward Gibbon, *The Decline and Fall of the Roman Empire*

It may very well happen that what seems for one group a period of decline may seem to another the birth of a new advance.

Edward Hallett Carr, *What Is History?*

CONTENTS

MAPS

PLATES

GENEALOGIES

FIGURES

ABBREVIATIONS, DATE CONVENTIONS, WEBSITE

ABBREVIATIONS

c. circa. Used to indicate that dates or other numbers are approximate.
cent. century
d. date of death
emp. emperor
fl. flourished. This is given when even approximate birth and death dates are unknown.
pl. plural form of a word
r. dates of reign
sing. singular form of a word

DATE CONVENTIONS

All dates are CE/AD unless otherwise noted (the two systems are interchangeable). The dates of popes are not preceded by r. because popes took their papal names upon accession to office, and the dates after those names apply only to their papacies.

The symbol / between dates indicates uncertainty: e.g., Boethius (d.524/526) means that he died some time between 524 and 526.

WEBSITE

http://www.utphistorymatters.com = The website for this book, which has practice short-answer and discussion questions (with sample answers provided), as well as maps, figures, and genealogies.

ACKNOWLEDGMENTS

I would like to thank all the readers, many anonymous, who made suggestions for improving earlier editions of *A Short History of the Middle Ages*. While I hope I will be forgiven for not naming everyone—a full list of names would begin to sound like a roll call of medievalists, both American and European—I want to single out two who were of special help for this edition: Dionysios Stathakopoulos and Julia Bray. Both sent me enormously helpful and often annotated bibliographies (on Byzantium and the Islamic world, respectively) for each chapter. I am indebted as always to Riccardo Cristiani for his help with and advice on every part and phase of this entire book. In addition, he prepared the inserts on Material Culture. Erik Goosmann was an exceptionally learned, creative, and willing cartographer. I thank as well Esther Cohen, who alerted me to some new interpretations; Albrecht Diem, who shared with me his classroom experiences with the book; Judith Earnshaw, editor extraordinaire; Natalie Fingerhut; and Matthew Jubb at Em Dash Design.

Finally, I thank my family, and I dedicate this book to my granddaughters Sophie and Natalie.

NOTE FOR THE FIFTH EDITION

Here students and teachers will find a much-enhanced map and artistic program and considerable expansion of the treatment of the Islamic and Byzantine worlds. To counter the tendency of textbook readers to imagine that everything therein is a "fact," I have singled out in each chapter at least one issue on which historians explicitly differ. The proponents of the various sides of those controversies are listed in the end-of-chapter Further Reading offerings, which have also been updated to take into account the most important new contributions.

ONE

PRELUDE: THE ROMAN WORLD TRANSFORMED (*c*.300–*c*.600)

At the beginning of the third century, the Roman Empire wrapped around the Mediterranean Sea like a scarf. (See Map 1.1.) Thinner on the North African coast, it bulked large as it enveloped what is today Spain, England, Wales, France, and Belgium, and then evened out along the southern coast of the Danube River, following that river eastward, taking in most of what is today called the Balkans (southwestern Europe, including Greece), crossing the Hellespont and engulfing in its sweep the territory of present-day Turkey, much of Syria, and all of modern Lebanon, Israel, and Egypt. All the regions but Italy comprised what the Romans called the "provinces."

This was the Roman Empire whose "decline and fall" was famously proclaimed by the eighteenth-century historian Edward Gibbon. Many historians today still think that judgment to be correct: consider the title of Bryan Ward-Perkins' book *The Fall of Rome: And the End of Civilization*. (For all modern author references, see Further Reading at the end of each chapter.) But many other historians follow Peter Brown in stressing the vitality of what he called "Late Antiquity." It is true that the old elites of the cities, especially of Rome itself, largely regretted the changes taking place around them *c*.250–350. They were witnessing the end of their political, military, religious, economic, and cultural leadership. That role was passing to the provincials (the Romans living outside of Italy) for whom this was in many ways a heady period, a long-postponed coming of age. They did not regret that Emperor Diocletian (r.284–305) divided the Roman Empire into four parts, each ruled by a different man. Called the Tetrarchy, the partition was tacit recognition of the importance of the provinces. But even the provinces eventually lost their centrality, as people still farther afield (whom the Romans called "barbarians") moved into the Roman Empire *c*.400–500. The barbarians, in turn, were glad to be the heirs of the Romans even as they contributed to the Empire's transformation.

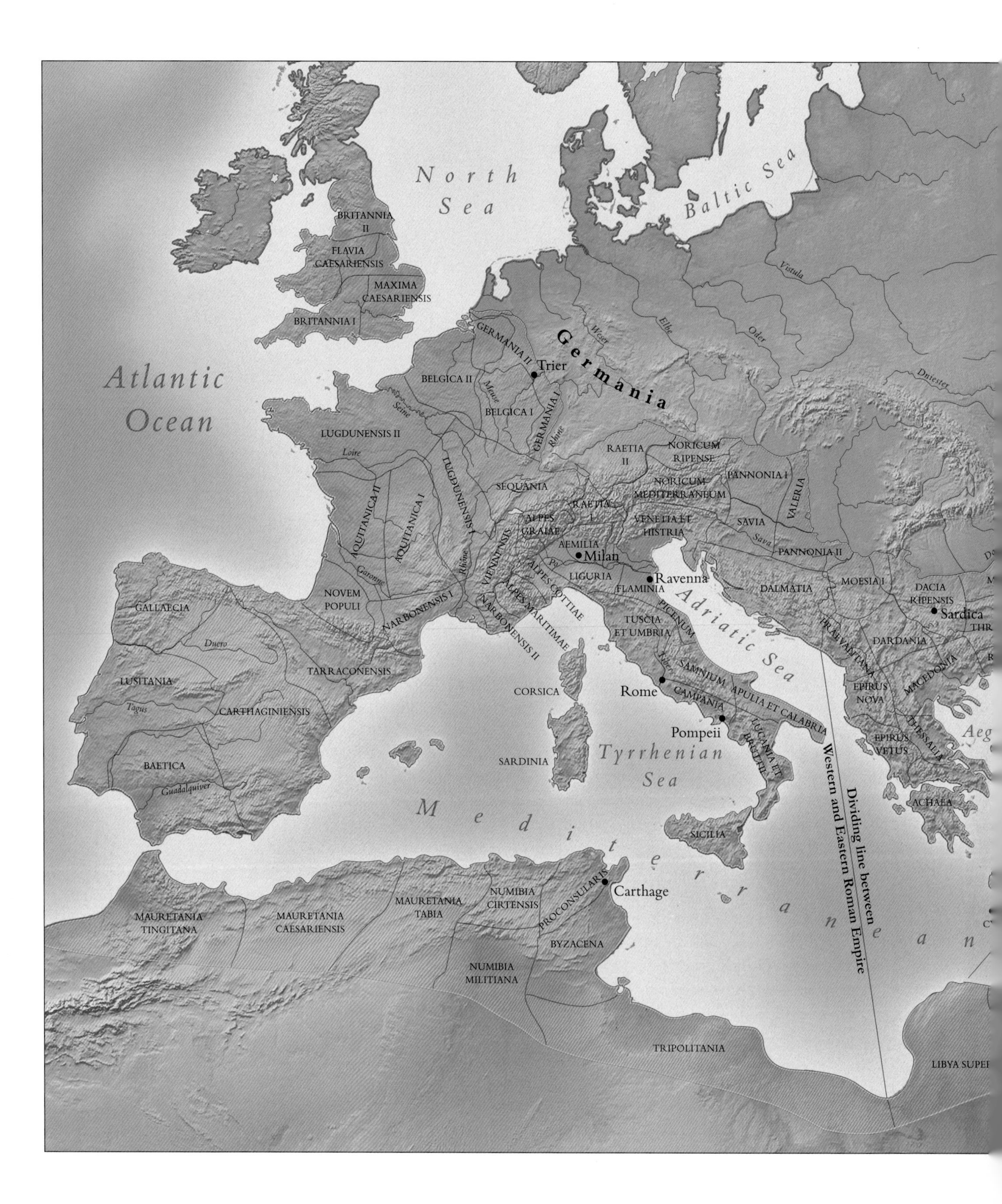
North Sea
Baltic Sea
BRITANNIA II
FLAVIA CAESARIENSIS
MAXIMA CAESARIENSIS
BRITANNIA I
Atlantic Ocean
Germania
GERMANIA II
Trier
Weser
Elbe
Oder
Vistula
Dniester
BELGICA II
Meuse
BELGICA I
GERMANIA I
Rhine
Seine
LUGDUNENSIS II
Loire
LUGDUNENSIS I
SEQUANIA
RAETIA II
NORICUM RIPENSE
PANNONIA I
NORICUM MEDITERRANEUM
VALERIA
RAETIA I
ALPES GRAIAE
VENETIA ET HISTRIA
SAVIA
Sava
PANNONIA II
AQUITANICA II
AQUITANICA I
Garonne
Rhône
VIENNENSIS
AEMILIA
Milan
Po
LIGURIA
Ravenna
FLAMINIA
ALPES COTTIAE
ALPES MARITIMAE
NOVEM POPULI
NARBONENSIS I
NARBONENSIS II
DALMATIA
MOESIA I
DACIA RIPENSIS
Sardica
Adriatic Sea
TUSCIA ET UMBRIA
PICENUM
PRAEVALITANA
DARDANIA
GALLAECIA
Duero
LUSITANIA
Tagus
TARRACONENSIS
CARTHAGINIENSIS
BAETICA
Guadalquiver
CORSICA
SARDINIA
Tiber
Rome
SAMNIUM
CAMPANIA
APULIA ET CALABRIA
Pompeii
LUCANIA ET BRUTTII
EPIRUS NOVA
MACEDONIA
THESSALIA
EPIRUS VETUS
ACHAEA
Tyrrhenian Sea
Mediterranean
SICILIA
Dividing line between Western and Eastern Roman Empire
MAURETANIA TINGITANA
MAURETANIA CAESARIENSIS
MAURETANIA TABIA
NUMIBIA CIRTENSIS
PROCONSULARIS
Carthage
BYZACENA
NUMIBIA MILITIANA
TRIPOLITANIA

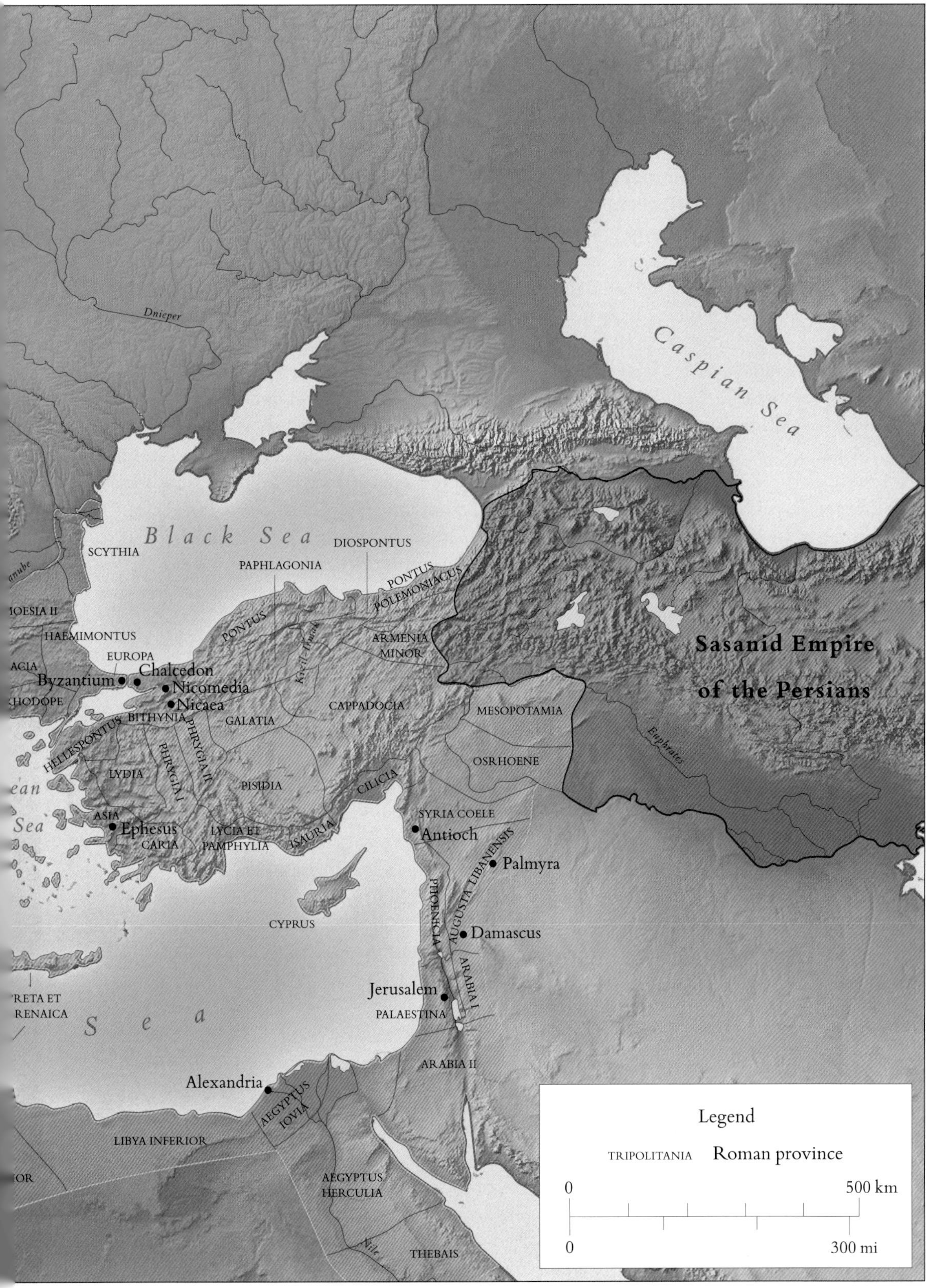

Map 1.1 The Roman Empire, *c.*300

THE PROVINCIALIZATION OF THE EMPIRE (*c.*250–*c.*350)

The Roman Empire was too large to be ruled by one man in one place, except in peacetime. This became clear during the so-called crisis of the third century, when two different groups from two different directions bore down on the frontiers of the Empire. From the north, beyond the Rhine and Danube Rivers, came the people the Romans dubbed barbarians; from the east came the Persians. To contend with these attacks, the Roman government responded with wide-ranging reforms that brought new prominence to the provinces.

Above all, the government expanded the army, setting up new crack mobile troops while reinforcing the standing army. Soldier-workers set up new fortifications, cities ringed themselves with walls, farms gained lookout towers and fences. It was not easy to find enough recruits to man this newly expanded defensive system. Before the crisis, the Roman legions had been largely self-perpetuating. The legionaries, drawn mainly from local provincial families, had settled permanently along the borders and raised the sons who would make up the next generation of recruits. Now, however, this supply was dwindling: the birthrate was declining, and *c.*252–267 an epidemic of smallpox ravaged the population further. Recruits would have to come from farther away, from Germania (the region beyond the northern borders of the Empire) and elsewhere. In fact, long before this time, Germanic warriors had been regular members of Roman army units; they had done their stints and gone home. But in the third century the Roman government began a new policy: it settled Germanic and other barbarian groups within the Empire, giving them land in return for military service.

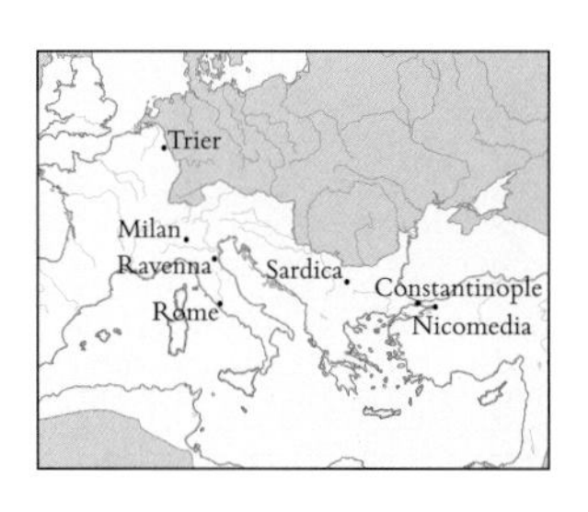

Map 1.2 The Capital Cities of the Empire

The term "crisis of the third century" refers not only to the wars that the Empire had to fight on its borders, but also to a political succession crisis that saw more than twenty men claim, then lose with their lives, the title of emperor between the years 235 and 284. Most of these men, often from the provinces, were creatures of the army, chosen to rule by their troops. Some of them led "breakaway empires," symptomatic of increasing decentralization, disaffection with Rome, and the power of the provincial army legions. The city of Rome itself was too far from any of the fields of war to serve as military headquarters. For this reason, Emperor Maximian (r.286–305) turned Milan into a new capital city, complete with an imperial palace, baths, walls, and circus. Soon other favored cities—Trier, Sardica, Nicomedia, Constantinople (formerly Byzantium), and much later Ravenna—joined Milan in overshadowing Rome.

The primacy of the provinces was further enhanced by the need to feed and supply the army. To meet its demand for ready money, the Roman government debased the currency, increasing the proportion of inferior metals to silver. While helpful in the short term, this policy produced severe inflation. Strapped for cash, the state increased taxes and used its power to requisition goods and services. To clothe the troops, it confiscated uniforms; to arm them it set up factories staffed by artisans who were required to produce a regular quota of weapons (spears, short swords, shields) for the state. Food for the army had to be produced and delivered; here too the state depended on the labor of growers, bakers, and haulers. New taxes assessed on both land and individual "heads" were collected.

The wealth and labor of the Empire moved inexorably toward the provinces, to the hot spots where armies were clashing.

The whole Empire, organized for war, became militarized. In about the middle of the third century, Emperor Gallienus (r.253–268) forbade the senatorial aristocracy—the old Roman elite—to lead the army; tougher men from the ranks were promoted to command positions instead. It was no wonder that those men also became the emperors. They brought new provincial tastes and sensibilities to the very heart of the Empire, as we shall see.

Diocletian, a provincial from Dalmatia (today Croatia), brought the crisis under control, and Constantine (r.306–337), from Moesia (today Serbia and Bulgaria), brought it to an end. For administrative purposes, Diocletian divided the Empire into four parts, later reduced to two. Although the emperors who ruled these divisions were supposed to confer on all matters (and even be the best of friends, as Plate 1.7 on p. 19 suggests), the administrative division was a harbinger of things to come, when the eastern and western halves of the Empire would go their separate ways. Meanwhile, the wars over imperial succession ceased with the establishment of Constantine's dynasty, and political stability put an end to the border wars.

A New Religion

The empire of Constantine was meant to be the Roman Empire restored. Yet it was nothing like the old Roman Empire. Constantine's rule marks the end of the classical era and the beginning of Late Antiquity, a period transformed by the culture and religion of the provinces.

The province of Palestine—to the Romans of Italy a most dismal backwater—had been in fact a hotbed of creative religious and social ideas around the beginning of the first millennium. Chafing under Roman domination, experimenting with new notions of morality and new ethical lifestyles, the Jews of Palestine gave birth to religious groups of breathtaking originality. One coalesced around Jesus. After his death, under the impetus of the Jew-turned-Christian Paul (d.*c.*67), a new and radical brand of monotheism in Jesus' name was actively preached to Gentiles (non-Jews), not only in Palestine, but also beyond. Its core belief was that men and women were saved—redeemed and accorded eternal life in heaven—by their faith in Jesus Christ.

At first Christianity was of nearly perfect indifference to elite Romans, who were devoted to the gods who had served them so well over years of conquest and prosperity. Nor did it attract many of the lower classes, who were still firmly rooted in old local religious traditions. The Romans had never insisted that the provincials whom they conquered give up their beliefs; they simply added official Roman gods into local pantheons. For most people, both rich and poor, the rich texture of religious life at the local level was both comfortable and satisfying. In dreams, they encountered their personal gods, who served them as guardians and friends. At home, they found their household gods, evoking family ancestors. Outside, on the street, they visited temples and monuments to local gods, reminders of home-town pride. Here and there could be seen monuments to the "divine emperor," put up by rich town benefactors. Everyone engaged in the festivals of the public cults, whose ceremonies gave rhythm to the year. Paganism was thus at one and the same time personal, familial, local, and imperial.

But Christianity had its attractions, too. Romans and other city-dwellers of the middle class could never hope to become part of the educated upper crust. Christianity gave them dignity by substituting "the elect" for the elite. Education, long and expensive, was the ticket into Roman high society. Christians had their own solid, less expensive knowledge. It was the key to an even "higher" society—the one in Heaven.

In the provinces, Christianity attracted men and women who had never been given the chance to feel truly Roman. (Citizenship was not granted to all provincials until 212.) The new religion was confident, hopeful, and universal. As the Empire settled into an era of peaceful complacency in the second century, its hinterlands opened up to the influence of the center, and vice versa. Men and women whose horizons in earlier times would have stretched no farther than their village now took to the roads as traders—or confronted a new cosmopolitanism right at their doorsteps. Uprooted from old traditions, they found comfort in small assemblies—churches—where they were welcomed as equals and where God was the same, no matter what region the members of the church hailed from.

The Romans persecuted Christians, but at first only locally, sporadically, and above all in times of crisis. At such moments, the Romans feared that the gods were venting their wrath on the Empire because Christians would not carry out the proper sacrifices. True, the Jews also refused to honor the Roman gods, but the Romans could usually tolerate—just barely—Jewish practices as part of their particular cultural identity. Christians, however, claimed their God not only for themselves but for all. Major official government persecutions of Christians began in the 250s, with the third-century crisis.

By 304, on the eve of the promulgation of Diocletian's last great persecutory edict, perhaps only 10 per cent of the population was Christian. (See Map 1.3.) But despite their tiny number, the Christians were well organized. Gathered into "churches" (from the Greek word, *ekklesia*, meaning "assembly"), they formed a two-tiered institution. At the bottom were the people (the "laity," from the Greek *laikos*, meaning "of the people"). Above them were the clergy (from the Greek word *kleros*, meaning "lot," or "inheritance," and referring to Deut. 18:2, where the Levitical priests have no inheritance but "the Lord himself"). In turn, the clergy were supervised by a regional bishop (in Greek *episkopos*, "overseer"), assisted by his "presbyters" (from the Greek *presbyteroi*, "elders," the priests who served with the bishops), deacons, and lesser servitors. Some bishops—those of Alexandria, Antioch, Carthage, Jerusalem, and Rome, whose bishop was later called the "pope"—were more important than others. No religion was better prepared for official recognition.

This it received in 313, in the so-called Edict of Milan. Emperors Licinius and Constantine declared toleration for all the religions in the Empire "so that whatever divinity is enthroned in heaven may be gracious and favorable to us."[1] In fact, the Edict

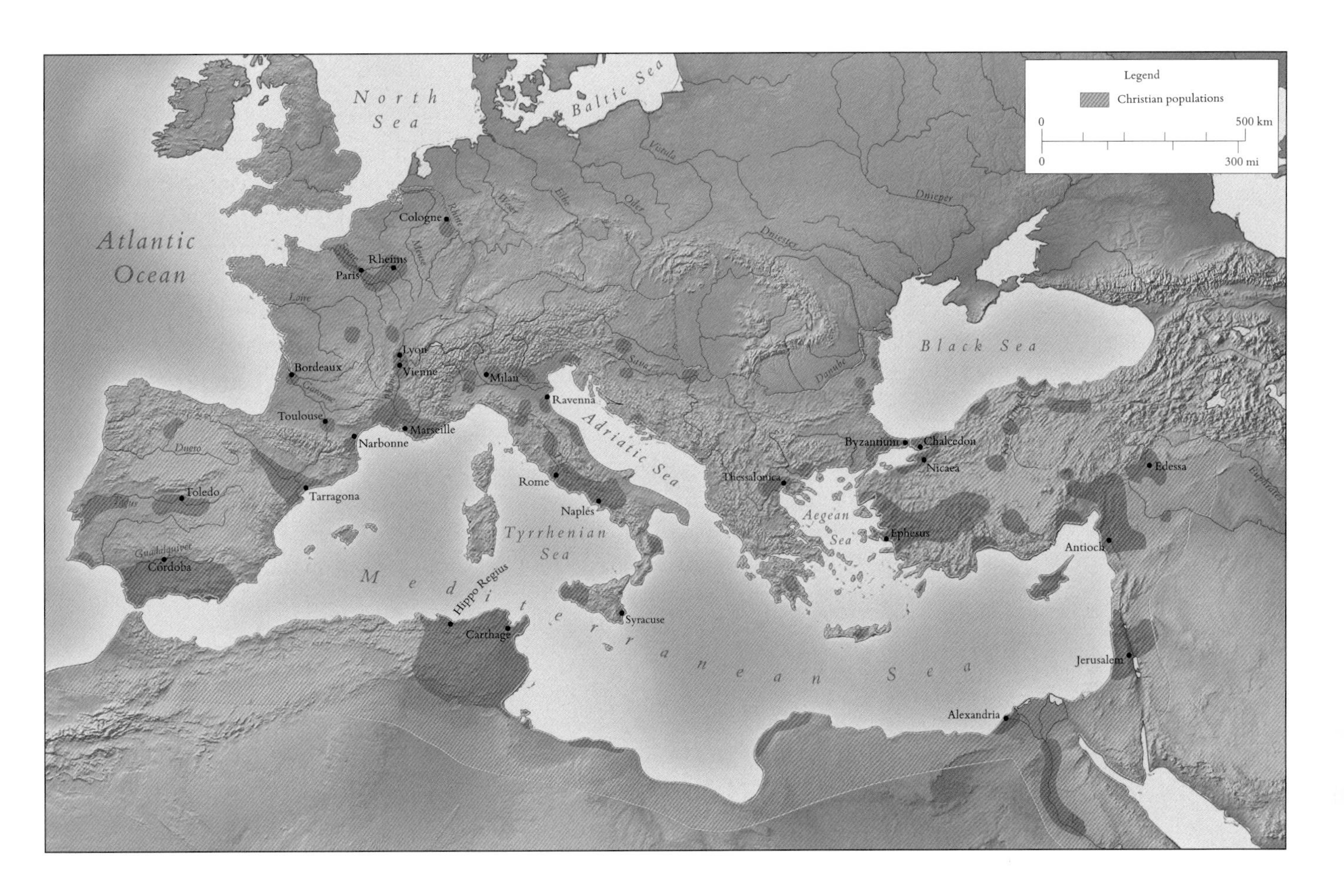

helped Christians above all: they had been the ones persecuted, and now, in addition to enjoying the toleration declared in the Edict, they regained their property. Constantine was the chief force behind the Edict: it was issued just after his triumphant battle at the Milvian Bridge against his rival emperor Maxentius in 312, a victory that he attributed to the God of the Christians. Constantine seems to have converted to Christianity; he certainly favored it, building and endowing church buildings, making sure that property was restored to churches that had been stripped during the persecutions, and giving priests special privileges. Under him, the ancient Greek city of Byzantium became a new Christian city, residence of emperors, and named for the emperor himself: Constantinople. The bishop of Constantinople became a patriarch, a "superbishop," equal to the bishops of Antioch and Alexandria, although not as important as the bishop of Rome. In one of the crowning measures of his career, Constantine called and then presided over the first ecumenical (universal) church council, the Council of Nicaea, in 325. There the assembled bishops hammered out some of the canon law and doctrines of the Christian church.

Map 1.3 Christian Populations at the End of the 3rd cent.

After Constantine, it was simply a matter of time before most people considered it both good and expedient to convert. Though several emperors espoused "heretical"—unacceptable—forms of Christianity, and one (Julian, the "Apostate") professed paganism, the die had been cast. In a series of laws starting in 380 with the Edict of Thessalonica and continuing throughout his reign, Emperor Theodosius I (r.379–395) declared that the form of Christianity determined at the Council of Nicaea applied to all Romans, and he outlawed all the old public and private cults. Christianity was now the official religion of the Roman Empire. In some places, Christian mobs took to smashing local pagan temples. In these ways—via law, coercion, and conviction—a fragile religion hailing from one of the most backward of the provinces triumphed everywhere in the Roman world.

But "Christianity" was not simply one thing. In North Africa, Donatists—who considered themselves purer than other Christians because they had not backpedaled during the period of persecutions—fought bitterly with Catholics all through the fourth century, willingly killing and dying to prevent priests and bishops from resuming their offices if they had handed over their Bibles, church furnishings, and other emblems of their faith to Roman authorities to escape death. As paganism gave way, Christian disagreements came to the fore: what was the nature of God? where were God and the sacred to be found? how did God relate to humanity? In the fourth and fifth centuries, Christians fought with each other ever more vehemently over doctrine and over the location of the holy.

Doctrine

The so-called Church Fathers were the victors in the battles over doctrine. Already in Constantine's day, Saint Athanasius (*c.*295–373)—then secretary to the bishop of Alexandria, later bishop there himself—had led the challenge against the beliefs of the Christians next door. He called them "Arians," rather than Christians, after the priest Arius (250–336), another Alexandrian and a competing focus of local loyalties. Athanasius promoted his views at the Council of Nicaea (325) and won. It is because of this that he is considered the orthodox catholic "Father," while Arius is the "heretic." For both Athanasius and Arius, God was triune, that is, three persons in one: the Father, the Son, and the Holy Spirit. Their debate was about the nature of these persons. For the Arians, the Father was pure Godhead while the Son (Christ) was created. Christ was, therefore, flesh though not quite flesh, neither purely human nor purely divine, but mediating between the two. To Athanasius and the assembled bishops at Nicaea, this was heresy—the wrong "choice" (the root meaning of the Greek term *hairesis*)—and a damnable faith. The Council of Nicaea wrote the party line: "We believe in one God, the Father almighty,... And in one Lord Jesus Christ, the Son of God, begotten from the Father,... begotten not made, of one substance [*homousios*] with the Father."[2] Arius was condemned and banished. His doctrine, however, persisted. It was the brand of Christianity that Ulfila (311–*c.*382), a Gothic bishop with Roman connections, preached to the Goths beyond the borders of the Empire, at the same time translating the Bible into the Gothic language.

Arianism was only the tip of the iceberg. Indeed, the period 350–450 might be called the "era of competing doctrines." Already the Council of Nicaea worried not only about Arians, who thought Christ to have a different substance from the Father, but also about groups (later called Monophysites or Miaphysites) who held that the "flesh" that God assumed as Christ was nevertheless entirely divine. Thus, the Nicene Creed went on to declare that Jesus Christ, "because of us men and because of our salvation came down and became incarnate,"—that is, became *human* flesh.[3] Despite that decision, ratified by later councils, especially one held at Chalcedon (451), Monophysite belief in the divinity of Christ's flesh nourished the Armenian, Coptic (Egyptian), and Ethiopian Christian churches.

Even Augustine (354–430), eventually the bishop of Hippo, a saint, and the most influential Western churchman of his day (and for many centuries thereafter), flirted in his youth with yet another variant of Christianity, Manichaeism. The Manichees, armed with a revelation from Mani, "apostle of Jesus Christ," believed in two cosmic principles, one godly, spiritual, and light; the other evil, material, and dark. For the Manichees, Jesus' human nature was not real; its materiality and suffering were only apparent. Human beings were mired in the material world, but they might liberate themselves from its shackles by fasting, renouncing sex, disdaining all forms of property, and clinging to the special knowledge brought to mankind by Christ's apostles. "The fasting that the saints fast," noted one Manichaean text, makes the soul "holy, cleansed, purified, and washed from the adulteration of the darkness that is mixed in with it." Other believers, too weak to be saints, showed their support of their pure brethren "by their faith and their alms."[4] They had the hope of being reborn in new bodies and eventually becoming one of the saints.

Pelagius (from Britain, d. after 418) was also interested in what human beings could do to achieve salvation. Pelagius thought that conversion bleached out sins, and thereafter people could follow God by their own will. But just as Augustine repudiated the Manichees for their dualism, which made God only one of two cosmic powers, so he rejected Pelagianism for its woeful misreading of human nature. In Augustine's view, human beings were capable of nothing good without God's grace working through them: "Come, Lord, act upon us and rouse us up and call us back! Fire us, clutch us, let your sweet fragrance grow upon us!"[5]

Like arguments over sports teams today, these disputes were more than small talk: they identified people's loyalties. They also brought God down to earth. God had debased himself to take on human flesh. It was critical to know how he had done so and what that meant for the rest of humanity.

For these huge questions, Augustine wrote most of the definitive answers for the West, though they were certainly modified and reworked over the centuries. In the *City of God*, a huge and sprawling work, he defined two cities: the earthly one in which our feet are planted, in which we are born, learn to read, marry, get old, and die; and the heavenly one, on which our hearts and minds are fixed. The first, the "City of Man," is impermanent, subject to fire, war, famine, and sickness; the second, the "City of God," is the opposite. Only there is true, eternal happiness to be found. Yet the first, however imperfect, is where the institutions of society—local churches, schools, governments—make possible the attainment of the second. Thus "if anyone accepts the present life in such a spirit that he uses it with the end in view of [the City of God],... such a man may without absurdity be called happy, even now."[6] In Augustine's hands, the old fixtures of the ancient world were reused and reoriented for a new Christian society.

The Sources of God's Grace

The City of Man was fortunate. There God had instituted his church. Christ had said to Peter, the foremost of his twelve apostles (his "messengers"):

> Thou art Peter [*Petros*, or "rock" in Greek]; and upon this rock I will build my church, and the gates of hell shall not prevail against it. And I will give to thee the keys of the kingdom of heaven. And whatsoever thou shalt bind upon earth, it shall be bound also in heaven; and whatsoever thou shalt loose on earth, it shall be loosed also in heaven. (Matt. 16:18–19)

Although variously interpreted (above all by the popes at Rome, who took it to mean that, as the successors of Saint Peter, the first bishop of Rome, they held the keys), no one doubted that this declaration confirmed that the all-important powers of binding (imposing penance on) and loosing (forgiving) sinners were in the hands of Christ's earthly heirs, the priests and bishops. In the Mass, the central liturgy of the earthly church, the bread and wine on the altar became the body and blood of Christ, the "Eucharist." Through the Mass the faithful were joined to one another; to the souls of the dead, who were remembered in the liturgy; and to Christ himself.

The importance of the Mass was made clear in the very architecture and decoration of Christian churches. In the sixth-century church of San Vitale in Ravenna, an apse (a semicircular niche) forms a brilliant marble and mosaic halo around the altar. Above the altar, a half dome presents an image of heaven, while just beneath the heavens, on either side of three lofty windows, are full-length figures of the emperor (on the left) and empress (on the right) along with their retinues. They are bringing offerings for the altar. (See Plate 1.12 and further discussion on pp. 31–33). In this way, imperial power was associated with the Eucharist and the Mass.

The Eucharist was one potent source of God's grace. There were others. Above all, there were certain people so beloved by God, so infused with his grace, that they were both models of virtue and powerful wonder-workers. These were the saints. In the early church, the saints had largely been the martyrs, who died for their faith. But Christian martyrdom ended with Constantine. The new saints of the fourth and fifth centuries had to find ways to be martyrs even while alive. Like Saint Symeon Stylites (*c*.390–459), they climbed tall pillars and stood there for decades; or, like Saint Antony (250–356), they entered tombs to fight, heroically and successfully, with the demons (whose reality was as little questioned as the existence of neutrons is today). They were the "athletes of Christ," greatly admired by the surrounding community. Purged of sin by their ascetic rigors—giving up their possessions, fasting, praying, not sleeping, not engaging in sex—holy men and women offered compelling role models. Twelve-year-old Asella, born into Roman high society, was inspired by such models to remain a virgin: she shut herself off from the world in a tiny cell where, as her admirer Saint Jerome put it, "fasting was her pleasure and hunger her refreshment."[7] This sounds a bit like Manichaeism, and the similarities are certainly real. But Jerome also spoke admiringly of Asella's devotion to martyrs' shrines, very much part of the material world and yet, in orthodox Christianity, godly as well.

Beyond offering models of Christian virtue, the saints interceded with God on behalf of their neighbors and acted as social peace-keepers. Saint Athanasius told the story of Saint Antony: after years of solitude and asceticism the saint emerged

> as if from some shrine, initiated into the mysteries and filled with God.... When he saw the crowd [awaiting him], he was not disturbed, nor did he rejoice to be greeted by so many people. Rather, he was wholly balanced, as if he were being navigated by the Word [of God] and existing in his natural state. Therefore, through Antony the Lord healed many of the suffering bodies of those present, and others he cleansed of demons. He gave Antony grace in speaking, and thus he comforted many who were grieved and reconciled into friendship others who were quarreling.[8]

Healer of illnesses, mediator of disputes, worker of wonders, Antony's power was spiritual, physical, and judicial combined.

But who was in charge of such power; who had the right to control it? Bishop Athanasius of Alexandria laid claim to Antony's legacy by writing about it. Yet writing was only one way to appropriate and harness the power of the saints. When holy men and women died, their power lived on in their relics (whatever they left behind: their bones, hair, clothes, sometimes even the dust near their tombs). Pious people knew this very well. They wanted access to these "special dead." Rich and influential Romans got their own holy monopolies simply by moving saintly bones home with them. Plate 1.9 on p. 21 shows the wall of just such a house, decorated with the image of an orant (a praying figure), perhaps a martyr-saint, and two kneeling women. Above them, hidden and yet tantalizingly present behind a grate, were the precious remains of martyrs.

Men like Saint Ambrose (339–397), bishop of Milan, tried to make clergymen, not pious laypeople, the overseers of relics. Ambrose had the newly discovered relics of Saints Gervasius and Protasius moved from their original resting place into his newly built cathedral and buried under the altar, the focus of communal worship. In this way, he allied himself, his successors, and the whole Christian community of Milan with the power of those saints. But laypeople continued to find private ways to keep precious bits of the saints near to them, wearing them in rings, lockets, purses, and belt buckles.

Art from the Provinces to the Center

Just as Christianity came from the periphery to transform the center, so too did provincial artistic traditions. Classical Roman art, nicely exemplified by paintings on the walls of ancient Roman villas (Plates 1.1, 1.2, and 1.3), was characterized by light and shadow, a sense of atmosphere—of earth, sky, air, light—and a feeling of movement, even in the midst of calm. Figures—sometimes lithe, sometimes stocky, always "plastic,"

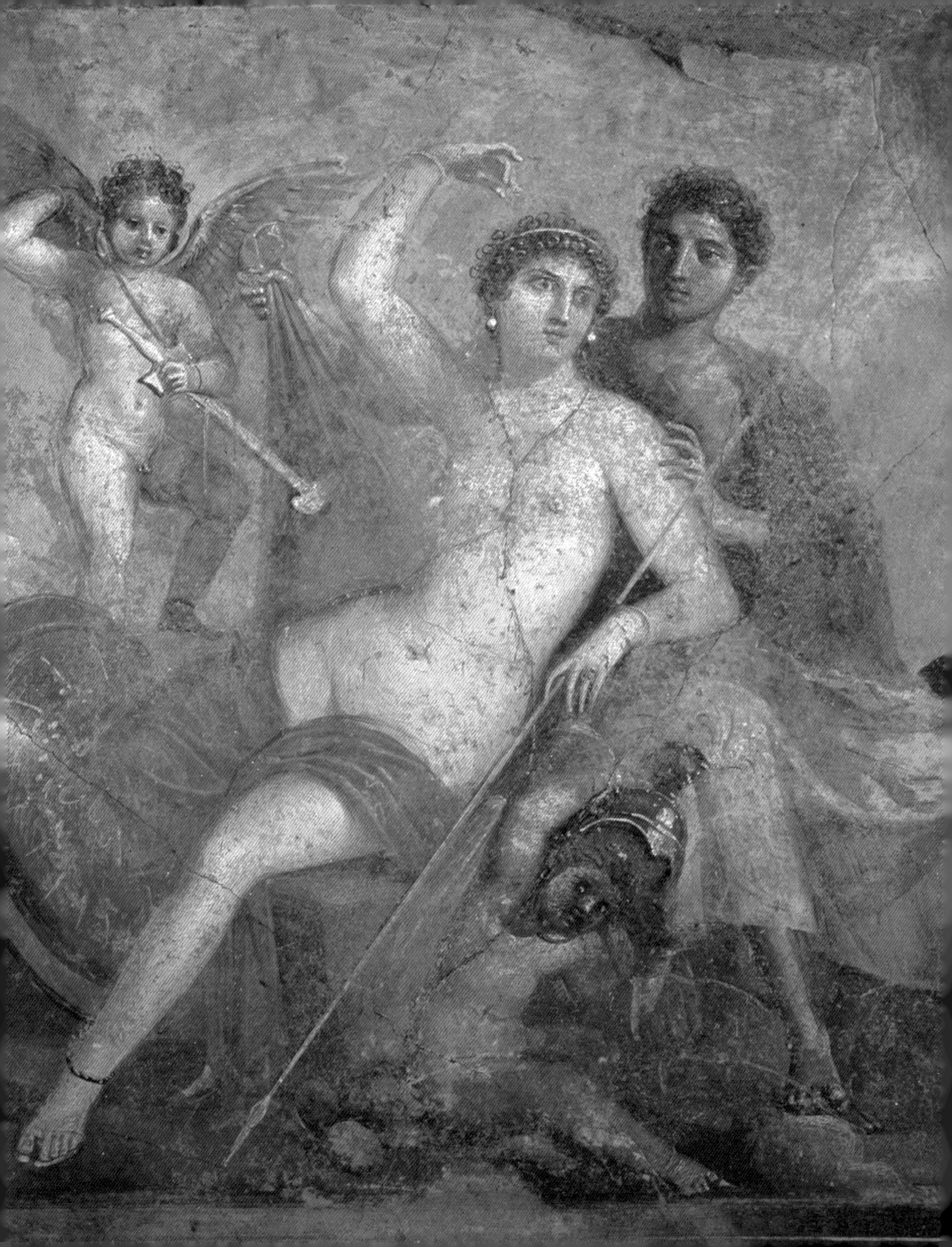

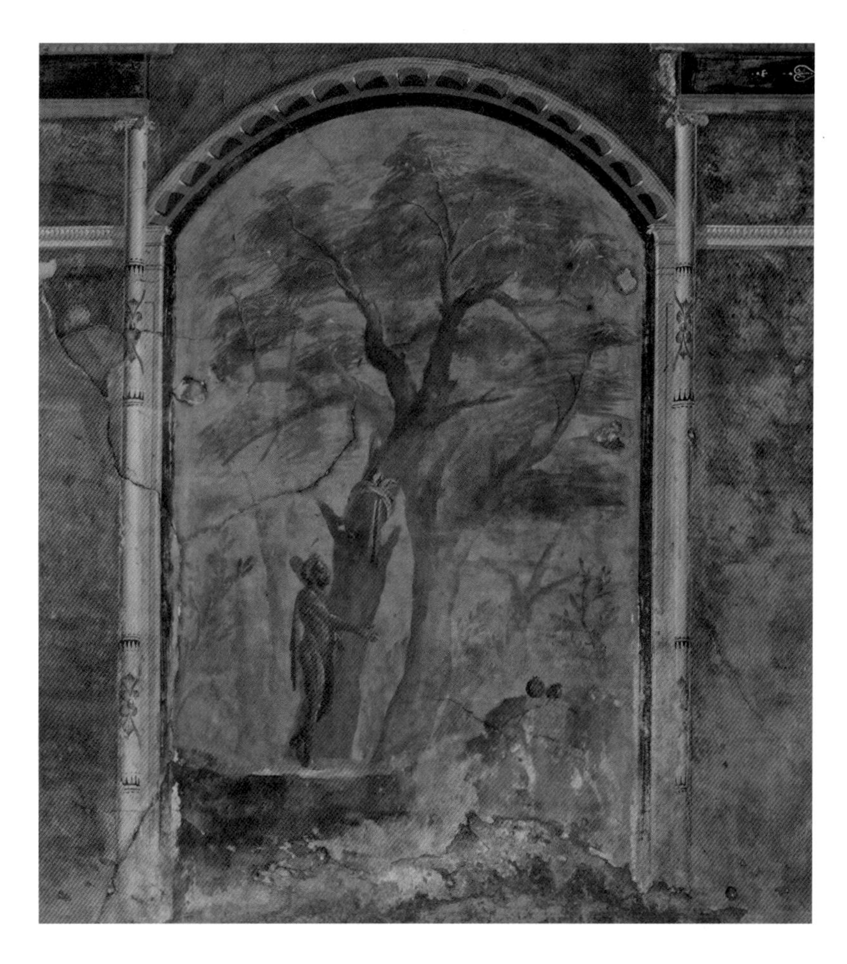

suggesting volume and real weight on the ground—interacted, touching one another or talking, and caring little or nothing about the viewer.

Plate 1.1 pictures an event well known to Romans from their myths. A handsome man lifts the veil that covers a beautiful woman, exposing her naked body to their mutual delight. A winged boy, a quiver strapped around his shoulder and an arrow in his hand, hovers nearby, while another boy, below the couple, plays with a man's helmet. Any Roman would know from the "iconography"—the symbolic meaning of the elements—that the man is the god Mars, the woman the goddess Venus, and the two boys are their sons, the winged one Cupid. Venus was married to Vulcan, but she and Mars carried on a passionate love affair until Vulcan caught them in a net as they were embracing and displayed them, to their shame, to all the other gods. The artist has chosen to depict a happy moment before their capture. Even though the story is illustrated for the pleasure of its viewers, the figures act as if no one is looking at them. They are self-absorbed, glimpsed as if through a window onto their private world.

That world was recognizably natural, much like the one the viewers lived in. In Plate 1.2 an orchard is the focus. A large tree dominates the scene, with an imposing figure, naked except for a lion skin. It's Hercules on one of his final labors: to gather the golden apples that will bring life after death. The golden scarf on the tree announces its sacredness. Two of the golden apples are already on a rock just visible at the lower right. Although this labor required Hercules to kill numerous opponents and, in the most common variant, to hold up the world on his shoulders in the place of Atlas, the artist shows none of that: his emphasis is on the natural world, here interpreted as both tranquil and grand.

Roman artists were also interested in busy, everyday life. Plate 1.3 is one panel of an extensive fresco painted in a corridor of the Villa Farnesina, located in a suburb of Rome. It features lithe figures painted with rapid brushstrokes and engaged in various activities. Some (on the far left) fill water jugs at a fountain. Others ready their fishing nets. Still others pass by a two-story villa delineated by interlocking blocks. Behind, connected by a bridge across the water, are the faint outlines of a building that may be a temple. The Villa Farnesina itself was too far from Rome's working port for this to represent its local

Plate 1.1 (facing page) Mars and Venus, Pompeii (1st cent.). Venus, goddess of love and beauty, and Mars, god of war, are utterly absorbed in both themselves and one another as they adorn the wall of a private house at Pompeii.

Plate 1.2 Hercules in the Garden of the Hesperides, Oplontis (*c.*10–1 BCE). Decorating one panel in the *caldarium* (hot tub room) of a villa at Oplontis (near Pompeii), this landscape features a hazy blue sky and trees that stretch into the distance. The artist of this painting created the illusion of space, air, and light directly on the flat surface of a wall.

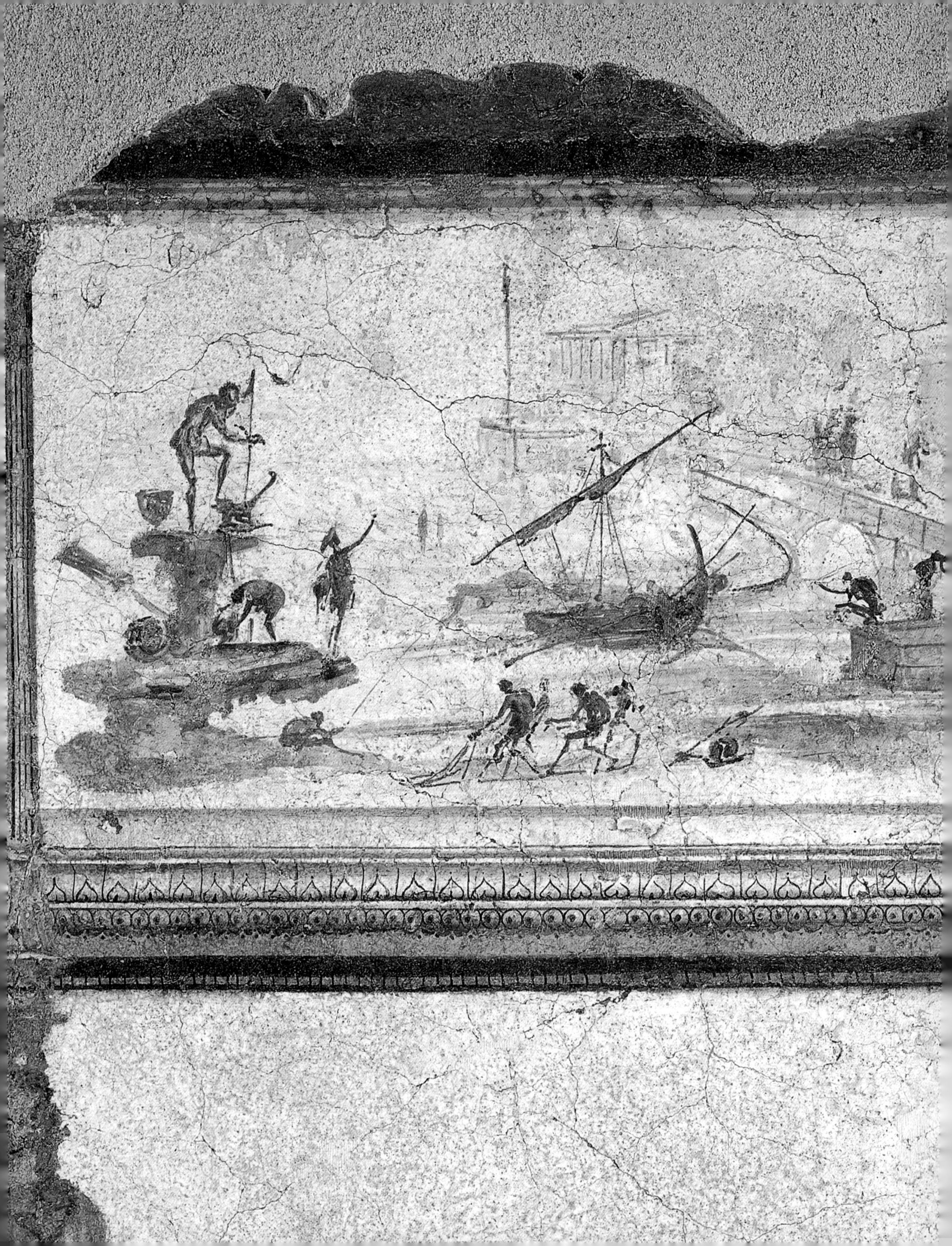

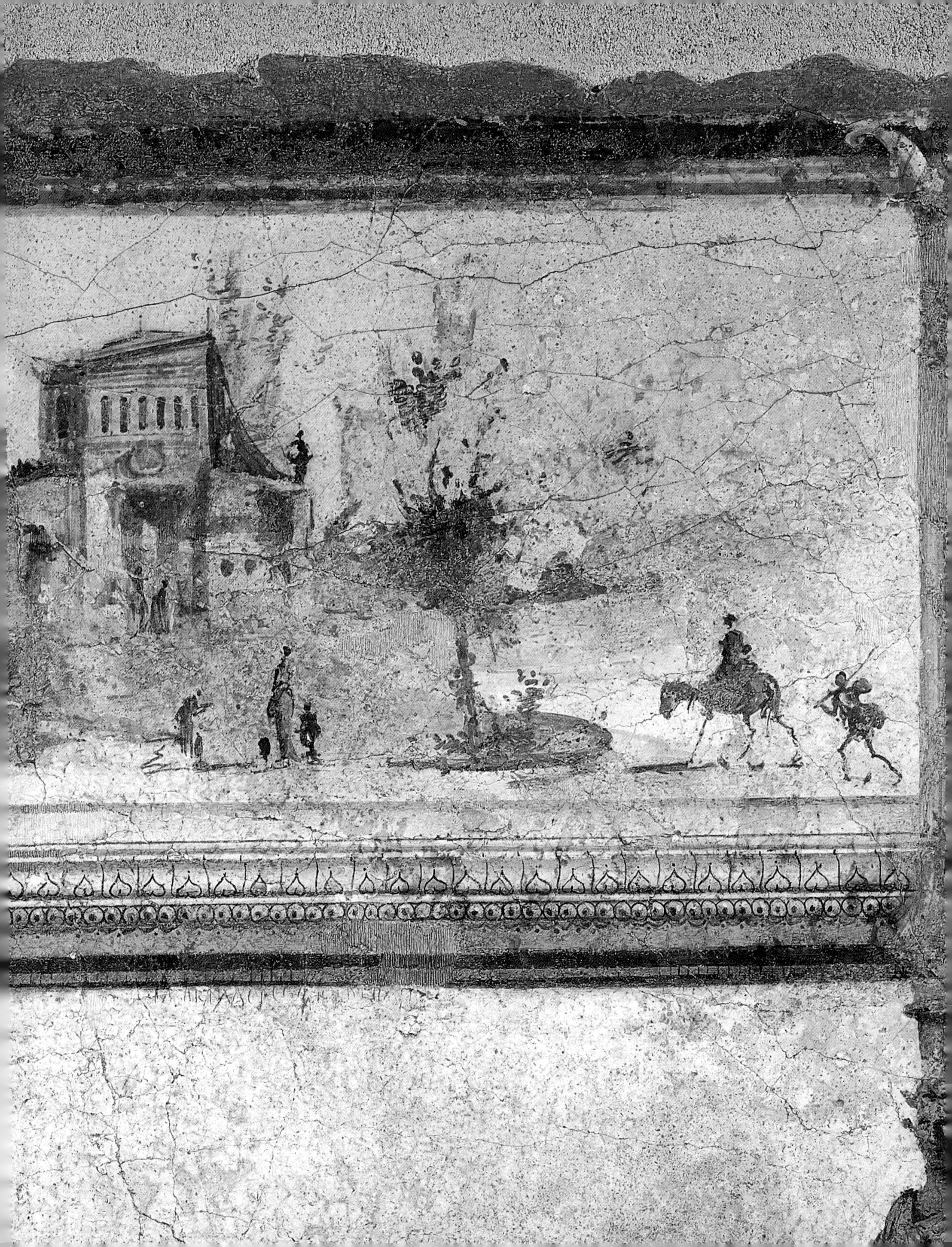

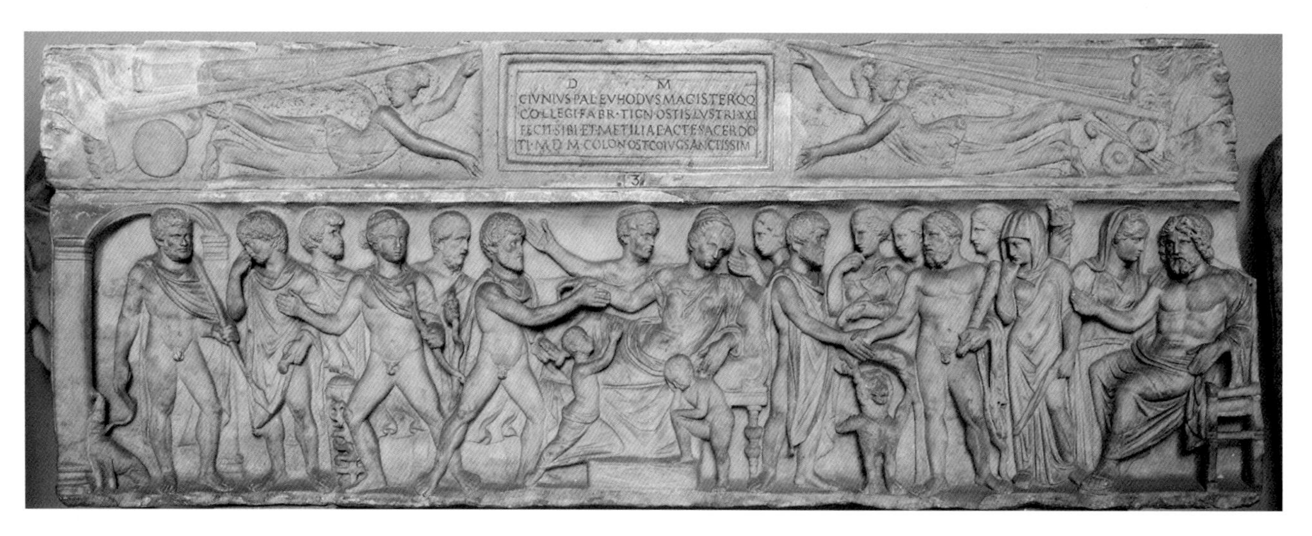

Plate 1.3 (previous page) Harbor Scene (late 1st cent. BCE). One of many painted panels in a long corridor at the Villa Farnesina, the scene seems to evoke the outside world even as it idealizes it.

Plate 1.4 Euhodus Sarcophagus (*c.*161–170). The sculptors have used a trick of perspective—carving the figures at different depths—to make some literally stand out and others recede. Note the veiled woman at the right: she is the spirit of Alcestis, returned from the dead.

landscape. But the likely owner, the Roman statesman and architect Agrippa, had in fact built a bridge over the Tiber and thus was personally involved in the very fabric of the city as depicted here.

Roman sculptors, like painters, were also interested in movement and three-dimensionality. They showed figures turning and interacting with one another, and they created space by playing on the optical illusion of "perspective," where some elements seem to recede while others—smaller, less precisely delineated—come to the fore. Consider a marble sarcophagus carved for Euhodus and his wife, Metilia Acte, both of whom were prestigious office-holders at Ostia (near Rome). Here the sculpture tells the story of Alcestis, a virtuous wife who volunteered to die in place of her young husband, King Admetus. After her death, the god Apollo persuaded the Fates to let her return to the world, and Hercules brought her back as a spirit. The sarcophagus's sculptors made Alcestis's death the central focus: she reclines on a long couch, while Admetus reaches toward her as if to embrace her one last time. To give the scene extra meaning and poignancy, the carvers have given Alcestis the face of Metilia Acte, while Admetus has the face of the old Euhodus. Like Mars and Venus in Plate 1.1, the sarcophagus shows two people utterly absorbed in one another. But the sarcophagus goes further, suggesting that the bond between the husband and wife will endure even beyond the grave.

Yet even in the classical period other artistic values and conventions existed in the Roman Empire—in the provinces. For many years these provincial styles had been tamped down, though not extinguished, by the juggernaut of Roman political and cultural hegemony. But in the third century, with the new importance of the provinces, regional traditions re-emerged. As provincial military men became the new heroes and emperors, artistic tastes changed as well. The center—Rome, Italy, Constantinople—began to borrow its artistic styles from the periphery.

To understand some of these regional traditions, consider the sculpted depiction of Venus from the north of Britain in Plate 1.5 and a tombstone from the region of Carthage—Tunis, Tunisia today—in Plate 1.6. Both of these were made under the shadow of Roman imperial rule. Yet they are little like Roman works of art. Above all, the artists who made these pieces valued clear hierarchies and decorative elements divorced from

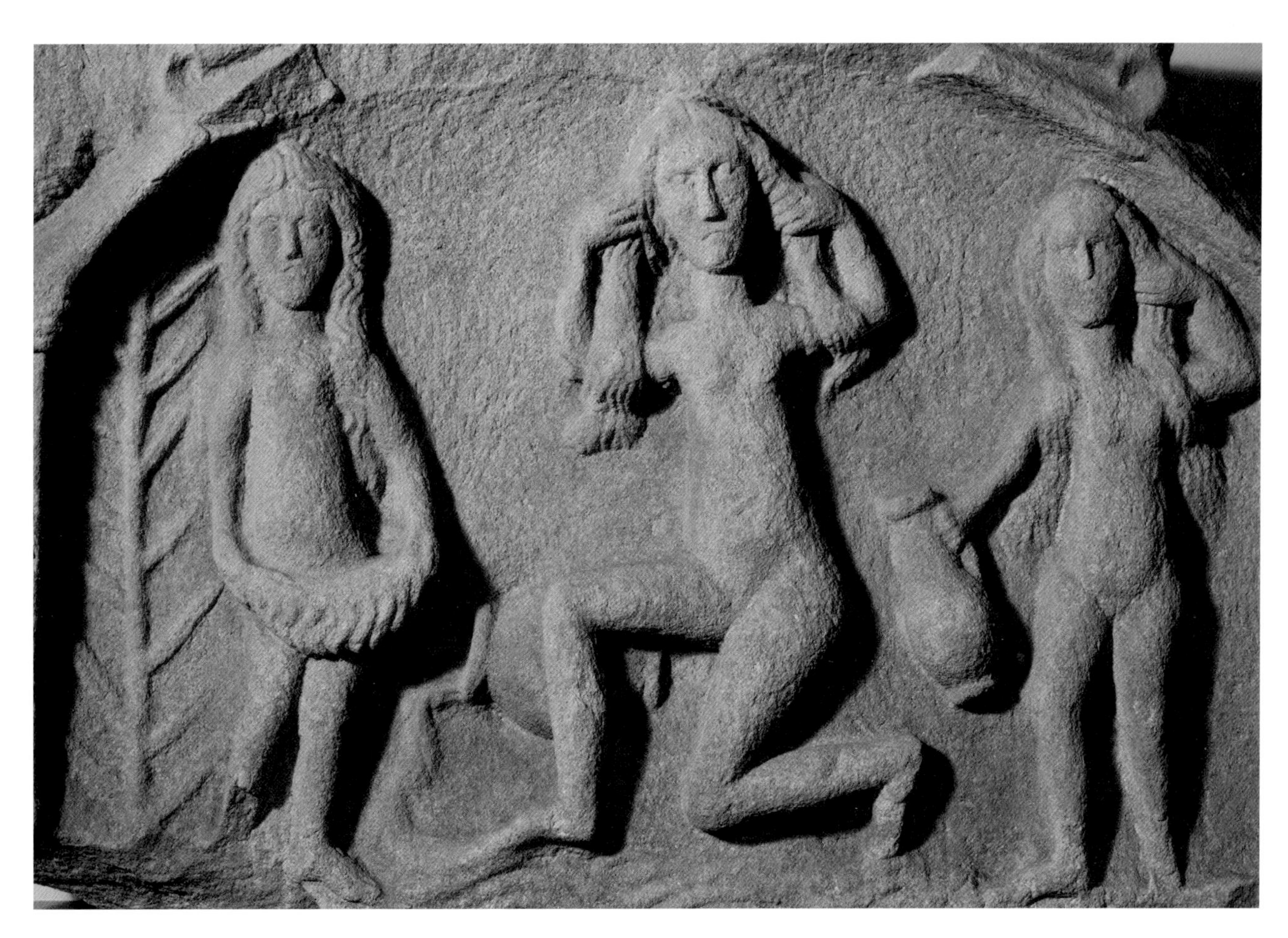

natural forms. The Venus from Britain is the center of attention not only because she is right in the middle of the relief but also because she looms over the two other women; she is too tall even to stand up straight. Although clearly based on a classical model, she was created by an artist in love with decoration. The "landscape" on this relief consists of wavy lines; a tree has become a series of diagonal sticks converging on a vertical. The figures do not interact; they look out—beyond one another and even beyond the viewer. All of this gives the relief an otherworldly feel, as if Venus existed in a place that transcended the here and now of the natural world.

Plate 1.5 Venus and Two Nymphs, Britain (2nd or early 3rd cent.). This relief was originally made to decorate the front of a water tank that stood before the headquarters of the Roman fort at High Rochester (today in Northumberland). This was an outpost of the Roman army, a fort on the road to Scotland. Compare the depiction of Venus here with that of Venus in Plate 1.1 to see the very different notions of the human body and of beauty that co-existed in the Roman Empire.

The same emphasis on transcendence explains the horizontal zones of the limestone tombstone in Plate 1.6, which announce a hierarchy. In the center of the top zone is a god. In the middle tier are people busying themselves with religious ceremonies. At the bottom, the lowest rung, three people are praying. The proper order of the cosmos, not the natural order, is the focus. The tombstone sculptors flattened their figures, varying them by cutting lines for folds, hands, and eyes. Any sense of movement here comes from the incised patterns, not from the rigidly frontal figures, who do not interact at all. Unlike the Venus and Mars fresco, this tombstone is no window onto a private world; unlike the Euhodus sarcophagus, it betrays no emotions. Rather, it teaches and preaches to those who look at it.

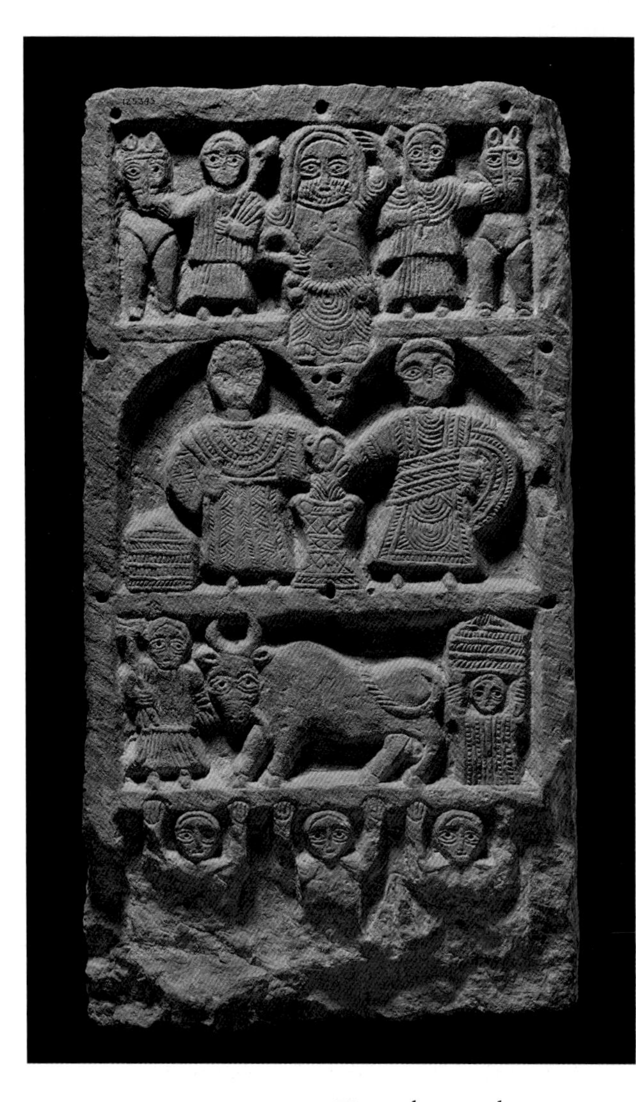

Plate 1.6 Tombstone, near Carthage (2nd cent.?). The stiff, frontal figures on this relief show the sculptors' delight in order, hierarchy, and decoration.

Plate 1.7 (facing page) Embracing Tetrarchs (*c*.300). Nearly two feet high, this imperial pair was accompanied by another nearly identical couple, both placed at the mid-point of two separate porphyry columns.

There may be something to the idea that such works of art were "inferior" to Roman products—but not much. The artists who made them had their own values and were not particularly interested in classical conventions. In the third century, even artists at the heart of the empire—at Rome, at Constantinople—adopted the provincial styles. Those conventions spoke best to new needs and interests. The "new" official style is nicely illustrated by the depiction of two emperors in Plate 1.7. Carved out of expensive, "imperial" porphyry stone, it was meant to telegraph amity and authority, not tell a story. When Diocletian divided the empire into four administrative districts, each ruled by a "Tetrarch" (ruler of a quarter), their unity was broadcast in a profusion of just such sculpted images. The two in Plate 1.7 are nearly identical; gone is the impulse (so evident in the Euhodus sarcophagus) to individualize. The sculptor is interested only in the gesture of embrace and the image of power, symbolized by the orbs both men hold in their left hands. Despite their friendliness, they do not look at each other but stare out, even beyond the viewer. Decorative elements—the details of their military garb, the leaves of their laurel wreaths—provide the only relief from the somber message here.

While the Tetrarchs were depicted as equals, other monuments of the fourth century telegraphed hierarchy. Consider a marble base made at Constantinople *c*.390 to support a gigantic ancient obelisk, transported at great cost from Egypt and set up with considerable difficulty at the Hippodrome, the great sports arena. (For the location of the Hippodrome, see Map 4.1 on p. 114.) The four-sided base depicts the games and races that took place in the stadium. The side shown in Plate 1.8 is decisively divided into two tiers. At the top are the imperial family and other dignitaries, all formal, frontal, staring straight ahead. Directly in the center is the imperial group, higher than all others. Beneath, in the lower tier, are bearded, hairy-coated barbarians, bringing humble offerings to those on high. The two levels are divided by a decorative frame, a rough indication of the "sky boxes" inhabited by the emperor and his retinue. The folds of the drapery are graceful but stylized. The hairstyles are caps. The ensemble is meant to preach eternal truths: the highness of imperial power and its transcendence of time and place.

Although this style of art was not initially Christian, it was quickly adopted by Christians. It was suited to a religion that saw only fleeting value in the City of Man, sought to transcend the world, and had a message to preach. A good example is the fourth-century wall painting decorating a small *confessio*—a place where martyrs or their

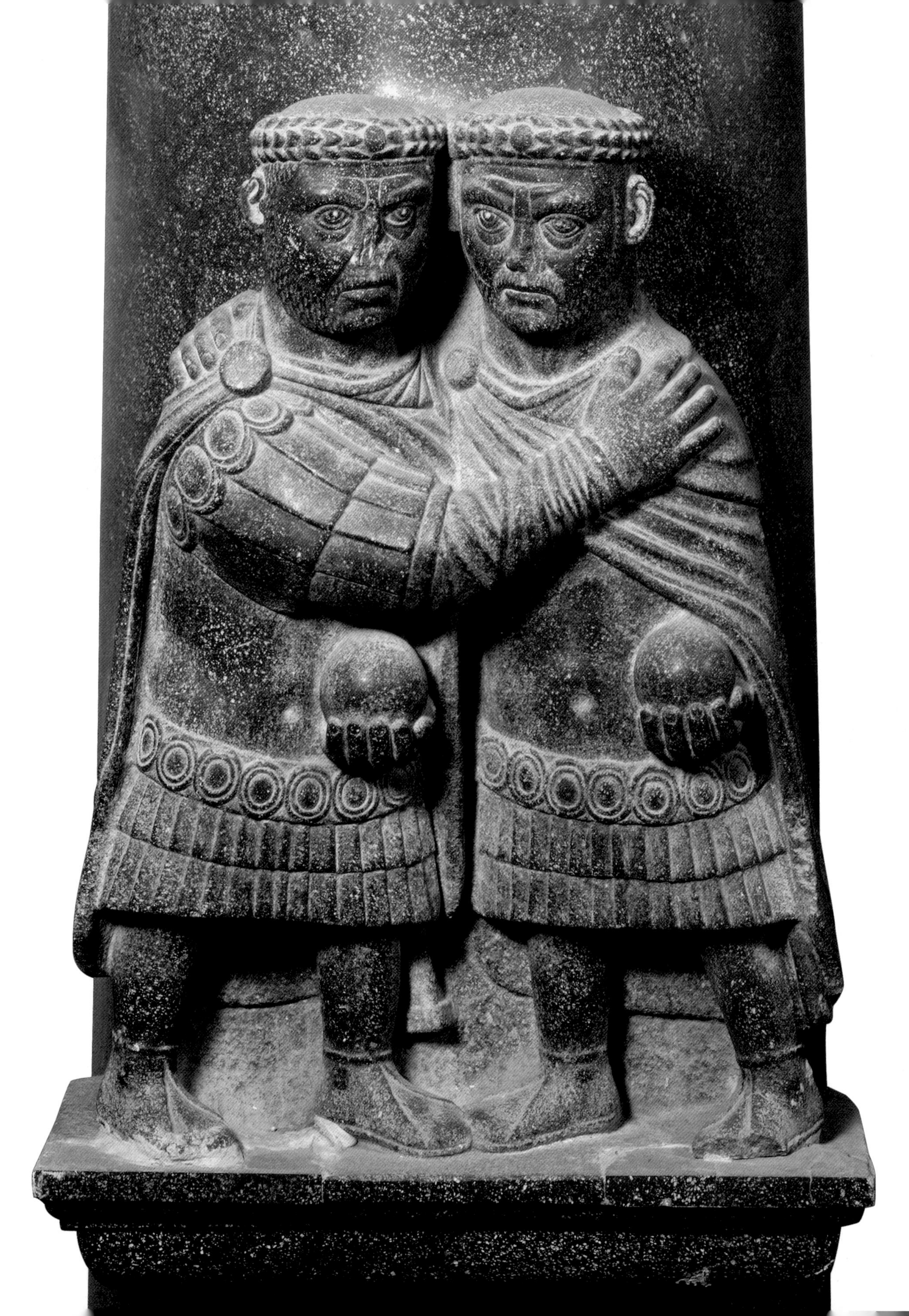

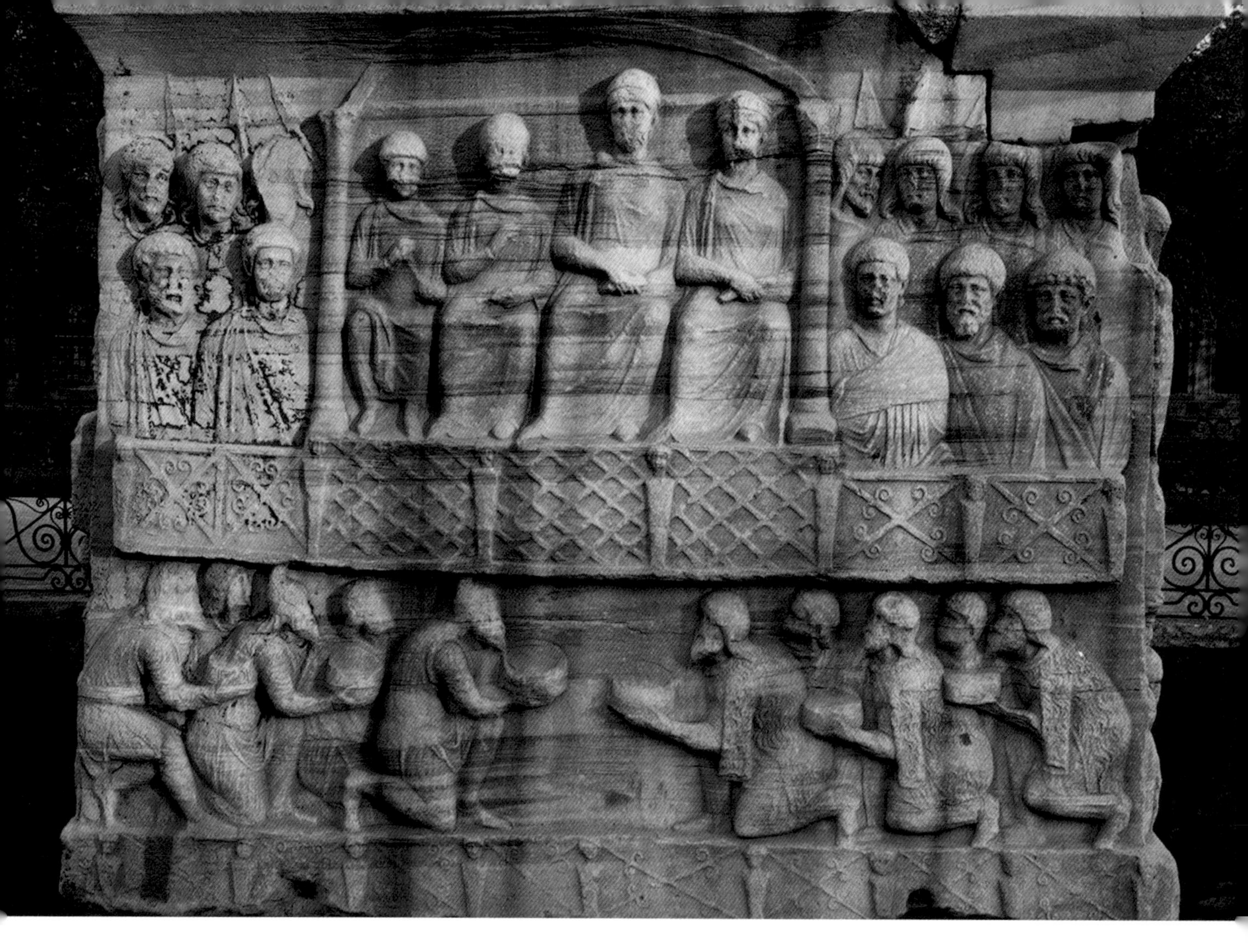

Plate 1.8 Base of the Hippodrome Obelisk (*c.*390). This carving, placed right in the middle of the most imperial part of Constantinople, was inspired more by the conventions of the Carthage tombstone (Plate 1.6) than by the traditional classical forms of the Euhodus sarcophagus (Plate 1.4).

relics were buried. (See Plate 1.9, also discussed earlier on p. 11.) The wall, originally in an alcove on the landing of a private house in Rome, is today beneath a church dedicated to two martyr-saints, John and Paul. Much like the figures on the tombstone in Plate 1.6, the painting immediately communicates a spiritual hierarchy. Whoever the standing orant might represent (there are conflicting interpretations), it is clear that he dominates the scene while two figures in postures of humility touch his feet. The curtains that frame the scene may symbolize a place of eternal rest. Certainly, the fresco, like the tombstone, marked a burial site, since behind the grill above the orant were the remains of a martyr or martyrs. Like the figures on the tombstone, those in the fresco have no weight, exist in no landscape, and interact with no one. We shall continue to see the influence of this transcendent style throughout the Middle Ages.

Nevertheless, around the very same time as this fresco was produced, classical artistic styles were making a brief comeback even in a Christian context. Sometimes called the "renaissance of the late fourth and early fifth centuries," this was the first of many recurring infusions of the classical spirit in medieval art. Consider the sarcophagus of Junius

Bassus, carved in 359 (Plate 1.10). Look at just the bottom central panel, which depicts a man on a horse-like donkey. Two young men greet him, one peeking out from behind an oak tree, the other laying down a cloak. The rider's garment drapes convincingly around his body, which has weight, volume, and plasticity. There is a sense of depth and lively human interaction, just as there was in the Euhodus sarcophagus (Plate 1.4). But this is a Christian coffin, and the rider is Christ, entering Jerusalem.

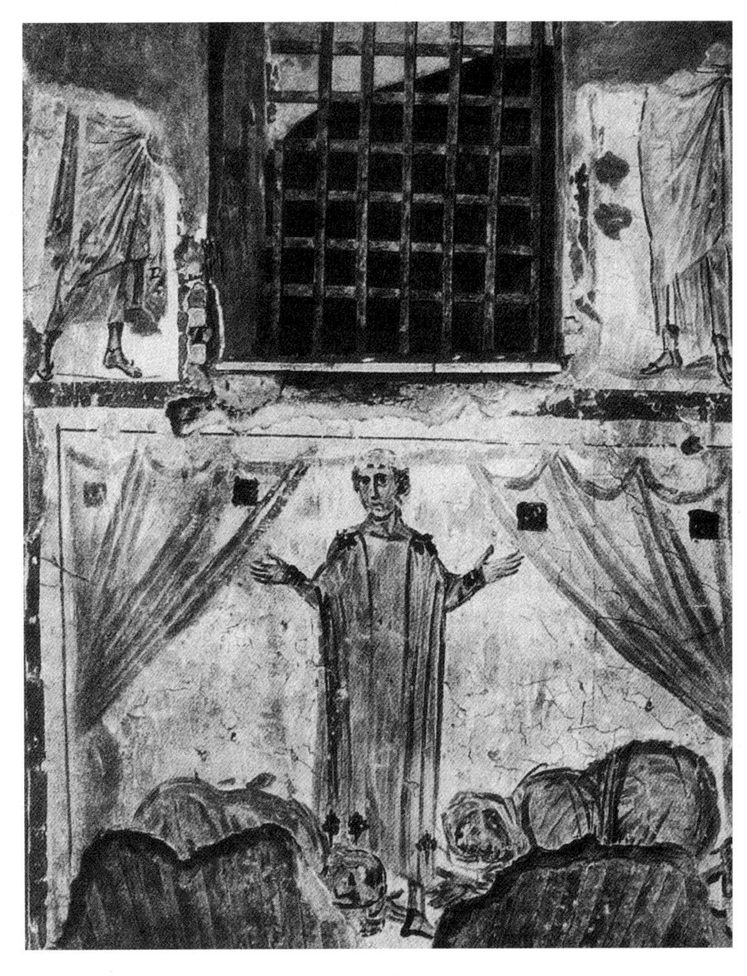

Plate 1.9 Orant Fresco (second half of 4th cent.). In a private house located in a posh neighborhood in Rome, an imposing figure commands the lower wall of a small room serving as a *confessio*, which contained the remains of martyrs. At the time, the house functioned as a *titulus*, or community church. We see here the sorts of lay devotional initiatives—a *confessio* in a private house—that Bishop Ambrose hoped to end.

THE BARBARIANS

The classicizing style exemplified by Junius Bassus's coffin did not long survive the sack of Rome by the Visigoths in 410. The sack was a stunning blow. Like a married couple in a bitter divorce, both Romans and Goths had once wooed one another; they then became mutually and comfortably dependent; eventually they fell into betrayal and strife. Nor was the Visigothic experience unique. The Franks, too, had been recruited into the Roman army, some of their members settling peacefully within the imperial borders. The Burgundian experience was similar.

The Romans called all these peoples "barbarians," though, borrowing a term from the Gauls, they designated those beyond the Rhine as "Germani"—Germans. Historians today tend to differentiate these peoples linguistically: "Germanic peoples" are those who spoke Germanic languages. Whatever name we give them (they certainly had no collective name for themselves), these peoples were not nomads (as an earlier generation of historians believed) but rather accustomed to a settled existence. Archaeologists have found evidence in northern Europe of some of their hamlets, built and inhabited for centuries before any Germanic groups entered the Empire. A settlement near Wijster, near the North Sea (today in the Netherlands; see p. 22), is a good example of one such community. Inhabited largely between *c.*150 and *c.*400, it consisted of well over fifty large rectangular wooden houses—these were partitioned so that they could be shared by humans and animals—and many smaller out-buildings, some of which were used as barns or workrooms, others as dwellings. Palisades—fences made of wooden stakes—marked off its streets and lanes. The people who lived at Wijster cultivated grains and raised cattle. They also raised horses, as we know from the fact that they frequently buried their horses

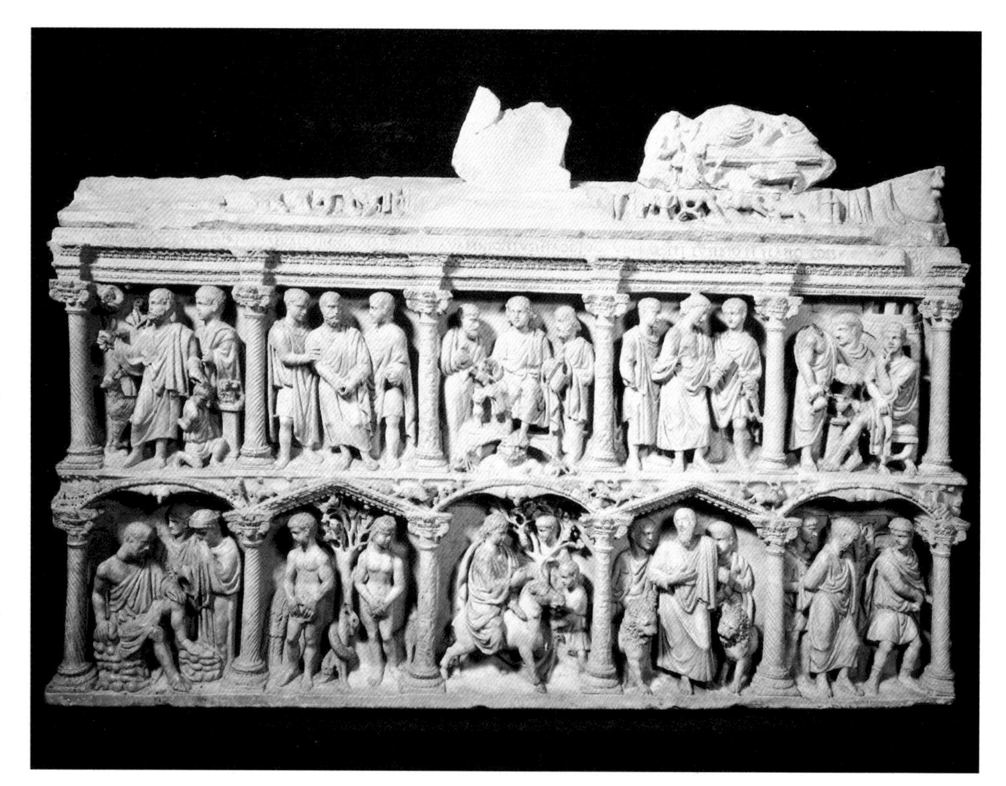

Plate 1.10 Sarcophagus of Junius Bassus (359). The figures of this relief are carved nearly in the round, and in that sense they are even more "classical" in inspiration than the Euhodus sarcophagus (Plate 1.4). However, the tight compartments in which the figures gesture and interact betray the fourth-century obsession with order. Although the figures could have almost been lifted from any classical sculpture, they are here involved in an entirely Christian story. Reading the scenes from left to right, they portray: (top) Abraham and Isaac; Peter's arrest; Christ enthroned between Saints Peter and Paul, his feet resting on the scarf of Heaven; Christ's arrest; the judgment of Pilate; (bottom) Job sitting on the dunghill, comforted by friends; Adam and Eve; Christ's triumphal entry into Jerusalem; Daniel (clothed by a later, prudish carver, but originally naked) in the lion's den; the arrest of Saint Paul.

in carefully dug rectangular pits. Some were craftsmen, like the carpenters who built the houses, the ironworkers who made the tools, and the cobbler who made a shoe found on the site. Some were craftswomen, like the spinners and weavers who used the spindle-whorls and loom-weights that were found there.

The disparate sizes of its houses suggest that the community at Wijster was hardly egalitarian. The cemetery there made the same point, since, while most of the graves contained no goods at all, a very few were richly furnished with weapons, necklaces, and jewelry. It seems that the wealthy few also had access to Roman products: archaeologists have unearthed a couple of Roman coins, bits of Roman glass, and numerous fragments of provincial Roman pottery. But even the rich at Wijster were probably not very powerful: it is very likely that here, as elsewhere in the Germanic world, kings leading military retinues lorded it over the community, commanding labor services and a percentage of its agricultural production.

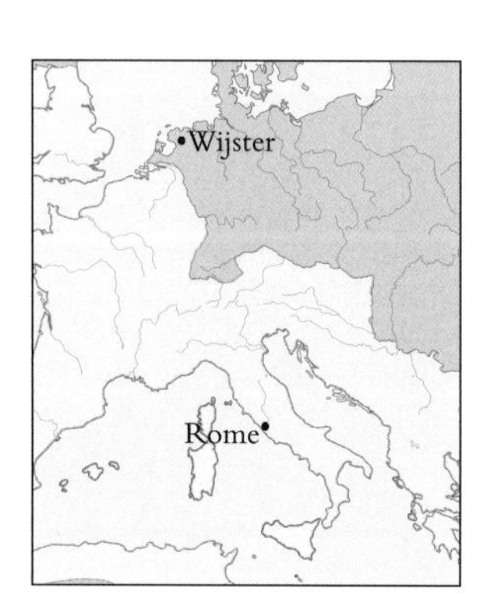

Map 1.4 Wijster

How did the better-off inhabitants of Wijster get their Roman dinnerware? They probably produced surplus enough to trade for other goods. All along the Empire's border, Germanic traders bartered with Roman provincials. No physical trait distinguished buyers from sellers. But barbarians and Romans had numerous *ethnic* differences—differences created by preferences and customs surrounding food, language, clothing, hairstyle, behaviors, and all the other elements that go into a sense of identity. Germanic ethnicities were often in flux as tribes came together and broke apart (and Roman ethnic identity also changed; for example, some began to sport Germanic clothing).

Consider the Goths. Their "ethnogenesis"—the ethnicities that came into being and changed over time—made them not one people but many. If it is true that a group called the "Goths" (Gutones) can be found in the first century in what is today northwestern Poland, that does not mean that they much resembled those "Goths" who, in the third century, organized and dominated a confederation of steppe peoples and forest dwellers of mixed origins north of the Black Sea (today Ukraine). The second set of Goths was a splinter of the first; by the time they got to the Black Sea, they had joined with many other groups. In short, the Goths were multiethnic.

Taking advantage—and soon becoming a part—of the crisis of the third century, the Black Sea Goths invaded and plundered the nearby provinces of the Roman Empire. The Romans responded at first with annual payments to buy peace, but before long they stopped, preferring confrontation. Around 250, Gothic and other raiders and pirates plundered parts of the Balkans and Anatolia (today Turkey). It took many years of bitter fighting for Roman armies, reinforced by Gothic and other mercenaries, to stop these raids. Afterwards, once again transformed, the Goths emerged in what historians have for convenience called two different groups: eastern (Ostrogoths), again north of the Black Sea, and western (Visigoths), in what is today Romania. By the mid-330s the Visigoths were allies of the Empire and fighting in their armies. Some rose to the position of army leaders. By the end of the fourth century, many Roman army units were made up of whole tribes—Goths or Franks, for example—fighting as "federates" for the Roman government under their own chiefs.

This was the marriage.

It fell apart, however, in the later fourth century, when first the Visigoths and soon other barbarian groups demanded entry into the Empire. They were fleeing the Huns, a nomadic people from the semi-arid, grass-covered plains (the "steppeland") of west-central Asia. After invading the Black Sea region in 376, the Huns moved west into what is today Romania, uprooting the Gothic groups living there and driving some to treat with the Romans and enter the Empire.

Barbarians had long been settled within the imperial borders as army recruits. But in this case the numbers were unprecedented: tens of thousands, perhaps even up to 200,000. The Romans were overwhelmed, unprepared, and resentful. They mistreated the refugees woefully, and in 378 a group of Visigoths and other barbarians rebelled, killing Emperor Valens (r.364–378) at the battle of Adrianople. The defeat meant more than the death of an emperor; it badly weakened the Roman army. Because the emperors needed soldiers and the Visigoths needed food and a place to settle, various arrangements were tried: treaties making the Visigoths federates; promises of pay and reward. None worked for long. Led by Alaric (d.410), an army of Visigoths set out to avenge their wrongs and to find land. Map 1.5 traces their long trek across Europe. Their sack of Rome in 410 inspired Augustine to write the *City of God*, but the Visigoths did not remain long in Italy. Joined by many other barbarian groups as well as Roman slaves taking advantage of the mayhem, they settled in southern Gaul by 418 and by 484 had taken most of Spain as well. The impact of the Visigoths on the Roman Empire was so decisive that some historians have taken the date 378 to mark the end of the Roman Empire, while others have chosen the date 410. (Other historians, to be sure, have disagreed with both dates!)

Meanwhile, beginning late in 406 and perhaps also impelled by the Huns, other barbarian groups—among them Vandals and Sueves—entered the Empire by crossing the Rhine River. They first moved into Gaul, then into Spain. The Vandals crossed into North Africa; the Sueves remained in Spain, though the Visigoths conquered most of their kingdom in the course of the sixth century. When, after the death in 453 of the powerful Hunnic leader Attila, the empire that he had created along the Danubian frontier collapsed, still other groups—Ostrogoths, Rugi, Gepids—moved into the Roman Empire. Each arrived with a "deal" from the Roman government; each hoped to work for Rome and reap its rewards. In 476 the last Roman emperor in the West, Romulus Augustulus (r.475–476), was deposed by Odoacer (433–493), a barbarian (from one of the lesser tribes, the Sciri) leading Roman troops. Odoacer promptly had himself declared king of Italy and, in a bid to "unite" the Empire, sent Romulus's imperial insignia to Emperor Zeno (r.474–491), ruler of the eastern half of the Roman Empire. But Zeno, in turn, authorized Theodoric, king of the Ostrogoths, to attack Odoacer in 489. Four years later, Theodoric's conquest of Italy was complete. Not much later the Franks, long used to fighting for the Romans, conquered Gaul under Clovis (r.481/482–511), a Roman official and king of the Franks, by defeating a provincial governor of Gaul and several barbarian rivals. Meanwhile, other barbarian groups set up their own kingdoms.

Around the year 500 the former Roman Empire was no longer like a scarf flung around the Mediterranean; it was a mosaic. (See Map 1.6.) Northwest Africa was now the Vandal kingdom, Spain the Visigothic kingdom, Gaul the kingdom of the Franks, and Italy the kingdom of the Ostrogoths. The Anglo-Saxons occupied southeastern Britain; the Burgundians formed a kingdom centered in what is today Switzerland. Only the eastern half of the Empire—the long end of the scarf—remained intact.

Map 1.5 The Huns and the Visigoths, *c.*375–450

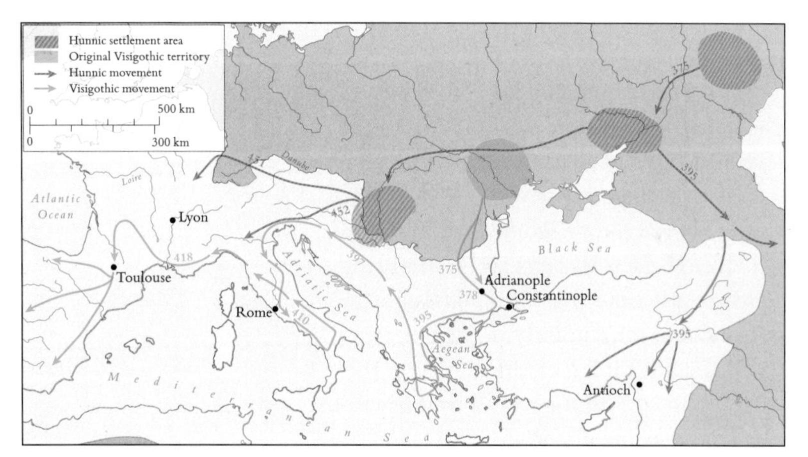

THE NEW ORDER

What was new about the "new order" of the sixth century was less the rise of barbarian kingdoms than it was, in the West, the decay of the cities balanced by the liveliness of the countryside, the increased dominance of the rich, and the quiet domestication of Christianity. In the East, the Roman Empire continued, made an ill-fated bid to expand, and finally retrenched as an autonomous entity: the Byzantine Empire.

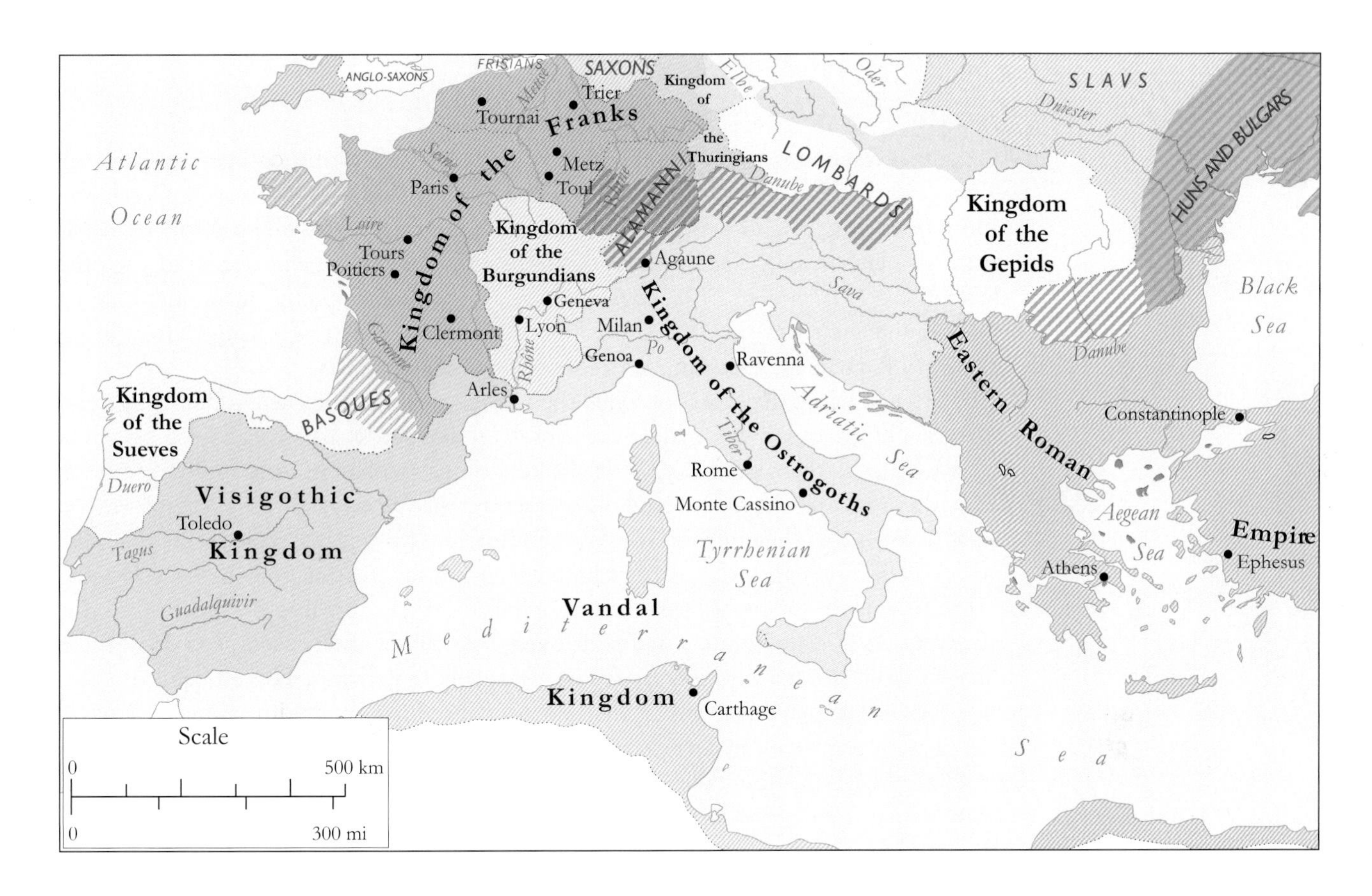

Map 1.6 The Former Western Empire, *c.*500

The Ruralization of the West

Where the barbarians settled, they did so with only tiny ripples of discontent from articulate Roman elites. How was that possible? Walter Goffart argues that taxes on Roman estates were shared between barbarian kings and their soldiers, with the allotments for the soldiers granted to their heirs as well. In this way, nothing upset traditional Roman property arrangements. Other historians—Matthew Innes is a good example—maintain that the barbarians were settled as "guests" directly on land of Roman property owners. In that case, barbarian kings, influenced by their Roman advisors, managed to defuse outright conflict. In either scenario, the end result was that elite "Romans" and "barbarians" gradually came to belong to the same community of free landowners.

But before this merging could take place, the great barrier to assimilation between Romans and barbarians—divergent religious beliefs—had to be overcome. Recall that Ulfila had preached Arianism to the Goths, and many of the other barbarian groups adopted this brand of Christianity as well. Clovis, king of the Franks, may have been the first Germanic king to choose the Roman version (though, if so, the king of Burgundy was close behind). Clovis had flirted with Arianism early on, but he soon converted to the Catholic Christianity of his Gallic neighbors. Bishop Avitus of Vienne welcomed this move with open arms: "Your faith is our victory."[9]

In other respects as well, the new rulers adopted Roman institutions, issuing laws that drew on Roman imperial precedents like *The Theodosian Code* (see below, p. 30), on regulations governing rural life found in Roman provincial law codes, and possibly on tribal customary law as well. *The Visigothic Code* was drawn up during the course of the fifth through seventh centuries. *The Burgundian Code* was issued in 517 by Sigismund, king of the Burgundians (r.516–524). A Frankish law code was compiled under King Clovis, fusing provincial Roman and Germanic procedures into a single whole.

Written in Latin, these laws revealed their Roman inspiration even in their language. Barbarian kings, some well-educated themselves, depended on classically trained advisors to write up their letters and laws. In Italy, in particular, an outstanding group of Roman administrators, judges, and officers served the Ostrogothic king Theodoric the Great (r.493–526). They included the learned Boethius (d.524/526), who wrote the tranquil *Consolation of Philosophy* as he awaited execution for treason, and the encyclopedic Cassiodorus (490–583), who wrote letters on behalf of Theodoric in the guise of a pious lawgiver. "As it is my desire, when petitioned, to give a lawful consent, so I do not like the laws to be cheated through my favors, especially in that area where I believe reverence for God to be concerned," Cassiodorus wrote (in Theodoric's name) to Jews at Genoa, allowing them, in accordance with Roman law and reverence for God, to add a roof to their synagogue, but nothing more.[10] Since the fourth century, Romans had become used to barbarian leaders; in the sixth, there was nothing very strange in having them as kings.

Far stranger was the disappearance of the urban middle class. The new taxes of the fourth century had much to do with this. The town councilors—the *curiales*, traditional leaders and spokesmen for the cities—had been used to collecting the taxes for their communities, making up any shortfalls, and reaping the rewards of prestige for doing so. In the fourth century, new land and head taxes impoverished the *curiales*, while very rich landowners—out in the countryside, surrounded by their bodyguards and slaves—simply did not bother to pay. Now the tax burdens fell on poorer people. Pressed to pay taxes they could not afford, families escaped to the great estates of the rich, giving up their free status in return for land and protection. By the seventh century, the rich had won; the barbarian kings no longer bothered to collect general taxes.

The cities, most of them walled since the time of the crisis of the third century, were no longer thriving or populous, though they remained political and religious centers. Tours (in Gaul), for example, protected its episcopal complex with a wall built *c*.400. (See Map 1.7.) But few people apart from the bishop and his entourage actually lived within those walls any longer. At the same time, in a cemetery that the Romans had carefully sited outside the city, a new church rose over the tomb of the local saint, Martin. This served as a magnet for the people of the surrounding countryside and even farther away. A baptistery was constructed nearby, to baptize the infants of pilgrims and others who came to the tomb hoping for a miracle. Sometimes people stayed for years. Gregory, bishop of Tours (r.573–594), our chief source for the history of Gaul in the sixth century, described Monegundis, a very pious woman:

> [she] left her husband, her family, her whole house, and went, full of faith, to the basilica of the holy bishop Martin. [After curing a sick girl on her way, she] arrived at the basilica of St Martin, and there, on her knees in front of the tomb, she gave thanks to God for being able to see the holy tomb with her own eyes. She settled herself in a small room [nearby] in which she gave herself every day to prayer, fasts and vigils.[11]

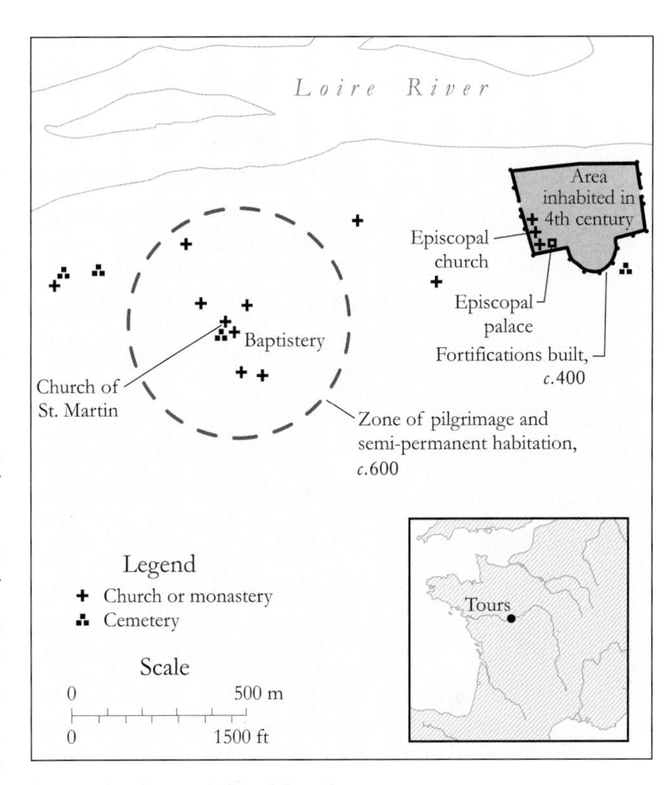

Map 1.7 Tours, *c.*600

With people like Monegundis flocking to the tomb, it is no wonder that archaeologists have found evidence of semi-permanent habitations right at the cemetery.

The shift from urban to rural settlements brought with it a new localism. The active long-distance trade of the Mediterranean slowed down, and although it did not stop, it penetrated very little beyond the coast. Consider the fate of pottery, a cheap necessity in the ancient world. In the sixth century, fine mass-produced African red pottery adorned even the humblest tables along the Mediterranean Sea coast. Inland, however, most people had to make do with local handmade wares, as regional networks of exchange eroded long-distance connections.

For some—the rich—the new disconnection of the rural landscape from the wider world hardly mattered. Bishop Gregory of Tours, who wrote about Monegundis, reported that greedy bishops sent an armed force against Bishop Victor right in the midst of his birthday celebration: "The attackers ripped his clothes, struck down servants and took away vessels and all the utensils of the feast, leaving the bishop grossly insulted."[12] Clearly Bishop Victor was used to living well. Indeed, bishops were among the rich; many rose to their episcopal status in their twilight years, after they had married and had sired children to inherit their estates. (Their wives continued to live with them but—or so it was expected—not to sleep with them.) Great lay landlords, kings, queens, warriors, and courtiers controlled and monopolized most of the rest of the wealth of the West, now based largely on land.

Monasteries, too, were becoming important corporate landowners. In the sixth century, many monks lived in communities just far enough away from the centers of power to be holy, yet near enough to be important. Monks were not quite laity (since they devoted their entire life to religion), yet not quite clergy (since they were only rarely ordained), but something in between and increasingly admired. It is often said that Saint Antony was the "first monk," and though this may not be strictly true, it is not far off the mark. Like Antony, monks lived a life of daily martyrdom, giving up their wealth, family ties, and worldly offices. Like Antony, who eventually gave up the solitary life, monks lived in communities. Some communities were of men only, some of women, some of both (in separate quarters). Whatever the sort, monks lived in obedience to a "rule" that gave them a stable and orderly way of life.

The rule might be unwritten, as it was at Saint-Maurice d'Agaune, a monastic community set up in 515 by Sigismund on the eve of his accession to the Burgundian throne. The monks at Agaune, divided into groups that went to the church in relay, carried out a grueling regime of non-stop prayer every day. Built outside the Burgundian capital of Geneva, high on a cliff that was held to be the site of the heroic martyrdom of a Christian Roman legion, this monastery tapped into a holy landscape and linked it to Sigismund and his episcopal advisors.

Other rules were written. Caesarius, bishop of Arles (r.502–542) wrote one for his sister, the "abbess" (head) of a monastery of women. He wrote another for his nephew, the "abbot" of a male monastery. In Italy, Saint Benedict (d.*c.*550/560) wrote the most famous of the monastic rules at some time between 530 and 560. With its adoption, much later, by the Carolingian kings of the ninth century, it became the monastic norm in the West. Unlike the rule of Agaune, where prayer was paramount, the Benedictine Rule divided the day into discrete periods of prayer, reading, and labor. Nevertheless, the core of its program, as at Agaune, was the "liturgy"—not just the Mass, but also an elaborate round of formal worship that took place seven times a day and once at night. At these specific times, the monks chanted—that is sang—the "Offices," most of which consisted of the psalms, a group of 150 poems in the Old Testament:

> During wintertime ... first this verse is to be said three times: "Lord, you will open my lips, and my mouth will proclaim your praise." To that should be added Psalm 3 and the Gloria [a short hymn of praise]. After that, Psalm 94 with an antiphon [a sort of chorus], or at least chanted. Then an Ambrosian hymn [written by Saint Ambrose of Milan] should follow, and then six psalms with antiphons.[13]

By the end of each week the monks would have completed all 150 psalms.

Benedict's monastery, Monte Cassino, was in the shadow of the city of Rome, far enough to be an "escape" from society but near enough to link it to the papacy. Pope Gregory the Great (590–604), arguably responsible for making the papacy the greatest power in Italy, took the time to write a biography of Benedict and praise his Rule. Monks may have renounced wealth and power individually, but monasteries became partners of the wealthy and powerful and benefited from their largess. The monks were seen as models of virtue, and their prayers were thought to reach God's ear. It was crucial to ally with them.

Little by little the Christian religion was domesticated to meet the needs of the new order, even as it shaped that order to fit its demands. Monegundis was not afraid to go to the cemetery outside of Tours. There were no demons there; they had been driven far away by the power of Saint Martin. Just as Benedict's monasteries had become perfectly acceptable alternatives to the old avenues of male prestige—armies and schools—so Monegundis's little cell became home to a group of pious women who found their vocation in the

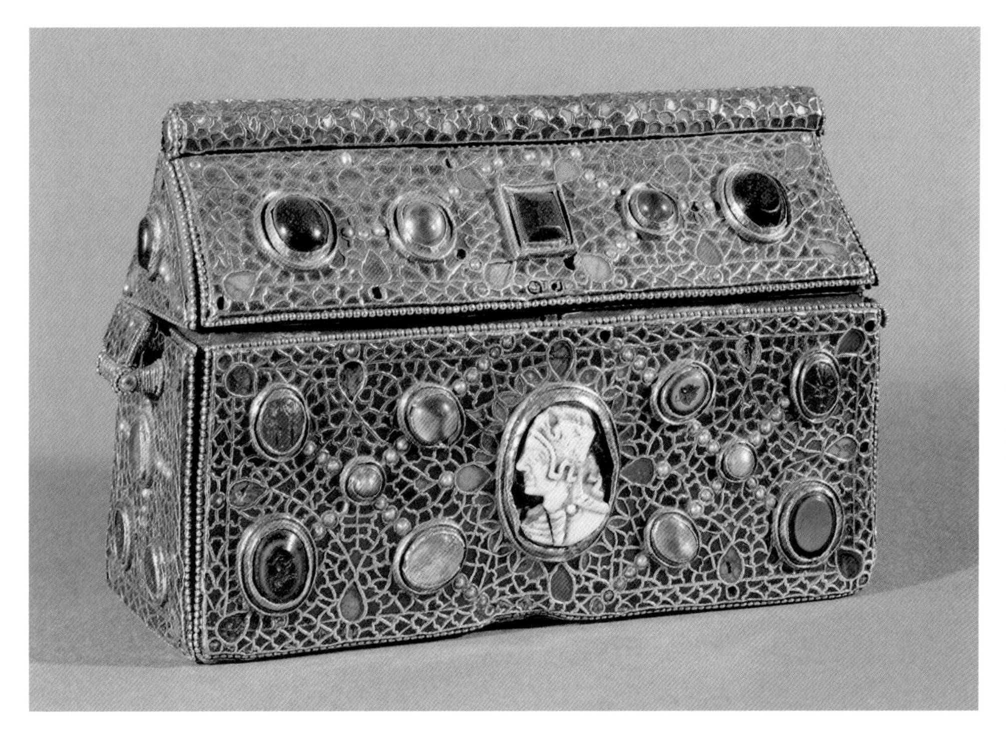

Plate 1.11 Reliquary of Theuderic (late 7th cent.). A small box shaped like a miniature sarcophagus and made of cloisonné enamel (bits of enamel framed by metal) richly adorned with semi-precious stones, this reliquary is inscribed on the back, "Theuderic the priest had this made in honor of Saint Maurice." Paying for the creation of a reliquary—suitable housing for the remains of the saints—was itself an act of piety.

religious life rather than marriage. When Monegundis was about to die, they acted to perpetuate the community she had founded, begging her "to bless some oil and salt that we can give to the sick who ask for a blessing." She did so, and they "preserved [it] with great care."[14] No doubt they kept the oil in a precious container, just as the monastery of Saint-Maurice d'Agaune kept some of its saintly relics in a gorgeous reliquary studded with garnets, glass gems, and a cameo (Plate 1.11). Relics like Monegundis's oil or Saint Martin's tomb brought the sacred into the countryside and into the texture of everyday life.

Retrenchment in the East

After 476 there was a "new order" in the East as well as the West, but initially the changes were less obvious. For one thing, there was still an emperor with considerable authority. The towns continued to thrive, and the best of the small-town educated elite went off to Constantinople, where they found good jobs as administrators, civil servants, and financial advisors. While barbarian kings in the West were giving in to the rich and eliminating general taxes altogether, the eastern emperors were collecting state revenues more efficiently than ever. Emperor Justinian (r.527–565) had the money to wage major wars—though failing to revive the Roman Empire of the first centuries—even as he rebuilt Hagia Sophia ("Holy Wisdom"), the great church of Constantinople, when it burned down. Ten thousand workers covered its domed ceiling with gold and used 40,000 pounds of silver for its decoration. When a terrible plague hit the whole Mediterranean region and beyond in the 540s, Justinian (after whom historians have named the plague) paid to dispose of

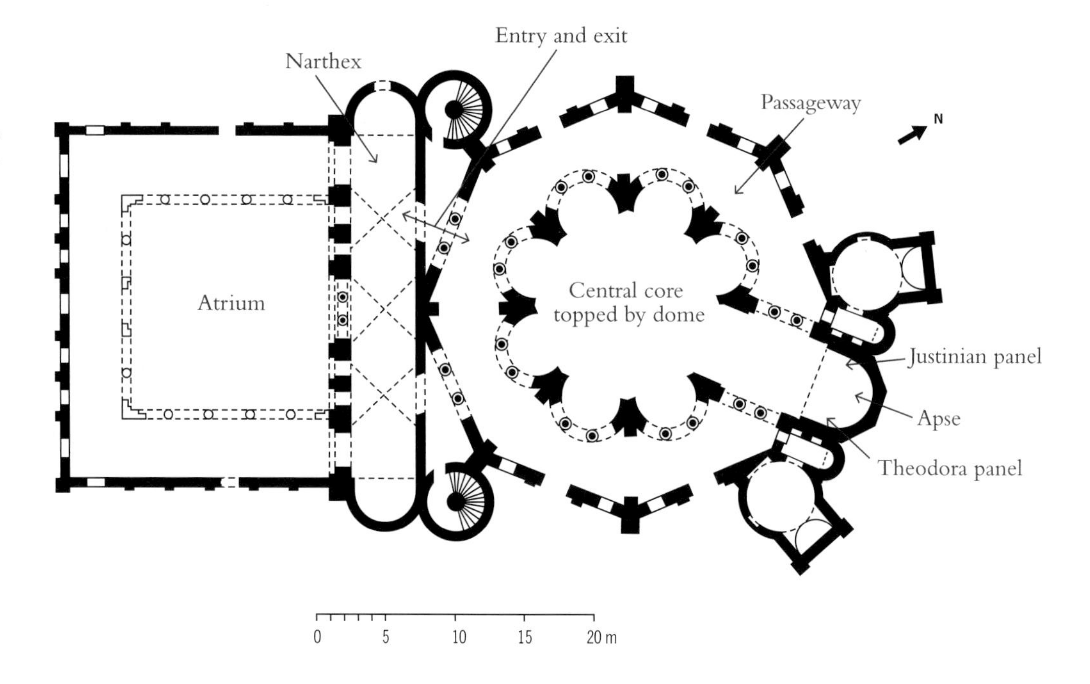

Figure 1.1 San Vitale, Ravenna, Reconstructed Original Ground Plan, 6th cent.

the rotting corpses piled up along the shore of Constantinople. He hired workers to build stretchers, carry out the bodies, and deposit the remains in burial pits. (Pope Gregory the Great had a more spiritual response to a later wave of the same plague: he called for "tears of penitence" rather than grave diggers.[15])

Nevertheless, the eastern Roman Empire was not the old Roman Empire writ small. When the Visigoths sacked Rome, the eastern emperor Theodosius II (r.408–450) did not send an army; he built walls around Constantinople instead. When the roads fell into disrepair, Justinian let many of them decay. When the Slavs pressed on the Roman frontier in the Balkans, Justinian let them enter. The Plague of Justinian, which continued to attack sporadically until the mid-eighth century, led to manpower and revenue shortages.

In the fifth and sixth centuries, the Eastern half of the Empire reorganized itself. For the first time, emperors issued compendia of Roman laws. *The Theodosian Code*, which gathered together imperial "constitutions" (general laws) alongside "rescripts" (rulings on individual cases), was published in 438. Western barbarian law codes of the sixth century attempted to match this achievement, but they were overshadowed by the great legal initiatives of Justinian, which included an imperial law code known as the *Codex Justinianus* (529, revised in 534), and the *Digest* (533), an orderly compilation of Roman juridical thought from the pre-imperial period onward. From then on the laws of the eastern Roman Empire were largely (though not wholly) fixed, though Justinian's books were soon eclipsed by short summaries in Greek, while in the West they had little impact until the twelfth century.

Above all, the emperor in the East took on the image of concentrated power associated with the ceremony and pomp of the Persian "king of kings," combining it with an exalted role in the Christian church. San Vitale at Ravenna offers a dazzling example. It was built by successive bishops of Ravenna: Ecclesius, Victor, and Archbishop Maximianus.

Constructed in the unusual form of an octagon (see Figure 1.1), San Vitale is topped by a lofty dome and glows with marble and mosaics. Its main apse—directly behind the altar—seamlessly merges heaven and earth, church and state. Plate 1.12 conveys an idea of the whole as the viewer (perhaps a priest entering to celebrate the Eucharist, or others entering the church in liturgical procession at one of the building's many doors) might have seen it. The plate shows the central half dome of the apse: beneath a youthful Christ, flanked by angels and sitting on a blue orb, run the Four Rivers of Paradise. Lilies and roses bloom on the rocky ground. The two angels flanking Christ look away from him, attending to the two men at their sides. These are, on the viewer's right, Bishop Ecclesius, who offers Christ a model of the very church of San Vitale; and on the left, Saint Vitalis (after whom the church is named), who accepts the crown of martyrdom from Christ.

Three large windows below this heavenly scene light the apse. On either side are mosaic panels depicting (on the viewer's left) Emperor Justinian and (on the right) Empress Theodora. Justinian, the central and largest figure in his panel, has a halo and wears a crown. He holds a large golden paten—the bowl that contains the bread of the Eucharist—and offers it in the direction of both Christ above him and the altar, which would have been below. To his left is a bishop carrying a gem-studded gold cross; the name MAXIMIANUS is boldly outlined above his head. Both the name and the face of Maximianus were added to the mosaic after it was first made. Maximianus was Justianian's appointee at Ravenna, and he here found a way to permanently associate himself with the imperial majesty. Behind Maximianus are other churchmen bringing more precious objects to the altar. On Justinian's right-hand side are members of his court: aristocrats and soldiers. It is no accident that the total number of people led by Justianian is twelve (or possibly thirteen), like the apostles of Jesus.

Facing the emperor's panel is a similar one for the empress. She, too, has a halo, and her garment (the same sort of purple *chlamys* that Justinian wears) has at the hem an image of the three Magi offering gifts to the Christ Child. Like them, Theodora is making an offering: she holds out to Christ (above her) and to the altar (below) a gold chalice, the vessel for the wine of the Eucharist. To her left are a group of splendidly dressed women, representing her retinue. To her right are two men of high rank.

The entire complex—reading it from the viewer's right to left—depicts a circle of gift-giving and mutual generosity: Theodora offers a chalice to Christ and the altar, Ecclesius gives a church to Christ, Christ presents a crown to Vitalis, and finally Emperor Justinian completes the circle by offering the paten back to Christ and the altar on which Christ's sacrifice is celebrated.

What were Justinian and Theodora doing in Ravenna? Hadn't the Ostrogoths conquered Italy in the fifth century, making Ravenna the seat of their royal government? The answer is that Justinian reconquered Italy as part of his bid to recapture the glory and territory of the old Roman Empire. His armies quickly took North Africa from the Vandals in 534. They added a strip of southeastern Spain in 552 and went on to wrench—but only with great difficulty—Italy from the Ostrogoths. Only the first enterprise was fairly successful; Eastern Roman rule lasted in North Africa for another century. The last venture, however,

Following pages:

Plate 1.12 San Vitale, Ravenna, Apse Mosaics (mid-6th cent.). The warm colors of the apse mosaics—especially greens and golds—emphasize the rich abundance of the offerings brought to the altar by emperor and empress, a theme mirrored by the intersecting cornucopias that frame the image of Christ and his companions in heaven.

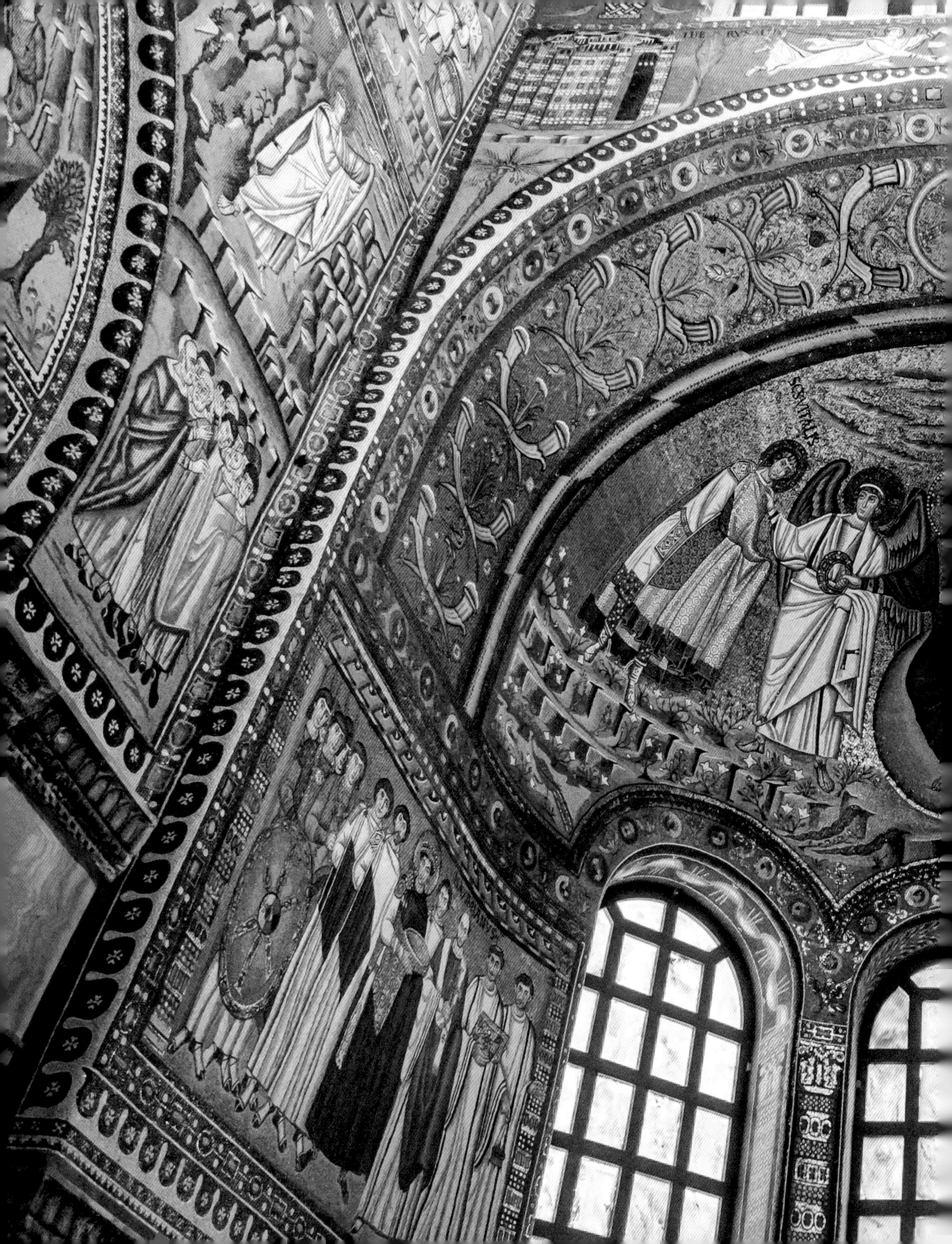
SCS VITALIS

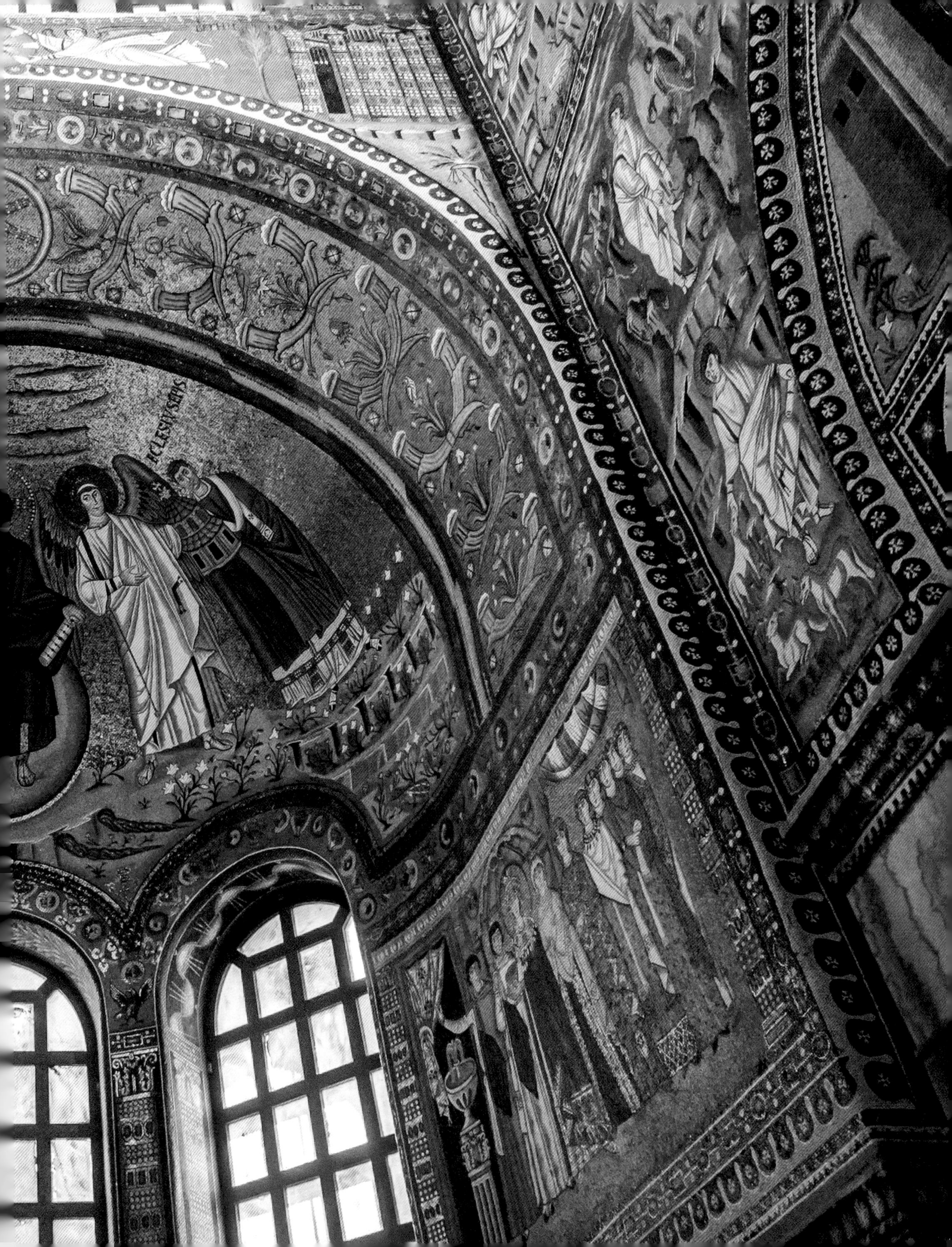

Map 1.8 Europe, the Eastern Roman Empire, and Persia, *c.*600

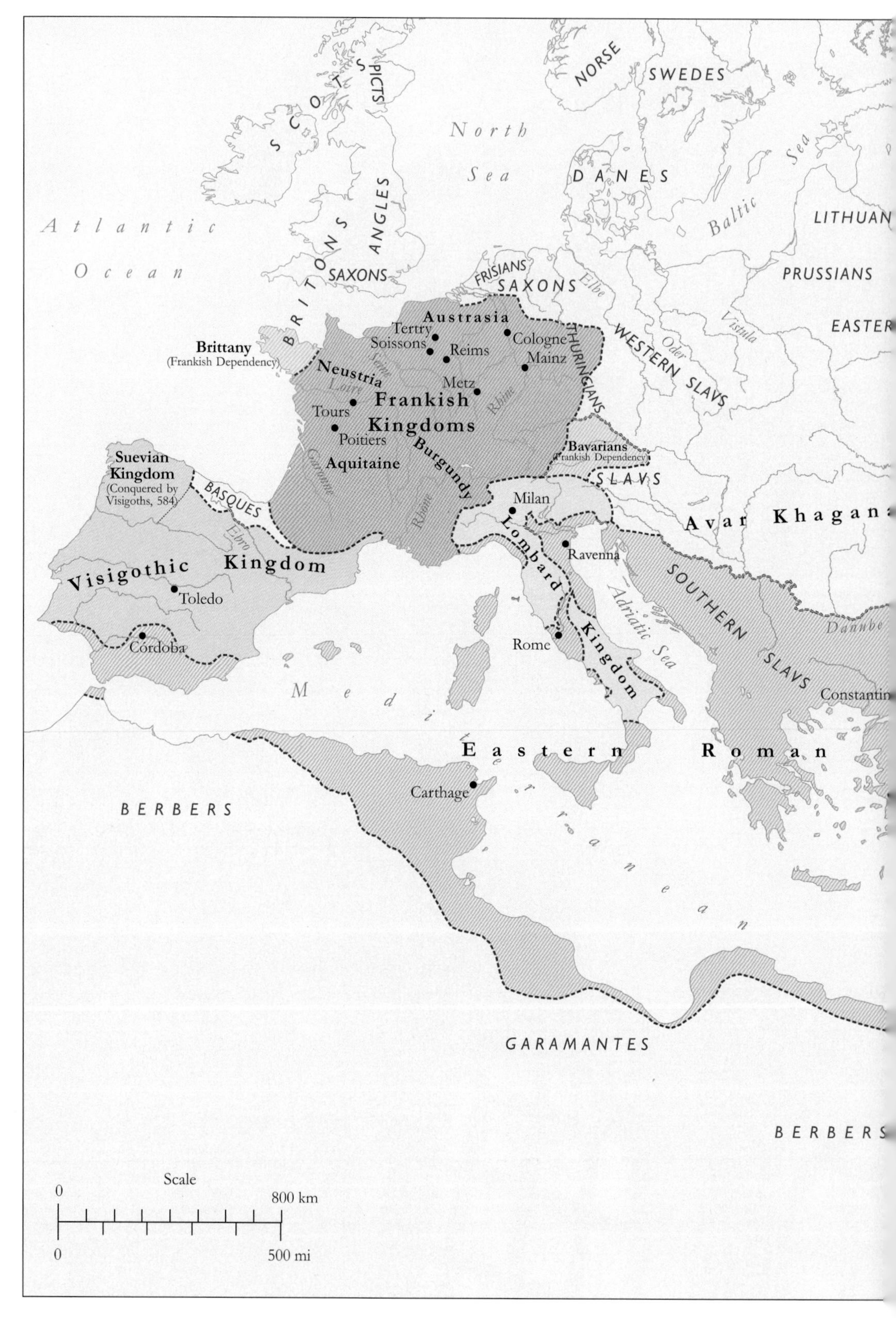

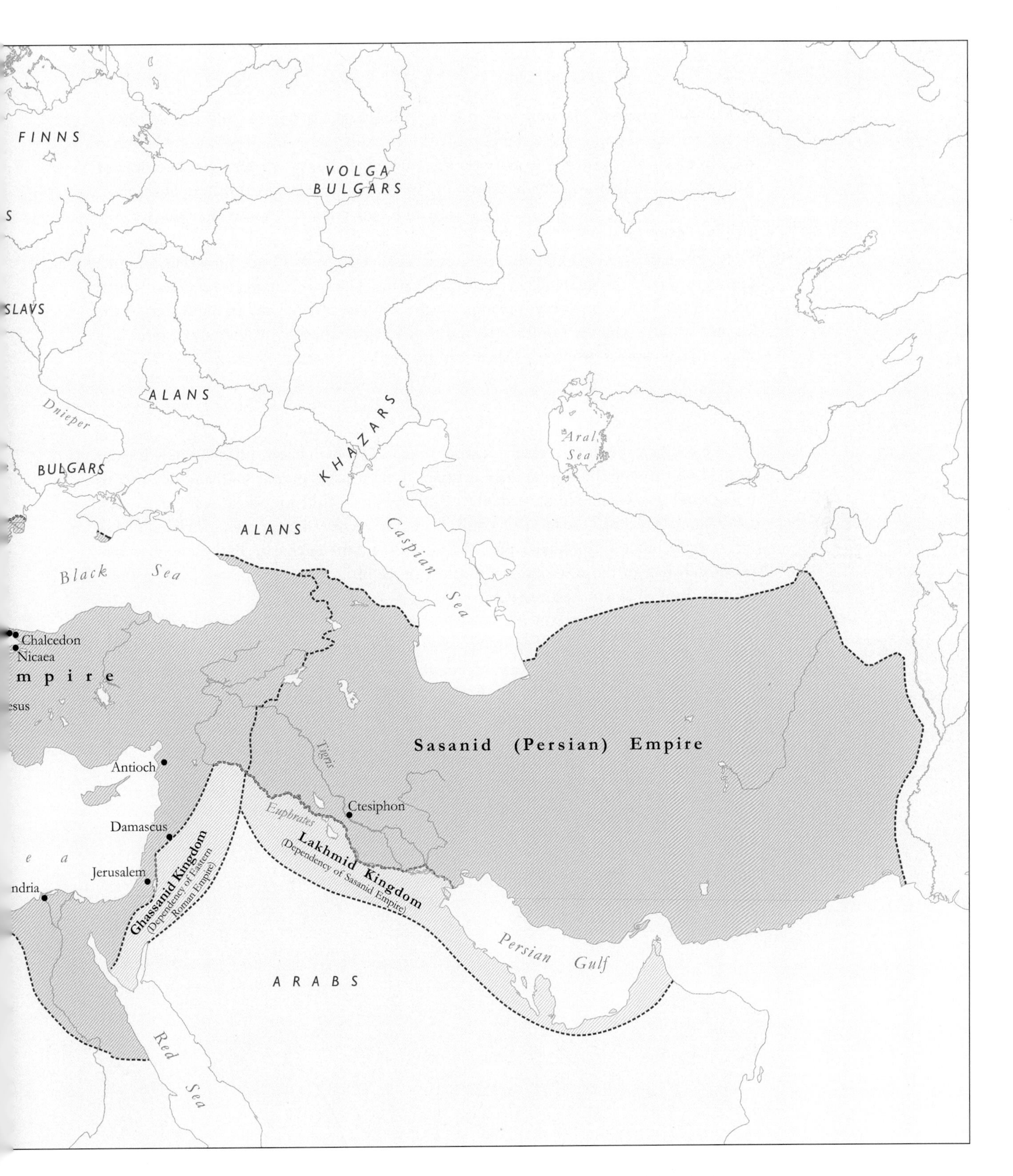

FINNS
VOLGA BULGARS
SLAVS
ALANS
Dnieper
KHAZARS
BULGARS
Aral Sea
ALANS
Caspian Sea
Black Sea
Chalcedon
Nicaea
mpire
Sasanid (Persian) Empire
Tigris
Antioch
Ctesiphon
Euphrates
Damascus
Lakhmid Kingdom
(Dependency of Sasanid Empire)
Ghassanid Kingdom
(Dependency of Eastern Roman Empire)
Jerusalem
Persian Gulf
ARABS
Red Sea

was nearly a disaster. The long war in Italy, which began in 535 and ended only in 553, devastated the country. Soon the Lombards, Germanic warriors employed by Justinian to help take Italy, returned to Italy on their own behalf. By 572 they were masters of part of northern Italy and, further south, of Spoleto and Benevento. Only an hour-glass-shaped strip of land running from Ravenna to Rome remained to the "Romans" of the East (See Map 1.8.)

For the Eastern Roman Empire, the western undertaking was a sideshow. The Empire's real focus was on the Sasanid Empire of the Persians. The two "super-powers" confronted one another with wary forays throughout the sixth century. They thought that to the winner would come the spoils. Little did they imagine that the real winner would be a new and unheard-of group: the Muslims.

★ ★ ★ ★ ★

The crisis of the third century demoted the old Roman elites, bringing new groups to the fore. Among these were the Christians, who insisted on one God and one way to understand and worship him. Made the official religion of the Empire under Theodosius, Christianity redefined the location of the holy: no longer was it in private households or city temples but in the precious relics of the saints and the Eucharist; in those who ministered on behalf of the church on earth (the priests, bishops, and emperors); and in those who led lives of ascetic heroism (the monks).

Politically the Empire, once a vast conglomeration of conquered provinces, was in turn largely conquered by its periphery. In spite of themselves, the Romans had tacitly to acknowledge and exploit the interdependence between the center and the hinterlands. They invited the barbarians in, but then declined to recognize the needs of their guests. That repudiation came too late. The barbarians were part of the Empire, and in the western half they took it over. In the next century, they would show how much they had learned from their former hosts.

CHAPTER ONE: ESSENTIAL DATES

306–337	Reign of Emperor Constantine
313	Edict of Milan; toleration of all religions in Empire
325	Council of Nicaea; laws and doctrines of Christianity declared
378	Battle of Adrianople; Emperor Valens killed by Visigoths
380	Edict of Thessalonica; Christianity becomes the official religion of the Roman Empire
410	Visigoths sack Rome
476	Deposition of Romulus Augustulus, last Roman emperor in the West
590–604	Pope Gregory the Great

NOTES

1 *The Edict of Milan*, in *Reading the Middle Ages: Sources from Europe, Byzantium, and the Islamic World*, 3rd ed., ed. Barbara H. Rosenwein (Toronto: University of Toronto Press, 2018), p. 3.
2 *The Nicene Creed*, in *Reading the Middle Ages*, p. 11.
3 Ibid.
4 *Manichaean Texts*, in *Reading the Middle Ages*, p. 10–11.
5 *The Confessions of Saint Augustine* 8.4, trans. Rex Warner (New York: Mentor, 1963), p. 166.
6 Augustine, *City of God*, in *Reading the Middle Ages*, p. 20.
7 Jerome, *Letter 24* (*To Marcella*), in *Reading the Middle Ages*, p. 29.
8 Athanasius, *Life of St. Antony of Egypt*, in *Reading the Middle Ages*, p. 34.
9 Avitus of Vienne, *Letter to Clovis*, in *Reading the Middle Ages*, p. 43.
10 Cassiodorus, *Variae (State Papers)*, in *Reading the Middle Ages*, p. 41.
11 Gregory of Tours, *The Life of Monegundis*, in *Reading the Middle Ages*, p. 40.
12 Gregory of Tours, *Histories*, in *Reading the Middle Ages*, p. 52.
13 *The Benedictine Rule*, in *Reading the Middle Ages*, p. 24.
14 Gregory of Tours, *The Life of Monegundis*, in *Reading the Middle Ages*, p. 40.
15 Gregory the Great, *Letter to Bishop Dominic of Carthage*, in *Reading the Middle Ages*, p. 7.

FURTHER READING

Brown, Peter. "Enjoying the Saints in Late Antiquity." *Early Medieval Europe* 9, no. 1 (2000): 1–24.

Burrus, Virginia, ed. *Late Ancient Christianity*. Minneapolis: Fortress Press, 2010.

Deliyannis, Deborah Mauskopf. *Ravenna in Late Antiquity*. Cambridge: Cambridge University Press, 2010.

Demacopoulos, George E. *Gregory the Great: Ascetic, Pastor, and First Man of Rome*. Notre Dame: University of Notre Dame Press, 2015.

Fleming, Robin. *Britain after Rome: The Fall and Rise, 400 to 1070*. London: Penguin, 2010.

Goffart, Walter. "The Technique of Barbarian Settlement in the Fifth Century: A Personal, Streamlined Account with Ten Additional Comments." *Journal of Late Antiquity* 3, no. 1 (2010): 65–98.

Heather, Peter. *Empires and Barbarians: Migrations, Development and the Birth of Europe*. London: Macmillan, 2009.

Heinzelmann, Martin. *Gregory of Tours: History and Society in the Sixth Century*. Trans. Christopher Carroll. Cambridge: Cambridge University Press, 2001.

Innes, Matthew. "Land, Freedom and the Making of the Medieval West." *Transactions of the Royal Historical Society* 16 (2006): 39–74.

Johnson, Scott Fitzegerald, ed. *The Oxford Handbook of Late Antiquity*. Oxford: Oxford University Press, 2012.

Little, Lester K., ed. *Plague and the End of Antiquity: The Pandemic of 541–750*. Cambridge: Cambridge University Press, 2007.

Mitchell, Stephen. *A History of the Later Roman Empire*. 2nd ed. Chichester: Wiley Blackwell, 2015.

O'Donnell, James J. *Pagans: The End of Traditional Religion and the Rise of Christianity*. New York: HarperCollins, 2015.

Potter, David. *Theodora: Actress, Empress, Saint*. Oxford: Oxford University Press, 2015.

Scott, Sarah, and Jane Webster, eds. *Roman Imperialism and Provincial Art*. Cambridge: Cambridge University Press, 2003.

Tuck, Steven L. *A History of Roman Art*. Chichester: Wiley Blackwell, 2014.

Ward-Perkins, Bryan. *The Fall of Rome: And the End of Civilization*. Oxford: Oxford University Press, 2005.

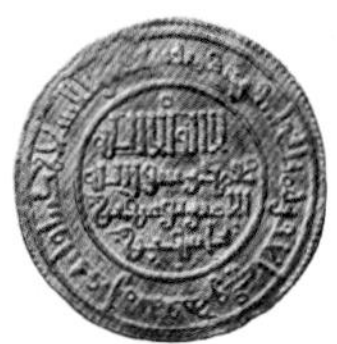

To test your knowledge of this chapter, please go to www.utphistorymatters.com for Study Questions.

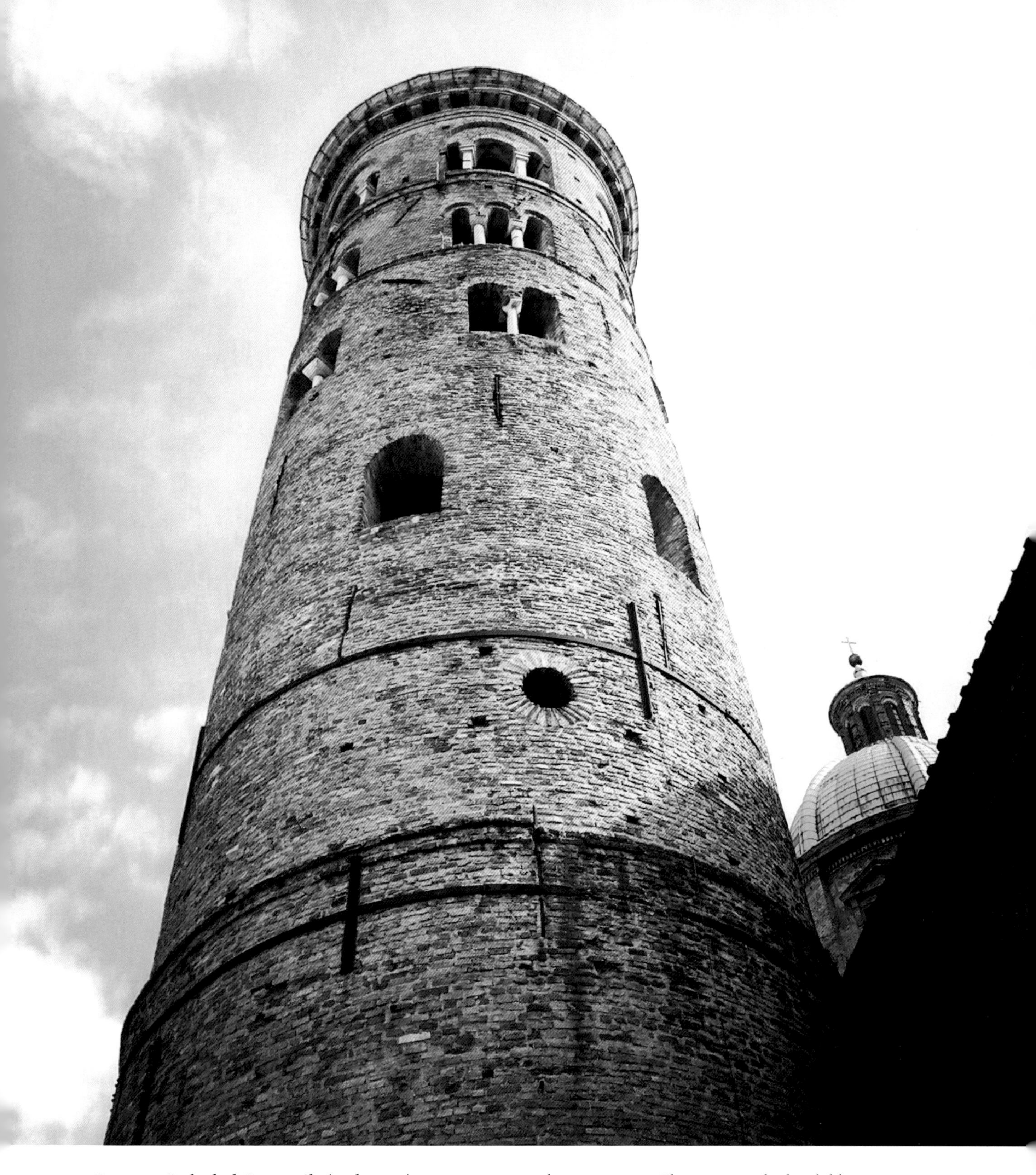

Ravenna Cathedral Campanile (10th cent.)
Although the original cathedral at Ravenna was built in late antiquity, the present church dates from the eighteenth century. But the campanile, or bell tower, was built in the late ninth or early tenth century, when Ravenna—once the Byzantine capital in Italy—still had a vibrant economy. The tower is cylindrical, like many others built in the city. Note how solid the wall is near the ground, while further up it is perforated by windows. These openings culminate in the arches and colonnades of the uppermost levels, making the tower seem to get lighter and even to soar. (Image courtesy of Riccardo Cristiani.)

TWO

THE EMERGENCE OF SIBLING CULTURES (*c*.600–*c*.750)

The rise of Islam in the Arabic world and its triumph over territories that for centuries had been dominated by either Rome or Persia is the first astonishing fact of the seventh and eighth centuries. The second is the persistence of the Roman Empire both politically, in what historians call the "Byzantine Empire," and culturally, in the Islamic world and Europe. By 750 three distinct and nearly separate civilizations—Byzantine, European, and Islamic—crystallized in and around the territory of the old Roman Empire. They professed different values, struggled with different problems, adapted to different standards of living. Yet all three bore the marks of common parentage—or, at least, of common adoption. They were sibling heirs of Rome.

SAVING BYZANTIUM

In the seventh century, the eastern Roman Empire was so transformed that by convention historians call it something new, the "Byzantine Empire," from the old Greek name for Constantinople: Byzantium. (Often the word "Byzantium" alone is used to refer to this empire as well.) War, first with the Sasanid Persians, then with the Arabs, was the major transforming agent. Gone was the ambitious imperial reach of Justinian; by 700, Byzantium had lost all its rich territories in North Africa and its tiny Spanish outpost as well. (See Map 2.2.) True, it held on tenuously to bits and pieces of Italy and Greece. But in the main it had become a medium-sized state, in the same location but about two-thirds the size of Turkey today. Yet, if small, it was also tough.

Sources of Resiliency

Byzantium survived the onslaughts of outsiders by preserving its capital city, which was well protected by high, thick, and far-flung walls that embraced farmland and pasture as well as the city proper. Within, the emperor (still calling himself the Roman emperor) and his officials serenely continued to collect the traditional Roman land taxes from the provinces left to them. This allowed the state to pay regular salaries to its soldiers, sailors, and court officials. The navy, well supplied with ships, patrolled the Mediterranean Sea. It was proud of its prestigious weapon, Greek fire—a mixture of crude oil and resin, heated and projected via a tube over the water, where it burned, engulfing enemy ships with its flames.[1] The armies of the empire, formerly posted as frontier guards, were pulled back in the face of the Arab invaders and set up as large regional defensive units within the empire itself. Called *strategiai* (literally, "commands of a general"), they were led by *strategoi* (generals), appointed by the emperors. Officials were posted throughout the empire to provide food and weapons to the army. They were authorized to collect foodstuffs as taxes in kind and to purchase materials for the army in the name of the state. Protected by fortresses, the *strategiai* managed to stave off Arab conquest. Well trained and equipped, Byzantium's troops served as reliable defenders of their newly compact state.

Invasions and Their Consequences

The Sasanid Empire of Persia, its capital at Ctesiphon, its ruler styled king of kings, was as venerable as the Roman Empire—and as ambitious. (See Map 2.1.) King Chosroes II (r.590–628), not unlike Justinian a half-century before him, dreamed of recreating past glories. In his case the inspiration was the ancient empire of Xerxes and Darius, which had sprawled from a lick of land just west of Libya to a great swathe of territory ending near the Indus River. When Byzantine Emperor Maurice was deposed by Phocas in 602, Chosroes took advantage of the ensuing political chaos to invade Byzantine territory. By 604 he had captured Dara and soon other cities nearby; he took Theodosiopolis in Byzantine Armenia in 606/607, Damascus by 613, Jerusalem by 614, and Alexandria by 619. By mid-621 the whole of Egypt was in his hands.

Map 2.1 Persian Expansion, 602–622

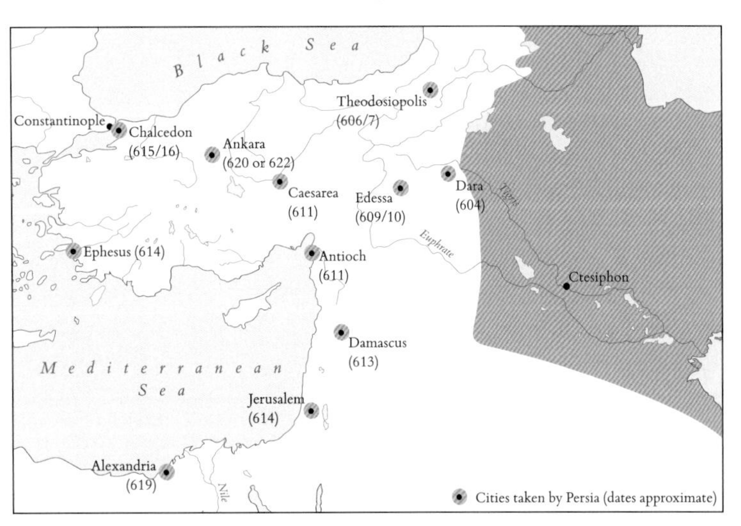

When Emperor Heraclius (r.610–641) went on the offensive, the Persians, in alliance with Avars and Slavs, attacked Constantinople itself. A chronicler of the event attributed their defeat to the city's protector, the Virgin Mary, whose image was displayed on all the city gates: "After

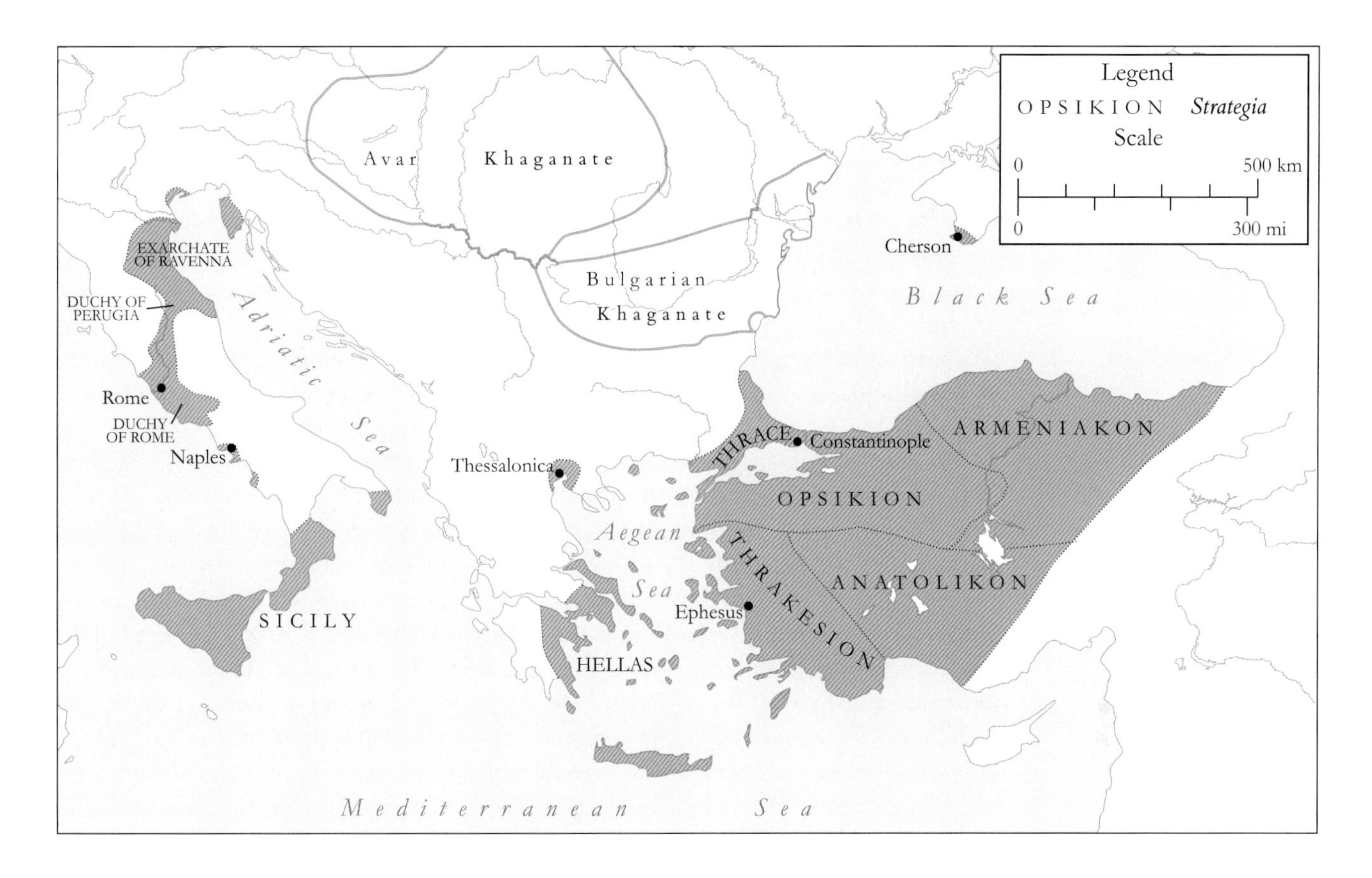

Map 2.2 The Byzantine Empire, c.700

approaching the church of our Lady the Mother of God and the Holy Reliquary, the enemy were completely unable to damage any of the things there, since God showed favor, at the intercession of his undefiled Mother."[2] Harder facts were at work as well: Heraclius's canny deployment of his army and use of diplomacy saved the city. By 630 all territories taken by the Persians were back in Byzantine hands. On a map, it would seem that nothing much had happened; in fact, the cities fought over were depopulated and ruined, and both Sasanid and Byzantine troops and revenues were exhausted.

Although the Persians were pushed back, the Slavs—farmers and stock-breeders in the main—moved into the Balkans, sometimes accompanied by the Avars, multi-ethnic horseback warriors and pastoralists. It took another half-century for the Bulgars, a Turkic-speaking nomadic group, to become a threat, but in the 670s they began moving into what is today Bulgaria, defeating the Byzantine army in 680 and again in 681. By 700 very little of the Balkan Peninsula was Byzantine. (See Map 2.2.) The place where once the two halves of the Roman Empire had met was now a wedge—created by Bulgars, Avars, and Slavs—that separated East from West.

An even more dramatic obliteration of the old geography took place when attacks by Arab Muslims in the century after 630 ended in the conquest of Sasanid Persia and the further shrinking of Byzantium. We shall soon see how and why the Arabs poured out of Arabia. But first we need to know what the shrunken Byzantium was like.

Decline of Urban Centers

The city-based Greco-Roman culture on which the Byzantine Empire was originally constructed had long been gradually giving way. Invasions and raids hastened this development. Many urban centers, once bustling nodes of trade and administration, disappeared or reinvented themselves. Some became fortresses; others were abandoned; still others remained as skeletal administrative centers. The public activities of marketplaces, theaters, and town squares yielded to the pious pursuits of churchgoers or the private affairs of the family.

The story of Ephesus (for its location see Map 2.2) is unique only in its details. Ephesus had once been an opulent commercial and industrial center. Turned to rubble by an earthquake near the end of the third century, it rebuilt itself on a grand scale during the course of the fourth and especially the fifth centuries. Imagine it in about 500. (See Figure 2.1, concentrating on the labels in red.) It had two main centers, both fitting comfortably within the old walls that had been constructed in the Hellenistic period. The most important center was the Embolos, a grand avenue paved with marble. Extending the length of more than two football fields, the Embolos began at its west end on a market square and the Library of Celsus, while it opened out on its east end onto the so-called State Agora, only bits of which were restored after the earthquake. All along the Embolos's length were statues, monumental fountains, and arcades. Along its north side were the Baths of Varius and other public buildings. Flanking its south were poor living quarters built over the rubble of once-elegant "terrace houses." There was no question about the religious affiliation of this sector of the city: the Embolos was well Christianized by numerous crosses etched onto the marble slabs of its fountains and paving stones. Small churches were scattered about the vicinity.

The second center of Ephesus around 500 was to the northwest, nearer the harbor. Here numerous old temples and cultural centers were now being reused for homes, baths, and churches. Richly furnished houses were erected in the Harbor Baths, while a chapel was built in the Byzantine palace and a church was constructed in the stadium. Above all, there was the new Church of St. Mary, the seat of the bishopric, which had been built into the southern flank of an old temple (the Olympieion) next to the bishop's palace and the baptistery.

In short, Ephesus around 500 suggests the comfortable integration of Christian and old Roman institutions. Baths expressed the traditional Roman value of cleanliness; temples were turned into churches; a chapel nestled in the shadow of the old stadium. Grand fountains and heroic statues continued to be built along the Embolos by proud city benefactors.

But the events of the sixth and seventh centuries transformed the city. The Persian wars disrupted Ephesus's trade and threatened its prosperity. Repeated visitations of the Plague of Justinian took their grim demographic toll. The residences along the length of the Embolos were destroyed in 614, as the result of the Persian invasions and perhaps an earthquake as well. Arab attacks on Ephesus began in 654–655.

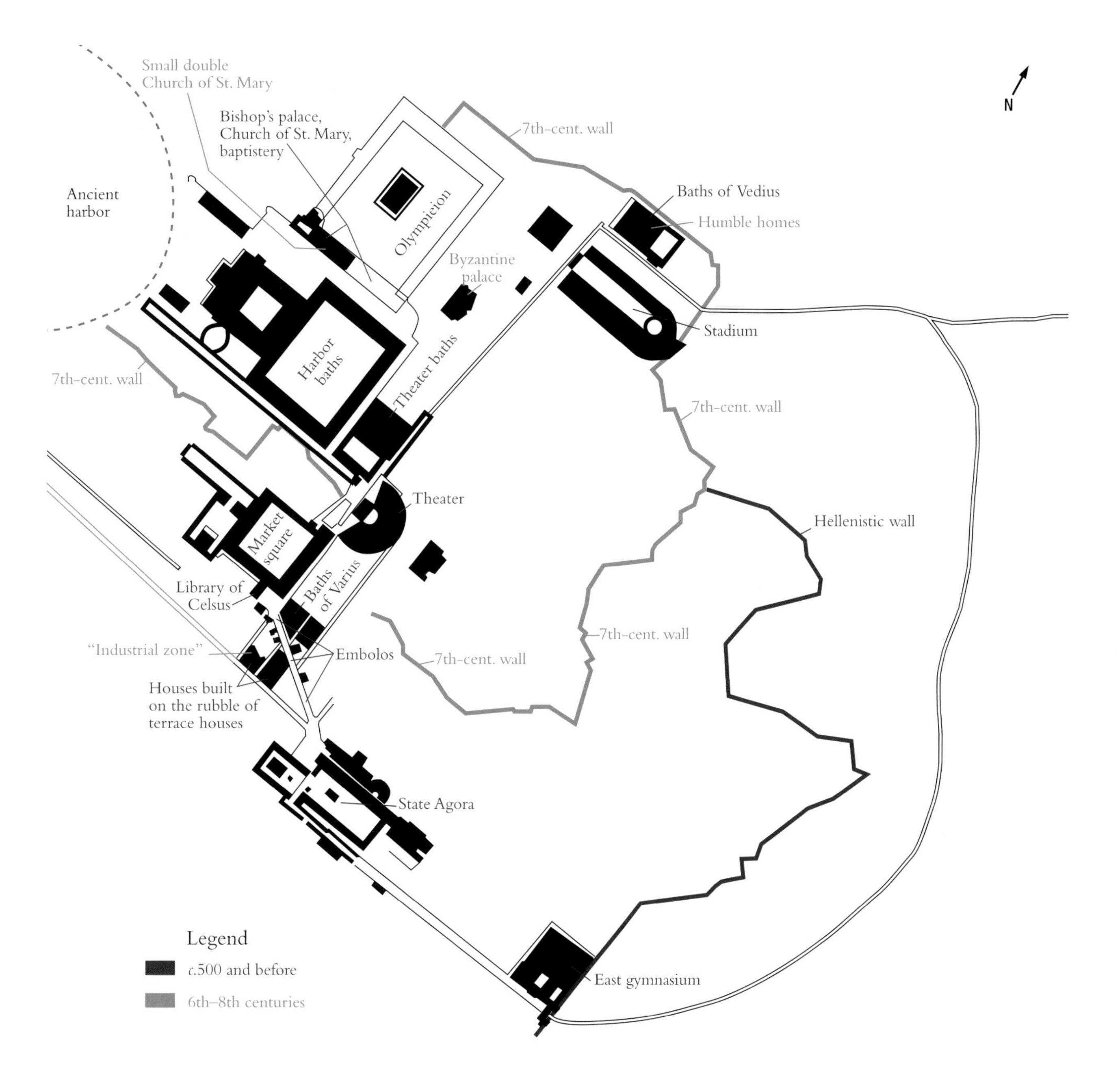

Figure 2.1 Late Antique Ephesus

In the face of these disasters, the face of Ephesus changed. (Consider Figure 2.1 again, now focusing on the elements in green.) As if tightening its belt, the city put up new walls to enclose the harbor area. The Embolos lost its centrality. Its southern flank became an "industrial zone," with mills and stone-cutting and ceramic factories, while other workshops were built on the edge of where the terrace houses had once stood. No doubt this location protected the harbor from both noise and pollution. A road south of the Embolos became the workaday thoroughfare, while the "Byzantine palace," closely protected by the seventh-century walls, became the new center of administration.

Yet the new walls did not stave off disaster and decay. The Baths of Vedius were destroyed—though some families made their homes in the rubble until the roof collapsed, probably at the end of the sixth century. The Church of St. Mary itself was partially destroyed—perhaps in the early seventh century—and rebuilt as two separate smaller churches within the original space. Finally, in the wake of Arab attacks, the bishop abandoned his palace by the harbor and moved to a church about a mile and a half outside of the city.

The fate of Ephesus—much reduced in size but nevertheless still a center of production and habitation—was echoed in many cities circling the eastern Mediterranean in Syria, Palestine, and Egypt. Elsewhere, the urban centers of the Byzantine Empire became little more than fortresses in the course of the seventh and eighth centuries. Constantinople itself was spared this fate only in part. As with other cities, its population shrank, and formerly inhabited areas right within the walls were abandoned or turned into farms. As the capital of both church and state, however, Constantinople boasted an extraordinarily thriving imperial and ecclesiastical upper class. It also retained some trade and industry. Even in the darkest days of the seventh-century wars, it had taverns, brothels, merchants, and a money economy. Its factories continued to manufacture fine silk textiles. Although Byzantium's economic life became increasingly rural in the seventh and eighth centuries, institutions vital to urban growth remained at Constantinople, ensuring a revival of commercial activity once the wars ended.

Ruralization

With the decline of cities came the rise of the countryside. Agriculture had all along been the backbone of the Byzantine economy. Apart from large landowners—the state, the church, and a few wealthy individuals—most Byzantines were free or semi-free peasant farmers. In the interior of Anatolia, on the great plateau that extends from the Mediterranean to the Black Sea, peasants must often have had to abandon their farms when Arab raiders came. Some may have joined the pastoralists of the region, ready to drive their flocks to safety. Elsewhere (and, in times of peace, on the Anatolian plains as well), peasants worked small plots (sometimes rented, sometimes owned outright), herding animals, cultivating grains, and tending orchards.

These peasants were subject as never before to imperial rule. With the disappearance of the traditional town councilors—the *curiales*—cities and their rural hinterlands were now controlled directly by the reigning imperial governor and the local "notables"—a new elite consisting of the bishop and big land owners favored by the emperor. Freed from the old buffers that separated it from commoners, the state adopted a thoroughgoing agenda of "family values," narrowing the grounds for divorce, setting new punishments for marital infidelity, and prohibiting abortions. Legislation gave mothers greater power over their offspring and made widows the legal guardians of their minor children. Education was still important, but now for many pious Christians, reading the ancient classics took second place to studying the Psalter, the book of 150 psalms in the Old Testament thought to have been written by King David.

New family values coexisted with old community practices. A church council that met at Constantinople in 691/692 (the so-called Quinisext) forbade, among other things, dancing on the first day of March, wearing comic masks at festivals, and cross-dressing in masquerade: "Moreover we drive away from the life of Christians the dances given in the names of those falsely called gods by the Greeks whether of men or women, and which are performed after an ancient and un-Christian fashion; decreeing that no man from this time forth shall be dressed as a woman, nor any woman in the garb suitable to men."[3]

Iconoclasm

Other popular practices centered on the saints. As in the West, so too in the East, saints' relics were housed in precious containers. Some were kept in churches, often under the altar; others were preserved at home by pious Christians. Many reliquaries were decorated with precious stones and metals and often, too, with images of saints, Christ, and his mother, Mary. Around 680, these images took on new importance in the Byzantine world. A cult of images became as important there as the cult of saints. The argument on their behalf was straightforward: the sacred could best be grasped by human beings when made visible and palpable. Stories circulated of saintly images that spoke; it became common for worshipers to bow down to sacred portraits. Images became more than representations of divine beings; they became—like relics, like reliquaries—containers of the holy.

These new ideas responded to the crises of the day. In the late seventh century, as we have seen, Byzantium was confronted by plagues, earthquakes, and (above all) wars. How could this happen to God's Chosen People (as the Byzantines thought of themselves)? The answer was clear: God was angry with them for their sins. What recourse did they have but to seek new avenues to access divine favor? While still depending on relics to protect and fortify them, many Byzantines sought the aid of holy images as well. Monks were especially enthusiastic patrons of these powerful works of art.

Soon there was a backlash against these new-fangled ideas. Emperor Leo III the Isaurian (r.717–741) agreed that the crises were God's punishment for the sins of the Byzantines. But he thought that their chief sin was idolatry—their cult of images. In 726, after a terrifying volcanic eruption in the middle of the Aegean Sea, Leo seems to have denounced sacred portraits publicly. Historians used to report that Leo had his soldiers tear down a great golden icon of Christ at the Chalke, the gateway to the imperial palace, and replace it with a cross. Newer research (by Leslie Brubaker, for example) notes that no contemporary sources record this incident. Most likely it was a legend invented much later. Nevertheless, around 726, or perhaps a bit before, Leo erected a cross in front of the imperial palace. It affirmed not only the Cross's salvific place in the lives of all Christians but also its unwavering role in imperial victories. This may be taken to signify the beginning of the "iconoclastic" (anti-icon or, literally, icon-breaking) period. In 730, Leo required

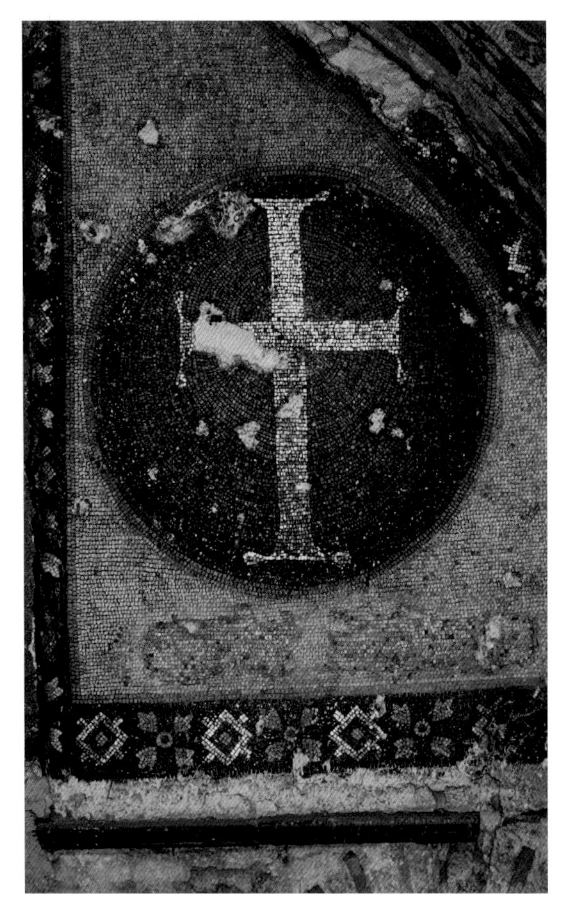

Plate 2.1 Cross at Hagia Sophia (orig. mosaic 6th cent.; redone 768/769). In this section of a mosaic just off the gallery at Hagia Sophia, the original mosaicist depicted a holy figure in a medallion. Beneath the image was an inscription identifying the saint. During the iconoclastic period, the figure and inscription were hacked out. The saint was replaced by a gold cross with flared arm tips; it was surrounded by a rainbow of colored tesserae (the bits of glass or stone used in mosaics) to make the cross seem to glow. Below the cross can be clearly seen the rectangular space in which the original inscription was replaced by tesserae to match the background color.

the pope at Rome and the patriarch of Constantinople to subscribe to a new policy: to remove sacred images, or at least to marginalize them, if they inspired the wrong kind of devotion.

Leo was the harbinger of a new religious current. There had always been churchmen who objected to compassing the divine in the limiting form of a material image, but they had been in the minority. By the end of Leo's reign, a majority was inspired to criticize images. At the Synod of 754, a meeting of over 300 bishops and Emperor Constantine V (r.741–775) held in Constantinople, sacred images were banned outright. Its decrees made clear how material representations threatened, according to iconoclasts, to befoul the purity of the divine. Christ himself had declared he should be represented through the bread and wine—and in no other way. As for the saints, they (in the words of the Synod)

> live on eternally with God, although they have died. If anyone thinks to call them back again to life by a dead art, discovered by the heathen, he makes himself guilty of blasphemy.... It is not permitted to Christians ... to insult the saints, who shine in so great glory, by common dead matter.[4]

Above all, iconoclastic churchmen worried about losing control over the sacred. Unlike relics, images could be reproduced infinitely and without clerical authorization. Their cultivation at monasteries threatened to encroach on clerical authority. Banning icons had multiple purposes.

However vehement they may have been, the iconoclasts seem rarely to have wiped out already-existing icons—though later propagandists on the iconophile (icon-loving) side accused them of great damage. One example of obliteration, however, certainly remains from Hagia Sophia. A room used by the patriarch—located just off the southwest corner of the gallery—was originally covered with mosaics, including medallions with images of saints. During the iconoclastic period, the images were cut out and replaced by crosses. (See Plate 2.1.) Elsewhere, new churches were decorated with crosses from the start, while artists of the iconoclastic period were commissioned to depict (depending on the use of the building) ornaments, trees, birds, hunting, horse races, and other non-sacred motifs. The iconoclasts thought that they thereby ensured God's favor—that, once again, the Byzantines were God's "Chosen People."

Ultimately, however, iconoclasm was an utter failure, though the ban on icons lasted until 787 and was revived, in modified form, between 815 and 843. Not only did the iconoclastic movement come to an end, but during the eighth century the position of those who supported icons, already argued at the Quinisext Council, would be elaborated at great length in learned treatises. The idea that icons held the "real presence" of the divine marked a watershed between the early Christian and the medieval Byzantine state.

THE RISE OF THE "BEST COMMUNITY": ISLAM

Like the Byzantines, the Muslims thought of themselves as God's people. In the Qur'an, the "recitation" of God's words, Muslims are "the best community ever raised up for mankind ... having faith in God" (3:110). The community's common purpose is "submission to God," the literal meaning of "Islam." The Muslim (a word that derives from "Islam") is "one who submits." Under the leadership of Muhammad (*c.*570–632) in Arabia, Islam created a new world power in less than a century.

The Shaping of Islam

"One community" was a revolutionary notion for the disparate peoples of Arabia (today Saudi Arabia), who converted to Islam in the course of the early seventh century. Pre-Islamic Arabia lay between the two great empires of the day—Persia and Byzantium—and felt the cross-currents as well as the magnetic pull of their economies and cultures. Its land supported Bedouins: nomads (the word "arab" is derived from the most prestigious of these, the camel-herders) and semi-nomads. But by far the majority of the population was neither; it was sedentary. To the southwest, where rain was adequate, farmers worked the soil. Elsewhere people settled at oases, where they raised date palms for their highly prized fruit; some of these communities were prosperous enough to support merchants and artisans. Both the nomads and the settled population were organized as tribes—communities whose members considered themselves related through a common ancestor.

Herding goats, sheep, or camels, the nomads and semi-nomads lived in small groups, largely making do with the products (leather, milk, meat) of their animals, and raiding one another for booty—including women. "Manliness" was the chief Bedouin virtue; it meant not sexual prowess (though polygyny—having more than one wife at a time—was practiced), but rather bravery, generosity, and a keen sense of honor.

By the time of Muhammad, the prophet of Islam, the Arabs had a well-developed literary as well as oral culture. Poetry was much honored (and remains so to this day); multipurpose, the ode alone (there were many other forms of poetry) could praise, mock, lament, and wax nostalgic about love. Most poets were "publicists" for their tribe, advertising its virtues. But a few were appreciated even beyond Arabia.

Islam began as a religion of the sedentary, but it soon found support and military strength among the nomads. The movement began at Mecca, a commercial center and the launching pad of caravans organized to sell Bedouin products—mainly leather goods and raisins—to the more urbanized areas at the Syrian border. (See Map 2.3.) Mecca was also a holy place. Its shrine, the Ka'ba, was rimmed with the images of hundreds of gods. Within its sacred precincts, where war and violence were prohibited, pilgrims bartered and traded.

Muhammad, born in this commercial and religious center, was orphaned as a child and came under the guardianship of his uncle, a leader of the Quraysh tribe that dominated Mecca and controlled access to the Ka'ba. Muhammad became a trader, married, had

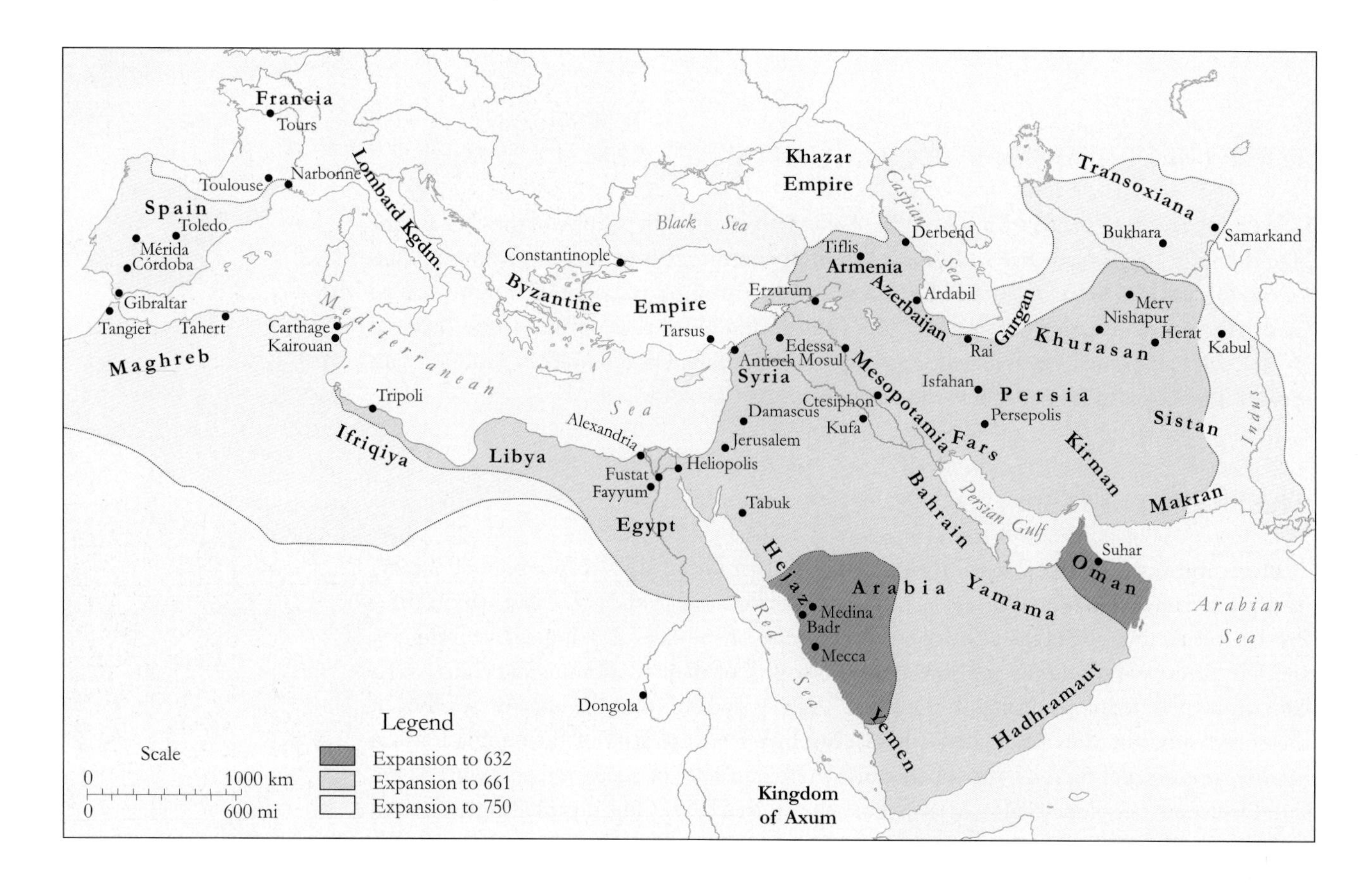

Map 2.3 The Islamic World to 750

children, and seemed comfortable and happy. But he sought something more: he would sometimes leave home, escaping to a nearby mountain to pray.

"In the Name of God the Compassionate the Caring / Recite in the name of your lord who created— / From an embryo created the human / Recite your lord is all-giving."[5] Thus began a sequence of searing words and visions that, beginning around 610 (as tradition has it), came to Muhammad during his retreats. The key word was God, *one* God (the Arabic word for God is Allah). The key command was to "recite." Muhammad obeyed, and later his recitations of God's word were written down on scraps of parchment and elsewhere by Muhammad's companions. Once arranged—a process that was certainly completed by the mid-seventh century—they became the Qur'an, the holy book of Islam. (See Plate 2.2.) The Qur'an is understood to be God's revelation as told to Muhammad by the angel Gabriel, and then recited in turn by Muhammad to others. Its first chapter—or sura—is the *fatihah*, or Opening:

> In the name of God
>   the Compassionate the Caring
> Praise be to God
>   lord sustainer of the worlds
> the Compassionate the Caring
> master of the day of reckoning

To you we turn to worship
and to you we turn in time of need
Guide us along the road straight
the road of those to whom you are giving
not those with anger upon them
not those who have lost the way.[6]

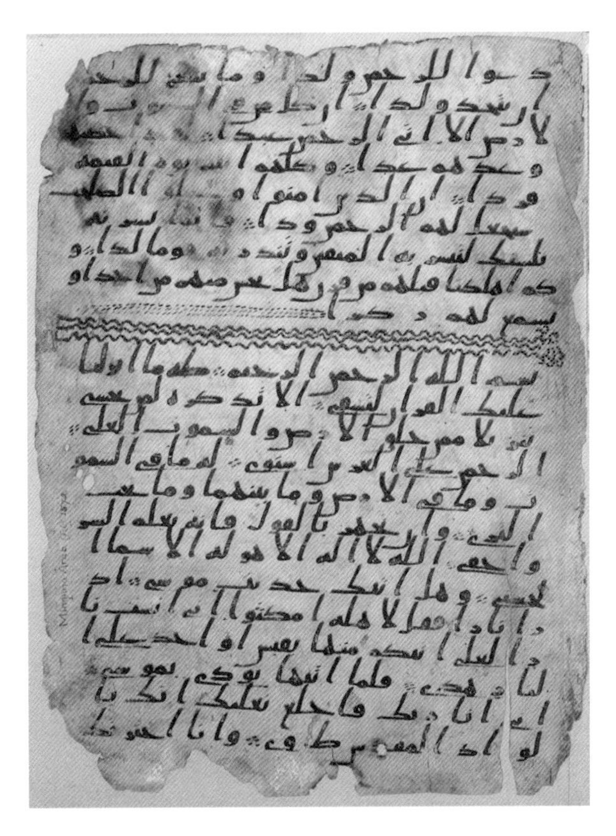

Plate 2.2 Page from an Early Qur'an (568–645). The parchment used for this Qur'an page has been radiocarbon dated to 568–645. Its precocity calls into question the traditional dating of Muhammad's revelations as well as when and how they were organized into an official text. Tradition gives the role of organization to Caliph Uthman (r.644–656), who had an authorized text prepared by a committee and issued *c.*650. These fragments (and other similar finds) suggest an earlier date and variant compilations of the Qur'an.

Reading from right to left and top to bottom, we see the end of sura 19 ("Maryam") and the beginning of sura 20 ("Ta Ha"). The verses of each sura are marked by little clusters of dots, and the division between the two suras is indicated by a decorative design in red ink.

The Qur'an continues with a far longer sura, followed by others (114 in all) of gradually decreasing length. For Muslims, the Qur'an covers the gamut of human experience—the sum total of history, prophecy, and the legal and moral code by which men and women should live—as well as the life to come.

Banning infanticide, Islam gave girls and women new dignity. It allowed for polygyny, but this was limited to four wives at one time, all to be treated equally. It mandated dowries and offered some female inheritance rights. At first women even prayed with men, though that practice ended in the eighth century. The nuclear family (newly emphasized, as was happening around the same time at Byzantium as well; see p. 46) became more important than the tribe. In Islam, there are three essential social facts: the individual, God, and the *ummah*, the community of the faithful. There are no intermediaries between the divine and human realms, no priests, Eucharist, or relics.

A community of believers coalesced around Muhammad as God's prophet. They adhered to a strict monotheism, prepared for the final Day of Judgment, and carried out the tasks that their piety demanded—daily prayers, charity, periods of fasting, and so on. Later these were institutionalized as the "five pillars" of Islam.[7] The early believers' idea of the righteous life included living in the world, marrying, and having children. For them, virtue meant mindfulness of God in all things. They could take moderate—though not excessive—pleasure in God's bounty. Their notions of righteousness did not call for asceticism.

At Mecca, where Quraysh tribal interests were bound up with the Ka'ba and its many gods, Muhammad's message was unwelcome. But it was greeted with enthusiasm at Medina, an oasis about 200 miles to the northeast of Mecca. Feuding tribes there invited Muhammad to join them and arbitrate their disputes. He agreed, and in 622 he made the *Hijra*, or flight from Mecca to Medina. There he became not only a religious but also a secular leader. This joining of the political and religious spheres set the pattern for Islamic government thereafter. After Muhammad's death, the year of the *Hijra*, 622, became the year 1 of the Islamic calendar, marking the establishment of the Islamic era.

Muhammad consolidated his leadership by asserting hegemony over three important groups: the Jews, the Meccans, and the nomads. At Medina itself, he took control by ousting and sometimes killing his main competitors, the Jewish clans of the city.

Against the Meccans he fought a series of battles; the battle of Badr (624), waged against a Meccan caravan, marked the first Islamic military victory. After several other campaigns, Muhammad triumphed and took over Mecca in 630, offering leniency to most of its inhabitants, who in turn converted to Islam. Meanwhile, Muhammad allied himself with numerous nomadic groups, adding their contingents to his army. Warfare was thus integrated into the new religion as a part of the duty of Muslims to strive in the ways of God; *jihad*, often translated as "holy war," in fact means "striving." Through a combination of military might, conversion, and negotiation, Muhammad united many, though by no means all, Arabic tribes under his leadership by the time of his death in 632.

Out of Arabia

"Strive, O Prophet," says the Qur'an, "against the unbelievers and the hypocrites, and deal with them firmly. Their final abode is Hell; And what a wretched destination" (9:73). Cutting across tribal allegiances, the Islamic *ummah* was itself a formidable "supertribe" dedicated to victory over the enemies of God. After Muhammad's death, armies of Muslims led by caliphs—a title that at first seems to have derived from *khalifat Allah*, "deputy of God," but that later came to mean "deputy of the Apostle of God, Muhammad"—moved into Sasanid and Byzantine territory, toppling or crippling the once-great ancient empires. (See Map 2.3.) Islamic armies captured the Persian capital, Ctesiphon, in 637 and continued eastward to take Persepolis in 648, Nishapur in 651, and then, beyond Persia, to conquer Kabul in 664 and Samarqand in 710. To the west, they picked off, one by one, the great Mediterranean cities of the Byzantine Empire: Antioch and Damascus in 635, Alexandria in 642, Carthage in 697. By the beginning of the eighth century, Islamic warriors held sway from Spain to India.

What explains their astonishing triumph? Above all, they were formidable fighters, and their enemies were relatively weak. The Persian and Byzantine Empires had exhausted one another after years of fighting. Nor were their populations particularly loyal; some—Jews and Christians in Persia; Monophysite (or Miaphysite) Christians in Syria and Egypt—even welcomed the invaders. Despite some harsh measures, as when the Muslim conqueror of Egypt "destroyed the houses of the Alexandrians who had fled" before his army, the Christians were largely proved right.[8] The Muslims made no attempt to convert them, imposing a tax on them instead. Then, too, the Muslims sometimes conquered through diplomacy rather than battle. In Spain, for example, they treated with a local leader, Theodemir (or Tudmir), offering him and his men protection—the promise that "[they will not] be separated from their women and children. They will not be coerced in matters of religion"—in return for loyalty and taxes.[9]

Although Arabic culture was only partly city-based, Muhammad himself was attached to Mecca and Medina, and the Muslims almost immediately fostered urban life in the regions that they conquered. In Syria and Palestine, most of the soldiers settled within existing coastal cities; their leaders, however, built palaces and hunting lodges in the countryside. Everywhere else the invaders created large permanent camps of their own, remaining separate from the indigenous populations. Some of these camps were eventually abandoned, but others—such as those at Baghdad and Cairo—became centers of new and thriving urban agglomerations.

The caliphate was well organized. Regional governors appointed by the caliphs worked with lower-level local officials to collect taxes, maintain law and order, and provision the military. Consider the administration of Egypt, for which we have a relatively large number of documents. Papyrus sheets, preserved for centuries beneath the ground (thanks to Egypt's dry climate), reveal a thriving bureaucracy. The Egyptian governor (the *amir*) sent out orders to local pagarchs (officials) who in turn ordered underlings to help them collect taxes, regulate water use (of utmost importance in this largely agricultural society), and settle claims. Numerous scribes dutifully wrote letters and instructions, for even though most transactions were oral, the written word was highly valued. Sails, nails, woolen cloth, and Egyptian wheat—formerly exported to feed the people at Constantinople—were requisitioned for the army and navy. The Egyptian tax system, too, required the movement not only of money but of vast amounts of goods in kind: grapes, oil, beans, barley. The pagarchs were evidently very much at the beck and call of the amir. As one of them wrote to an underling: "The *amir* ... wrote to me with what he has calculated for me, of the amount in coin of the people of the province [and] of their taxes in kind. So pay this to him and ... hurry to me the amount in money."[10]

Thus, men and women who had been living along the Mediterranean—in Syria, Palestine, North Africa, and Spain—went back to work and play much as they had done before the invasions. In return for a heavy tax, Christians and Jews could worship in their traditional ways. Safe in Muslim-controlled Damascus, Saint John of Damascus (d.749) was able to thunder against iconoclasm as he would never have been allowed to do in iconoclastic Byzantium. Another Christian, al-Akhtal (*c*.640–710), found employment at the court of Caliph 'Abd al-Malik (r.685–705), where he poured forth verses of praise:

So let him in his victory
    long delight!
He who wades into the deep of battle,
    auspicious his augury,
The Caliph of God
    through whom men pray for rain.[11]

Maps of the Islamic conquest divide the world into Muslims and Christians. But the "Islamic world" was only slightly Islamic; Muslims constituted a minority of the population. Then, even as their religion came to predominate, they were themselves absorbed, at least to some degree, into the cultures that they had conquered.

The Culture of the Umayyads

Dissension, triumph, and disappointment followed the naming of Muhammad's successors. The caliphs were not chosen from the old tribal elites but rather from a new inner circle of men close to Muhammad. The first two caliphs, Abu-Bakr and Umar, ruled without serious opposition. They were the fathers of two of Muhammad's wives. But the third caliph, Uthman, husband of two of Muhammad's daughters and great-grandson of the Quraysh leader Umayyah, aroused resentment. (See Genealogy 2.1.) His family had come late to Islam, and some of its members had once even persecuted Muhammad. The opponents of the Umayyads supported Ali, the husband of Muhammad's daughter Fatimah. After a group of discontented soldiers murdered Uthman, civil war broke out between the Umayyads and Ali's faction. It ended when Ali was killed in 661 by one of his own erstwhile supporters. Thereafter, the caliphate remained in Umayyad hands until 750.

Yet the *Shi'ah*, the supporters of Ali, did not forget their leader. They became the "Shi'ites," faithful to Ali's dynasty, mourning his martyrdom, shunning the "mainstream" caliphs of the other Muslims ("Sunni" Muslims, as they were later called), awaiting the arrival of the true leader—the *imam*—who would spring from the house of Ali.

Meanwhile, the Umayyads made Damascus, previously a minor Byzantine city, into their capital. Here they adopted many of the institutions of the culture that they had conquered, issuing coins like those of the Byzantines (in the east they used coins based on Persian models), and employing former Byzantine officials as administrators. Caliph 'Abd al-Malik (who, as we have seen, won high praise from the poet al-Akhtal) turned Jerusalem—already sacred to Jews and Christians—into an Islamic holy city as well. His successor, al-Walid I (r.705–715) built major mosques (places of worship for Muslims) at Damascus, Medina, and Jerusalem. The one at Damascus retains most of its original elements; Plate 2.3 demonstrates how effortlessly Byzantine motifs were absorbed—yet also transformed—in their new Islamic context. Cityscapes and floral motifs drawn from Byzantine traditions were combined to depict an idealized world created by the triumph of Islam.

Arabic, the language of the Qur'an, became the official tongue of the Islamic world. As translators rendered important Greek and other texts into this newly imperial language, it proved to be both flexible and capacious. Around this time, Muslim scholars began to compile pious narratives about the Prophet's sayings, or *hadith*. A new literate class—composed mainly of the old Persian and Syrian elite, now converted to Islam and schooled in Arabic—created new forms of prose and poetry. A commercial revolution in China helped to vivify commerce in the Islamic world. At hand was a cultural flowering in a land of prosperity.

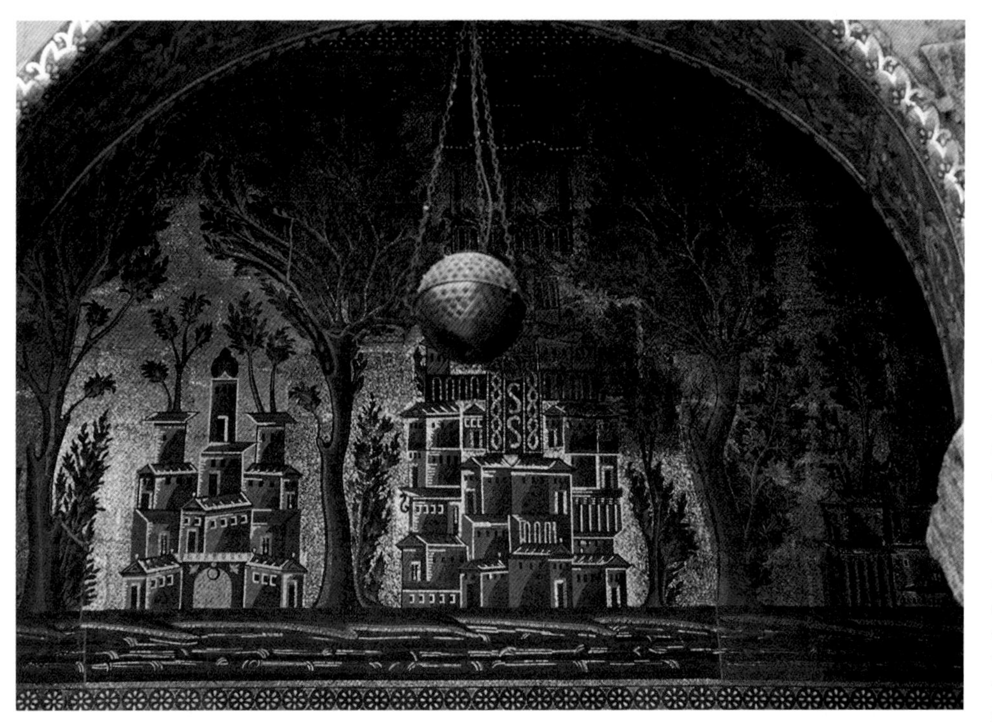

Plate 2.3 Damascus Great Mosque Mosaic (706). It is likely that Byzantine artisans were hired to cover the mosque at Damascus with mosaics both inside and out. Even if not from Byzantium, the mosaicists drew on Byzantine artistic traditions that were still recognizably based on classical Roman motifs. Compare this detail of the western portico of the Damascus mosque, which shows two cities separated by trees, with the harbor scene in Plate 1.3. We see here buildings similar to the depiction of the villa at Villa Farnesina, composed of blocks, topped by slanting roofs, and pierced by numerous windows. The way in which the trees work to divide the scene in the Damascus portico is also Romano-Byzantine. But in another way, the mosaicists rejected that ancient inheritance, imposing a different—an Islamic—ideal: they depicted no human being or animal. To be sure, we should not expect that Mars would seduce Venus here (recall Plate 1.1)! But more remarkably, no living being whatsoever paraded on this or any mosque's walls. In what ways might this ideal have affected Byzantium itself?

THE MAKING OF WESTERN EUROPE

No reasonable person in the year 750 would have predicted that, of the three heirs of the Roman Empire, Western Europe would, by 1500, be well on its way to dominating the world. While Byzantium cut back, reorganized, and forged ahead, while Islam spread its language and rule over a territory that stretched nearly twice the length of the United States today, Western Europe remained an impoverished backwater. Fragmented politically and linguistically, its cities (left over from Roman antiquity) mere shells, its tools primitive, its infrastructure—what was left of Roman roads, schools, and bridges—collapsing, Europe lacked identity and cohesion. That these and other strengths did indeed eventually develop over a long period of time is a tribute in part to the survival of some Roman traditions and institutions and in part to the inventive ways in which people adapted those institutions and made up new ones to meet their needs and desires.

Impoverishment and Its Variations

Taking in the whole of Western Europe around this time means dwelling long on its variety. Dominating the scene was Gaul, now taken over by the Franks; we may call it Francia. To its south were Spain (ruled first by the Visigoths, and then, after *c.*715, by the Muslims) and Italy (divided between the pope, the Byzantines, and the Lombards). To the north, joined to, rather than separated from, the Continent by the lick of water

Following pages:
Genealogy 2.1 Muhammad's Relatives and Successors to 750

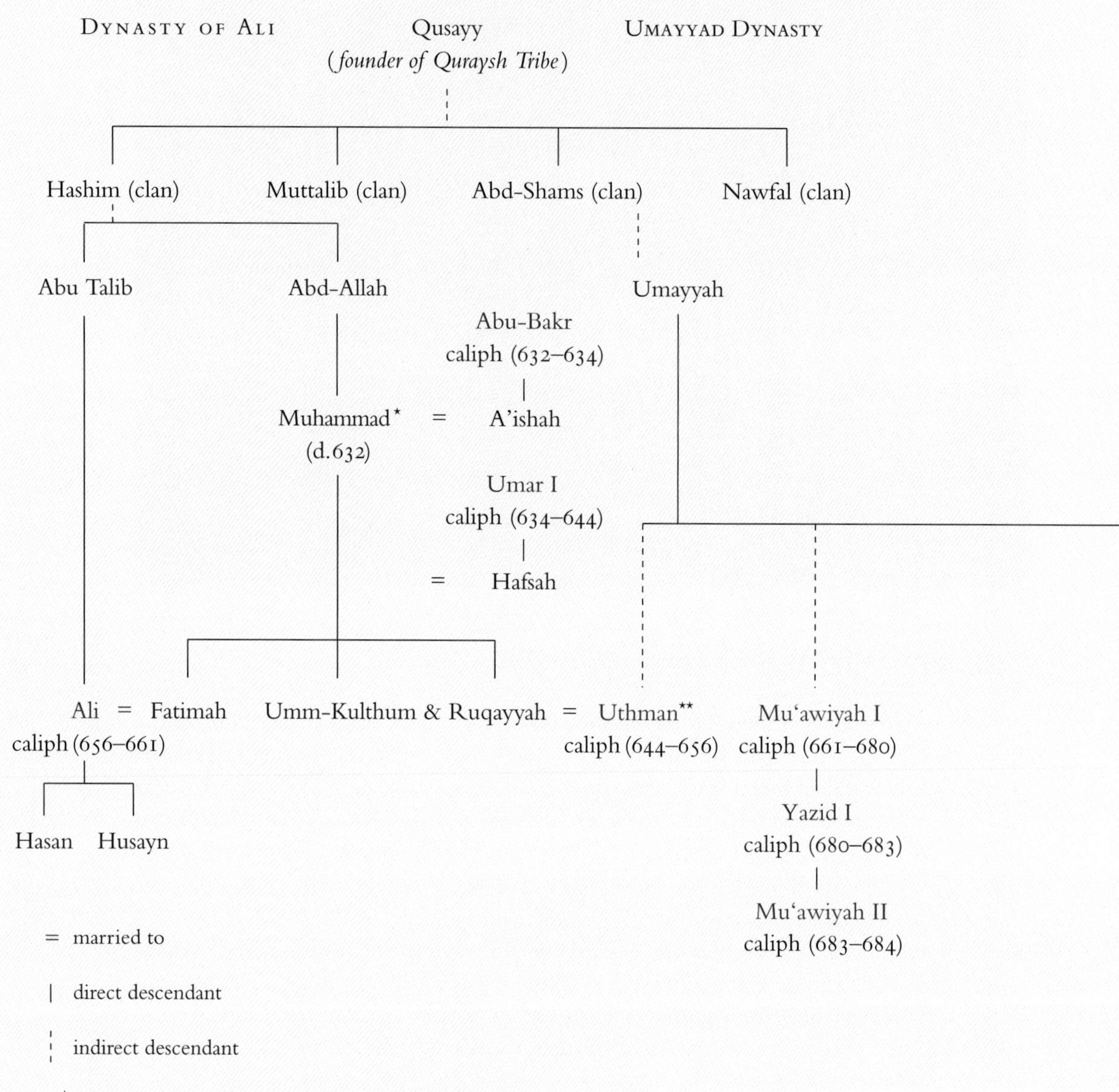

* Muhammad was married to both A'ishah and Hafsah, as well as others

** Uthman was married to two of Muhammad's daughters, Umm-Kulthum and Ruqayyah

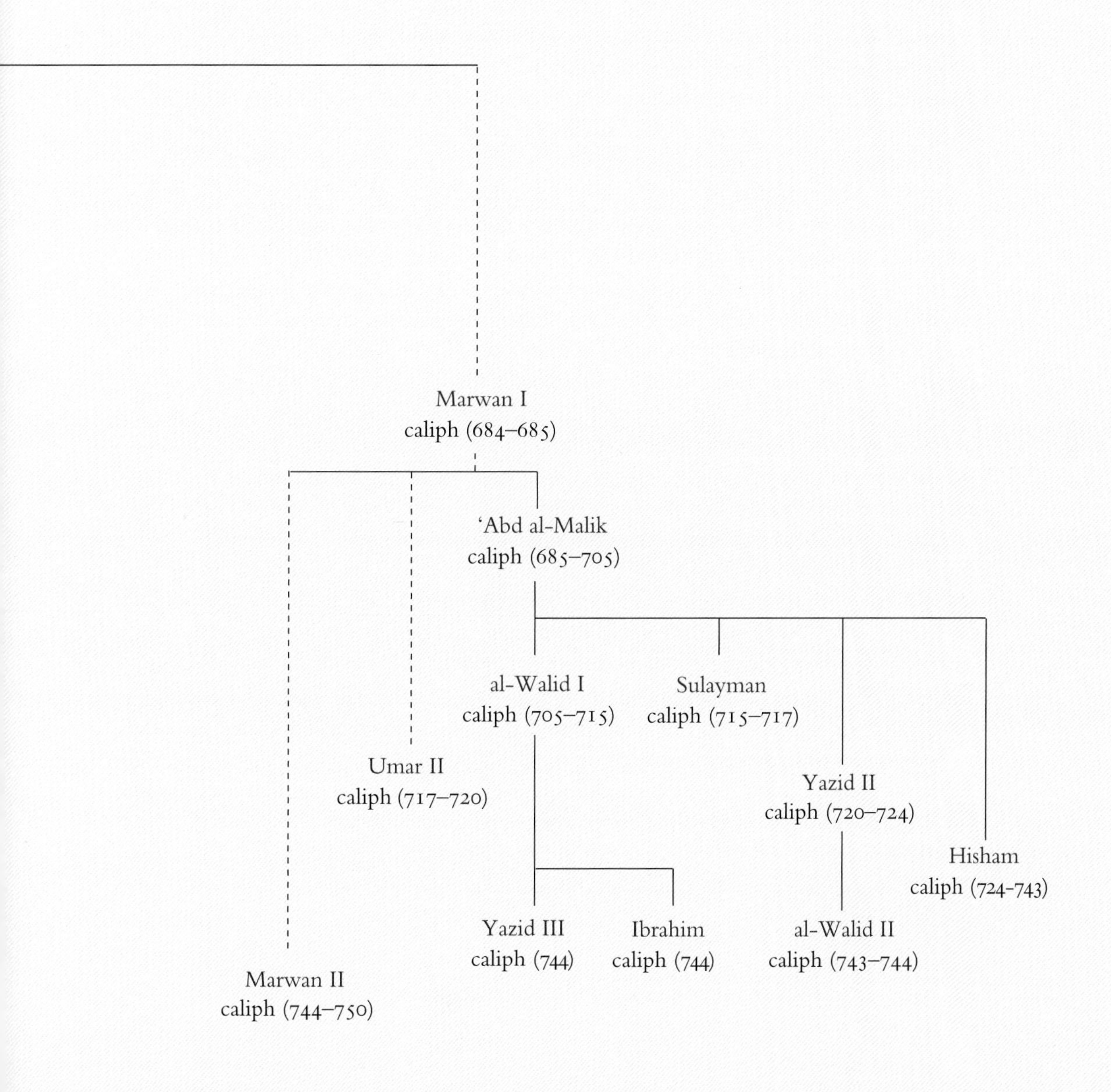

Marwan I
caliph (684–685)
'Abd al-Malik
caliph (685–705)
al-Walid I
caliph (705–715)
Sulayman
caliph (715–717)
Umar II
caliph (717–720)
Yazid II
caliph (720–724)
Hisham
caliph (724-743)
Yazid III
caliph (744)
Ibrahim
caliph (744)
al-Walid II
caliph (743–744)
Marwan II
caliph (744–750)

called the English Channel, the British Isles were home to a plethora of tiny kingdoms, about three quarters of which were native ("Celtic") and the last quarter Germanic ("Anglo-Saxons").

There were clear differences between the Romanized south—Spain, Italy, southern Francia—and the north. (See Map 2.4.) Travelers going from Anglo-Saxon England to Rome would have noticed them. There were many such travelers: some, like the churchman Benedict Biscop, were voluntary pilgrims; others were slaves on forced march. Making their way across England, voyagers such as these would pass fenced wooden farmsteads much like the ones at Wijster (see pp. 21–22). Even royal estates were made of wood, however impressive in size they must have been. Figure 2.2 on p. 60 shows an artist's recreation of Yeavering (England) based on archaeological excavations there. Built within a landscape dominated by a great twin-peaked hill, it was occupied—and used as a burial site—for millennia without having any special regional status. In the early seventh century, however, it became a major royal estate center that included a great hall, a theater (a feature clearly drawing on Roman precedents), and a large enclosure probably used for keeping animals but also serviceable for defense. The estate belonged to the king of the northern Anglo-Saxon kingdom of Bernicia, who probably stayed there once or twice a year, hunting in the nearby woods, feasting in the great hall, and calling his chief men together in the theater. Right at the narrow point of this wedge-shaped wooden edifice was a small platform marked by a high post; the best guess is that from this acoustically well-placed spot the king greeted foreign dignitaries and declared his judgments and decisions. Even in the absence of the king, officials might have used the theater in this way to carry out business in his name.

More typical farmsteads consisted of a relatively large house, outbuildings, and perhaps a sunken house, its floor below the level of the soil, its damp atmosphere suitable for weaving. Ordinarily built in clusters of four or five, such family farmsteads made up tiny hamlets. Peasants planted their fields with barley (used to make a thick and nourishing ale) as well as oats, wheat, rye, beans, and flax. Two kinds of plows were used. One was heavy: it had a coulter and moldboard, often tipped with iron, to cut through and turn over heavy soils. The other was a light "scratch plow," suitable for making narrow furrows in light soils. Because the first plow was hard to turn, the fields it produced tended to be long and rectangular in shape. The lighter plow was more agile: it was used to cut the soil in one direction and then at right angles to that, producing a square field. There were many animals on these farms: cattle, sheep, horses, pigs, and dogs. In some cases, the peasants who worked the land and tended the animals were relatively independent, owing little to anyone outside their village. In other instances, regional lords—often kings—commanded a share of the peasants' produce and, occasionally, labor services. But all was not pastoral or agricultural in England: here and there, and especially toward the south, were commercial settlements—real emporia.

Crossing the Channel, travelers would enter northern Francia, also dotted with emporia (such as Quentovic and Dorestad) but additionally boasting old Roman cities, now mainly religious centers. Paris, for example, was largely an agglomeration of churches: Montmartre, Saint-Laurent, Saint-Martin-des-Champs—perhaps thirty-five churches

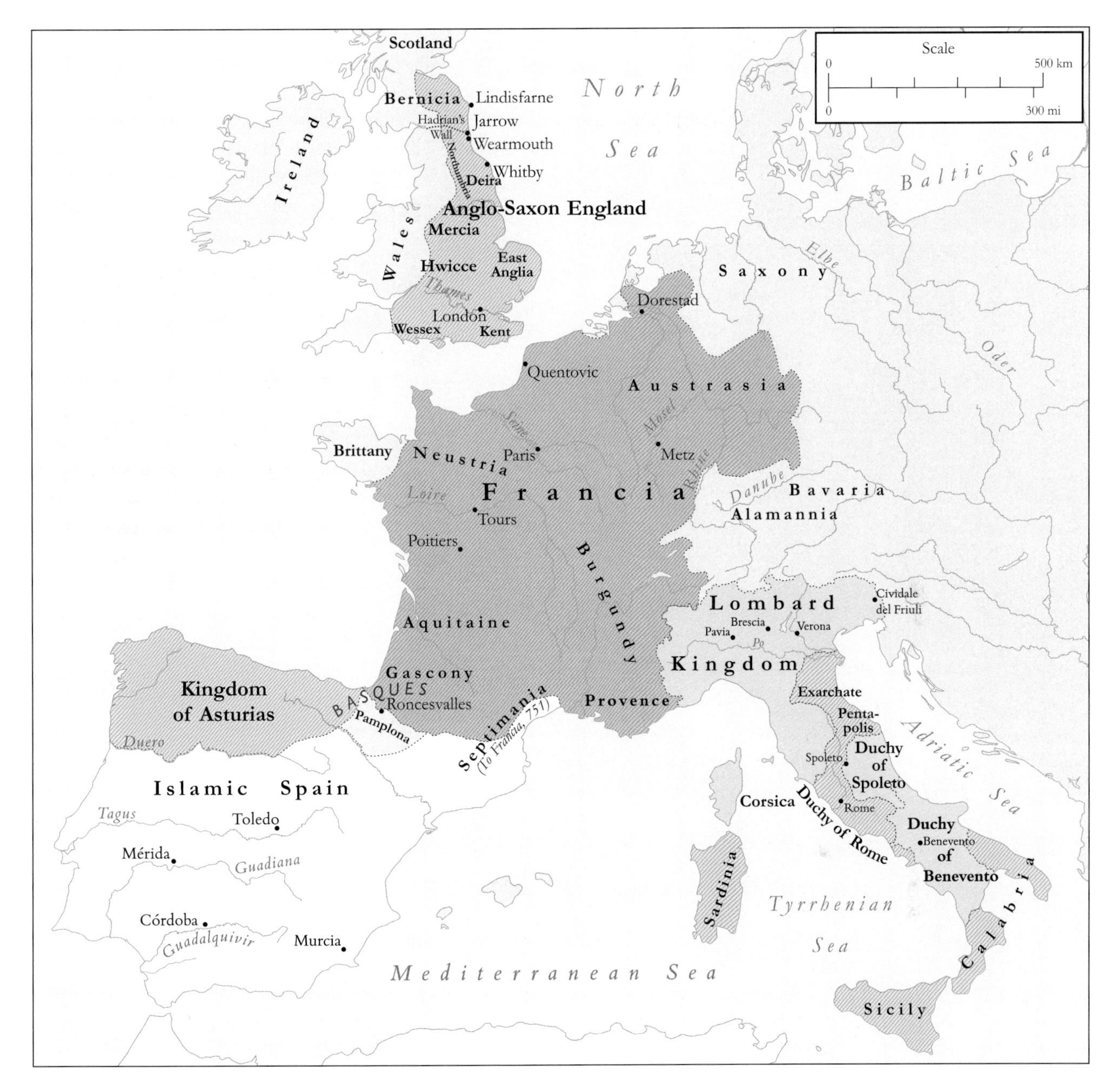

Map 2.4 Western Europe, *c.*750

were jammed into an otherwise nearly abandoned city. In the countryside around Paris, peasant families, each with its own plot, tended lands and vineyards that were generally owned by aristocrats. Moving eastward, our voyagers would pass through thick forests and land more often used as pasture for animals than for cereal cultivation. Along the Mosel River they would find villages with fields, meadows, woods, and water courses, a few supplied with mills and churches. Some of the peasants in these villages would be tenants or slaves of a lord; others would be independent farmers who owned all or part of the land that they cultivated.

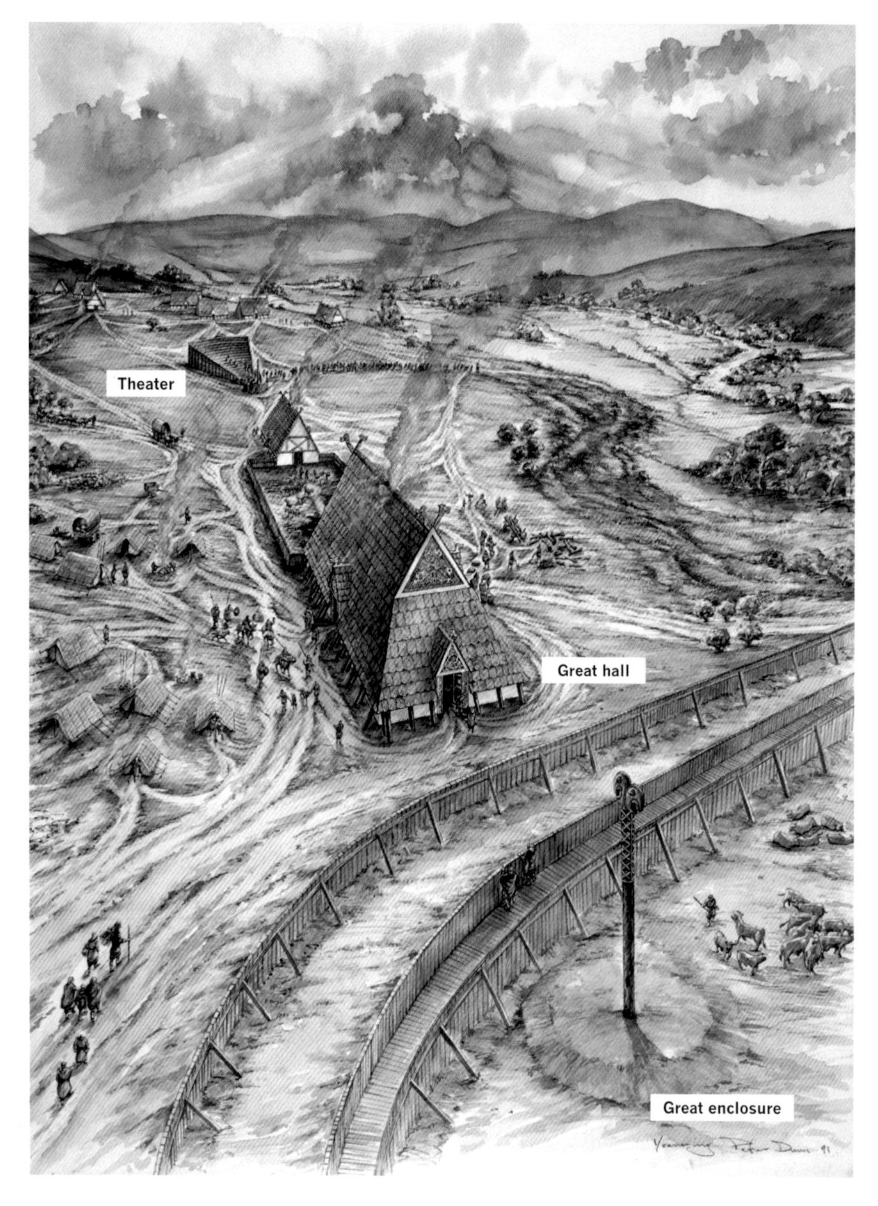

Figure 2.2 Yeavering, Northumberland, Anglo-Saxon Royal Estate, 7th cent.

Near the Mediterranean, by contrast, the terrain still had an urban feel. Here the great hulks of Roman cities, with their stone amphitheaters, baths, and walls, dominated the landscape even though, as at Byzantium, their populations were much diminished. Peasants, settled in small hamlets scattered throughout the countryside, cultivated their own plots of land. In Italy, many of these peasants were real landowners; aristocratic landlords were less important there than in Francia. The soil of this region was lighter than in the north, easily worked with scratch plows to produce the barley and rye (in northern Italy) and wheat (elsewhere) that were the staples—along with meat and fish—of the peasant diet.

By 700, there was little left of the old long-distance Mediterranean commerce of the ancient Roman world. Nevertheless, although this was an impoverished society, it was not without wealth or lively patterns of exchange. In the first place, money was still minted—increasingly in silver rather than gold. The change of metal was due in part to a shortage of gold in Europe. But it was also a nod to the importance of small-scale commercial transactions—sales of surplus wine from a vineyard, say, for which small coins were the most practical. In the second place, North Sea merchant-sailors—carrying, for example, ceramic plates and glass vessels—had begun to link together through commerce northern Francia, the east coast of England, Scandinavia, and the Baltic Sea. Brisk trade gave rise to new emporia and revivified older Roman cities along the coasts. In the third place, a gift economy—that is, an economy of give and take—flourished. Booty was seized, tribute demanded, harvests hoarded, and coins struck, all to be redistributed to friends, followers, dependents, and the church. Kings and other rich and powerful men and women amassed gold, silver, ornaments, and jewelry in their treasuries and grain in their storehouses to give out in ceremonies that marked their power and added to their prestige. Even the rents that peasants paid to their lords, mainly in kind, were often couched as "gifts."

Politics and Culture

If variations were plentiful in even so basic a matter as material and farming conditions, the differences were magnified by political and cultural conditions. We need now to take Europe kingdom by kingdom.

FRANCIA

Francia comes first because it was the major player, a real political entity that dominated what is today France, Belgium, the Netherlands, Luxembourg, and much of Germany. In the seventh century, it was divided into three related kingdoms—Neustria, Austrasia, and Burgundy—each of which included parts of a fourth, southern region, Aquitaine. By 700, however, the political distinctions between them were melting, and Francia was becoming one kingdom.

The line of Clovis—the Merovingians—ruled these kingdoms. (See Genealogy 2.2.) The dynasty owed its longevity to biological good fortune and excellent political sense: it allied itself with the major lay aristocrats and ecclesiastical authorities of Gaul—men and women of high status, enormous wealth, and marked local power. To that alliance, the kings brought their own sources of power: a skeletal Roman administrative apparatus, family properties, appropriated lands once belonging to the Roman state, and the profits and prestige of leadership in war.

The royal court—which moved with the kings as they traveled from one place to another, as they had no capital city—was the focus of political life. Here gathered talented young men; they were aristocrats on the rise and many of them later became bishops. The most important courtiers had official positions: there were, for example, the referendary and the cupbearer. Highest of all was the "mayor of the palace," who controlled access to the king and brokered deals with aristocratic factions.

Queens were an important part of the court as well. One of them, Balthild (d.680), had once been among the unwilling travelers from England. Purchased there as a slave by the mayor of the palace of Neustria, she parlayed her beauty into marriage with the king himself. (Merovingian kings often married slaves or women captured in war. By avoiding wives with powerful kindred, they staved off challenges to their royal authority.) Balthild's biographer praised her for ministering to all the men at court. When her husband, King Clovis II, died in 657, Balthild served as regent for her minor sons, acting, in effect, as king during this time. Meanwhile, she gave generously to churches and monasteries. In an era before formal canonization processes, Balthild was nevertheless deemed a saint: "Without

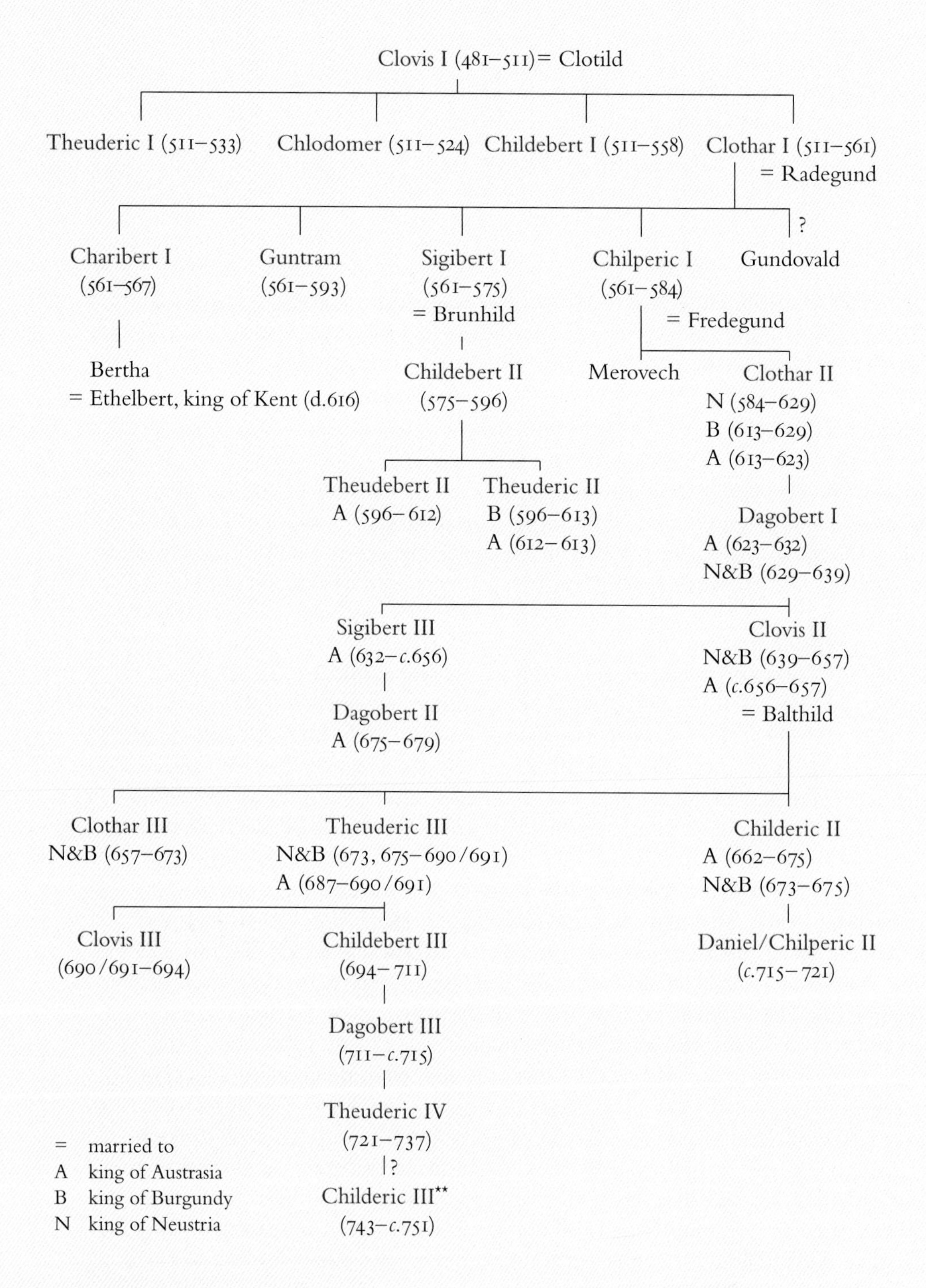

* Many of the Merovingian kings had more than one wife. The children listed (selected as only the most important of the fathers' progeny) are those of the king but not necessarily of the wife named here.

** The parentage of Childeric III is not clear. His father may equally well have been Daniel/Chilperic II as Theuderic IV.

doubt this holy soul was gloriously received by a chorus of angels," was the dramatic way in which her hagiographer ended his account of her life.[12]

Genealogy 2.2 (facing page) The Merovingians*

Just as a king's power radiated outward from his court, so too did aristocrats command their own lordly centers. Like kings, they had many "homes" at one time, scattered throughout Francia. Tending to their estates, honing their skills in the hunt, aristocratic men regularly led armed retinues to war. They proved their worth in the regular taking of booty and rewarded their faithful followers afterwards at generous banquets.

And they bedded down. The bed—or rather procreation—was the focus of marriage, the key to the survival of aristocratic families and the transmission of their property and power. Though churchmen had many ideas about the value of marriage, they had nothing to do with the ceremony; no one married in a church. Rather, marriage was a family affair, and often a very expensive one. There was more than one form of marriage: in the most formal, the husband-to-be gave his future bride a handsome dowry of clothes, bedding, livestock, and land. Then, after the marriage was consummated, he gave his wife a morning gift of furniture and perhaps the keys to the house. Very rich men often had, in addition to their wife, one or more "concubines" at the same time. These enjoyed a less formal type of marriage, receiving a morning gift but no dowry.

The wife's role was above all to maintain the family. A woman passed from one family (that of her birth) to the next (that of her marriage) by parental fiat. When they married, women left the legal protection of their father for that of their husband. Did women have any freedom of action? Yes. For one thing, they had considerable control over their dowries. Some participated in family land transactions: sales, donations, exchanges, and the like. Upon the death of their husbands, widows received a portion of the household property. Although inheritances generally went from fathers to sons, many fathers left bequests to their daughters, who could then dispose of their property more or less as they liked. In 632, for example, the nun Burgundofara, who had never married, drew up a will giving to her monastery the land, slaves, vineyards, pastures, and forests that she had received from her two brothers and her father. In the same will, she gave other property near Paris to her brothers and sister.

Burgundofara's generous piety was extraordinary only in degree. The world of kings, queens, and aristocrats intersected with that of the church. The arrival (*c.*590) on the Continent of the fierce Irish monastic reformer Saint Columbanus (543–615) marked a new level of association between the two. Columbanus's brand of monasticism, which stressed exile, devotion, and discipline, made a powerful impact on Merovingian aristocrats. They flocked to the monasteries that he established in both Francia and Italy, and they founded new ones on their own lands in the countryside. In Francia alone there was an explosion of monasteries: between the years 600 and 700, an astonishing 320 new houses were established, most of them outside of the cities. Some of the new monks and nuns were grown men and women; others were young children, given to a monastery by their parents. This latter practice, called oblation, was well accepted and even considered essential for the spiritual well-being of both children and their families.

The Irish monks introduced aristocrats on the Continent to a deepened religious devotion. Those who did not actively join or patronize a monastery still read—or listened to others read—books preaching penance, and they chanted the psalms. Irish and Anglo-Saxon clerics cultivated private penance; using books called "penitentials," they reminded people of their possible sins and assigned penances, usually fasting on bread and water for a certain length of time. The *Penitential of Finnian*, for example, assigns six years of fasting, three of them on bread and water and the last three abstaining from wine and meat, to "any cleric or woman who practices magic [and has] led astray anyone by their magic."[13]

Deepened piety did not, in this case, lead to the persecution of others—something that (as we shall see) happened in later centuries. In particular, where Jews were settled in Western Europe—along the Mediterranean coast and inland, in Burgundy, for example—they remained integrated into every aspect of secular life. They used Hebrew in worship, but otherwise they spoke the same languages as Christians and used Latin in their legal documents. Their children were often given the same names as Christians (and Christians often took biblical names, such as Solomon); they dressed as everyone else dressed; and they engaged in the same occupations. Many Jews planted and tended vineyards, in part because of the importance of wine in synagogue services, in part because the surplus could easily be sold. Some were rich landowners, with slaves and dependent peasants working for them; others were independent peasants of modest means. While some Jews lived in the few cities that remained, most, like their Christian neighbors, lived on the land.

THE BRITISH ISLES

Celtic groups from the north and west had often attacked Roman Britain. When the last of the Roman garrisons left Britain *c.*410, new immigrants—Saxon and other Germanic groups—arrived piecemeal. They came as families, in boats that held about forty persons, to settle and farm along Britain's east coast. Irish immigrants gradually settled in the west. Elsewhere—in what is today the north and west of England, Scotland, and Ireland—Celtic kingdoms survived.

Where the Germanic tribes settled, their tastes, expectations, styles, and religious practices affected the indigenous British population, and vice versa. In the eighth century, the monk-historian Bede portrayed this amalgamated culture as utterly pagan: Anglo-Saxon England was, in his words, "a barbarous, fierce, and unbelieving nation."[14] But the story that archaeology tells is more nuanced: holy sites dedicated to the saints remained magnets for pilgrimage, burial, and settlement. Most, perhaps all, of the British Isles remained Christian. Wales was already Christian when, in the course of the fifth century, missionaries converted Ireland and Scotland. (Saint Patrick, apostle to the Irish, is only the most famous of these.) However, in contrast to Bede's vision of a highly organized church led by the pope, post-Roman Britain's Christianity was decentralized and local. The same was true in the Celtic kingdoms—Wales, Ireland, and Scotland—which supported relatively non-hierarchical church organizations. Rural monasteries normally served as the seats of bishoprics as well as centers of population and settlement. Abbots and abbesses, often members of powerful families, enjoyed considerable power and prestige.

At the end of the sixth century the Roman form of Christianity arrived to compete with the diverse forms already flourishing in the British Isles. In 597 missionaries sent by Pope Gregory the Great, led by Augustine (not the fifth-century bishop of Hippo!), arrived at the court of King Ethelbert of Kent (d.616). According to Bede, Ethelbert was a pagan. Yet he was married to a Christian Frankish princess, and he welcomed the missionaries kindly: "At the king's command they sat down and preached the word of life to himself and all his officials and companions there present." While he refused to convert because "[I cannot] forsake those beliefs which I and the whole people of the Angles have held so long," the king did give the missionaries housing and material support.[15]

Above all, the king let them preach. This was key: Augustine had in mind more than the conversion of a king: he wanted to set up an English church on the Roman model, with ties to the pope and a clear hierarchy. Successful in his work of evangelization, he divided England into territorial units (dioceses) headed by an archbishop and bishops. Augustine himself became the first archbishop of Canterbury. There he constructed the model English ecclesiastical complex: a cathedral, a monastery, and a school to train young clerics.

There was nothing easy or quick about the conversion of England to the Roman brand of Christianity. The old and the new Christian traditions clashed over matters as large as the organization of the church and as seemingly small as the date of Easter. Everyone agreed that they could not be saved unless they observed the day of Christ's Resurrection properly and on the right date. But what was the right date? Each side was wedded to its own view. A turning point came at the Synod of Whitby, organized in 664 by the Northumbrian king Oswy to decide between the Roman and Irish dates. When Oswy became convinced that Rome spoke with the very voice of Saint Peter, the heavenly doorkeeper, he opted for the Roman calculation of the date and embraced the Roman church as a whole.

The pull of Rome—the symbol, in the new view, of the Christian religion itself—was almost physical. In the wake of Whitby, Benedict Biscop, a Northumbrian aristocrat-turned-abbot and founder of two important English monasteries, Wearmouth and Jarrow, made numerous arduous trips to Rome. He brought back books, saints' relics, liturgical vestments, and even a cantor to teach his monks the proper melodies in a time before written musical notation existed. A century later, the Anglo-Saxon monk Wynfrith changed his name to the more Roman-sounding Boniface (672/675–754) after he went to Rome to get a commission from Pope Gregory II (715–731) to preach the Word to people living east of the Rhine. Though they were already Christian, their brand of Christianity was not Roman enough for Saint Boniface.

As Roman culture confronted Anglo-Saxon forms, the results were particularly eclectic. This is best seen in the visual arts. The Anglo-Saxons, like other barbarian (and, indeed, Celtic) tribes, had artistic traditions particularly well suited to adorning flat surfaces. Belt buckles, helmet nose-pieces, brooches, and other sorts of jewelry of the rich were embellished with semi-precious stones and enlivened with decorative patterns, often made up of animal parts or intertwining snakes (see Plate 2.4). When Benedict Biscop (and others like him) returned to England with books from Rome, they challenged scribes and artists there to combine traditions. The imported books contained not only texts but also illustrations that relied, at least distantly, on ancient Roman artistic traditions (see Plates 1.1–1.4). English artists soon combined their native decorative impulses with the classical interest in human forms. The result was perfectly suited to flat pages. Consider the Lindisfarne Gospels, which were probably made at the monastery of Lindisfarne in the first third of the eighth century. (The Gospels are the four canonical accounts of Christ's life and death in the New Testament.) The artist of this sumptuous book was clearly uniting Anglo-Saxon, Irish, and Roman artistic traditions when he introduced each Gospel with three full-page illustrations: first, a portrait of the "author" (the evangelist); then an entirely ornamental "carpet" page; finally, the beginning words of the Gospel text. Plates 2.5 to 2.7 illustrate the sequence for the Gospel of Luke. The figure of Luke (see Plate 2.5), though clearly human, floats in space. His "throne" is a square of ribbons, his drapery a series of looping lines. The artist captures the essence of an otherworldly saint without the distraction of three-dimensionality. The carpet page (see Plate 2.6), with its geometrical and animal forms, has some of the features of the Great Square-Headed brooch as well as Irish interlace patterns. It is more than decorative, however: the design clearly evokes a cross. The next page (see Plate 2.7) begins with a great letter, Q (for the first word, "quoniam"), as richly decorated as the cross of the carpet page; gradually, in the course of the next few words, the ornamentation diminishes. In this way, after the fanfare of author and carpet pages, the reader is ushered into the Gospel text itself.

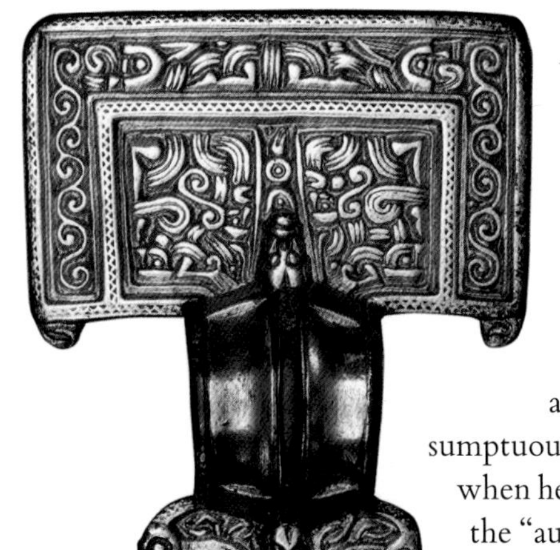

Plate 2.4 Great Square-Headed Brooch (early 6th cent.). This brooch—one of many found in the graves of wealthy women in Anglo-Saxon England and elsewhere in the North and Baltic Sea regions—was heavy and imposing. Made of silver gilt and niello (a black metallic alloy), it measures over five inches long. A framed panel adorned with scrolls and stylized animals forms the top, while the foot is decorated with many face masks: there is one on each of the side lobes, and a larger one in the middle of the diamond. Two more are at the top and bottom of the bow (the center clip).

Just as the Anglo-Saxons held on to their artistic styles, so too did they retain their language. In England, the vernacular—the language of the people, as opposed to Latin—was quickly turned into a written language and used in every aspect of English life, from government to entertainment. If you look closely at Plate 2.7 you will see tiny words written in the spaces between the large Latin words of the text: these are in Anglo-Saxon (or Old English). Even Bede praised the common speech of the people, telling the story of Caedmon, a simple monk who dreamed a song in Anglo-Saxon about God's creation. Bede himself provided only a Latin translation of the poem in his *Ecclesiastical History*, but Anglo-Saxon versions were soon available. Indeed, two manuscripts of Bede's work from the eighth century still survive today with Caedmon's hymn in both Latin and Anglo-Saxon.

THE SOUTH: SPAIN AND ITALY

The mix of cultures characteristic of England was doubly the case in Spain and Italy. In Spain, especially in the south and east, some Roman cities had continued to flourish after the Visigothic invasions. Merchants from Byzantium regularly visited Mérida, and the sixth-century bishops there constructed lavish churches and set up a system of regular food distribution. Under King Leovigild (r.569–586), all of Spain came under Visigothic control.

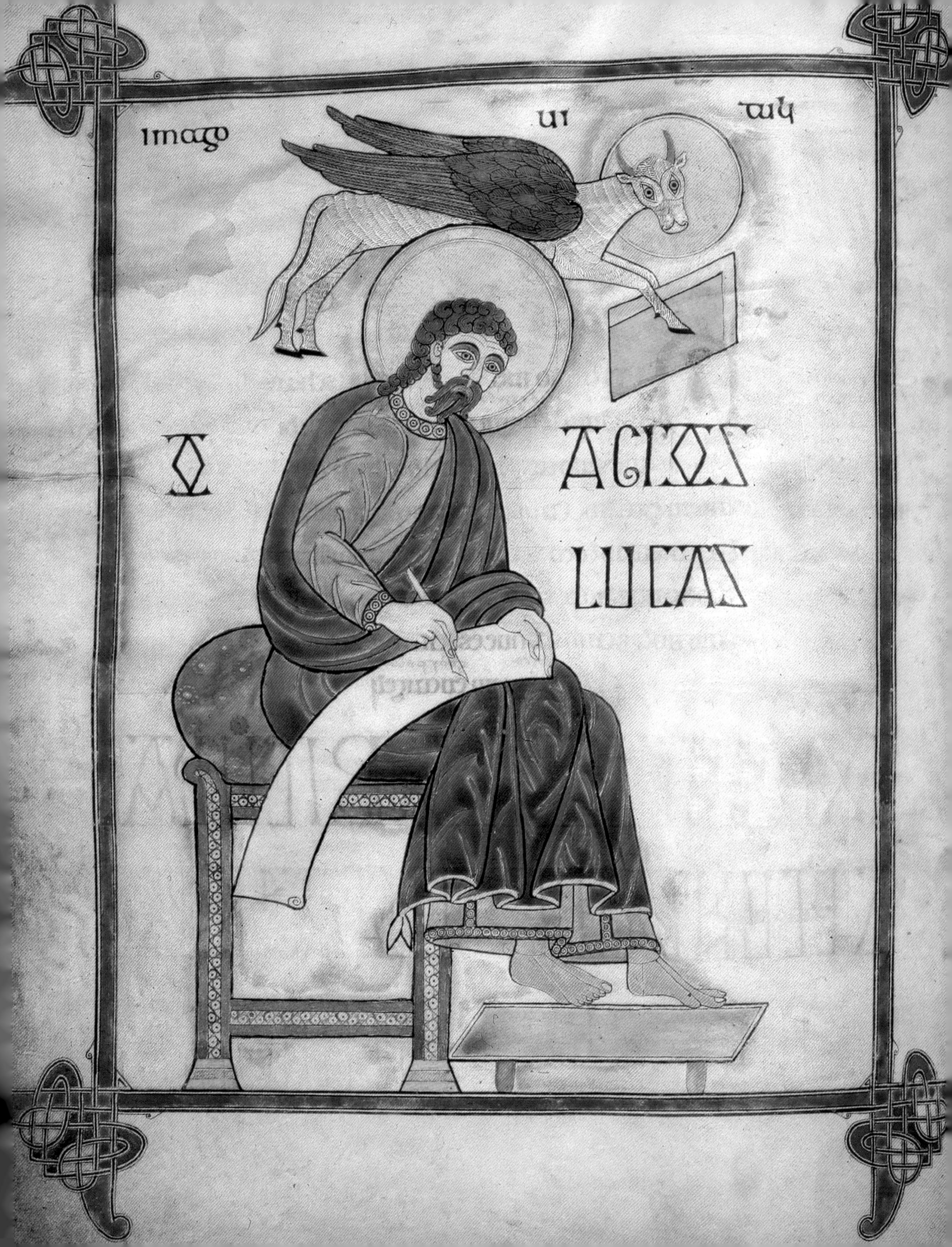
imago ui tuli
O AGIOS
LUCAS

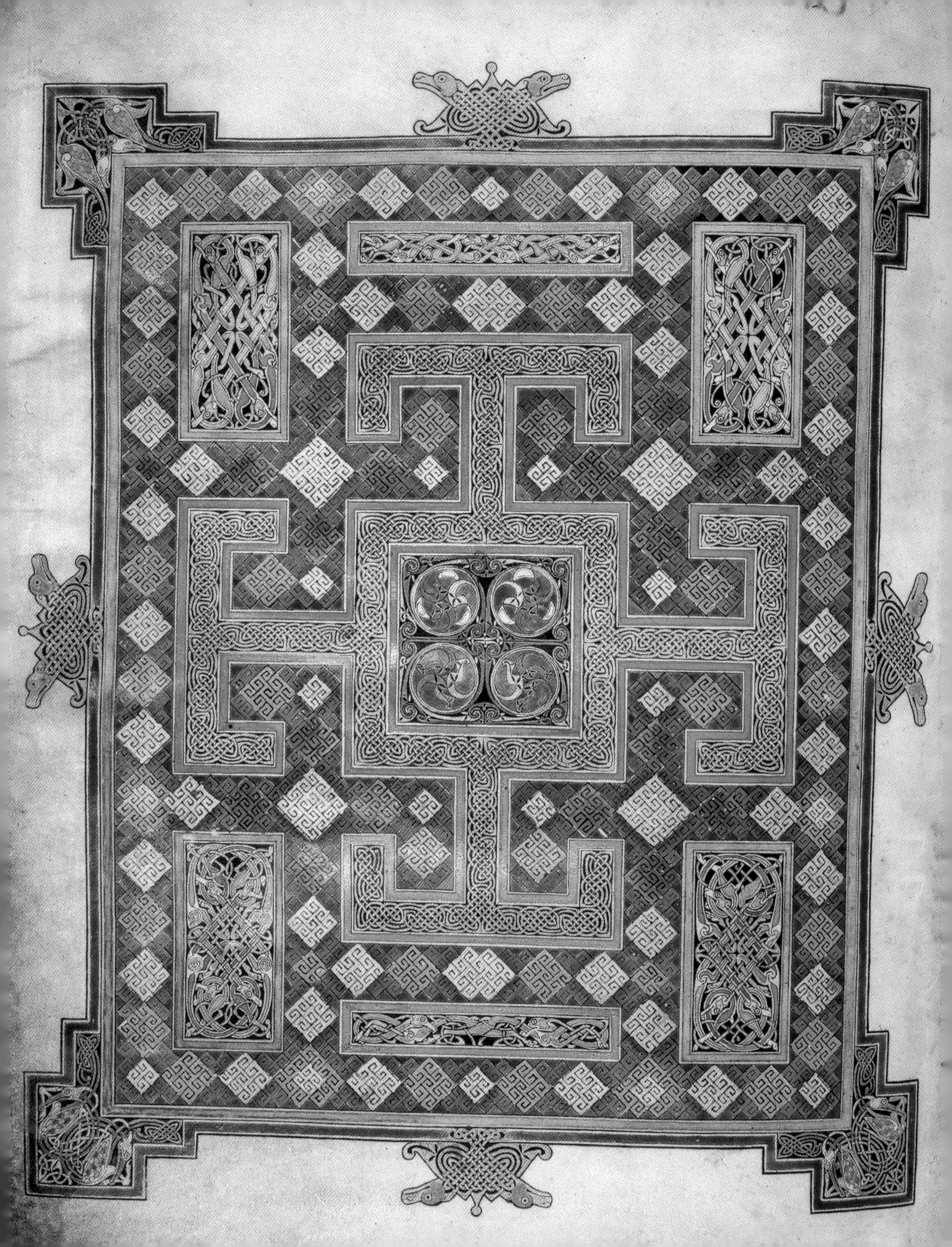

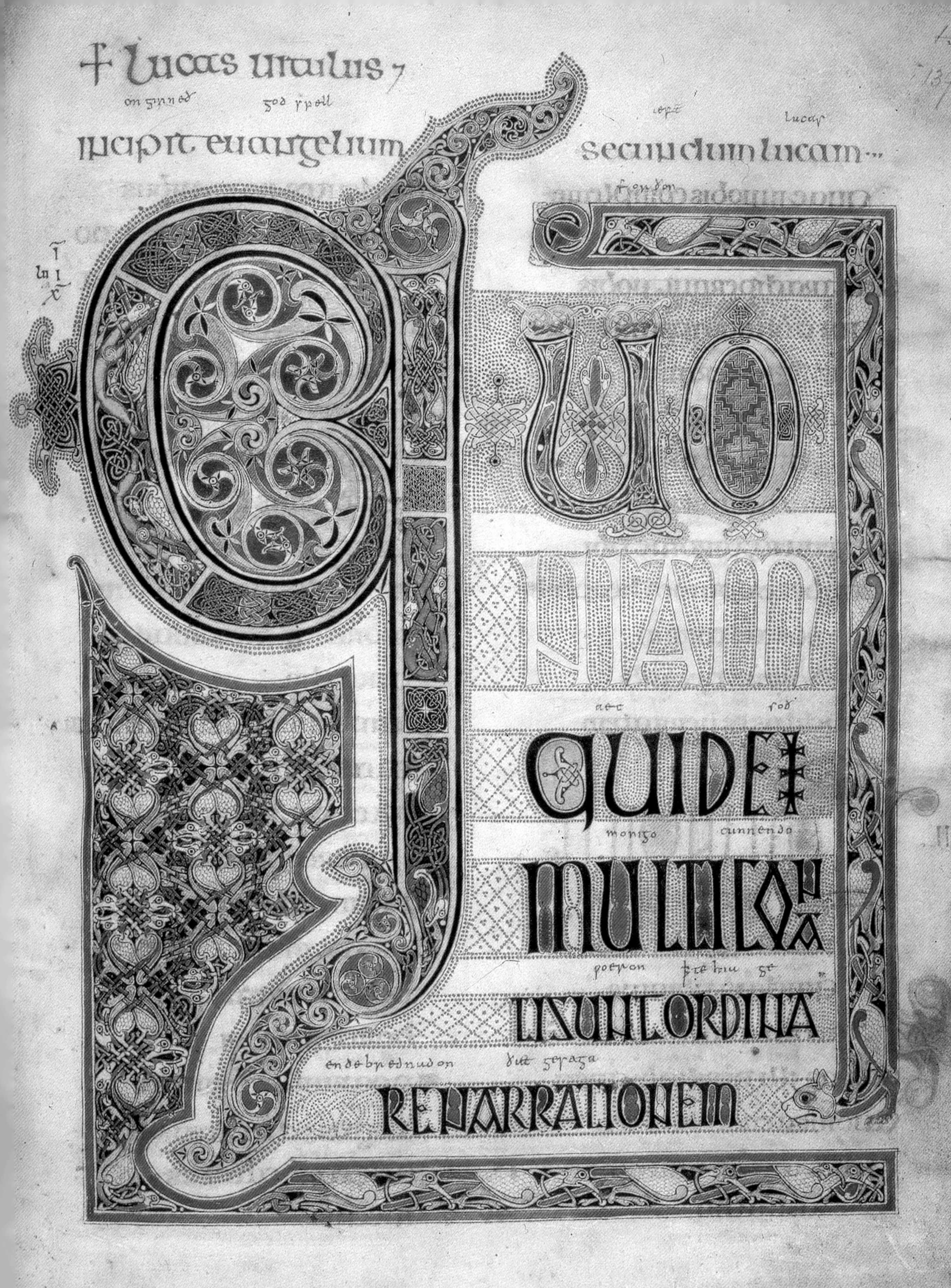
+ lucas uitulus 7
incipit euangelium
secundum lucam
QUONIAM
QUIDEM
NARRATIONEM

Previous pages:

Plate 2.5 Saint Luke, Lindisfarne Gospels (first third of 8th cent.?). Inspired by Late Roman traditions, the artist—who was also the scribe of this book—introduced the Gospel of Luke with an author's portrait. The winged calf perched on Luke's halo is his symbol.

Plate 2.6 Carpet Page, Lindisfarne Gospels (first third of 8th cent.?). Anglo-Saxon and Celtic artistic ornamental traditions lie behind this elaborate cross, which follows Luke's portrait in Plate 2.5 and faces (as here) the first text page, depicted in Plate 2.7.

Plate 2.7 First Text Page, Gospel of Saint Luke, Lindisfarne Gospels (first third of 8th cent.?). The third page in the Luke Gospel sequence begins the text itself: "Quoniam quidem multi conati sunt ordinare narrationem," "Since many have undertaken to put in narrative order...."

Under his son Reccared (r.586–601), the monarchy converted from Arian to Catholic Christianity. This event (587) cemented the ties between the king and the Hispano-Roman population, which included the great landowners and leading bishops. Two years later, at the Third Council of Toledo, most of the Arian bishops followed their king by announcing their conversion to Catholicism, and the assembled churchmen enacted decrees for a united church in Spain, starting with the provision "that the statutes of the Councils and the decrees of the Roman Pontiffs be maintained."[16] Here, as in England a few decades later, Rome and the papacy had become the linchpins of the Christian religion.

The Roman inheritance in Spain was clear not only in the dominance of the Hispano-Roman aristocracy and the adoption of its form of Christianity but also in the legal and intellectual culture that prevailed there. Nowhere else in Europe were church councils so regular or royal legislation so frequent. Nowhere else were the traditions of classical learning so highly regarded. Only in seventh-century Spain could a man like Isidore of Seville (*c.*560–636) draw on centuries of Latin learning to write the encyclopedic *Etymologies*, in which the essence of things was explained by their linguistic roots. His book was wildly popular.

Unlike the Merovingians the Visigothic kings were not able to establish a stable dynasty. The minority of a king's son almost always sparked revolts by rival families, and the child's deposition was often accompanied by wholesale slaughter of his father's followers and confiscation of their lands. Even so, the kings were able to control their realm from the top more effectively than most barbarian kings because of their partnership with the Spanish church. While the king gave the churchmen free rein to set up their own hierarchy (with the bishop of Toledo at the top) and to meet regularly at synods to regulate and reform the church, the bishops in turn supported the king. They even anointed him, daubing him with holy oil in a ritual that paralleled the ordination of priests and echoed the anointment of kings in the Old Testament. While the bishops in this way made the king's cause their own, their lay counterparts, the great landowners, helped supply the king with troops.

It was precisely the centralization of the Visigothic kingdom that proved its undoing. In 711, a small Islamic raiding party killed the Visigothic king and thereby dealt the whole state a decisive blow. Between 712 and 715, as we have seen, armies led by Arabs took over the peninsula through a combination of war and diplomacy.

The conquest of Spain was less Arab or Islamic than Berber. The generals who led the invasion of Spain were Arabs, to be sure, but the rank-and-file fighters were Berbers from North Africa. While the Berbers were converts to Islam, they did not speak Arabic. The Arabs considered them crude mountainfolk, only imperfectly Muslim. Perhaps a million people settled in Spain in the wake of the invasions, the Arabs taking the better lands in the south, the Berbers getting less rich properties in the center and north. Most of the conquered population consisted of Christians, along with a sprinkling of Jews. A thin ribbon of Christian states—Asturias, Pamplona, and so on—survived in the north. There was thus a great variety of religions on the Iberian Peninsula. (See Map 2.4 on p. 59.) The history of Spain would for many centuries thereafter be one of both acculturation and war.

Unlike Visigothic Spain, Lombard Italy presented no united front. In the center of the peninsula was a swathe of territory claimed by the Byzantines (the Exarchate) and dominated on its southwestern end by the papacy, always hostile to the Lombard kings in the north. To Rome's east and south were the dukes of Benevento and Spoleto. Although theoretically the Lombard king's officers, in fact they were virtually independent rulers. Although many Lombards were Catholics, others, including important kings and dukes, were Arians. The "official" religion varied with the ruler in power. Rather than signal a major political event, then, the conversion of the Lombards to Catholic Christianity occurred gradually, ending only in the late seventh century. Partly as a result of this slow development, the Lombard kings, unlike the Visigoths, Franks, or even Anglo-Saxons, never enlisted the wholehearted support of any particular group of churchmen.

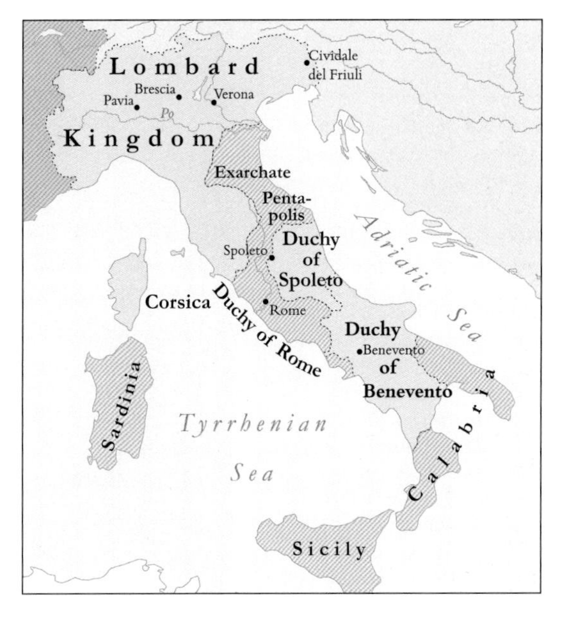

Map 2.5 Lombard Italy, *c.*750

Yet the Lombard kings did not lack advantages. They controlled extensive estates, and they made use of the Roman institutions that survived in Italy. The kings made the cities their administrative bases, assigning dukes to rule from them and setting up one, Pavia, as their capital. Recalling emperors like Constantine and Justinian, the kings built churches and monasteries at Pavia, maintained city walls, and issued law codes.

When the Lombards settled in Italy, they found the artifacts and lingering traditions of Rome's city-based culture. The newcomers tried to preserve these to some degree, as at Brescia and Verona, where they maintained some Roman roads. On the other hand, cities taken over by the Lombards were no longer commercially active, even though the urban centers of Byzantine Italy (the narrow strip running from Ravenna to Rome) were still alive with trade. The Lombards also allowed Roman houses and apartment blocks to crumble, their places taken by burial plots, vegetable gardens, and, more ambitiously, new churches and monasteries.

The influence of both classical Roman and "barbarian" or at least "provincial" artistic sensibilities in Lombard Italy is clear in two monuments from the period: the altar of King Ratchis (r.744–749) from the church of San Giovanni at Cividale del Friuli and carved figures in Cividale's Tempietto (i.e., small temple). Both probably date from the eighth century (though the Tempietto's date may be later), and both involve religious themes. At first glance, they seem very different. The altar (Plate 2.8) is made of slabs of marble carved in very low relief. The sculptors, here depicting the theme of the Three Magi bringing gifts to the Christ Child, showed no interest in the volume and weight of ordinary human bodies. Nevertheless, considering that most Lombard art was purely decorative, the figures on the altar may be seen as a real concession to Roman traditions.

The Tempietto (Plate 2.9), located right next to San Giovanni in Cividale, is in a rather different style. Unlike the Mary of the Ratchis Altar, the women here have weight and volume. When they were originally made, they were part of an array of such female saints all along the Tempietto's walls. One turns toward another (see the two figures flanking

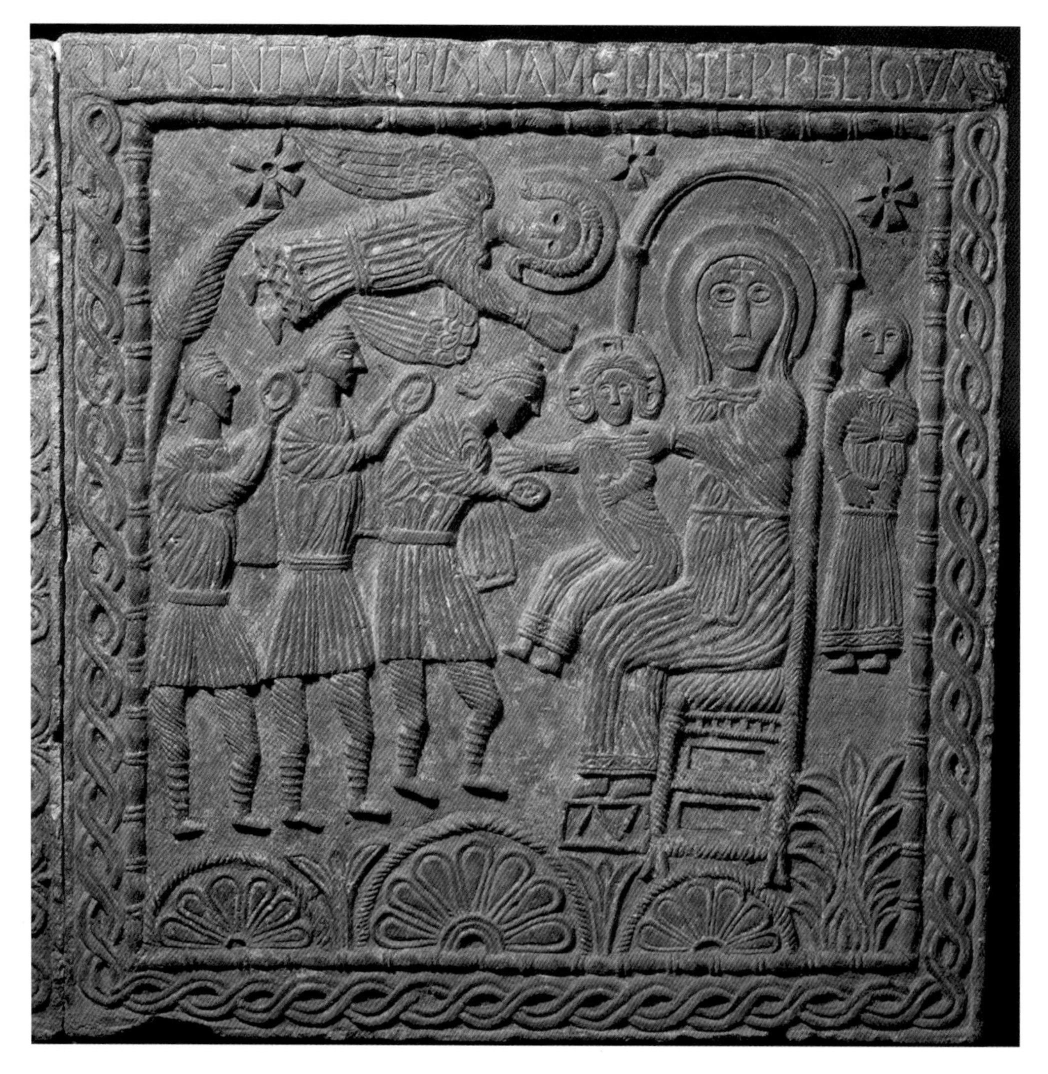

Plate 2.8 The Altar of Ratchis (737–744). Like the provincial artists of the Roman Empire (see Plates 1.5 and 1.6 on pp. 17–18), the sculptors of this marble slab—one end of a four-sided carved altar—were interested in pattern and transcendence. The three magi advance toward Mother and Child in lock step, their short tunics forming identical triangles, the folds of their clothing turned into incised lines. Mary, mother of God, and the Christ Child look outward, beyond the viewer, interacting with no one. The otherworldly character of the relief is stressed by the landscape—three "half daisy-wheels" rising from a decorative border—and an angel hovering above. A tiny Joseph, husband of Mary, hovers mid-air behind her throne. Originally the altar was studded with gems and brightly painted in blues, yellows, and reds; traces of polychrome remain. An opening in the back panel of the altar allowed worshipers to view the relics within. A dedicatory inscription running along the top border of the entire altar declares that it was King Ratchis's gift to San Giovanni (Saint John).

the open space, the lunette). Yet even in the case of these Tempietto carvings, the artists' interest in design and decoration is clear: above and below the saints are decorative borders with flowers that recall the "daisy-wheels" of the Altar of Ratchis (Plate 2.8), and their robes fall into folds created by incised lines.

Cividale was not the only Lombard center to boast significant artistic activity. The monastery of San Salvatore at Brescia, for example, also built in the eighth century, was comparably decorated. The importance of both classical and Roman provincial styles in Lombard Italy suggests that the elites there welcomed artists not only from Europe but also from the Byzantine and Islamic worlds. This should not be surprising: Byzantium ran through the middle of Italy, while the Umayyad caliphs, not far from Sicily and Southern Italy, were themselves enthralled with Romano-Byzantine traditions, as we saw in the case of their mosque at Damascus (Plate 2.3).

Emboldened by their achievements in the north, the Lombard kings tried to make some headway against the independent dukes of southern Italy. But that threatened to

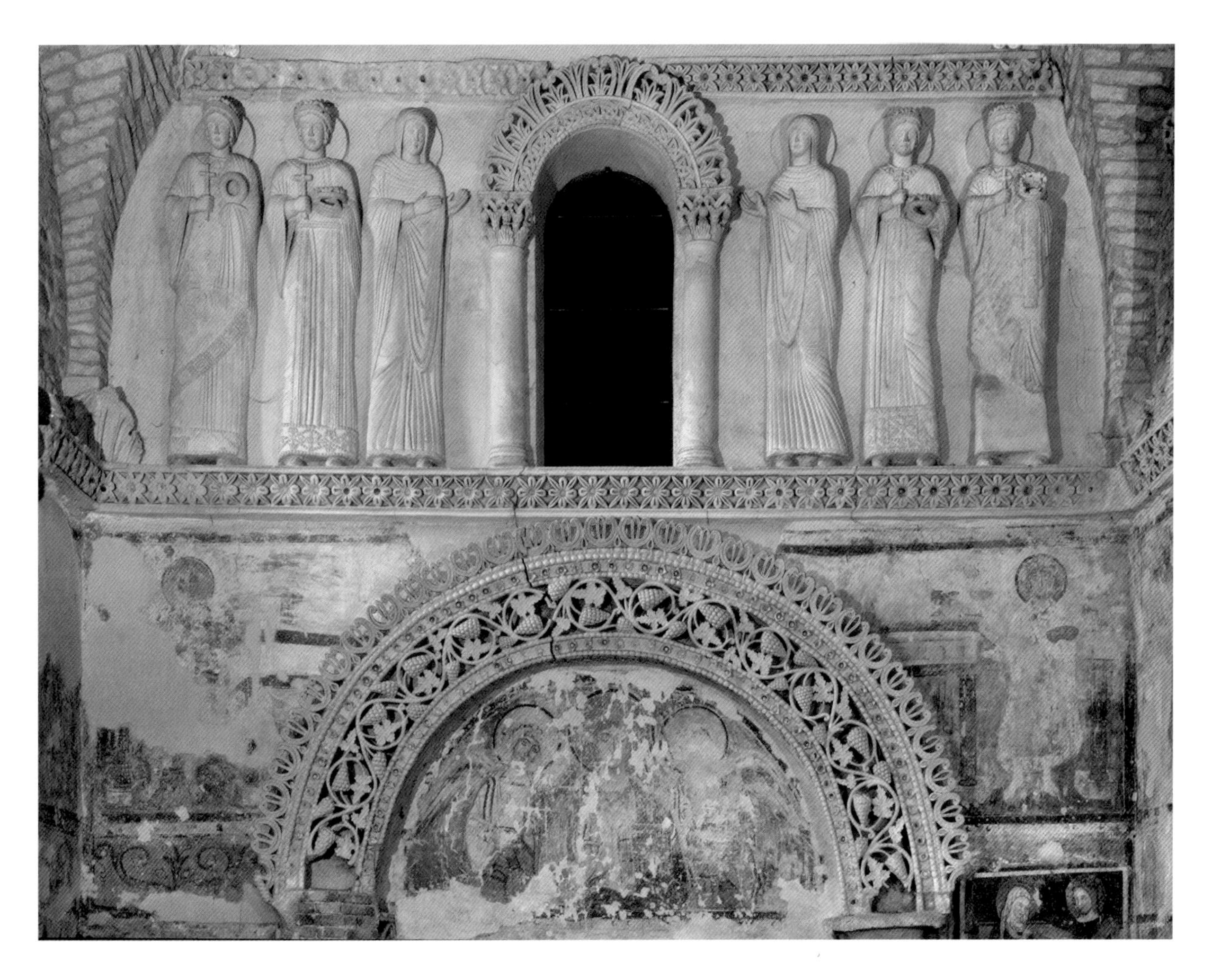

Plate 2.9 The Cividale Tempietto (8th cent.?). These stucco figures stand above the main entrance of the small church of Santa Maria in Valle, originally an oratory for the church of San Giovanni.

surround Rome with a unified Lombard kingdom. The pope, fearing for his own position, called on the Franks for help.

THE POPE: A MAN IN THE MIDDLE

By the end of the sixth century, the pope's position was ambiguous. As bishop of Rome, he wielded real secular power within the city as well as a measure of spiritual leadership farther afield. Yet in other ways he was subordinate to Byzantium. Pope Gregory the Great (590–604), whom we have already met a number of times, laid the foundations for the papacy's later spiritual and temporal ascendancy. During Gregory's tenure, the pope became the greatest landowner in Italy; he organized Rome's defense and paid for its army; he heard court cases, made treaties, and provided welfare services. The missionary expedition he sent to England was only a small part of his involvement in the rest of Europe. A prolific author of spiritual works, Gregory digested and simplified the ideas of Church Fathers such as Saint Augustine, making them accessible to a wider audience. In his *Moralia in Job*, he set forth a model of biblical exegesis that was widely imitated for centuries. His

MATERIAL CULTURE: FORGING MEDIEVAL SWORDS

The medieval sword was more than a weapon on which the warrior's life depended. It had magical, sacred, even moral significance. Usually expensive, it was available only to richer men and often handed down over generations. Medieval epic poetry sometimes made swords their very focus. Consider the story of Sigurd (or Siegfried) in the *Volsunga Saga*. His father's sword, Gram (in epic tales the hero's sword had names; e.g., Excalibur, Durendal), broke in two, but the swordsmith Regin forged the two halves together, making Gram better than ever. Now unbreakable, it made possible Sigurd's slaying of the treasure-guarding dragon, Fafnir.

A carved wooden panel, originally part of a twelfth-century (or perhaps early thirteenth-century) church portal in Norway, shows how Gram was forged (see Plate 2.10).

The carvings seem to display a "pattern-welded" blade, an early technique in which twisted strips of natural steel (iron with heterogeneous carbon content) and wrought iron (iron low in carbon) were welded together on a forge fire at a temperature of no less than 2100° F/1150°C. The result was a distinctive serpentine pattern on the blade surface and the unique attributes of durability and resistance to fracture. The sword in the carvings also shows a "fuller," a groove that runs along almost the entire length of the blade to make the sword lighter.

Temperature control was key during the forging process. The lower roundel in Plate 2.10 shows an assistant (or perhaps Sigurd) manning two bellows. These blowing devices—generally made of wood and leather—provided constant air flow into the forge to keep the fire going. The swordsmith needed to reach top forging temperatures of *c.*2400–2500° F/1315–1370° C. Moreover, the swordsmith used heat-control techniques (and not just mechanical ones, like hammering) to modify the distribution of carbon inside the blade. He repeatedly quenched and then tempered the blade. Quenching had to be performed when the blade was cherry red (at a minimum temperature of 1375° F/745° C) by rapidly immersing it in cool water (or sometimes brine or oil) to improve its hardness, while tempering called for the blade to be reheated at lower temperatures (300° to 1200° F/150° to 650° C) to relieve brittleness.

Swords were much on the minds of ninth-century Carolingian kings, who were constantly waging war. While the Norwegian portal romanticized the making of the blade, in the ninth century whole workshops were dedicated to the task, often employing slaves to operate both forge and bellows. Some produced very fine blades, like the shop that made swords boasting on their fuller the name Vlfberht or Ulfberht along with one or two crosses in various positions (e.g., +Vlfberht+; +Vlfberh+t). They were exceptionally popular: their remains have been found in more than twenty different European countries. Scholars have long debated the identity of Ulfberht. Some (like Ewart Oakeshott) think that he was the sword maker, a Frankish blacksmith operating in the lower or middle Rhine area (Germany). Other scholars (such as Anne Stalsberg) believe he was the master, or supervisor, of a local sword-blade workshop where illiterate slaves did the actual forging. If so, this may explain the many variants of the Ulfberht signatures. In one case (see Plate 2.11)—one of the oldest extant Ulfberht blades—the "wrong" spelling +Vlfbeht+ (with the "r" missing) has been attributed to imitation or even to a forgery to make the sword more valuable. But it is even more likely that it was the simple mistake of an illiterate smith.

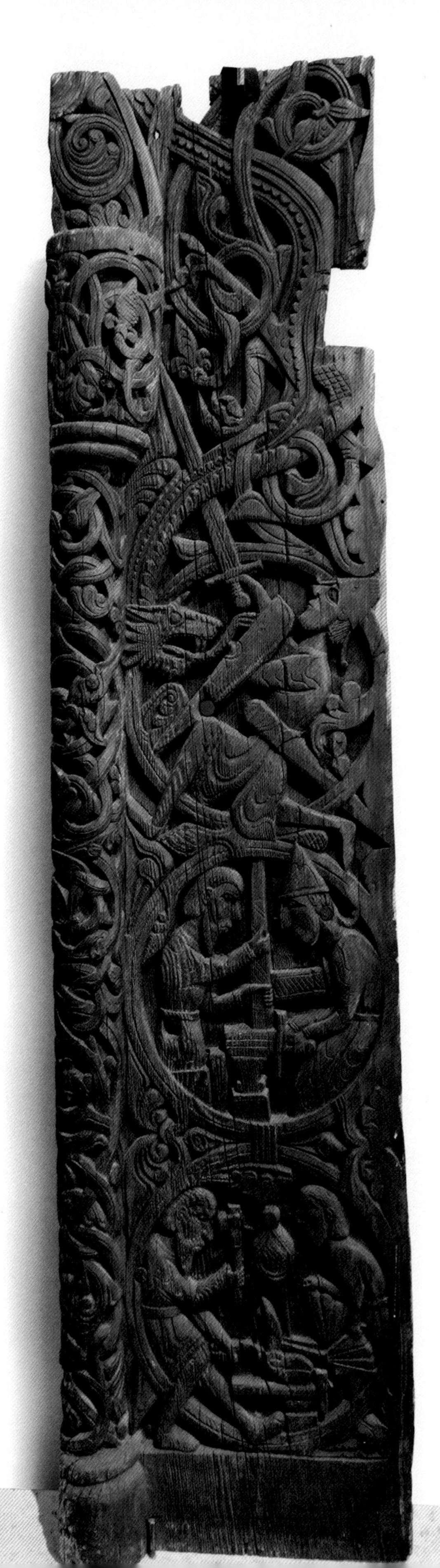

Plate 2.10 The Sigurd Portal, Hylestad Stave Church, Norway (12th–13th cent.). Shown here is the right-hand column of the portal, which reads from bottom to top. At the bottom, Gram is being forged. In the middle roundel, Sigurd (with the helmet) tests the sword, while in the top roundel he slays the dragon Fafnir.

A Carolingian Psalter illustration sheds light on the final step in the production of a sword: sharpening the blade. Plate 2.12 shows two techniques. On the right, the side where the psalmist himself stands inspired by a winged angel above, members of the army of the righteous sharpen a sword on a hand-operated rotary grindstone. That was the most up-to-date method, and this drawing is the first we have of it. On the left, the enemy army, the "wicked," as the psalmist puts it, uses an "old-fashioned" whetstone. The artist seems to be saying that virtue and advanced technology go hand-in-hand.

The invention of the blast furnace, a new technology for smelting iron ores, allowed for transformations in the production of weaponry, and—in particular—made all-steel swords a reality. Scholars now seem to agree that prototypes of this kind of shaft furnace were probably introduced earlier than *c.*1350 (the traditional date). It was in use at some point between the eleventh and thirteenth century in central Swabia (southwest Germany). However, from the late fourteenth century, it heralded an "industrial revolution." The transition from the traditional direct process smelting furnace—the small, low-shaft bloomery that could operate at *c.*1470–1650° F/800–900° C—to the blast furnace occurred when shafts were pitched higher and made larger, and air was blasted into the furnace with water-powered bellows. The furnace temperature could now go far above 2100° F/1150° C (the melting point of cast iron), and even up to the melting point of pure iron (2795°F/1535° C). This method produced massive quantities of liquid cast iron (or "pig iron"): a single blast furnace could yield up to nine tons of iron from a single "charge"—the load of iron ore and charcoal fed into the top of the furnace. The high carbon content (up to 3–4 per cent) in the liquid cast iron was then reduced in a refining furnace to obtain high quality wrought iron and/or natural steel. With these sweeping, "proto-industrial" improvements, medieval weaponry could include steel plate armor, wrought iron bombards (cannons that hurled stones) and handguns, and cast iron cannons, eventually giving way to modern warfare.

FURTHER READING

Peirce, Ian. *Swords of the Viking Age*, Introduction by Ewart Oakeshott. Woodbridge: Boydell Press, 2002.

Stalsberg, Anne. "The identity of Vlfberht and how the swords with his signature were spread in Europe." In *Tverrfaglige perspektiver*, ed. Marianne Nitter and Einar Solheim Pedersen, 21–36. Stavanger: University of Stavanger, 2009.

Williams, Alan. *The Sword and the Crucible. A History of the Metallurgy of European Swords up to the 16th Century*. Leiden: Brill, 2012.

Plate 2.12 (facing page) The Utrecht Psalter (first half of 9th cent.). This drawing of the two techniques of blade-sharpening depicts a passage in Psalm 64 (Douay 63):1–4, "Preserve my life from dread of the enemy, hide me from the secret plots of the wicked, from the scheming of evildoers, who whet their tongues like swords, who aim bitter words like arrows, shooting from ambush at the blameless."

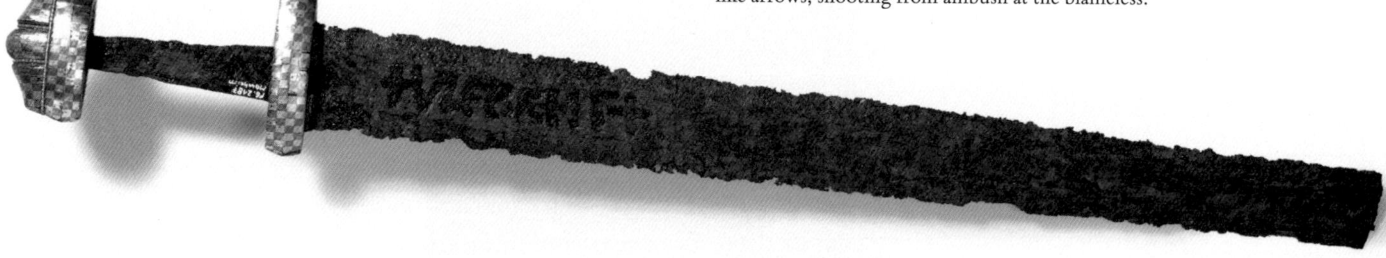

Plate 2.11 Ulfberht Sword (9th cent.). This sword was found in the Rhine, near Mannheim, in 1960.

LXII PSALMUS DD CUMESSETINDE SERTOIDUMEAE

DSDSMEUS
ADTEDELUCEUIGILO SI
TIUITINTEANIMAMEA
QUAMMULTIPLICITER
TIBICAROMEA;
INTERRADESERTAETIN
UIAETININAQUOSA·
SICINSCOAPPARUITTIBI
UTUIDEREMUIRTUTEM
TUAMETGLORIĀTUAM;
QMMELIORESTMISERICOR
DIATUASUPERUITAS·
LABIAMEALAUDABITTE;

SICBENEDICAMTEINUITA
MEA· ETINNOMINETUO
LEUABOMANUSMEAS;
SICUTADIPEETPINGUIDI
NEREPLEATURANIMA
MEA· ETLABIAEXSULTATI
ONISLAUDABITOSMEŪ;
SIMEMORFUITUISUPER
STRATUMMEŪINMATU
TINISMEDITABORINTE
QUIAFUISTIADIUTORMS
ETINUELAMENTOALARŪ
TUARUMEXSULTABO·

ADHAESITANIMAMEA
POSTTE· MESUSCEPITDEX
TERATUA;
IPSIUEROINUANŪQUAE
SIERUNTANIMĀMEĀ·
INTROIBUNTININFERIORA
TERRAE· TRADENTURIN
MANUSGLADIIPARTES
UULPIUMERUNT;
REXUEROLAETABITURINDŌ·
LAUDABUNTOMSQUIIU
RANTINEO· QUIAOBSTRUC
TŪEOSLOQUENTIŪINIQUA·

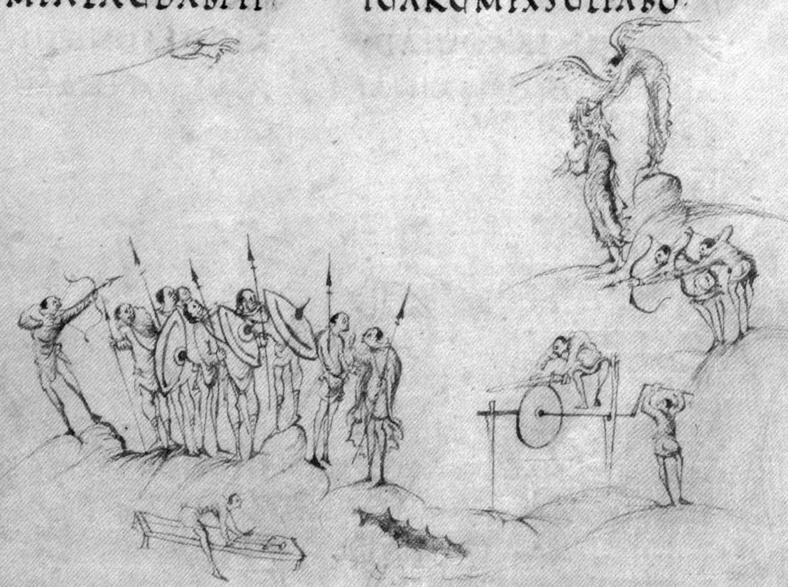

LXIII INFINEM PSALMUS DAUID

EXAUDIDSORATI
ONEMMEAMCUMDE
PRECOR· ATIMOREINI
MICIERIPEANIMĀMEĀ
PROTEXISTIMEACONUEN
TUMALIGNANTIUM·
AMULTITUDINEOPERAN
TIUMINIQUITATEM·
QUIAEXACUERUNTUTGLA

handbook for clerics, *Pastoral Care*, went hand-in-hand with his practical church reforms in Italy, where he tried to impose regular episcopal elections and enforce clerical celibacy.

At the same time, even Gregory was only one of many bishops in the Byzantine Empire. For a long time the emperor's views on dogma, discipline, and church administration largely prevailed at Rome. However, this authority began to unravel in the seventh century. In 691/692, the Quinisext council did not just ban dancing on the first day of March (see p. 48), but in fact drew up 102 rules of discipline for both churchmen and laity. Emperor Justinian II (r.685–695; 705–711) convened the council with the hope that the pope would attend, but Pope Sergius I (687–701) did not, nor would he agree to the canons produced by the council. He objected in particular to two, one permitting priests to have wives if their marriages had occurred before ordination and the other prohibiting fasting on Saturdays in Lent (which the Roman church required). Outraged by Sergius's refusal, Justinian tried to arrest the pope, but the imperial army in Italy (theoretically under the emperor's command) came to the pontiff's aid instead. Justinian's arresting officer was reduced to cowering under the pope's bed. Clearly Constantinople's influence and authority over Rome had become tenuous. Sheer distance as well as diminishing imperial power in Italy meant that the popes had in effect become the leaders of non-Lombard Italy.

The gap between Byzantium and the papacy widened in the early eighth century, when Emperor Leo III tried to increase the taxes on papal property to pay for his wars against the Arabs. Gregory II, the pope who later commissioned Saint Boniface's evangelical work (see above, p. 65), responded by leading a general tax revolt. Meanwhile, Leo's fierce policy of iconoclasm collided with the pope's tolerance of images. For Gregory, holy images could and should be venerated, though not worshiped. Increasing friction with Byzantium meant that when the pope felt threatened by the Lombard kings, as he did in the mid-eighth century, he looked elsewhere for support. Pope Stephen II (752–757) appealed to the Franks—not to the Merovingians, who had just lost the throne, but to Pippin III, the king who had taken the royal crown. Pippin listened to the pope's entreaties and marched into Italy with an army to fight the Lombards. The new Frankish/papal alliance would change the map of Europe in the coming decades.

★ ★ ★ ★ ★

The "fall" of the Roman Empire meant the rise of its heirs. In the East, the Muslims swept out of Arabia—and promptly set up a Roman-style government where they conquered. The bit that they did not take—the part ruled from Constantinople—still considered itself the Roman Empire. In the West, impoverished kingdoms looked to the city of Rome for religion, culture, and inspiration. However much East and West, Christian and Muslim, would come to deviate from and hate one another, they could not change the fact of shared parentage.

CHAPTER TWO: ESSENTIAL DATES

622	*Hijra*; Muhammad's migration from Mecca to Medina
624	Battle of Badr; first Islamic military victory
632	Death of Muhammad the Prophet
661–750	Umayyad caliphate
664	Synod of Whitby; Roman form of Christianity adopted in England
711–715	Conquest of Spain by Islamic-led armies
726–787, 815–843	Iconoclasm at Byzantium

NOTES

1 For "Greek fire," see "Reading through Looking," in *Reading the Middle Ages: Sources from Europe, Byzantium, and the Islamic World*, 3rd ed., ed. Barbara H. Rosenwein (Toronto: University of Toronto Press, 2018), pp. X–XII.
2 The *Easter Chronicle*, in *Reading the Middle Ages*, p. 59.
3 *The Quinisext Council*, Canon 62, in *Reading the Middle Ages*, p. 61.
4 *The Synod of 754*, in *Reading the Middle Ages*, pp. 64–65.
5 *Qur'an Sura* 96 ("The Embryo"), in *Reading the Middle Ages*, p. 68.
6 *Qur'an Sura* 1, in *Reading the Middle Ages*, p. 67.
7 The five pillars are: 1) the *zakat*, a tax to be used for charity; 2) Ramadan, a month of fasting to mark the battle of Badr (624); 3) the *hajj*, an annual pilgrimage to Mecca to be made at least once in a believer's lifetime; and 4) the *salat*, formal worship at least three times a day (later increased to five), including 5) the *shahadah*, or profession of faith: "There is no god but God, and Muhammad is His prophet."
8 John of Nikiu, *Chronicle*, in *Reading the Middle Ages*, p. 73.
9 *The Treaty of Tudmir*, in *Reading the Middle Ages*, p. 79.
10 *Letters to 'Abd Allah b. As'ad*, in *Reading the Middle Ages*, p. 80.
11 Al-Akhtal, *The Tribe Has Departed*, in *Reading the Middle Ages*, p. 83.
12 *The Life of Queen Balthild*, in *Reading the Middle Ages*, p. 91.
13 *Penitential of Finnian*, in *Reading the Middle Ages*, p. 87.
14 Bede, *The Ecclesiastical History of the English People*, in *Reading the Middle Ages*, p. 96.
15 Ibid., p. 97.
16 *The Third Council of Toledo*, in *Reading the Middle Ages*, p. 46.

FURTHER READING

Al-Azmeh, Aziz. *The Emergence of Islam in Late Antiquity: Allah and His People*. Cambridge: Cambridge University Press, 2014.

Brown, Peter. *The Ransom of the Soul: Afterlife and Wealth in Early Western Christianity*. Cambridge, MA: Harvard University Press, 2015.

Brubaker, Leslie, and John Haldon. *Byzantium in the Iconoclast Era c. 680–850: A History*. Cambridge: Cambridge University Press, 2011.

Donner, Fred M. *Muhammad and the Believers: At the Origins of Islam*. Cambridge, MA: Harvard University Press, 2010.

Eger, A. Asa. *The Islamic-Byzantine Frontier: Interaction and Exchange among Muslim and Christian Communities*. London: I.B. Tauris, 2015.

Evans, Helen C. with Brandie Ratliff. *Byzantium and Islam: Age of Transition, 7th–9th Century*. New Haven, CT: Yale University Press, 2012.

Fleming, Robin. *Britain after Rome: The Fall and Rise, 400 to 1070*. London: Penguin, 2010.

Fox, Yaniv. *Power and Religion in Merovingian Gaul: Columbian Monasticism and the Frankish Elites*. Cambridge: Cambridge University Press, 2014.

Haldon, John. *The Empire That Would Not Die: The Paradox of Eastern Roman Survival, 640–740*. Cambridge, MA: Harvard University Press, 2016.

Hoyland, Robert G. *In God's Path: The Arab Conquests and the Creation of an Islamic Empire*. Oxford: Oxford University Press, 2015.

Kaegi, Walter E. *Muslim Expansion and Byzantine Collapse in North Africa*. Cambridge: Cambridge University Press, 2015.

Meens, Rob. *Penance in Medieval Europe, 600–1200*. Cambridge: Cambridge University Press, 2014.

Reimitz, Helmut. *History, Frankish Identity and the Framing of Western Ethnicity, 550–850*. Cambridge: Cambridge University Press, 2015.

Reynolds, Gabriel Said, ed. *The Qur'an in Its Historical Context*. Abingdon: Routledge, 2008.

Robinson, Chase F. *'Abd al-Malik*. Oxford: Oxford University Press, 2005.

Stathakopoulos, Dionysios. *A Short History of the Byzantine Empire*. London: I.B. Tauris, 2014.

Stevens, Susan T., and Jonathan P. Conant, eds. *North Africa under Byzantium and Early Islam*. Washington, DC: Dumbarton Oaks, 2016.

Storr, Jim. *King Arthur's Wars: The Anglo-Saxon Conquest of England*. Solihull, UK: Helion & Company, 2016.

Wagner, Walter. *Opening the Qur'an: Introducing Islam's Holy Book*. South Bend, IN: University of Notre Dame Press, 2008.

Wickham, Chris. *The Inheritance of Rome: Illuminating the Dark Ages, 400–1000*. New York: Viking, 2009.

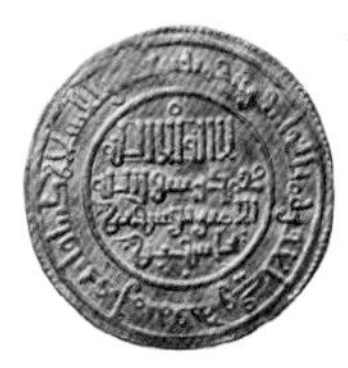

To test your knowledge of this chapter, please go to www.utphistorymatters.com for Study Questions.

THREE

CREATING NEW IDENTITIES (*c*.750–*c*.900)

In the second half of the eighth century the periodic outbreaks of the Plague of Justinian, which had devastated half of the globe for two centuries, came to an end. In their wake came a gradual but undeniable upswing in population, land cultivation, and general prosperity. At Byzantium an empress took the throne, in the Islamic world the Abbasids displaced the Umayyads, while in Francia the Carolingians deposed the Merovingians. New institutions of war and peace, learning, and culture developed, giving each culture—Byzantine, Islamic, and European—its own characteristic identity (though with some telling similarities).

BYZANTIUM: FROM TURNING WITHIN TO CAUTIOUS EXPANSION

In 750 Byzantium was a state with its back to the world: its iconoclasm isolated it from other Christians; its *strategiai* focused its military operations on internal defense; and its abandonment of classical learning set it apart from its past. By 900, all this had changed. Byzantium was iconophile (icon-loving), aggressive, and cultured.

New Icons, New Armies, New Territories

Within Byzantium, iconoclasm sowed dissension. In the face of persecution and humiliation, men and women continued to venerate icons, even in the very bedrooms of the imperial palace. The tide turned in 780 when Leo IV died and his widow, Irene, became head of the Byzantine state as regent for her son Constantine VI, and sole ruler 797–802 after her son was deposed. Long a secret iconophile, Irene immediately moved to replace important iconoclast bishops. Then she called a council at Nicaea in 787, the first there since the famous one of 325. The meeting went as planned, and the assembled bishops condemned iconoclasm. But iconoclastic fervor still lingered, and a partial ban on icons was put into effect between 815 and 843.

At first the end of iconoclasm displeased the old guard in the army, but soon a new generation was in charge. Already before Irene's rule, Byzantium's territorial *strategiai* had been reformed. That system had given too much power to a few *strategoi*, who dominated their regions and often rebelled against imperial power. In the eighth century, the emperors began to divide the imperial army into smaller regional units (and led by less powerful *strategoi*). Drawing the recruits for each unit from its immediate neighborhood, they made the nearby rural communities pay for the equipment of soldiers unable to foot the bill. By the early ninth century, each local army and its district both were given the name *thema* (pl. *themata*): theme. Rooted in the rural landscape, the theme's very organization made clear how fully the once city-based Roman East had become agricultural. Indeed, the eighth-century landowner Philaretos was considered a saint because he gave away or lost most of his extensive lands, "so that he was left with no more than one yoke of oxen and one horse and one ass and one cow with its calf and one slave and one slave-girl."[1] Soon he gave those away as well.

One key element of the newly reformed army was not, however, grounded in the countryside: the *tagmata* (sing. *tagma*). Created by Emperor Constantine V (r.741–775), they consisted of two new mobile regiments of heavy cavalry. At first deployed largely around Constantinople itself to shore up the emperors, the *tagmata* were eventually used in cautious frontier battles. Under the ninth- and tenth-century emperors, they helped Byzantium to expand.

In Greece, where Slavs had settled, the emperors made inroads by trying to impose their rule and taxes. To the north, in the Balkans, the emperors used military force against the Bulgars, sometimes successfully. But when Emperor Nicephorus I (r.802–811) attempted in 810 to take Sardica (today Sofia, Bulgaria), which had long been outside Byzantine control, his soldiers mutinied. To secure at least his northern border, Nicephorus uprooted thousands of families from Anatolia and elsewhere, sending them to settle and serve as soldiers in the Balkans and offering them new lands and fiscal privileges.

A year later, still keen to knock out Bulgarian power in the region, Nicephorus marshaled a huge army. Escorted by the luminaries of his court, he plundered the Bulgarian capital, Pliska, and then coolly made his way west. But the Bulgarians blockaded his army as it passed through a narrow river valley, fell on the imperial party, and killed the emperor. The toll on the fleeing soldiers and courtiers was immense, and Theophanes the Confessor said that the Bulgarian ruler, Krum (r.803–814), covered Nicephorus's skull with silver and turned it into a ceremonial drinking cup. But Theophanes, who detested both Nicephorus (because of his iconoclastic policies) and the Bulgars, may well have made up the story. In the end, Byzantine territory north- and westward swelled mightily, as a comparison of Map 3.1 with Map 2.2 on p. 43 makes clear.

Another glance at the two maps reveals a second area of modest expansion, this time on Byzantium's eastern front. In the course of the ninth century the Byzantines worked

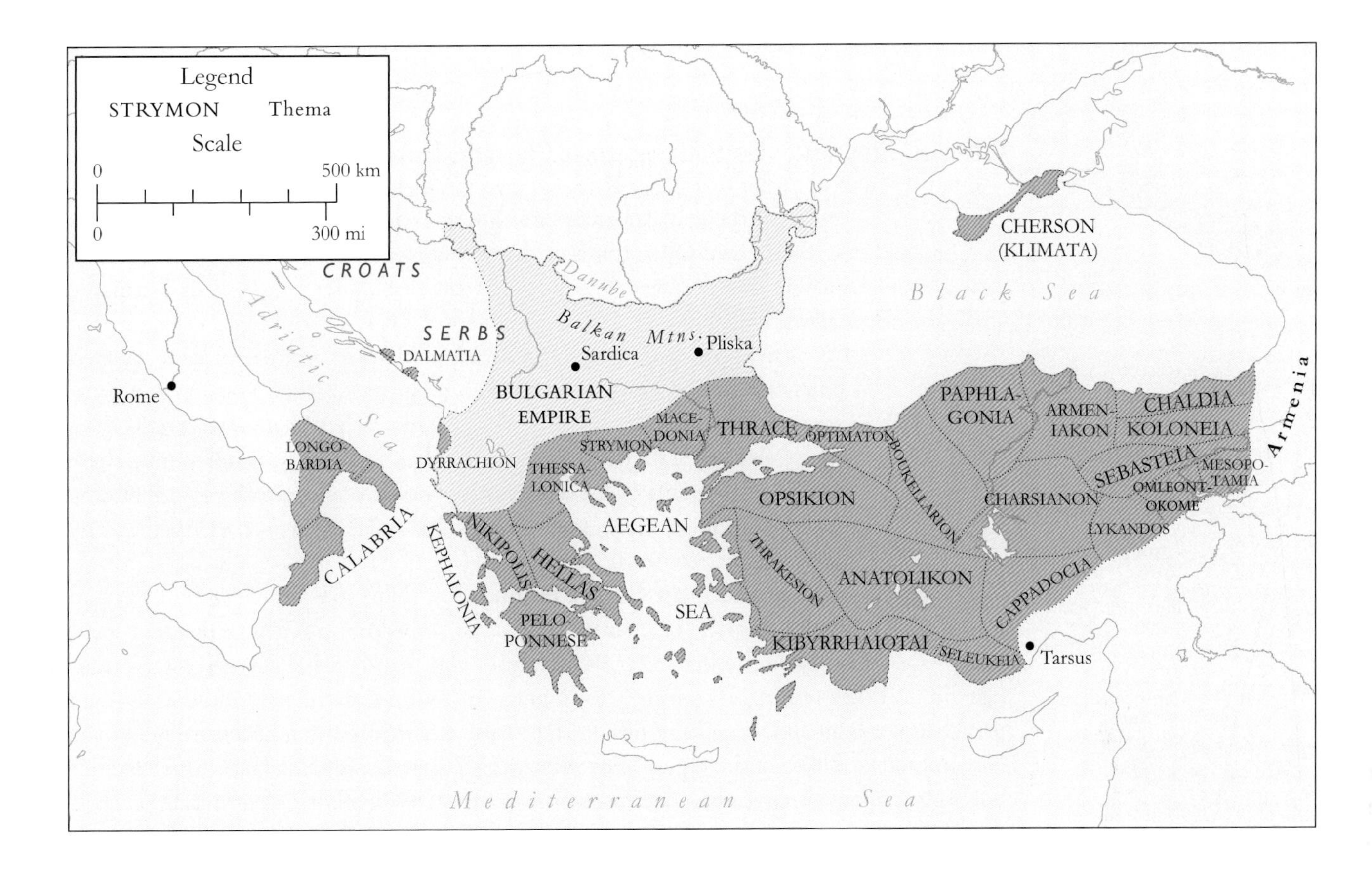

Map 3.1 The Byzantine and Bulgarian Empires, *c*.920

out a strategy of skirmish warfare in Anatolia. When Muslim raiding parties attacked, the *strategoi* evacuated the population, burned the crops, and, while sending out a few troops to harass the invaders, largely waited out the raid within their local fortifications. But by 860, the threat of invasion was largely over (though the menace of Muslim navies—on Sicily and southern Italy, for example—remained very real). In 900, Emperor Leo VI (r.886–912) was confident enough to go on the offensive, sending the *tagmata* in the direction of Tarsus. The raid was a success, and in its wake at least one princely family in Armenia broke off its alliance with the Arabs, entered imperial service, and ceded its principality to Byzantium. Reorganized as the theme of Mesopotamia, it was the first of a series of new themes that Leo created in an area that had been largely a no-man's-land between the Islamic and Byzantine worlds.

The rise of the *tagmata* eventually had the unanticipated consequence of downgrading the *themata*. The soldiers of the themes did the "grunt work"—the inglorious job of skirmish warfare—without much honor or (probably) extra pay. The *tagmata* were the professionals, gradually taking over most of the fighting, especially as the need to defend the interior of Anatolia receded. By the same token, the troops of the themes became increasingly inactive, and the *strategoi*, whose original job had been to lead the themes, gradually also became regional governors. These were new men, not drawn from the traditional elites. They formed a military aristocracy that mirrored (as we shall see) the rise of a similar class in Europe and the Islamic world.

Christianity and the Rise of East Central Europe

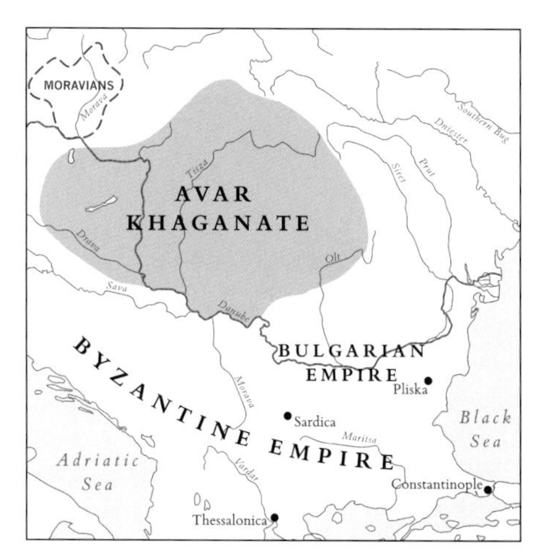

Map 3.2 The Avar Khaganate, 7th–8th cent.

To the north of Byzantium was a huge swathe of territory stretching to the Baltic Sea. Once states coalesced there, it would become East Central Europe. But while such polities (in this case under the aegis of Germanic leaders) were forming in Europe's west, the east-central region remained in flux as new groups, mainly of Slavic and Turkic origins, entered, created ephemeral political entities, and then disappeared. The Slavs made up the majority of these immigrants. As farmers rather than warriors (on the whole), however, they were normally subject to others. Chief among these were the Avars, Turkic-speaking warrior nomads who created a great empire on the Pannonian Plain. (See Map 3.2.) But the Avars were wiped out by the Franks in 796 (see below, p. 99).

Thereafter, East Central Europe took shape like a carpet unrolled from south to north; Lithuania was the last to become a fairly permanent state, Bulgaria the first. Christianization went hand-in-hand with state formation; in the ninth century Byzantines (following Orthodox Christianity) and Franks (who preached the Roman Catholic brand of Christianity) competed to take advantage of the new political stability in the region. For these proselytizers, spreading the Gospel had not only spiritual but also political advantages: it was a way to bring border regions under their respective spheres of influence. For the fledgling East Central European states, conversion to Christianity meant new institutions to buttress the ruling classes, recognition by one or another of the prestigious heirs of Rome, and enhanced economic and military opportunities.

The process of Christianization began in Moravia and Bulgaria. In Moravia, Duke Ratislav (r.846–870) made a bid for autonomy from Frankish hegemony by calling on Byzantium for missionaries. The imperial court was ready. Two brothers, Constantine (later called Cyril) and Methodius, set out in 863 armed with translations of the Gospels and liturgical texts. Born in Thessalonica, they well knew about the Slavic languages, which had been purely oral. Constantine devised an alphabet using Greek letters to represent the sounds of one Slavic dialect (the "Glagolitic" alphabet). He then added Greek words and grammar where the Slavic lacked Christian vocabulary and suitable expressions. The resulting language, later called Old Church Slavonic, was an effective tool for conversion: "What man can tell all the parables / Denouncing nations without their own books / And who do not preach in an intelligible tongue? / ... Whoever accepts these letters, / To him Christ speaks wisdom," reads the prologue to Constantine-Cyril's translation of the Gospels.[2] However much Byzantium valued the Greek language, and however keen it was to control all matters from Constantinople, it was nevertheless willing at times to work with different regional linguistic and cultural traditions. The Roman church, by contrast, was more rigid, insisting that the Gospels and liturgy be in Latin. In the end, however, Moravia opted for Rome.

But the Byzantine brand of Christianity prevailed in Bulgaria, Serbia, and later (see Chapter 4) Russia. We have seen how hostile the relations between the Bulgar ruler and the Byzantine emperors were. Yet *c.*864, Khan Boris (r.852–889) not only converted to Christianity under Byzantine auspices but also adopted the name of the Byzantine emperor of the time, Michael III (r.842–867), becoming Boris-Michael. How did Bulgaria end up in the Byzantine camp? To answer this question, consider the position of the Bulgar khan. Leader of warrior nomads, he claimed heaven's mandate; but as ruler of a state that embraced a large Christian population of Greek-speaking former Byzantines, he was obliged to take on the trappings of a Byzantine ruler as well: he employed Greeks to administer his state, used Greek officials in his writing-office, authenticated his documents with Byzantine-style seals, and adopted Byzantine court ceremonies.[3] In addition, in the course of the ninth century, Bulgar contact with Byzantines increased as a result of Greek refugees fleeing—and war-prisoners being forced—into the Bulgar state. The religion of these newcomers began to "rub off" on the ruling classes. Finally, as questions Boris-Michael put to the pope in 866 suggest, the pagan religion of the Bulgars involved practices rather than dogma. It was therefore possible (though hardly easy) to convert by exchanging one sort of act with another: "When you used to go into battle," the pope wrote, "you indicated that you carried the tail of a horse as your military emblem, and you ask what you should carry now in its place. What else, of course, but the sign of the cross?"[4] By writing to the pope, Boris made clear that he had no intention of becoming subservient to Byzantium. Similarly, he arranged for an archbishop independent of Constantinople to live near him at Pliska, his capital city.

Cultural Flowering at Byzantium

The creation of the Glagolitic alphabet in the mid-ninth century was one of many scholarly and educational initiatives taking place in the Byzantine Empire in the ninth century. Constantinople had always had schools, books, and teachers dedicated above all to training civil servants. But in the eighth century the number of bureaucrats was dwindling, schools were decaying, and books, painstakingly written out on papyrus, were disintegrating. Ninth-century confidence reversed this trend, while fiscal stability and surplus wealth in the treasury greased the wheels. So did competition with the rulers and elites of the Islamic world, who supported the translations of hundreds of classical Greek texts into Arabic. Emperor Theophilus (r.829–842) opened a public school in the palace headed by Leo the Mathematician, a master of geometry, mechanics, medicine, and philosophy. Controversies over iconoclasm sent churchmen scurrying to the writings of the Church Fathers to find passages that supported their cause. With the end of iconoclasm, the monasteries, staunch defenders of icons, garnered renewed prestige and gained new recruits. Because their abbots insisted that they read Christian texts, the monks had to get new manuscripts in a hurry. Practical need gave impetus to the creation of a new kind of script: minuscule. This was made up of lower-case letters, written in cursive, the letters strung together. It was faster and easier to write than the formal capital uncial letters that had previously been used. Words were newly separated by spaces, making them easier to read. Papyrus was no longer easily available from Egypt, so the new manuscripts were made out of parchment—animal skins scraped and treated to create a good writing surface. (See The Making of an Illuminated Manuscript on pp. 152–55.) Far more expensive than papyrus, parchment was nevertheless much more durable, making possible books' preservation over the long haul.

A general cultural revival was clearly under way by the middle of the century. As a young man, Photius, later patriarch of Constantinople (r.858–867; 877–886), had already read hundreds of books, including works of history, literature, and philosophy. As patriarch, he gathered a circle of scholars around him; wrote sermons, homilies, and theological treatises; and tutored Emperor Leo VI. He taught Constantine-Cyril, the future missionary to the Slavs, who was already a brilliant student in his home town, Thessalonica.

The new importance of classical Greek texts helped inspire an artistic revival. Even during the somber years of iconoclasm, artistic activity did not entirely end at Byzantium. But the new exuberance and sheer numbers of mosaics, manuscript illuminations, ivories, and enamels after 870 suggest a new era. Sometimes called the Macedonian Renaissance, after the ninth- and tenth-century imperial dynasty that fostered it, the new movement found its models in both the hierarchical style that was so important during the pre-iconoclastic period (see Plate 1.12 on pp. 32–33) and the natural, plastic style of classical art and its revivals (see Plates 1.2, 1.3, and 1.10 on pp. 13, 14–15, and 22).

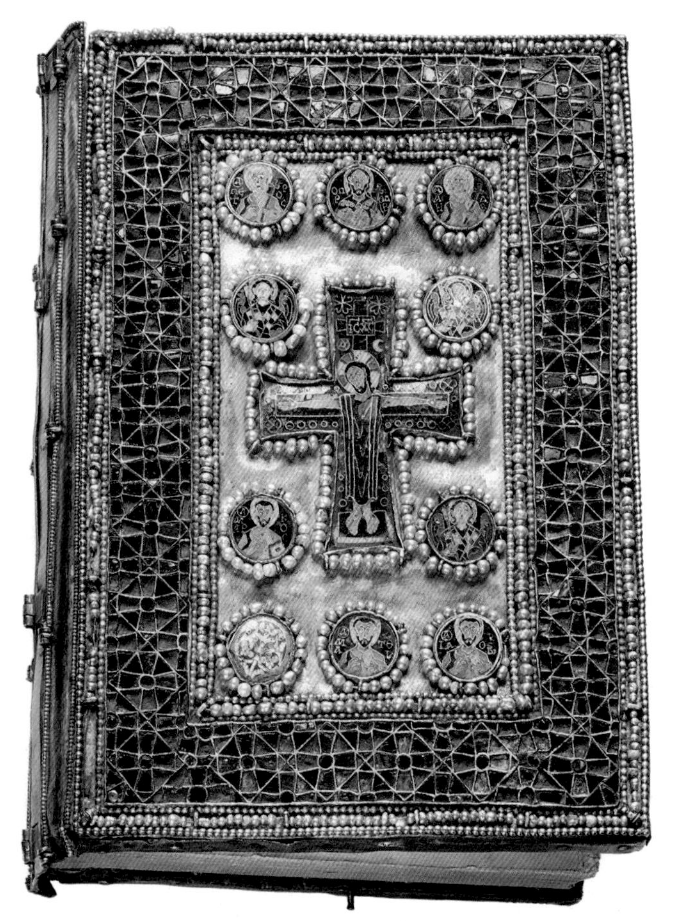

Plate 3.1 Christ on the Cross amid Saints (9th–early 10th cent.). Today this is the front cover of a liturgical book, joined to a matching portrayal of Mary, Mother of God, serving as the back cover. Perhaps originally the two together formed an icon diptych, with Mary, like Christ, standing within a cross, her arms raised in prayer, while roundels originally holding images of saints surround her.

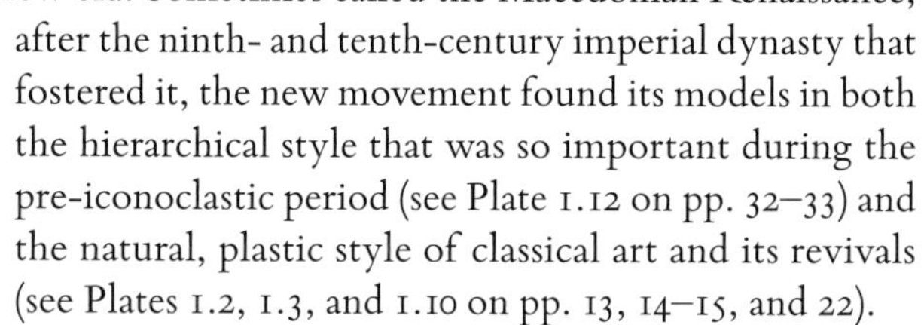

Thus, both styles harked back to the past. In Plate 3.1, Christ is entirely flat and perpendicular except for his bent head. Images of the saints and angels appear in roundels. Made of cloisonné enamel and outlined with strung pearls, the figures are complex and glowing. Their richness is set off by the simplicity of the silver-gilt flat surface of the plaque and its frame, which is made of cut glass and beads of gold and pearl. No one looks at anyone else; the figures are totally isolated from one another. The artist is far more interested in patterns and color than in delineating bodies. At the same time, the very weightlessness of Christ and the others stresses a permanent, transcendental reality, so that the event of Christ's crucifixion is as triumphant as Justinian's procession in Plate 1.12 (pp. 32–33).

In Plate 3.2, however, a very different—and more classical—artistic spirit is in play. Painted in a manuscript of homilies (sermons) given by a revered figure of the Byzantine church, the figures gesture and interact, and they exist in a landscape beneath a hail-filled sky.

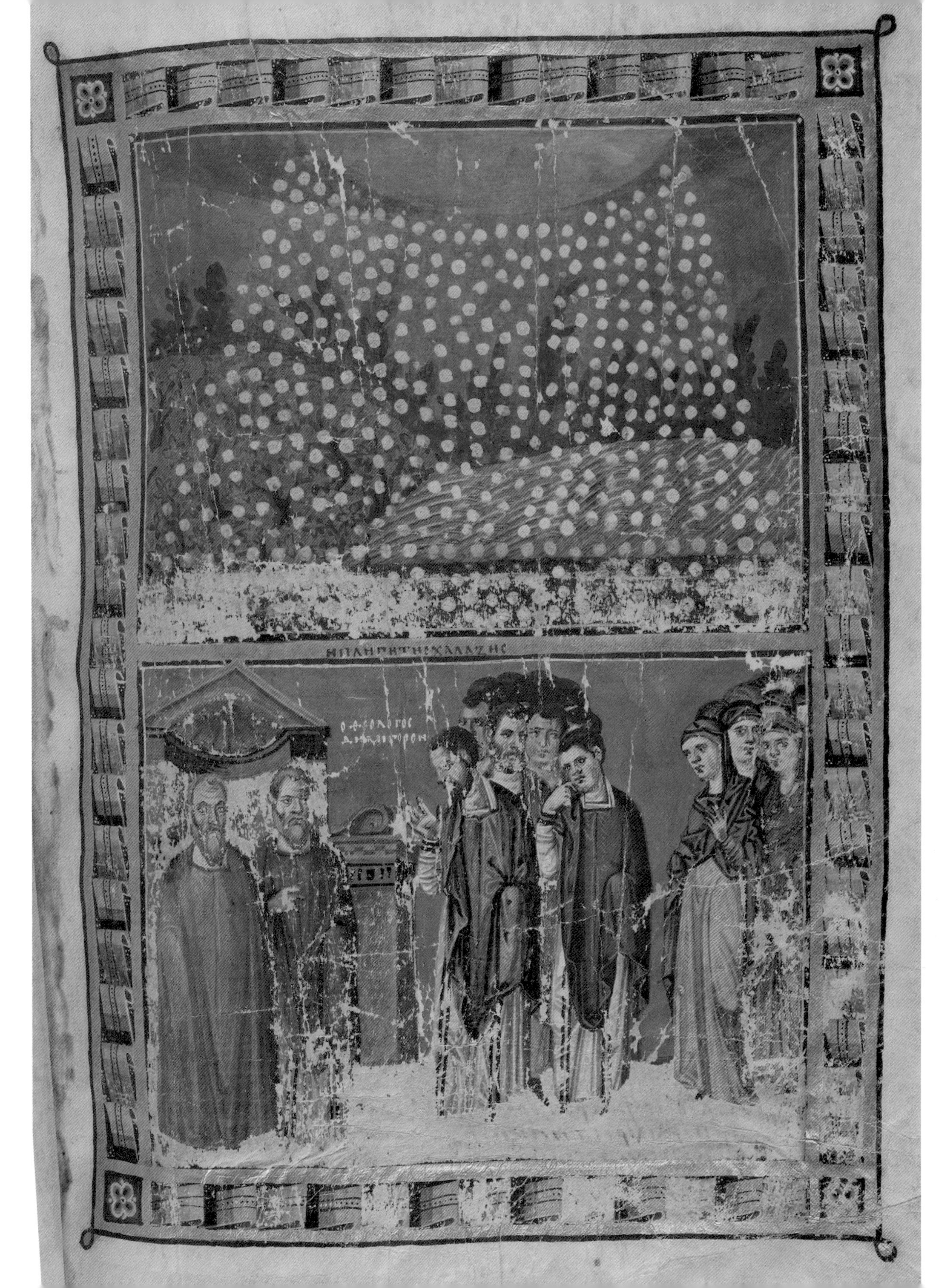
ΗΠΛΗΓΗΤΗϹΧΑΛΑΖΗϹ
Ο ΘΕΟΛΟΓΟϹ

Plate 3.2 (previous page) Gregory of Nazianzus Preaches on the Plague of Hail, Gregory's *Homilies* (*c.*880). There is a human-interest story behind this miniature, which illustrates Gregory's Homily 16: "On the plague of hail and his father's silence." There had been a hailstorm in 373 that ruined the harvests in Nazianzus, a small town in the province of Cappadocia. Gregory's father, who as local bishop should have delivered the sermon, was too depressed by the events to do so. Gregory preached in his stead. In the miniature, the hail falls from the sky, a rare instance of the portrayal of a real natural disaster. Below are three groups: on the left are Gregory and his father, in the middle are men—villagers, no doubt—and to their right are women. Gregory's father hides his hands beneath his cloak to show that he cannot preach; Gregory gestures with his right hand to indicate that he is speaking. The central man gestures that the people demand an official response to the disaster; the other people indicate their sorrow. In the homily Gregory admits the horror of the event, attributes it to God's just chastisement of sinners, and counsels weeping, prayer, and confession.

All have roundness and weight; they turn and interact. It is true that the hail is depicted as a polka-dotted veil, and the picture's frame is made of decorative curls of ribbon. But it is in just this way that the Byzantines melded classical traditions to their overriding need to represent transcendence.

Not surprisingly, the same period saw the revival of monumental architecture. Emperor Theophilus was known for the splendid palace that he commissioned on the outskirts of Constantinople, and Basil I was famous as a builder of churches. Rich men from the court and church imitated imperial tastes, constructing palaces, churches, and monasteries of their own.

THE SHIFT TO THE EAST IN THE ISLAMIC WORLD

Just as at Byzantium the imperial court determined both culture and policies, so too in the Islamic world of the ninth century were the caliph and his court the center of power. The Abbasids, who ousted the Umayyad caliphs in 750, moved their capital city to Iraq (part of the former Persia) and stepped into the shoes of the Sasanid king of kings, the "shadow of God on earth." Yet much of their time was spent less in imposing their will than in conciliating different interest groups.

The Abbasid Reconfiguration

Years of Roman rule had made Byzantium relatively homogeneous. Nothing was less true of the Islamic world, made up of regions wildly diverse in geography, language, and political, religious, and social traditions. Each tribe, family, and region had its own expectations and desires for a place in the sun. The Umayyads paid little heed. Their power base was Syria, formerly a part of Byzantium. There they rewarded their hard-core followers and took the lion's share of conquered land for themselves. They expected every other region to send its taxes to their coffers at Damascus. This annoyed regional leaders, even though they probably managed to keep most of the taxes that they raised. Moreover, with no claims to the religious functions of an *imam*, the Umayyads could never gain the adherence of the followers of Ali. Soon still other groups began to complain. Where was the equality of believers preached in the Qur'an? The Umayyads privileged an elite; Arabs who had expected a fair division of the spoils were disappointed. So too were non-Arabs who converted to Islam: they discovered that they had still to pay the old taxes of their non-believing days.

The discontents festered, and two main centers of resistance emerged: Khurasan (today eastern Iran) and Iraq. (See Map 3.3.) Both had been part of the Persian Empire; the rebellion represented the convergence of old Persian and newly "Persianized" Arab factions. In the 740s this defiant coalition at Khurasan decided to support the Abbasid family. This was

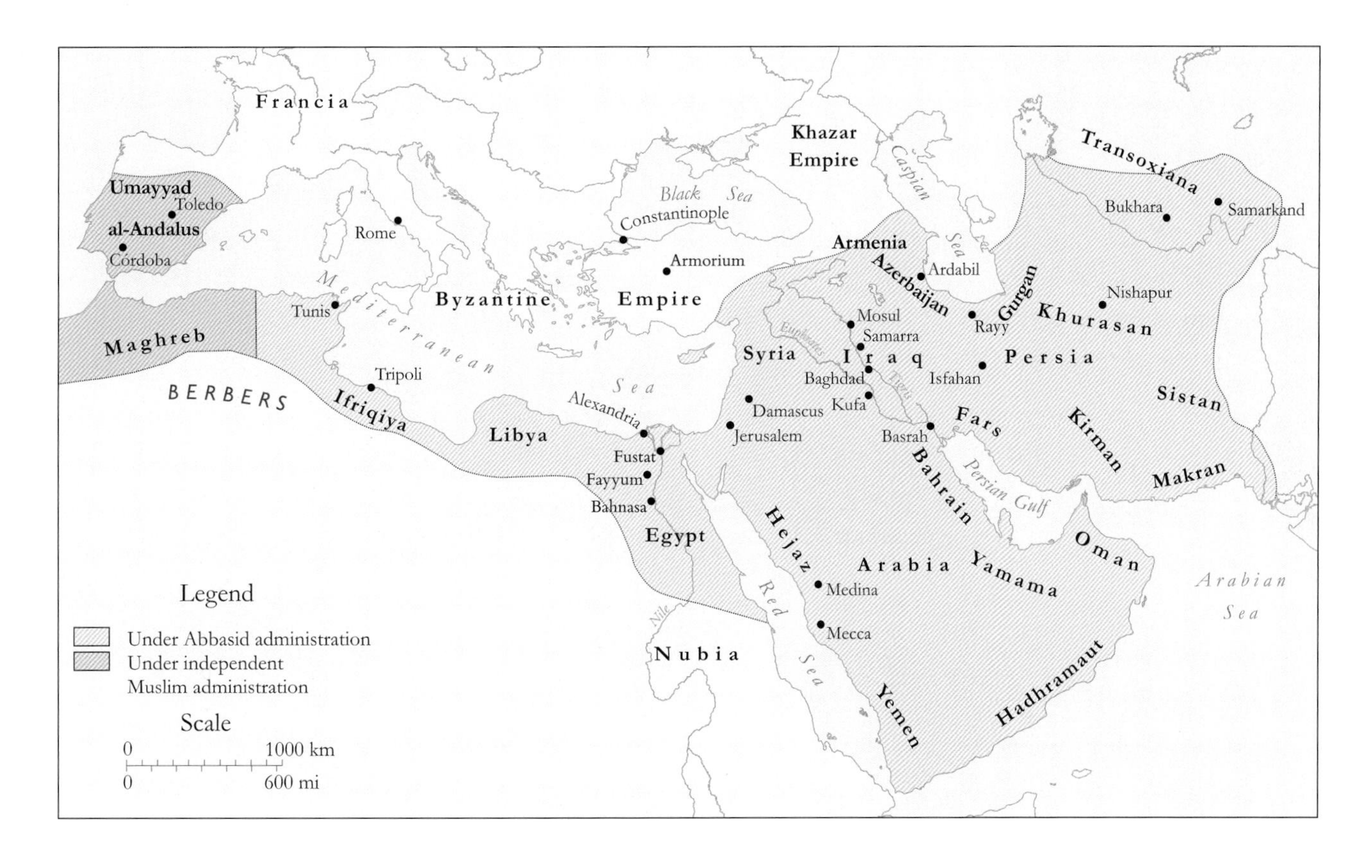

Map 3.3 The Islamic World, *c.*800

an extended kin group with deep-rooted claims to the caliphate, tracing its lineage back to the very uncle who had cared for the orphaned Muhammad. With militant supporters, considerable money, and the backing of a powerful propaganda organization, the Abbasids organized an army in Khurasan and, marching undefeated into Iraq, picked up more support there. In 750 the last Umayyad caliph, Marwan II, abandoned by almost everyone and on the run in Egypt, was killed in a short battle. Al-Saffah was then solemnly named the first Abbasid caliph.

The new dynasty seemed to signal a revolution. Most importantly, the Abbasids recognized the crucial centrality of Iraq and built their capital cities there: Baghdad became the capital in 762, Samarra in the 830s in the aftermath of a bitter civil war. The Abbasids took the title of *imam* and even, at one point, wore the green color of the Shi'ites.

Yet, as they became entrenched, the Abbasids in turn created their own elite, under whom other groups chafed. In the eighth century most of their provincial governors, for example, came from the Abbasid family itself. When building Baghdad, Caliph al-Mansur (r.754–775) allotted important tracts of real estate to his Khurasan military leaders. In the course of time, as Baghdad prospered and land prices rose, the Khurasani came to constitute a new, exclusive, and jealous elite. At the same time as they favored these groups, the Abbasids succeeded in centralizing their control even more fully than the Umayyads had done. This is clearest in the area of taxation. The Umayyads had demanded in vain that all taxes come to them. But the Abbasid caliph al-Mu'tasim (r.833–842) was able to control and direct provincial revenues to his court in Iraq. (For the Abbasids, see Genealogy 3.1).

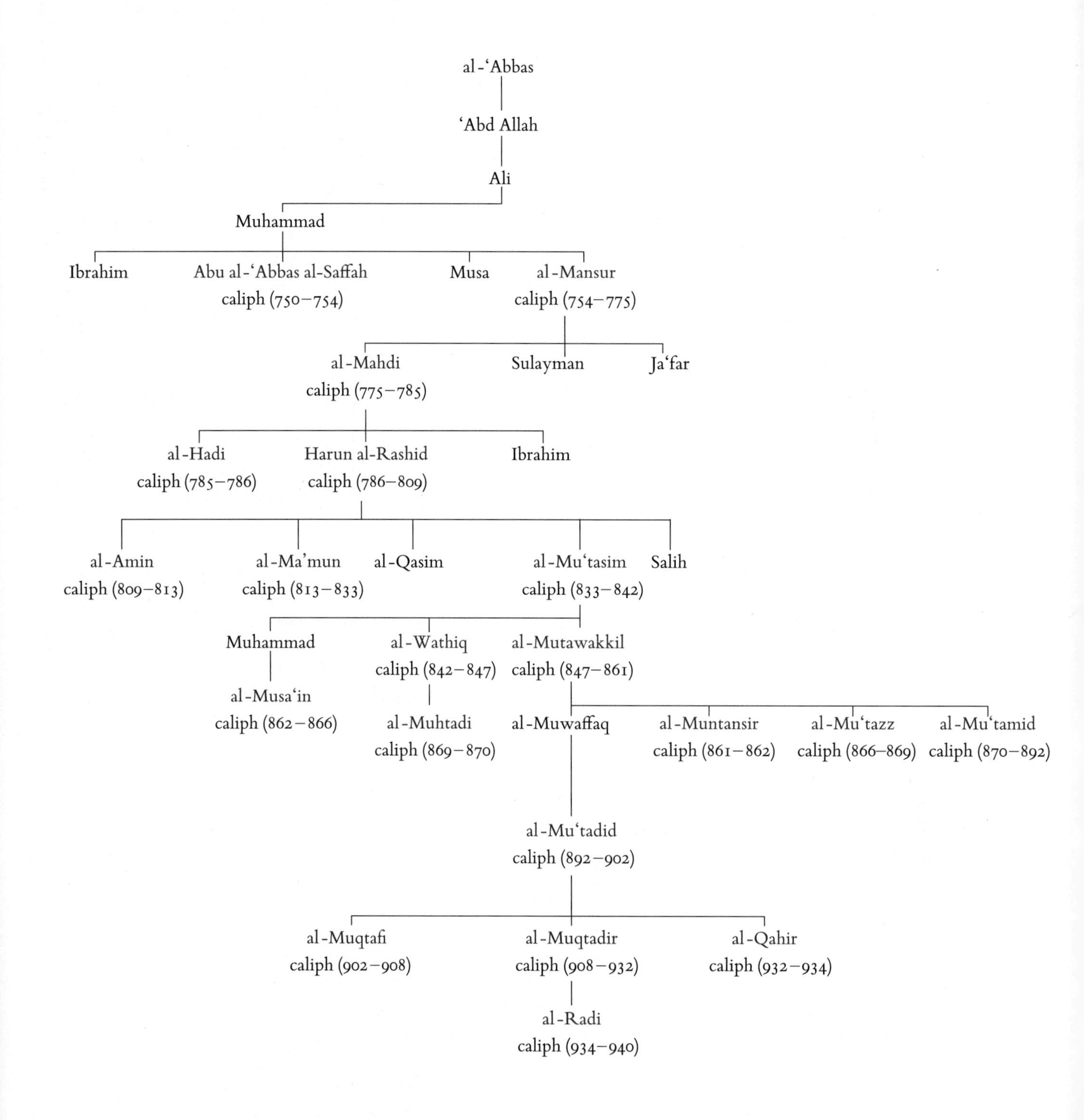

* Abbasid caliphs continued at Baghdad—with however, only nominal power—until 1258. Thereafter, a branch of the family in Cairo held the caliphate until the sixteenth century.

Control, however, was uneven. Until the beginning of the tenth century, the Abbasid caliphs generally could count on ruling Iraq (their "headquarters"), Syria, Khurasan, and Egypt. But they never had the Iberian Peninsula; they lost Ifriqiya (today Tunisia) by about 800; and they never controlled the Berbers in the soft underbelly of North Africa. In the course of the tenth century, they would lose effective control even in their heartlands. That, however, was in the future (see Chapter 4).

Whatever control the Abbasids had depended largely on their armies. Unlike the Byzantines, the Abbasids did not need soldiers to stave off external enemies or to expand outwards. (The Byzantine strategy of skirmish warfare worked largely because the caliphs led raids to display their prowess, not to take territory. The serious naval wars that took Sicily from Byzantium were launched from Ifriqiya, independent of the caliphs.) Rather, the Abbasids needed troops to collect taxes in areas already conquered but weakly controlled.

Well into the ninth century the caliphs' troops were paid, but not mustered, by them. Generals recruited their own troops from their home districts, tribes, families, and clients. When the generals were loyal to the caliphs, this military system worked well. In the dark days of civil war, however, when two brothers fought over the caliphate (811–819), no one controlled the armies. After al-Ma'mun (r.813–833) won this civil war, he had no reliable army to back him up. His brother and successor, al-Mu'tasim, found the solution in a new-style, private army. He bought and trained his own slaves, many of them Turks and thus unrelated to other tribal groups. These men were given governorships as well as military posts. They were the reason that al-Mu'tasim was able to collect provincial taxes so effectively. He could not foresee that in time the Turks would come to constitute a new elite, one that would eventually help to overpower the caliphate itself.

Under the Abbasids, the Islamic world became wealthy. The Mediterranean region had always been a great trade corridor; in the ninth century, Baghdad, at the crossroads of East and West, drew that trade into a wider network that included India, China, and the Khazar Empire to its north. Eclectic, open to numerous traditions of arts and crafts, the Abbasid world was cosmopolitan. Dining off ornate plates and bowls, pouring their water from richly decorated pitchers, the Islamic upper and middle classes could boast splendid tableware (see Plate 3.3). Their clothes, made of richly woven fabrics, were luxurious. Wall-hangings and rugs adorned their homes, and elaborately carved censers spread their perfume. Luxury followed them even into the graveyard. (See Plate 3.4.)

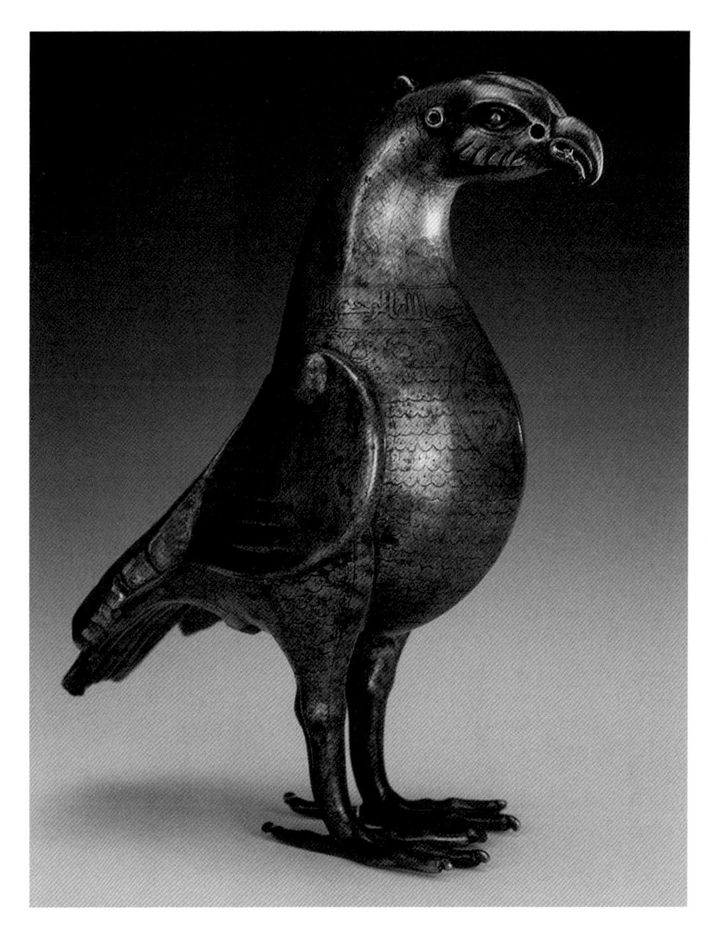

Genealogy 3.1 (facing page) The Abbasids*

Plate 3.3 Water Pitcher in the Shape of an Eagle (796–797). At one time this brass eagle had a handle and was no doubt used as a water pitcher by a well-to-do Syrian or Iraqi family. Inlaid with silver and copper, most of which has disappeared, it includes the name of the craftsman who made it (Suleiman) along with a blessing and the date of its manufacture.

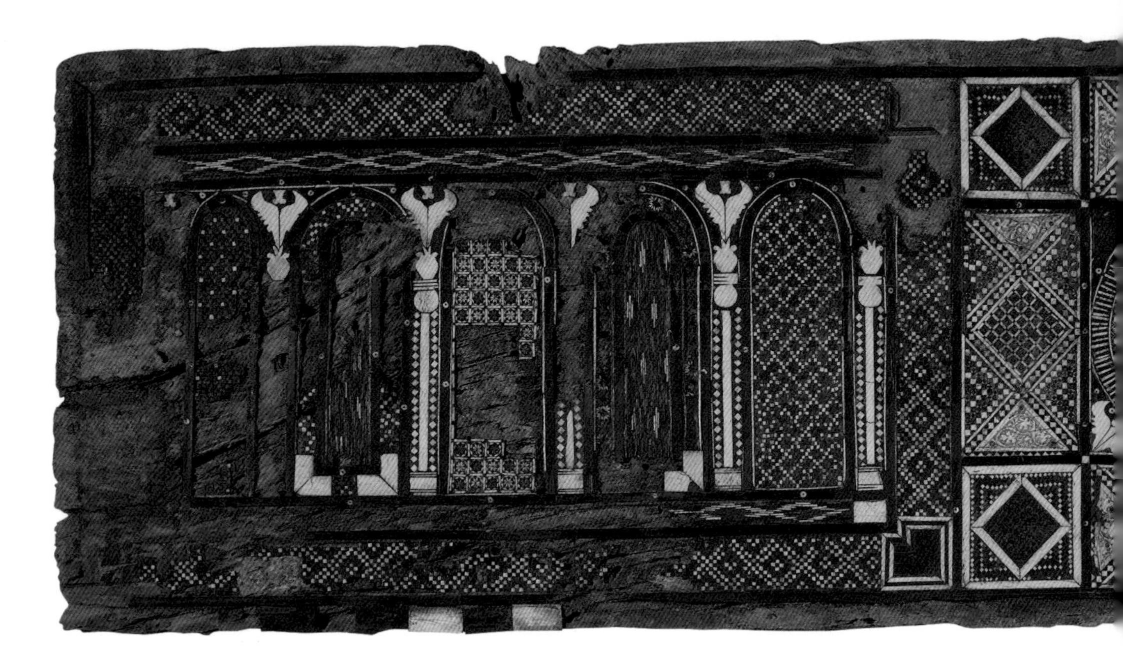

Plate 3.4 Chest or Cenotaph Panel (second half of 8th cent.). This inlaid wood panel, found in a cemetery near Fustat (Old Cairo), brings together numerous different traditions. Marquetry, which uses thousands of pieces of tiny bone and woods of different shades to create an intricate design, was a skill practiced by the Coptic Christians in Egypt. The wings at the top of the columns and holding up the central wheel drew on a Sasanid Persian motif. The geometric pattern was pre-Islamic. In the center of the wheel is a late classical vine scroll. The sequence of arches is Romano-Byzantine. Perhaps this remarkable piece may be connected to a military garrison established in the vicinity in the mid-eighth century.

New Forms of Literature

With revenues from commerce and (above all) taxes from agriculture in their coffers, the Abbasid caliphs paid their armies, salaried their officials (drawn from the many talented men—but, in this relentlessly male-dominated society, not women—in the Persian, Arab, Christian, and Jewish population), and presided over a cultural revival that, as we have seen, inspired a similar one at Constantinople.

In the ninth century, most spectacularly under caliphs Harun al-Rashid and al-Ma'mun, literature, science, law, and other forms of scholarship flourished. Books of all sorts were relatively cheap (and therefore accessible) in the Islamic world because they were written on paper. The caliphs launched scientific studies via a massive translation effort that brought the philosophical, medical, mathematical, and astrological treatises of the Indian and Greek worlds into Islamic culture. They encouraged poetry of every sort.

Thus after Caliph al-Mu'tasim conquered the Byzantine city of Amorium (838), he paid the poet Abu Tammam handsomely for a long poem that praised both the victory and the victors:

> A victory of victories, so sublime
>   prose cannot speak nor verse can utter it;
> A victory at which Heaven threw wide its gates,
>   which Earth put on new dress to celebrate:
> O battle of Amorium, for which
>   our hopes returned engorged with milk and honey.
> The Muslims hast thou fixed in the ascendant,
>   pagans and pagandom fixed in decline![5]

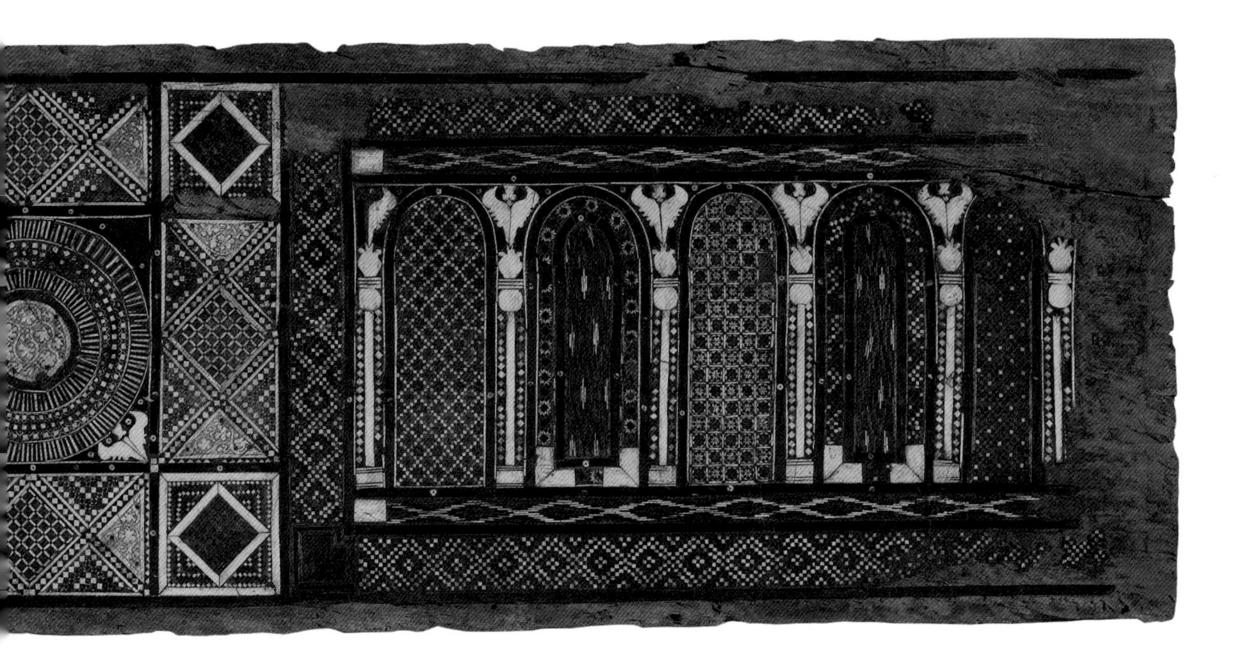

It is obvious why such laudatory poetry, beautifully and cleverly written, should be cultivated under the Abbasids. But other kinds of poetry were equally prized: those celebrating wine and love, for example, were appreciated as *adab*, a literature (both in verse and prose) of refinement. (*Adab* means "good manners.")

Shoring up the regime with astrological predictions; winning theological debates with the pointed weapons of Aristotle's logical and scientific works; understanding the theories of bridge-building, irrigation, and land-surveying with Euclid's geometry—these were just some of the reasons why scholars in the Islamic world labored over translations and created original scientific works. Their intellectual pyrotechnics won general support. Patrons of scientific writing included the caliphs, their wives, courtiers, generals, and ordinary people with practical interests. Al-Khwarizmi (d.*c.*850), author of a book on algebra (a term derived from *al-jabr*, a word in its title), explained all its practical uses. Even handier was his treatise on the Indian method of calculation—Indian numerals are what *we* call Arabic numerals—and the use of the zero, essential (to give just one example) for distinguishing 100 from 1.

How should one live to be pleasing to God? This was the major question that inspired the treatises on *hadith* (traditions about the Prophet) that began to appear in the Abbasid period. Each *hadith* began with the chain of oral transmitters (the most recent listed first) that told a story about Muhammad; there then followed the story itself. Thus, for example, in the compilation of *hadith* by al-Bukhari (810–870) on the issue of fasting during Ramadan (the yearly period of fasting from sunrise to sunset), he took up the question of the distracted "faster who eats and drinks from forgetfulness":

> 'Abdan related to us [saying], Yazid b. Zurai' informed us, saying, Hisham related to us, saying: Ibn Sirin related to us from Abu Huraira, from the Prophet—upon

whom be blessing and peace—that he said: "If anyone forgets and eats or drinks, let him complete his fast, for it was Allah who caused him thus to eat or drink."[6]

Here 'Abdan was the most recent witness to a saying of the Prophet, with Abu Huraira the closest to the source. A well-known "Companion" of the Prophet Muhammad, Abu Huraira was named as the ultimate authority for thousands of *hadith*.

Even the Qur'an did not escape scholarly scrutiny. While some interpreters read it literally as the word of God and thus part of God, others viewed it as something (like humankind) created by God and therefore separate from Him. For Caliph al-Ma'mun, taking the Qur'an literally undermined the caliph's religious authority. Somewhat like the Byzantine emperor Leo III (see pp. 47–48), whose iconoclastic policies were designed to separate divinity from its representations, al-Ma'mun determined to make God greater than the Qur'an. In 833 he instituted the Mihna, or Inquisition, demanding that the literalists profess the Qur'an's createdness. But al-Ma'mun died before he could punish those who refused, and his immediate successors were relatively ineffective in pursuing the project. The scholars on the other side—the literalists and those who looked to the *hadith*—carried the day, and in 848 Caliph al-Mutawakkil (r.847–861) ended the Mihna, emphatically reversing the caliphate's position on the matter. Sunni Islam thus defined itself against the views of a caliph who, by asserting great power, lost much. The caliphs ceased to be the source of religious doctrine; that role went to the scholars, the *ulama*. It was around this time that the title "caliph" came to be associated with the phrase "deputy of the Prophet of God" rather than the "deputy of God." The designation reflected the caliphate's decreasing political as well as religious authority (see Chapter 4).

Al-Andalus: A Society in the Middle

Taking advantage of the caliphs' waning prestige was the ruler of al-Andalus (Islamic Spain). In the mid-eighth century Abd al-Rahman I, an Umayyad prince on the run from the Abbasids, managed to gather an army, make his way to Iberia, and defeat the provincial governor at Córdoba. In 756 he proclaimed himself "emir" (commander) of al-Andalus. His dynasty governed al-Andalus for two and a half centuries. In 929, emboldened by his growing power and the depletion of caliphal power at Baghdad, Abd al-Rahman III (r.912–961) took the title caliph. Nevertheless, like the Abbasid caliphs, the Umayyad rulers of Spain headed a state poised to break into its regional constituents.

Al-Andalus under the emirs was hardly Muslim and even less Arab. As the caliphs came to rely on Turks, so the emirs relied on a professional standing army of non-Arabs, the *al-khurs*, the "silent ones"—men who could not speak Arabic. They lived among a largely Christian—and partly Jewish—population; even by 900, only about 25 per cent of the people in al-Andalus were Muslim. This had its benefits for the regime, which taxed Christians and Jews heavily. Although, like Western European rulers, they did not have the land tax that the Byzantine emperors and caliphs could impose, the emirs did draw some of their revenue from Muslims, especially around their capital at Córdoba. (See Map 3.4 on p. 96.)

Money allowed the emirs to pay salaries to their civil servants and to preside over a cultural efflorescence that reflected the region's unique ethnic and religious mix. The Great Mosque in Córdoba is a good example. Begun under Abd al-Rahman I and expanded by his successors, its square form was much like other early mosques. (See Figure 3.1). Yet it drew on the design of the Roman aqueduct at Mérida for its rows of columns connected by double arches. (See Plate 3.5 on p. 97.) For the shape of the arches, however, it borrowed a form—the "Visigothic" horseshoe arch—from the Christians.

The cultural "mix" went beyond architectural forms. Some Muslim men took Christian wives, and religious practices seem to have melded a bit. In fact, the Christians who lived in al-Andalus were called "Mozarabs"—"would-be Arabs"—by Christians elsewhere. It is likely that Christians and Muslims on the whole got along fairly well. Christians dressed like Muslims, worked side-by-side with them in government posts, and used Arabic in many aspects of their life. In the mid-ninth century, there were in the region of Córdoba alone at least four churches and nine monasteries. No doubt there were synagogues as well, but our sources for Jewish life in Islamic Iberia are very fragmentary until the tenth century, when at least a few high-ranking Jews burst onto the public stage.

To the north of al-Andalus, beyond the Duero River, were tiny Christian principalities. Their spokesmen donned the mantle of the Visigoths, claiming to be the legitimate rulers of Spain. A chronicler from the ninth century celebrated their triumphs as God-given: "Alfonso was elected king by all the people, receiving the royal sceptre with

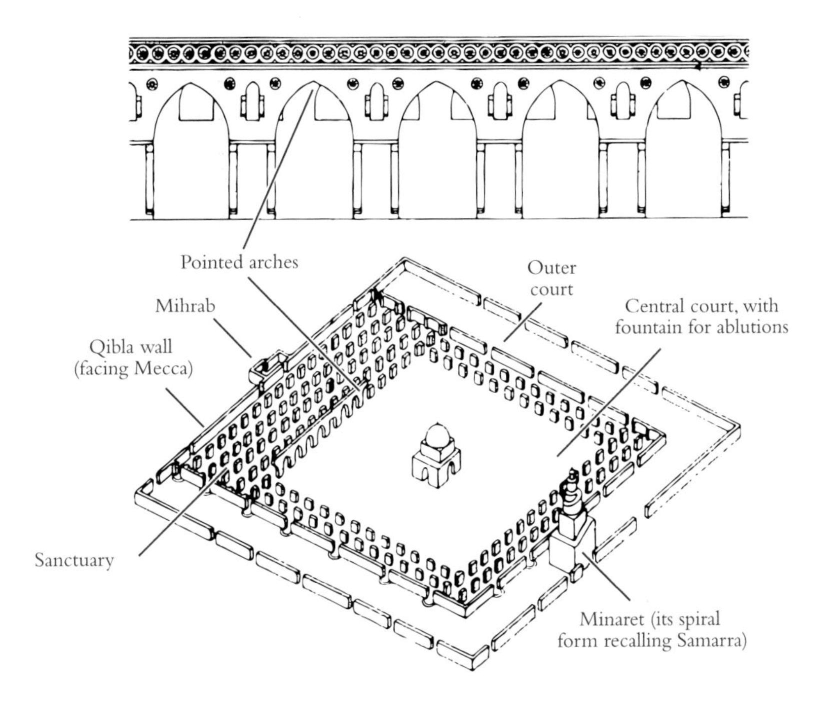

Figure 3.1 Mosque Plan (Cairo, Ibn Tulum Mosque, built 876–879)

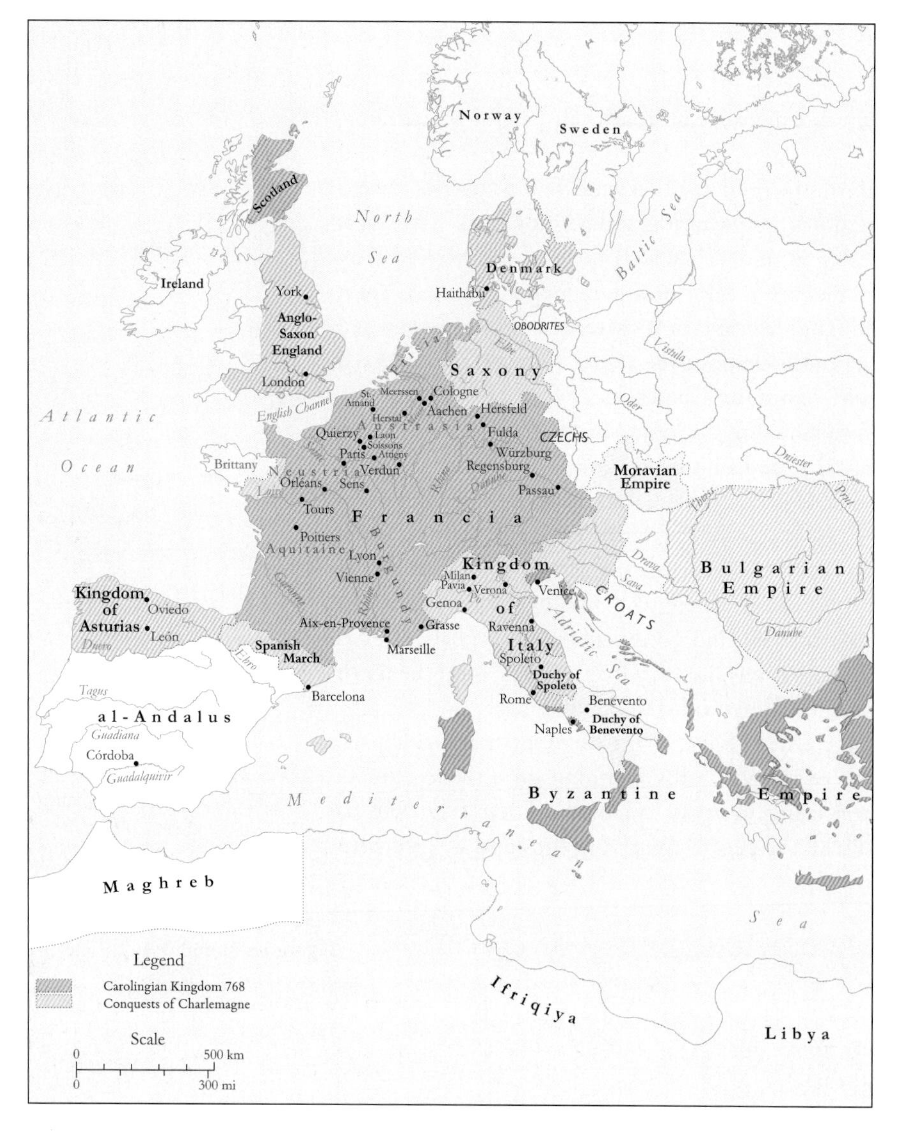

Map 3.4 Europe, *c.*814

Plate 3.5 (facing page) Great Mosque, Córdoba (785–787). The Great Mosque of Córdoba gave monumental identity to the new Umayyad rulers in al-Andalus. Note the two tiers of arches, the first set on pre-Islamic columns despoiled from Roman and Visigothic buildings, the second springing from high piers. With their alternating red and white stones and repeated pattern, the arches suggest lively arcades leading from west to east, but the overall effect is tranquil.

divine grace. He always crushed the audacity of his enemies.... Killing all the Arabs with the sword, he led the Christians back with him to his country."[7] The hero here was Alfonso I (r.739–757), whose kingdom of Asturias partook in the general demographic and economic growth of the period. Alfonso and his successors built churches, encouraged monastic foundations, collected relics, patronized literary efforts, and welcomed Mozarabs from the south. As they did so, they looked to Christian models still farther north—to Francia, where Charlemagne and his heirs ruled as kings "by grace of God."

AN EMPIRE IN SPITE OF ITSELF

Between Byzantium and the Islamic world was Francia. While the first two were politically centralized, subject to sophisticated tax systems, and served by salaried armies and officials, Francia inherited the centralizing traditions of the Roman Empire without its order and efficiency. Francia's kings could not collect a land tax, the backbone of the old Roman and the more recent Byzantine and Islamic fiscal systems. There were no salaried officials or soldiers in Francia. Yet the new dynasty of kings there, the Carolingians, managed to muster armies, expand their kingdom, encourage a revival of scholarship and learning, command the respect of emperors and caliphs, and forge an identity for themselves as leaders of the Christian people. Their successes bore striking resemblance to contemporary achievements at Constantinople and Baghdad. How was this possible? The answer is at least threefold: the Carolingians took advantage of the same gentle economic upturn that seems to have taken place generally; they exploited to the full the institutions of Roman culture and political life that remained to them; and at the same time, they were willing to experiment with new institutions and take advantage of unexpected opportunities.

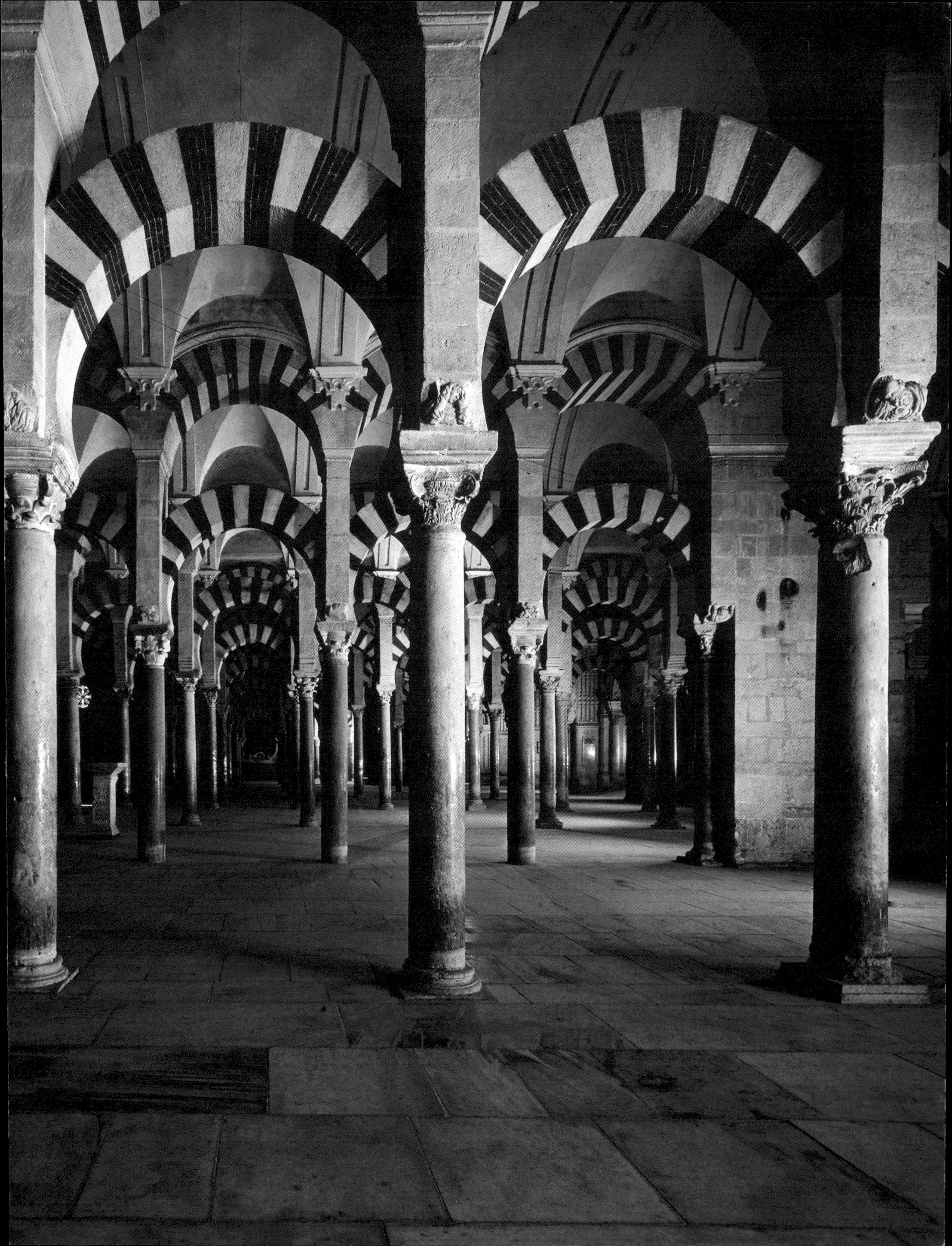

The Making of the Carolingians

The Carolingian take-over was a "palace coup." After a battle (at Tertry, in 687) between Neustrian and Austrasian noble factions, one powerful family with vast estates in Austrasia came to monopolize the high office of mayor for the Merovingian kings in both places. In the first half of the eighth century these mayors took over much of the power and most of the responsibilities of the kings.

Charles Martel (mayor 714–741) gave the name Carolingian (from *Carolus*, Latin for Charles) to the dynasty. In 732 he won a battle near Poitiers against an army led by the Muslim governor of al-Andalus, ending further raids. But Charles had other enemies: he spent most of his time fighting vigorously against regional Frankish aristocrats intent on carving out independent lordships for themselves. Playing powerful factions against one another, rewarding supporters, defeating enemies, and dominating whole regions by controlling monasteries and bishoprics that served as focal points for both religious piety and land donations, the Carolingians created a tight network of supporters.

Moreover, they chose their allies well, reaching beyond Francia to the popes and to Anglo-Saxon churchmen, who (as we have seen) were closely tied to Rome. When the Anglo-Saxon missionary Boniface (d.754) wanted to preach in Frisia (today the Netherlands) and Germany, the Carolingians readily supported him as a prelude to their own conquests. Although many of the areas where Boniface missionized had long been Christian, their practices were local rather than tied to Rome. By contrast, Boniface's newly appointed bishops were loyal to Rome and the Carolingians, not to regional aristocracies. They knew that their power came from papal and royal fiat rather than from local power centers.

Men like Boniface opened the way to a more direct alliance between the Carolingians and the pope. Historians used to think that Pippin III (d.768), the son of Charles Martel, obtained approval from Pope Zacharias (741–752) to depose the reigning Merovingian king. Recent research by Rosamond McKitterick suggests that such an early liaison between the pope and the Carolingians was manufactured by later writers. But it is certain that after Pippin took the throne in 751, Pope Stephen II (752–757) traveled to Francia. He anointed Pippin, blessed him, and begged him to send an army against the encircling Lombards: "Hasten, hasten, I urge and protest by the living and true God, hasten and assist! ... Do not suffer this Roman city to perish in which the Lord laid my body [i.e., the body of Saint Peter, with whom the pope identified himself] and which he commended to me and established as the foundation of the faith. Free it and its Roman people, your brothers, and in no way permit it to be invaded by the people of the Lombards."[8]

In the so-called Donation of Pippin (756), the new king forced the Lombards to give some cities back to the pope. The arrangement recognized that the papacy was now the ruler in central Italy of a territory that had once belonged to Byzantium. Before the 750s, the papacy had been part of the Byzantine Empire; by the middle of that decade, it had become part of the West. It was probably soon thereafter that members of the papal chancery (writing office) forged a document, the *Donation of Constantine*, which had the fourth-century Emperor Constantine declare that he was handing the western half of the Roman Empire to Pope Sylvester.

The chronicler of Charles Martel had already tied his hero's victories to Christ. The Carolingian partnership with Rome and Romanizing churchmen added to the dynasty's Christian aura. Anointment—daubing the kings with holy oil—provided the finishing touch. It reminded contemporaries of David, king of the Israelites: "Then Samuel took the horn of oil and anointed him in the midst of his brethren; and the spirit of the Lord came upon David from that day forward" (1 Sam. [or Vulgate 1 Kings] 16:13).

Charlemagne

The most famous Carolingian king was Charles (r.768–814), called "the Great" ("le Magne" in Old French). Large, tough, wily, and devout, he was everyone's model king. Einhard (d.840), his courtier and scholar, saw him as a Roman emperor: he patterned his *Life of Charlemagne* on the *Lives of the Caesars*, written in the second century by the Roman biographer Suetonius. Alcuin (d.804), also the king's courtier and an even more famous scholar, emphasized Charlemagne's religious side, nicknaming him "David," the putative author of the psalms, victor over the giant Goliath, and king of Israel. Empress Irene at Constantinople saw Charlemagne as a suitable husband for herself (though the arrangement eventually fell through).

Charlemagne's fame was largely achieved through warfare. While the Byzantine and Islamic rulers clung tightly to what they had, Charlemagne waged wars of plunder and conquest. He invaded Italy, seizing the Lombard crown and annexing northern Italy in 774. He moved his armies northward, fighting the Saxons for more than thirty years, forcibly converting them to Christianity, and annexing their territory. To the southeast, he sent his forces against the Avars, capturing their strongholds, forcing them to submit to his overlordship, and making off with cartloads of plunder. His expedition to al-Andalus gained Charlemagne a band of territory north of the Ebro River, a buffer between Francia and the Islamic world called the "Spanish March." Even his failures were the stuff of myth: a Basque attack on Charlemagne's army as it returned from Spain became the core of the epic poem *The Song of Roland*.

Ventures like these depended on a good army. Charlemagne's was led by his *fideles*, faithful aristocrats, and manned by free men, many the "vassals" (clients) of the aristocrats. The king had the *bannum*, the ban, which was the right to call his subjects to arms (and, more generally, to command, prohibit, punish, and collect fines when his ban was not obeyed). Soldiers provided their own equipment; the richest went to war on horseback, the poorest had to have at least a lance, shield, and bow. There was no standing army; men had to be mobilized for each expedition. No *tagmata* or Turkish soldier-slaves were to be found here! Yet, while the empire was expanding, it was a very successful system; men were glad to go off to war when they could expect to return enriched with booty.

Genealogy 3.2 (facing page)
The Carolingians*

By 800, Charlemagne's kingdom stretched 800 miles from east to west, even more from north to south when Italy is counted. (See Map 3.4 on p. 96.) On its eastern edge was a strip of "buffer regions" extending from the Baltic to the Adriatic; they were under Carolingian overlordship. Such hegemony was reminiscent of an empire, and Charlemagne began to act according to the model of Roman emperors, sponsoring building programs to symbolize his authority, standardizing weights and measures, and acting as a patron of intellectual and artistic enterprises. He built a capital "city"—a palace complex, in fact—at Aachen, complete with a chapel patterned on San Vitale, the church built by Justinian at Ravenna (see pp. 31–33). So keen was Charlemagne on Byzantine models that he had columns, mosaics, and marbles from Rome and Ravenna carted up north to use in his own buildings.

Further drawing on imperial traditions, Charlemagne issued laws in the form of "capitularies," summaries of decisions made at assemblies held with the chief men of the realm. He appointed regional governors, called "counts," to carry out his laws, muster his armies, and collect his taxes. Chosen from Charlemagne's aristocratic supporters, they were compensated for their work by temporary grants of land rather than with salaries. This was not Roman; but Charlemagne lacked the fiscal apparatus of the Roman emperors (and of his contemporary Byzantine emperors and Islamic caliphs), so he made land substitute for money. To discourage corruption, he appointed officials called *missi dominici* ("those sent out by the lord king") to oversee the counts on the king's behalf. The *missi*—abbots, bishops, and counts, aristocrats all—traveled in pairs across Francia. They were to look into the affairs—large and small—of the church and laity.

In this way, Charlemagne set up institutions meant to echo those of the Roman Empire. It was a brilliant move on the part of Pope Leo III (795–816) to harness the king's imperial pretensions to papal ambitions. In 799, accused of adultery and perjury by a hostile faction at Rome, Leo narrowly escaped blinding and having his tongue cut out. Fleeing northward to seek Charlemagne's protection, he returned home under escort, the king close behind. Charlemagne arrived in late November 800 to an imperial welcome orchestrated by Leo. On Christmas Day of that year, Leo put an imperial crown on Charlemagne's head, and the clergy and nobles who were present acclaimed the king "Augustus," the title of the first Roman emperor. In one stroke the pope managed to exalt the king of the Franks, downgrade Irene at Byzantium, and enjoy the role of "emperor maker" himself.

About twenty years later, when Einhard wrote about this coronation, he said that the imperial titles at first so displeased Charlemagne "that he stated that, if he had known in advance of the pope's plan, he would not have entered the church that day, even though it was a great feast day."[9] In fact, Charlemagne continued to use the title "king" for about a year; then he adopted a new one that was both long and revealing: "Charles, the most serene Augustus, crowned by God, great and peaceful emperor who governs the Roman Empire and who is, by the mercy of God, king of the Franks and the Lombards." According to this title, Charlemagne was not the Roman emperor crowned by the pope but rather God's emperor, who governed the Roman Empire along with his many other duties.

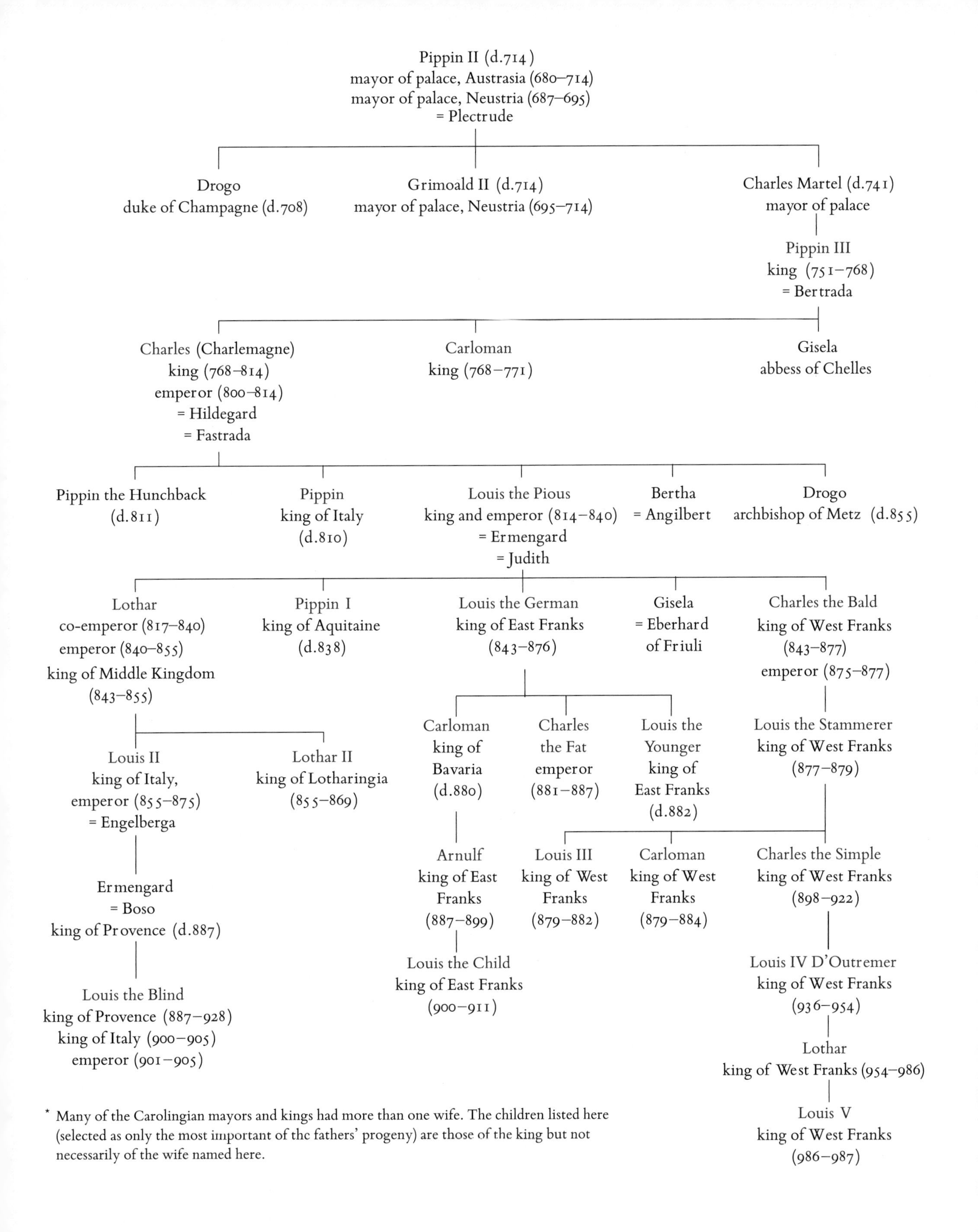

* Many of the Carolingian mayors and kings had more than one wife. The children listed here (selected as only the most important of the fathers' progeny) are those of the king but not necessarily of the wife named here.

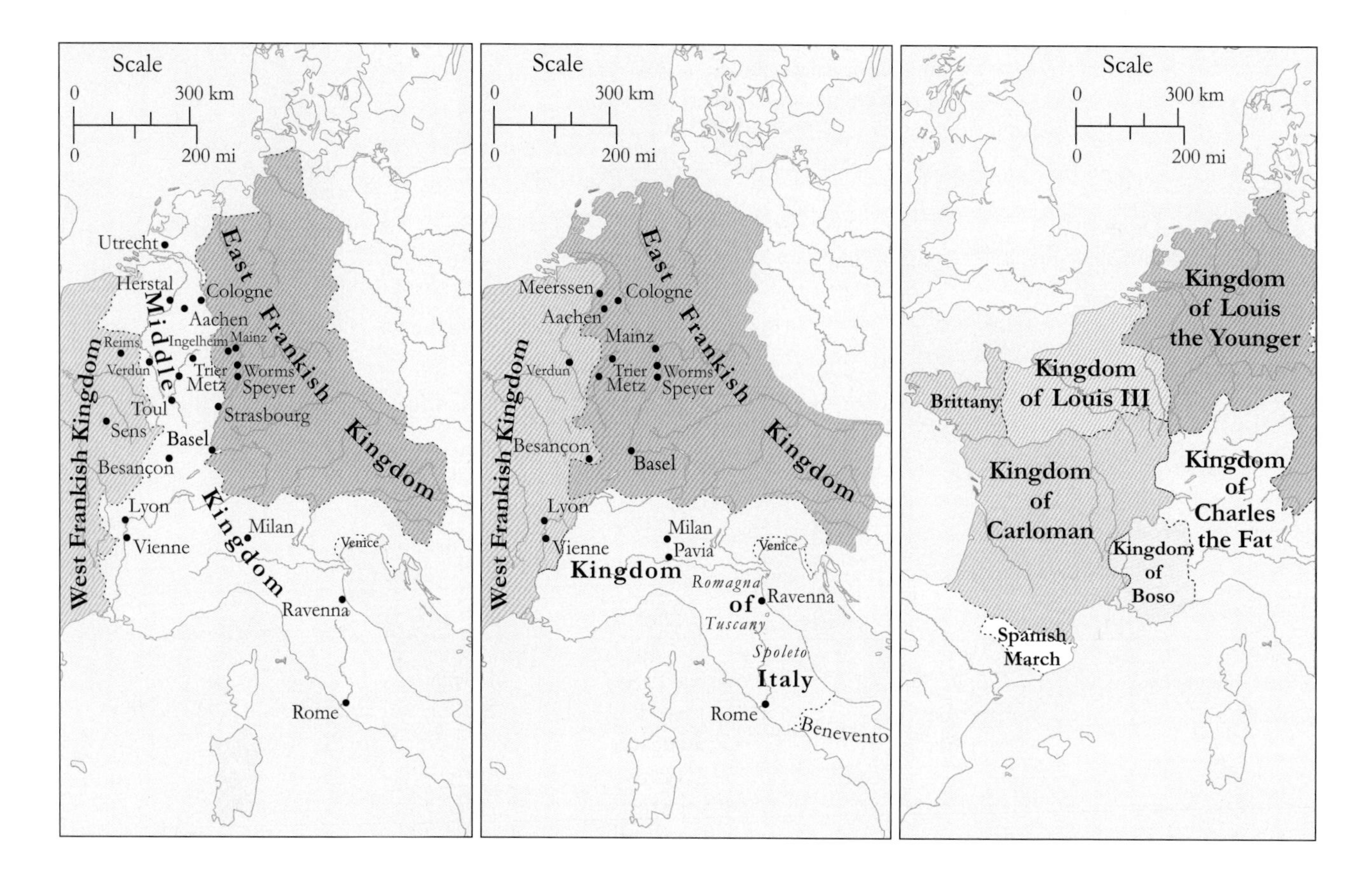

Map 3.5a Partition of 843 (Treaty of Verdun)

Map 3.5b Partition of 870 (Treaty of Meerssen)

Map 3.5c Partition of 880

Charlemagne's Heirs

When Charlemagne died, only one of his sons remained alive: Louis, nicknamed "the Pious." (See Genealogy 3.2.) Emperor he was (from 814 to 840), but over an empire that was a conglomeration of territories with little unity. He had to contend with the revolts of his sons, the depredations of outside invaders, the regional interests of counts and bishops, and above all an enormous variety of languages, laws, customs, and traditions, all of which tended to pull his empire apart. He contended with gusto, his chief unifying tool being Christianity. Calling on the help of the monastic reformer Benedict of Aniane (d.821), Louis imposed the Benedictine Rule on all the monasteries in Francia. Monks and abbots served as his chief advisors. Louis's imperial model was Theodosius I, who had made Christianity the official religion of the Roman Empire (see pp. 7–8). Organizing inquests by the *missi*, Louis looked into allegations of exploitation of the poor, standardized the procedures of his chancery, and put all Frankish bishops and monasteries under his control.

Charlemagne had employed his sons as "sub-kings," but Louis politicized his family still more. Early in his reign he had his wife crowned empress; named his first-born son, Lothar, emperor and co-ruler; and had his other sons, Pippin and Louis (later called "the German"), agree to be sub-kings under their older brother. It was neatly planned. But when Louis's first wife died he married Judith, daughter of a relatively obscure kindred (the Welfs) that stemmed from the Saxon and Bavarian nobility and would later become enormously powerful. In 823 she and Louis had a son, Charles (later "the Bald"), and this upset the earlier division of the empire. A family feud turned into bitter civil war as brothers fought one another and their father for titles and kingdoms. In 833 matters came to a head when Louis, effectively taken prisoner by Lothar, was forced to do public penance. Lothar expected the ritual to get his father off the throne for life. But Louis played one son against the other and made a swift comeback. The episode showed how Carolingian rulers could portray themselves as accountable to God and yet, in that very act of subservience, make themselves even more sacred and authoritative in the eyes of their subjects.

After Louis's death, a period of war and uncertainty (840–843) among the three remaining brothers (Pippin had died in 838) ended with the Treaty of Verdun (843). (See Map 3.5a.) The empire was divided into three parts, an arrangement that would roughly define the future political contours of Western Europe. The western third, bequeathed to Charles the Bald (r.843–877), would eventually become France, and the eastern third, given to Louis the German (r.843–876), would become Germany. The "Middle Kingdom," which became Lothar's portion (r. as co-emperor 817–840; as emperor 840–855), had a different fate: parts of it were absorbed by France and Germany, while the rest eventually coalesced into the modern states of Belgium, the Netherlands, and Luxembourg—the so-called Benelux countries—as well as Switzerland and Italy. All this was far in the future. As the brothers had their own children, new divisions were tried: one in 870 (the Treaty of Meerssen), for example, and another in 880. (See Maps 3.5b and 3.5c.) After the death of Emperor Charles the Fat (888), various kings and lesser rulers, many of them non-Carolingians, came to the fore in the irrevocably splintered empire.

Dynastic problems contributed to the breakup of the Carolingian Empire. So did invasions by outsiders—Vikings, Muslims, and, starting in 899, Magyars (Hungarians)—which harassed the Frankish Kingdom throughout the ninth century. These certainly weakened the kings: without a standing army, they were unable to respond to lightning raids, and what regional defense there was fell into the hands of local leaders, such as counts. A monk at Paris named Abbo, an eyewitness to Viking attacks there, wrote a poem in praise of the defenders of his city: "Among all the warriors, there were two most outstanding / For their valor: one was a count, the other an abbot."[10]

The Carolingians lost prestige and money as they paid out tribute to stave off further attacks. Above all, the Carolingian Empire atomized because linguistic and other differences between regions—and familial and other ties within regions—were simply too strong to be overcome by directives from a central court. Even today a unified Europe is only a distant ideal. Anyway, as we shall see, fragmentation had its own strengths and possibilities.

The Wealth of a Local Economy

The Carolingian economy was based on plunder, trade, and agriculture. After the Carolingians could push no further and the raids of Charlemagne's day came to an end,

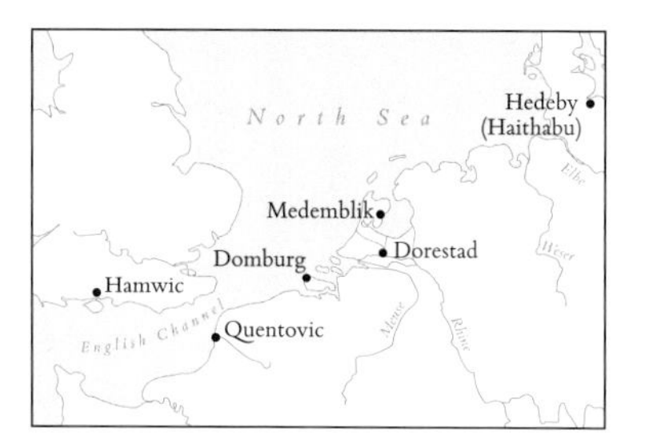

Map 3.6 Northern Emporia in the Carolingian Age

trade and land became the chief resources of the kingdom. To the north, in Viking trading stations such as Haithabu (see Map 3.6), archaeologists have found Carolingian glass and pots alongside Islamic coins and cloth, showing that the Carolingian economy meshed with that of the Abbasid caliphate. Silver from the Islamic world probably came north from the Caspian Sea, up the Volga River to the Baltic Sea. There the coins were melted down and the silver traded to the Carolingians in return for wine, jugs, glasses, and other manufactured goods. The Carolingians turned the silver into coins of their own, to be used throughout the empire for small-scale local trade. Baltic Sea emporia such as Haithabu supplemented those—Quentovic and Dorestad, for example—that served the North Sea trade.

Nevertheless, the backbone of the Carolingian economy was land. A few written records, called *polyptyques*, document the output of the Carolingian great estates—"villae," as they were called in Latin, "manors," as we term them. On the far-flung and widely scattered manors of rich landowners—churches, monasteries, kings, and aristocrats—a major reorganization and rationalization was taking place. The most enterprising landlords instituted a three-field rather than a two-field cultivation system. It meant that two-thirds of the land rather than one-half was sown with crops each year, yielding a tidy surplus.

Consider Lambesc, near Aix-en-Provence, one of the many manors belonging to the cathedral of Saint Mary of Marseille. It was not a compact farm but rather a conglomeration of essential parts, with its lands, woods, meadows, and vineyards scattered about the countryside. All were worked by peasant families, some legally free, some unfree, each settled on its own holding—here called a *colonica*; elsewhere often called a *mansus*, or "manse"—usually including a house, a garden, small bits of several fields, and so on. The peasants farmed the land that belonged to them and paid yearly dues to their lord—in this case the Church of Saint Mary, which, in its *polyptyque*, kept careful track of what was owed:

> [There is a] holding [*colonica*] at Nemphas. Martinus, *colonus*. Wife Dominica. Bertemarus, an adult son. Desideria, an adult daughter. It pays the tax: 1 pig, 1 suckling [pig]; 2 fattened hens; 10 chickens; 40 eggs. Savarildis, an adult woman. Olisirga, a daughter 10 years old. Rica, a daughter 9 years old.[11]

Martinus and his family apparently did not work the *demesne*—the land, woods, meadows, and vineyards directly held by Saint Mary—but they paid a yearly tax of animals and animal produce. Other tenants farmed the demesne, as at Nidis, in the region of Grasse, where Bernarius owed daily service and also paid a penny (1 *denarius*) in yearly dues. On many manors women were required to feed the lord's chickens or busy themselves in the *gynecaeum*, the women's workshop, where they made and dyed cloth and sewed garments.

Clearly the labor was onerous and the accounting system complex and unwieldy; but manors organized on the model of Saint Mary made a profit. Like the Church of Saint Mary and other lords, the Carolingian kings benefited from their own extensive manors.

Nevertheless, farming did not return great surpluses, and as the lands belonging to the king were divided up in the wake of the partitioning of the empire, Carolingian dependence on manors scattered throughout their kingdom proved to be a source of weakness.

The Carolingian Renaissance

With the profits from their manors, some monasteries and churches invested in books. These were not made of paper—a product that, although already used in the Islamic world, did not reach the West until the eleventh century—but rather of parchment: animal skins soaked, scraped, and cut into sheets (see The Making of an Illuminated Manuscript on pp. 152–55). Nor were Carolingian books printed, since the printing press was not invented until around 1450. Rather, books were written by hand; they were "manuscripts" from manus = hand and scriptus = written. This was taxing work, and scribes often shared in the production of just one manuscript, working together in scribal workshops (*scriptoria*; sing. *scriptorium*). Consider the monastery of Saint-Amand (today in northern France), which made books both for its own use and for the needs of many other institutions: its *scriptorium* produced Gospels, works of the Church Fathers, grammars, and above all liturgical books for the Mass and other church services.

Plate 3.6 on p. 106 shows a page from a Sacramentary (a liturgical book) that was produced at Saint-Amand for the Parisian monastery of Saint-Germain-des-Prés (where Abbo, above p. 103, wrote about the Viking attacks). For the most part, Saint-Amand provided only the texts of Mass chants. But in one instance the scribe added some "dots and dashes" above the word *Exaudi* (Hear!). They illustrate one early form of musical notation. These "notes" did not indicate pitches to the monks who sang the melodies. Nor did they suggest rhythms. They simply reminded the monks of the melody associated with one chant beginning with the word *Exaudi*.

The development of written music was a response to royal policy. Before the Carolingians came to power, the music at churches and monasteries had been determined by local oral traditions. But the special relationship that the Carolingians had with Rome included importing Roman chant melodies to Francia. This reform—the imposition of the so-called Gregorian chant—posed great practical difficulties. It meant that every monk and priest had to learn a year's worth of Roman music; but how? A few cantors were imported from Rome, but without a system of notation, it was easy to forget new tunes. The monks of Saint-Amand were part of a revolution in musical technology.

The same Sacramentary reveals another key development of the era: the use of minuscule writing. As at Byzantium, and around the same time, the Carolingians experimented with letterforms that were quick to write and easy to read. "Caroline minuscule" lasted into the eleventh century, when it gave way to a more angular script, today called "Gothic." But the Carolingian letter forms were rediscovered in the fifteenth century—by scholars who thought that they represented ancient Roman writing!—and they became the model for modern lower-case printed fonts.

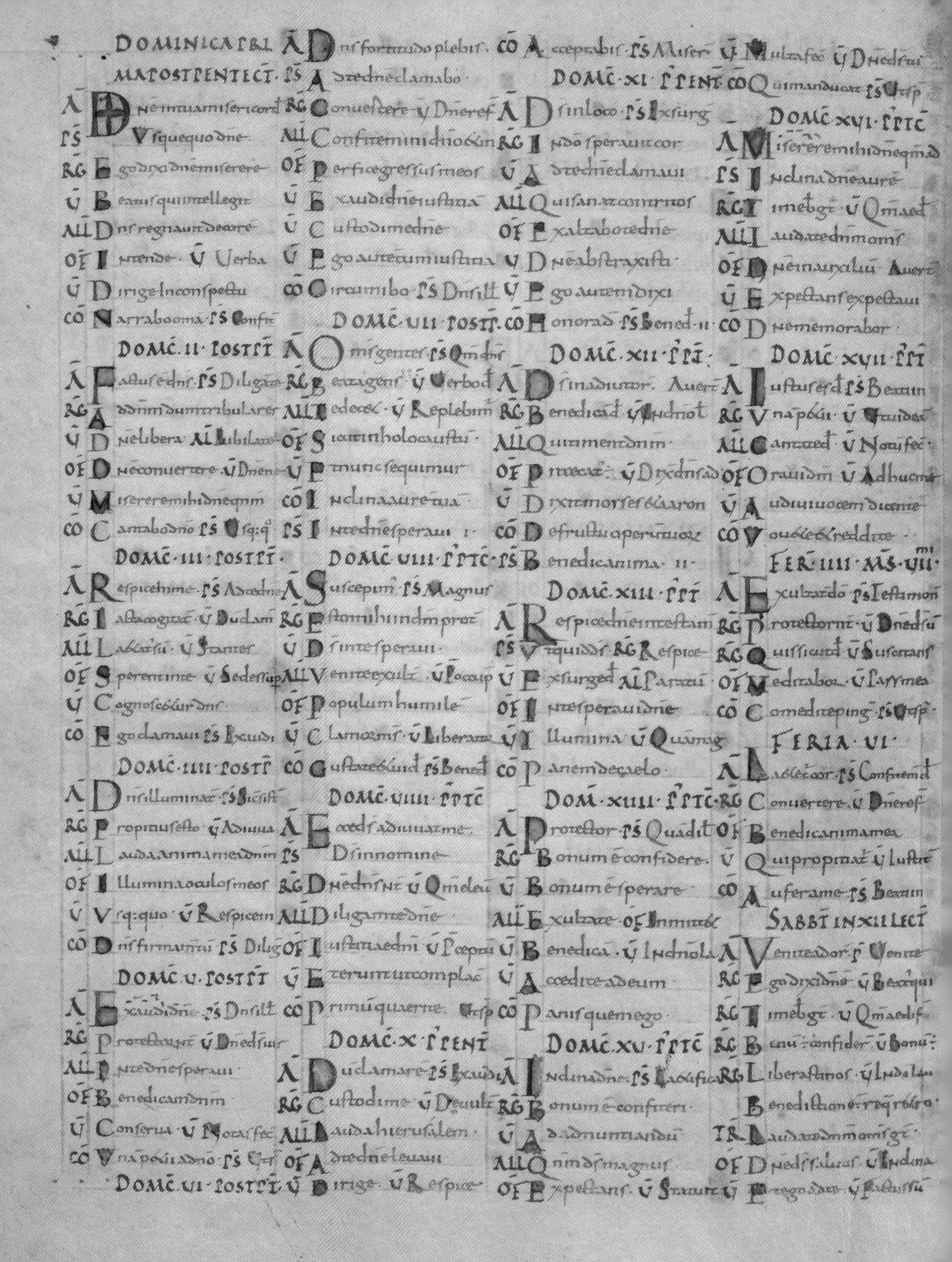

Plate 3.6 (facing page) Sacramentary of Saint-Germain-des-Prés (early 9th cent.). The scribe of this list of incipits (the "first words") of Mass chants provided a musical reminder of one (seven lines from the bottom, on the left) by adding neumes above the first words, "Exaudi Domine," "Hear, O Lord."

The Carolingian court was behind much of this activity. Most of the centers of learning, scholarship, and book production began under men and women who at one time or another were part of the royal court. Alcuin, perhaps the most famous of the Carolingian intellectuals, was "imported" by Charlemagne from England—where, as we have seen (p. 65), monastic scholarship flourished—to head up the king's palace school. Chief advisor to Charlemagne and tutor to the entire royal family, Alcuin eventually became abbot of Saint-Martin of Tours, grooming a new generation of teachers. More unusual but equally telling was the experience of Gisela, Charlemagne's sister. She too was a key royal advisor, the one who alerted the others at home about Charlemagne's imperial coronation at Rome in 800. She was also abbess of Chelles, near Paris, a center of manuscript production in its own right. Chelles had a library, and its nuns were well educated. They wrote learned letters and composed a history (the "Prior Metz Annals") that treated the rise of the Carolingians as a tale of struggle between brothers, sons, and fathers eased by the wise counsel of mothers, aunts, and sisters.

Women and the poor made up the largely invisible half of the Carolingian Renaissance. But without doubt some were part of it. One of Charlemagne's capitularies ordered that the cathedrals and monasteries of his kingdom should teach reading and writing to all who could learn. There were enough complaints (by rich people) about upstart peasants who found a place at court that we may be sure that some talented sons of the poor were getting an education. A few churchmen expressed the hope that schools for "children" would be established even in small villages and hamlets. Were they thinking of girls as well as boys? Certainly the noblewoman Dhuoda proves that education was available even to laywomen. We would never know about her had she not worried enough about her absent son to write a *Handbook for Her Son* full of advice. It is clear in this deeply felt moral text that Dhuoda was drawing on an excellent education: she obviously knew the Bible, writings of the Church Fathers, Gregory the Great, and "moderns," like Alcuin. Her Latin was fluent and sophisticated. And she understood the value of the written word:

> My great concern, my son William, is to offer you helpful words. My burning, watchful heart especially desires that you may have in this little volume what I have longed to be written down for you, about how you were born through God's grace.[12]

The original manuscript of Dhuoda's text is not extant. Had it survived, it would no doubt have looked like other "practical texts" of the time: the "folios" (pages) would have been written in Caroline minuscule, each carefully designed to set off the poetry—Dhuoda's own and quotes from others—from the prose; the titles of each chapter (there are nearly a hundred, each very short) would have been enlivened with delicately colored capital letters. The manuscript would probably not have been illuminated (illustrated); fancy books were generally made for royalty, for prestigious ceremonial occasions, or for books that were especially esteemed, such as the Gospels.

There were, however, many such lavish productions. In fact, Carolingian art and architecture mark a turning point. For all its richness, Merovingian culture had not stressed

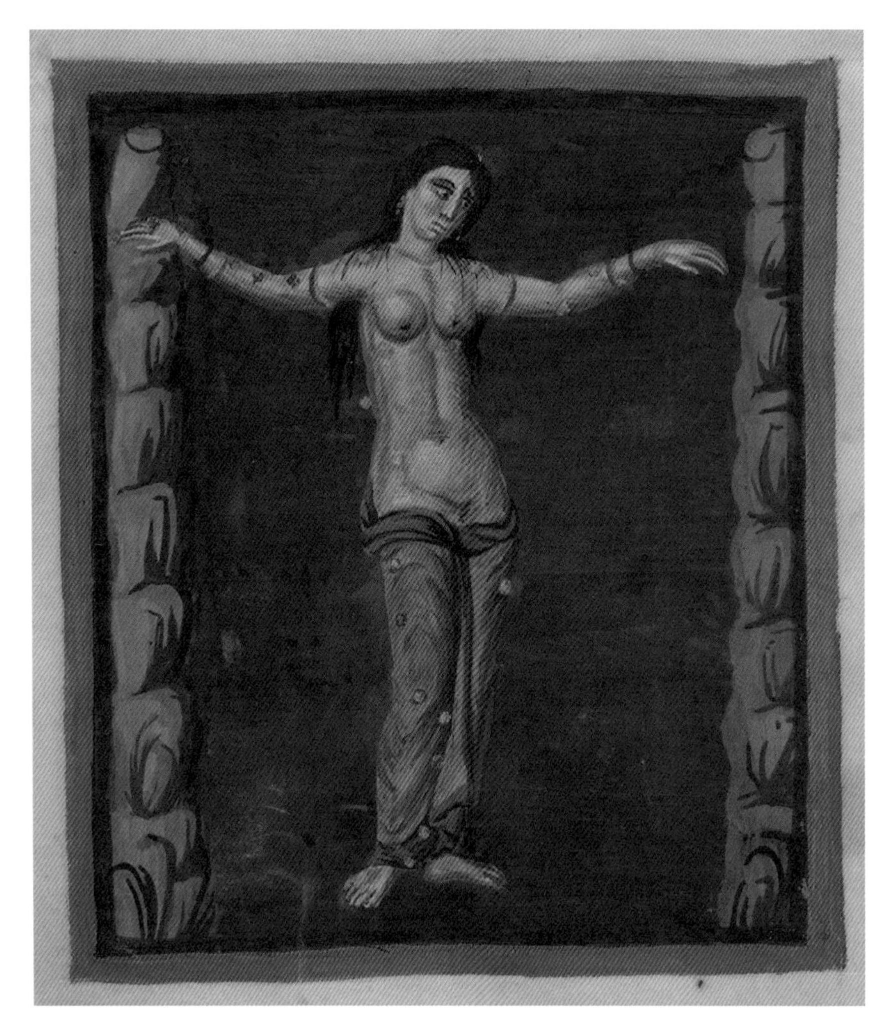

Plate 3.7 Andromeda (840s?). In this notebook-sized (about 9 × 8 inch) Carolingian manuscript, probably made at Aachen or Metz, an artist painted nearly forty miniatures of the constellations named in a poem by Aratos.

artistic expression, though some of the monasteries inspired by Saint Columbanus produced a few illuminated manuscripts. By contrast, the Carolingians, admirers and imitators of Christian Rome, vigorously promoted a vast, eclectic, and ideologically motivated program of artistic work. They were reviving the Roman Empire. We have already seen how Charlemagne brought the very marble of Rome and Ravenna home to Aachen to build his new palace complex. A similar impulse inspired Carolingian art.

As with texts, so with pictures: the Carolingians revered and imitated the past while building on and changing it. Their manuscript illuminations were inspired by a vast repertory of models: from the British Isles (where, as we have seen, a rich synthesis of decorative and representational styles had a long tradition), from late-antique Italy (which yielded its models in old manuscripts), and from Byzantium (which may have inadvertently provided some artists, fleeing iconoclasm, as well as manuscripts).

In Plate 3.7, a beautiful woman, nearly naked, stands with her arms outstretched, bound at their wrists by chains. Small stars are scattered over her body. She is the galaxy Andromeda. In Greek mythology she was the daughter of Cepheus and Cassiopeia, king and queen of Aethiopia. When Cassiopeia boasted that Andromeda was more beautiful than even the daughters of the sea god, that god took his revenge on Aethiopia and forced Cepheus to sacrifice his daughter by stripping off her clothes and chaining her to a rock. She was saved by the hero Perseus, who married her, and after her death Athena turned her into a constellation in the northern sky. The Carolingian artist took his inspiration not only from the text he (or she) was illustrating—the *Phainomena* by the classical Greek poet Aratos (*fl.* 3rd cent. BCE) in the later Latin version by Germanicus Caesar (*fl.* 1st cent. CE)—but also from the ancient classical models. Compare Andromeda to Venus in Plate 1.1. Both women have weight and flesh; both are absorbed in their own story and care nothing about hierarchy, ideology, or a world beyond their own.

An entirely different tradition lies behind the grand letters on the opening page of a Psalter (Plate 3.8). Painted around the same time as Plate 3.7, the only "classical" element here is the Latin language. Rather, the page owes much to the decorative style of the British Isles. "Beatus vir," ("Blessed is the man"), the first words of the first psalm, are here given luminous treatment with the use of gold leaf and a restrained palette. The page is then framed with designs of the same colors, with interlaced birds and dragon heads at the corners.

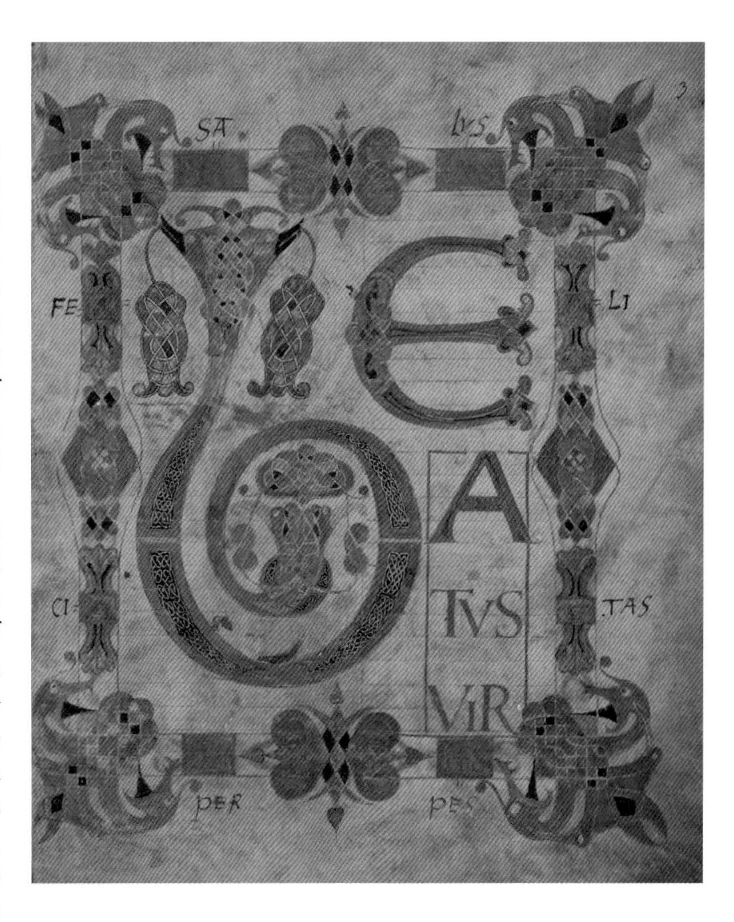

Plate 3.8 Psalter Page (second quarter of 9th cent.). In this sumptuous manuscript dedicated to King Louis the German (r.843–876) the artist (a monk at the monastery of Saint Omer, today in northern France) drew on the decorative, abstract traditions of the British Isles. Nevertheless, following the principle of "less is more," he pared down the colors and the "busyness" of his model, as a quick comparison with Plate 2.7, p. 69, illustrates.

In Plate 3.9, combining the two traditions in a startlingly original manner, an artist at Saint-Amand created a classically inspired scene framed by columns sporting the stylized birds and interlace designs of the Insular style—the style of the British Isles. Much as in an ancient Roman wall painting, the figure—the evangelist John—has volume and weight. He seems to live in a world of his own, separate from the viewer. But unlike an ancient wall painting, his world does not evoke an illusionistic atmosphere (as, for example, at Oplontis [see Plate 1.2 on pp. 14–15]) but rather is composed of three well-defined zones: at the bottom, earth of brushy brown; in the middle, a huge swathe of blue broken by ornamental trees; above, clouds of bright yellow and orange. The figure, too, has an unclassical twist, its pleated drapery giving it a somewhat frenetic urgency. By mixing various styles, the artist found a new mode of expressing the transcendent.

In this portrait, Saint John seems to be caught in the act of listening to a voice dictating what he is to write down. The artist is almost telling us a story about John. But the narrative impulse is given its fullest expression in the Utrecht Psalter, a Carolingian manuscript commissioned by Archbishop Ebbo of Reims and executed at a nearly monastery. Not only does it contain all 150 psalms and 16 other songs known as canticles, but it accompanies each poem with drawings that bring it to life. In Plate 2.12 (above, p. 77), the illustration for Psalm 64 (Douay 63), lively figures render the words of the first four verses literally:

> Preserve my life from dread of the enemy, / hide me from the secret plots of the wicked, from the scheming of evildoers, / who whet their tongues like swords, who aim bitter words like arrows, / shooting from ambush at the blameless.

In the middle is the psalmist standing on a mountain and holding forth. An angel above him stretches almost on tip-toe, bending over in order to hold a protective cloth over psalmist's head. Beneath them are the members of God's army, getting ready to do battle. On the left is the enemy, the "scheming evildoers": one soldier whets a sword, while another is about to shoot an arrow. But, as the discussion of this plate on p. 76 points out, the wicked army has the outdated equipment; it is no surprise that a later line in the psalm predicts the enemy's defeat.

It may plausibly be said that the various artistic styles elaborated during the Carolingian Renaissance—fed by classical, decorative, abstract traditions but combined in new and original ways—formed the basis of all subsequent Western art.

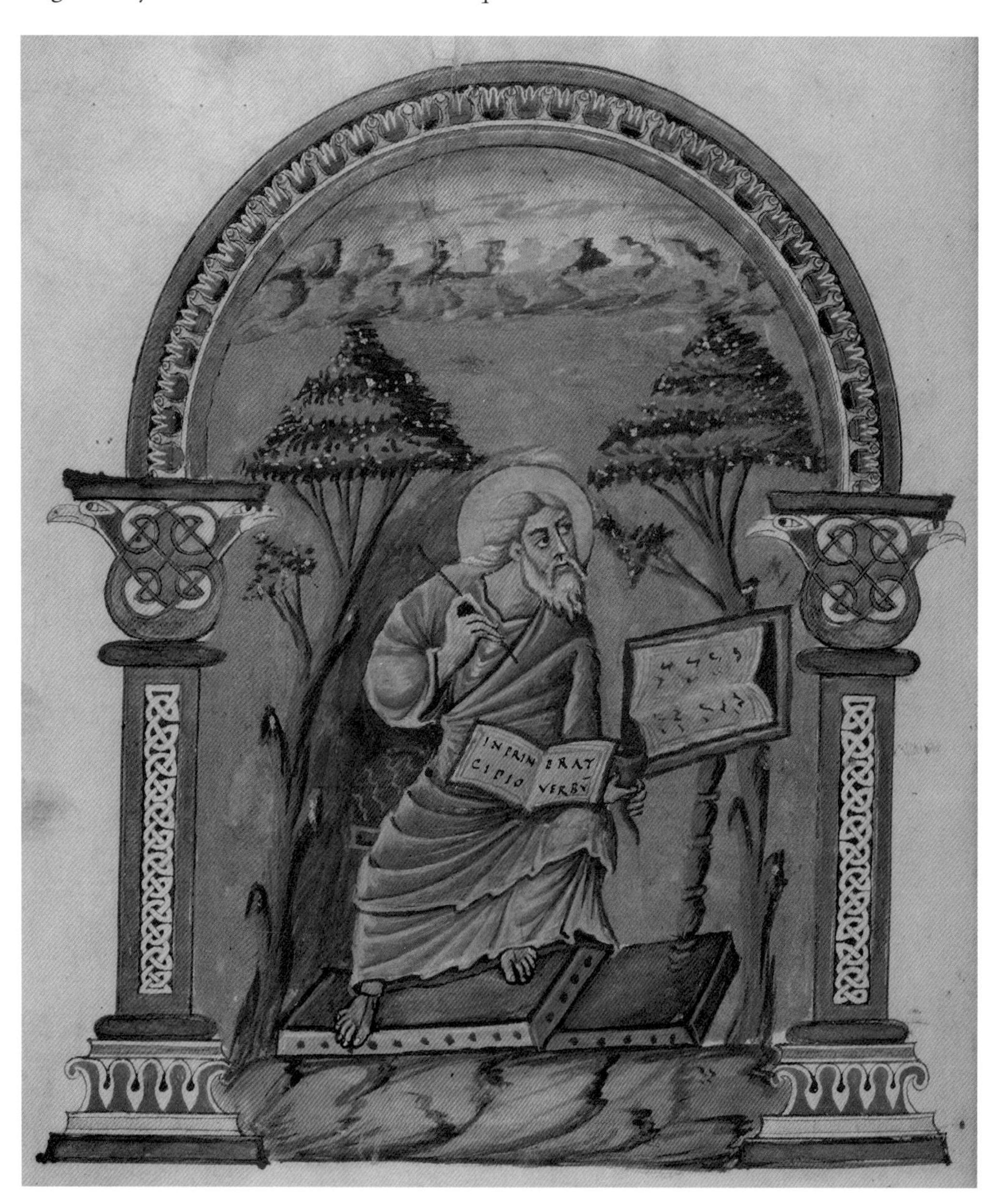

Plate 3.9 Saint John (second half of 9th cent.). Neither classically naturalistic nor entirely decorative in inspiration, this painting of the evangelist Saint John evokes a heavenly reality that is only vaguely anchored in earthly things. The book that John is writing (note the ink horn in his left hand) gives the opening line of his Gospel: "In principio erat verbum" ("In the beginning was the Word").

CHAPTER THREE: ESSENTIAL DATES

750	Abbasid caliphate begins
751	Pippin III (the first Carolingian king) elevated to kingship
762	Baghdad founded as the Abbasid capital city
768–814	Reign of Charlemagne (Charles the Great)
800	Charlemagne crowned emperor
843	End of iconoclasm in Byzantine Empire
843	Treaty of Verdun; Carolingian Empire divided
*c.*864	Bulgarian Khan Boris-Michael converts to Christianity

NOTES

1 *The Life of Saint Philaretos*, in *Reading the Middle Ages: Sources from Europe, Byzantium, and the Islamic World*, 3rd ed., ed. Barbara H. Rosenwein (Toronto: University of Toronto Press, 2018), p. 108.
2 Constantine-Cyril, *Prologue to the Gospel*, in *Reading the Middle Ages*, pp. 162–63.
3 For one of Boris-Michael's seals, see "Reading through Looking," in *Reading the Middle Ages*, p. II.
4 Pope Nicholas I, *Letter to Answer the Bulgarians' Questions*, in *Reading the Middle Ages*, p. 167.
5 Abu Tammam, *The sword gives truer tidings*, in *Reading the Middle Ages*, p. 125.
6 Al-Bukhari, *On Fasting*, in *Reading the Middle Ages*, p. 151.
7 *The Chronicle of Alfonso III*, in *Reading the Middle Ages*, p. 135.
8 Pope Stephen II, *Letters to King Pippin III*, in *Reading the Middle Ages*, p. 158.
9 Einhard, *Life of Charlemagne*, in *Reading the Middle Ages*, p. 123.
10 Abbo of Saint-Germain-des-Prés, *Battles of the City of Paris*, in *Reading the Middle Ages*, p. 139.
11 *Polyptyque of the Church of Saint Mary of Marseille*, in *Reading the Middle Ages*, p. 106.
12 Dhuoda, *Handbook for Her Son*, in *Reading the Middle Ages*, p. 129.

FURTHER READING

Bennison, Amira K. *The Great Caliphs: The Golden Age of the 'Abbasid Empire*. New Haven, CT, and London: Yale University Press, 2009.

Benson, Bobrick. *The Caliph's Splendor: Islam and the West in the Golden Age of Baghdad*. New York: Simon and Schuster, 2012.

Berend, Nora, ed. *Christianization and the Rise of Christian Monarchy: Scandinavia, Central Europe and Rus' c.900–1200*. Cambridge: Cambridge University Press, 2007.

Betti, Maddalena. *The Making of Christian Moravia (858–882): Papal Power and Political Reality*. Leiden: Brill, 2014.

Cameron, Averil. *Byzantine Christianity: A Very Brief History*. London: SPCK, 2017.

Cooperson, Michael. *Al-Ma'mun*. Oxford: Oneworld, 2005.
Costambeys, Marios, Matthew Innes, and Simon MacLean. *The Carolingian World*. Cambridge: Cambridge University Press, 2011.
Davis, Jennifer R. *Charlemagne's Practice of Empire*. Cambridge: Cambridge University Press, 2015.
DeJong, Mayke. *The Penitential State: Authority and Atonement in the Ages of Louis the Pious, 814–840*. Cambridge: Cambridge University Press, 2009.
Faulkner, Thomas. *Law and Authority in the Early Middle Ages: The Frankish* leges *in the Carolingian Period*. Cambridge: Cambridge University Press, 2016.
Fried, Johannes. *The Middle Ages*. Trans. Peter Lewis. Cambridge, MA: Harvard University Press, 2015.
Goldberg, Eric J. *Struggle for Empire: Kingship and Conflict under Louis the German, 817–876*. Ithaca, NY: Cornell University Press, 2006.
Hallaq, Wael B. *The Origins and Evolution of Islamic Law*. Cambridge: Cambridge University Press, 2005.
Heather, Peter. *The Restoration of Rome: Barbarian Popes & Imperial Pretenders*. London: Macmillan, 2014.
Herrin, Judith. *Women in Purple: Rulers of Medieval Byzantium*. Princeton, NJ: Princeton University Press, 2002.
Levy, Kenneth. *Gregorian Chant and the Carolingians*. Princeton, NJ: Princeton University Press, 1998.
McCormick, Michael. *Origins of the European Economy: Communications and Commerce, AD 300–900*. Cambridge: Cambridge University Press, 2001.
McKitterick, Rosamond. "The Illusion of Royal Power in the Carolingian Annals." *English Historical Review* 115, no. 460 (2000): 1–20.
———. *Charlemagne: The Formation of a European Identity*. Cambridge: Cambridge University Press, 2008.
Phelan, Owen Michael. *The Formation of Christian Europe: The Carolingians, Baptism, and the Imperium Christianum*. Oxford: Oxford University Press, 2014.
Turner, John P. *Inquisition in Early Islam: The Competition for Political and Religious Authority in the Abbasid Empire*. London: I.B. Tauris, 2013.
Verhulst, Adriaan. *The Carolingian Economy*. Cambridge: Cambridge University Press, 2002.
Wormald, Patrick, and Janet L. Nelson, eds. *Lay Intellectuals in the Carolingian World*. Cambridge: Cambridge University Press, 2011.

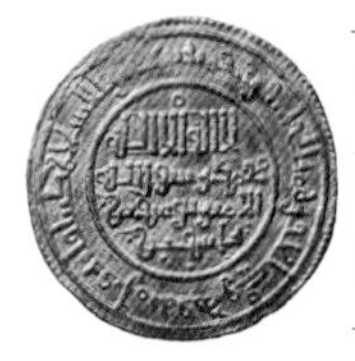

To test your knowledge of this chapter, please go to www.utphistorymatters.com for Study Questions.

FOUR

POLITICAL COMMUNITIES REORDERED (*c.*900–*c.*1050)

The large-scale centralized governments of the ninth century dissolved in the tenth. The fission was least noticeable at Byzantium, where, although important landowning families emerged as brokers of patronage and power, the primacy of the emperor was never effectively challenged. In the Islamic world, however, new dynastic groups established themselves as regional rulers. In Western Europe, Carolingian kings ceased to control land and men, while new political entities—some extremely local and weak, others quite strong and unified—emerged in their wake.

BYZANTIUM: THE STRENGTHS AND LIMITS OF CENTRALIZATION

By 1025 the Byzantine Empire once again touched the Danube and Euphrates Rivers. Its emperors maintained the traditional cultural importance of Constantinople by carefully orchestrating the radiating power of the imperial court. At the same time, however, powerful men in both town and countryside gobbled up land and dominated the peasantry, challenging the dominance of the center.

The Imperial Court

The Great Palace of Constantinople, a sprawling building complex begun under Constantine, was expanded and beautified under his successors. (See Map 4.1.) Far more than the symbolic emplacement of imperial power, it was the central command post of the empire. Servants, slaves, and grooms; top courtiers and learned clergymen; cousins,

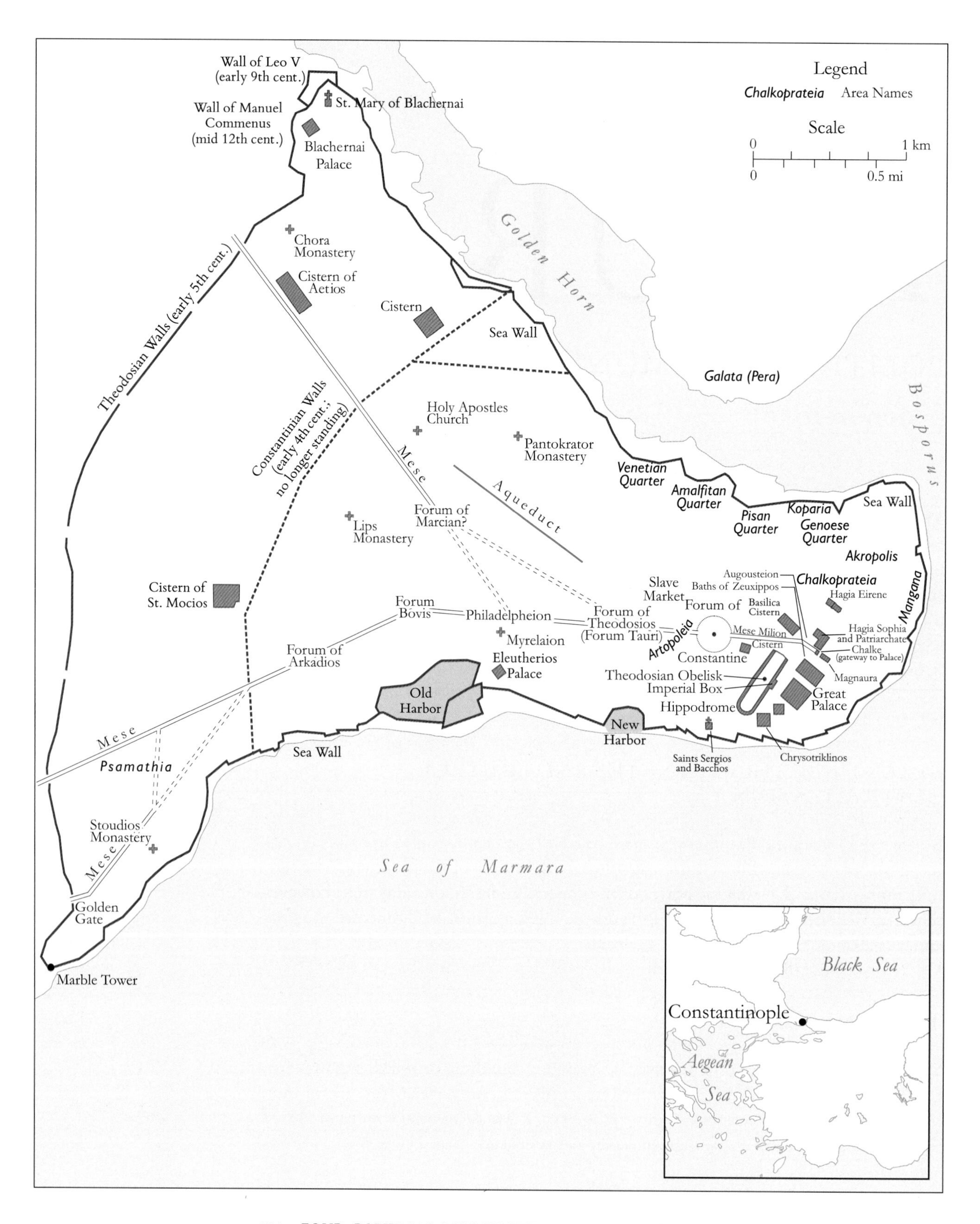

Legend
Chalkoprateia Area Names
Scale
0 1 km
0 0.5 mi
Wall of Leo V (early 9th cent.)
St. Mary of Blachernai
Wall of Manuel Commenus (mid 12th cent.)
Blachernai Palace
Golden Horn
Chora Monastery
Cistern of Aetios
Cistern
Sea Wall
Theodosian Walls (early 5th cent.)
Constantinian Walls (early 4th cent.; no longer standing)
Galata (Pera)
Bosporus
Holy Apostles Church
Pantokrator Monastery
Mese
Aqueduct
Venetian Quarter
Amalfitan Quarter
Pisan Quarter
Koparia
Genoese Quarter
Sea Wall
Akropolis
Forum of Marcian?
Lips Monastery
Cistern of St. Mocios
Augousteion
Baths of Zeuxippos
Chalkoprateia
Slave Market
Forum of Constantine
Basilica Cistern
Hagia Eirene
Mangana
Forum Bovis
Philadelpheion
Forum of Theodosios (Forum Tauri)
Mese Milion
Hagia Sophia and Patriarchate
Chalke (gateway to Palace)
Cistern
Artopoleia
Myrelaion
Forum of Arkadios
Eleutherios Palace
Theodosian Obelisk
Imperial Box
Magnaura
Old Harbor
Great Palace
Hippodrome
New Harbor
Mese
Sea Wall
Saints Sergios and Bacchos
Chrysotriklinos
Psamathia
Stoudios Monastery
Mese
Sea of Marmara
Golden Gate
Marble Tower
Black Sea
Constantinople
Aegean Sea

Map 4.1 (facing page)
Constantinople, *c.*1100

siblings, and hangers-on of the emperor and empress lived within its walls. Other courtiers—civil servants, officials, scholars, military men, advisers, and other dependents—lived as near to the palace as they could manage. They were "on call" at every hour. The emperor had only to give short notice and all assembled for impromptu but nevertheless highly choreographed ceremonies. These were in themselves instruments of power; the emperors manipulated courtly formalities to indicate new favorites or to signal displeasure.

The court was mainly a male preserve, but there were powerful women at the Great Palace as well. Consider Zoe (d.1050), the daughter of Constantine VIII. Contemporaries acknowledged her right to rule through her imperial blood, and through her marriages, she "made" her husbands into legitimate emperors. She and her sister even ruled jointly for one year (1042). But their biographer, Michael Psellus, a courtier who observed them with a jaundiced eye, was happy only when Zoe married: "The country needed a man's supervision—a man at once strong-handed and very experienced in government, one who not only understood the present situation, but also any mistakes that had been made in the past, with their probable results."[1]

There was also a "third gender" at the Great Palace: eunuchs—men who had been castrated, normally as children, and raised to be teachers, doctors, or guardians of the women at court. Their status began to rise in the tenth century. Originally foreigners, they were increasingly recruited from the educated upper classes in the Byzantine Empire itself, even from the imperial families. In addition to their duties in the women's quarter of the palace, some of them accompanied the emperor during his most sacred and vulnerable moments—when he removed his crown; when he participated in religious ceremonies; even when he dreamed, at night. They hovered by his throne, like the angels flanking Christ in the apse of San Vitale (Plate 1.12 on pp. 32–33). No one, it was thought, was as faithful, trustworthy, or spiritually pure as a eunuch.

The imperial court assiduously cultivated the image of perfect, stable, eternal order. The emperor wore the finest silks, decorated with gold. In artistic representations, he was the largest figure. Sometimes he was shown seated on a high throne with admiring officials beneath him. At other times he stood, as in Plate 4.1, which depicts Emperor Basil II (r.976–1025), broad of shoulder and well-armed, as figures grovel beneath his feet, and Christ, helped by an archangel, places a crown on his head.

This sort of image of Basil—as Christian emperor—has led historians such as Paul Magdalino to emphasize the Orthodox identity of Byzantium. Other historians, impressed by the fact that the Byzantines spoke and wrote in Greek, see Byzantine culture as a distant heir of Hellenism. Still others—Anthony Kaldellis is one—emphasize continuities with Roman political forms. All of these identities (and a few others besides) are surveyed in Averil Cameron's recent book (see Further Reading, p. 157), which argues against seeking a single Byzantine identity. She prefers to find it in constant dialogue with its own many traditions and those of the other cultures—Persian, Slavic, European, Islamic—with whose histories it was a part.

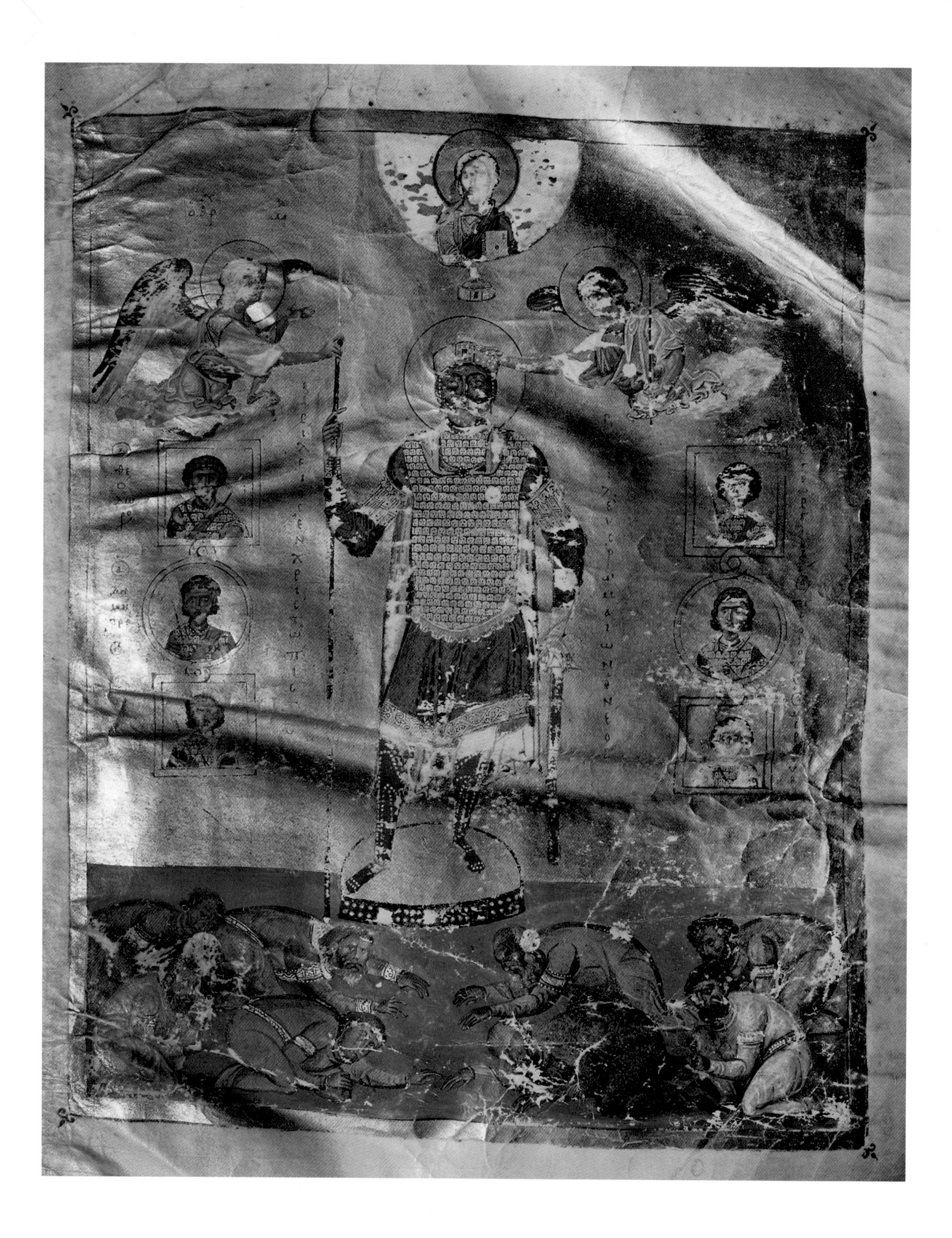

A Wide Embrace and Its Tensions

The artist who painted the image of Basil at the start of a Psalter was imagining him as a sort of King David, the presumed author of the psalms. Like the biblical slayer of Goliath, Basil liked to present himself as a giant-slayer: a tireless warrior. Certainly his epitaph reads that way:

> nobody saw my spear at rest,...
> but I kept vigilant through the whole span of my life ...
> marching bravely to the West,
> and as far as the very frontiers of the East.[2]

Ruling longer than any other Byzantine emperor, Basil built on the achievements of his predecessors. Nicephorus II Phocas (r.963–969) and John I Tzimisces (r.969–976) pushed the Byzantine frontiers north to the Danube (taking half of the Bulgarian Empire), east beyond the Euphrates, and south to Antioch, Crete, and Cyprus (see Map 4.2). Basil thus inherited a fairly secure empire except for the threat from Rus' further to the north. This he defanged through a diplomatic and religious alliance, as we shall see (p. 119). (Rus' is used for the polity; Rus, without the apostrophe, for the peoples.)

But if his borders were secure, Basil's position was not. It was challenged by powerful landowning families from whose ranks his two predecessors had come. Members of the provincial elite—military and government officers, bishops, abbots, and others—benefitted from a general quickening of the economy and the rise of new urban centers. They took advantage of their ascendency, buying land from still impoverished peasants as yet untouched by the economic upswing. No wonder they were called *dynatoi* (sing. *dynatos*), "powerful men." Already, some forty years before Basil came to the throne, Emperor Romanus I Lecapenus (r.920–944) had bewailed in his *Novel* (New Law) of 934 the "intrusion" of the rich

> into a village or hamlet for the sake of a sale, gift, or inheritance.... For the domination of these persons has increased the great hardship of the poor ... [and] will cause no little harm to the commonwealth unless the present legislation puts an end to it first.[3]

The *dynatoi* made military men their clients (even if they were not themselves military men) and, as in the case of Nicephorus Phocas and John Tzimisces, sometimes seized the imperial throne itself.

Basil had two main political goals: to stifle the rebellions of the *dynatoi*, and to swell the borders of his empire. When the powerful Phocas and Scleros families of Anatolia, along with much of the Byzantine army, rebelled against him in 987, he created his own personal Varangian Guard, made up of troops from Rus'. Once victorious, Basil moved to enervate the *dynatoi* as a group. He reinforced the provisions of Romanus's *Novel* and

Plate 4.1 (facing page) Emperor Basil II (1018). Commissioned by Basil II to celebrate his final victory over the Bulgarians in 1018, this picture, painted on shiny gold leaf, shows the emperor triumphant over cowering Bulgarians. Beneath his armor, Basil wears a long-sleeved purple tunic trimmed with gold. Medallions of saints flank his sides, much as they surround the cross of Christ in Plate 3.1 (p. 86). Two archangels hover above. Gabriel, on the left, gives Basil a lance, while Michael, on the right, transmits to him the crown offered by Christ. The emperor grasps a sword in one hand, while in the other he holds a staff that touches the neck of one of the semi-prone figures beneath his feet.

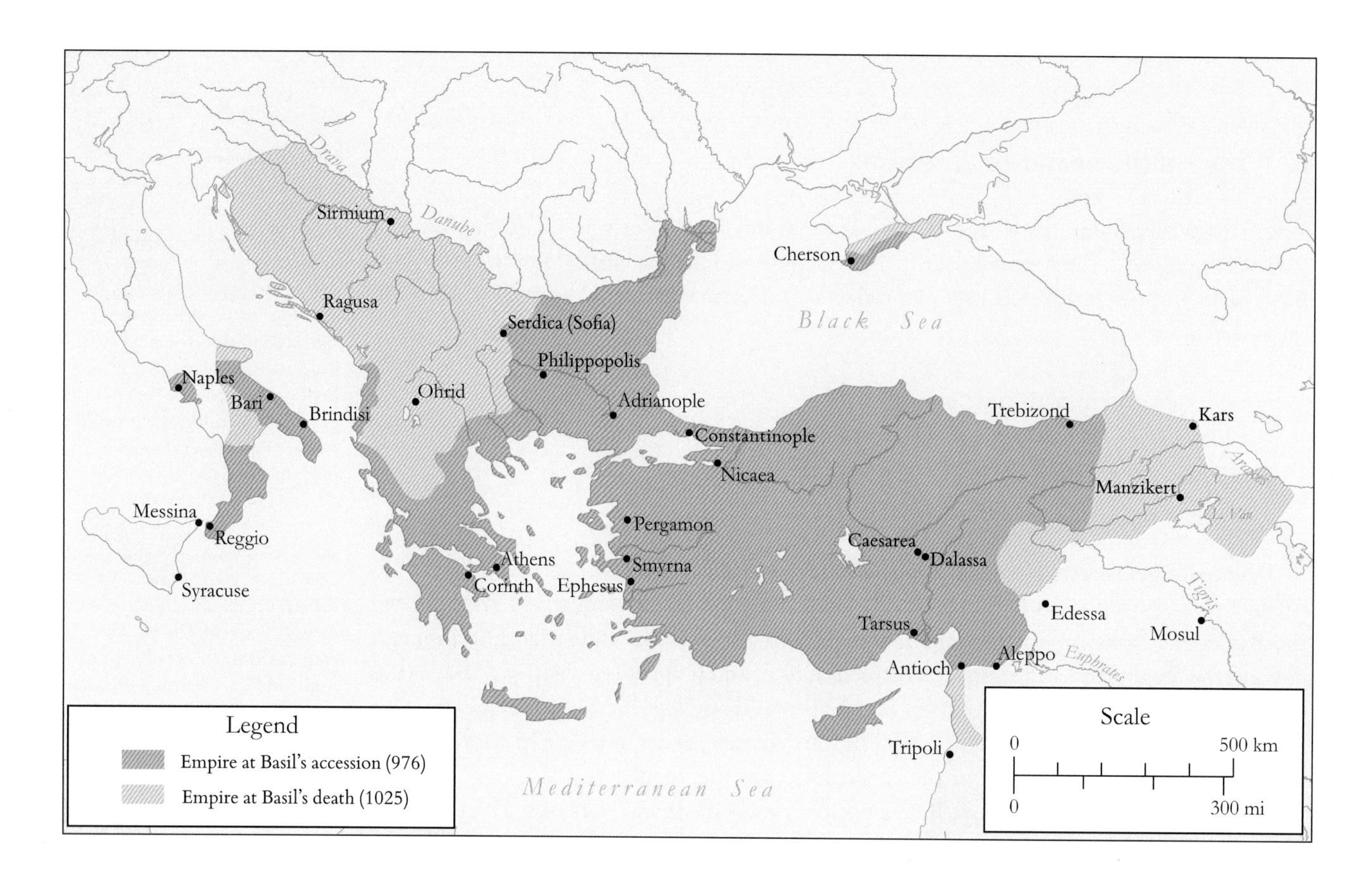

Map 4.2 The Byzantine Empire during the Reign of Basil II, 976–1025

others like it by threatening to confiscate and destroy the villas of those who transgressed the rules. He changed the system of taxation so that the burden fell on large landowners rather than on the peasants. He relieved the peasants and others of local military duty in the themes by asking for money payments instead. This allowed him to shower wealth on the Varangian Guard and other mercenary troops.

At the same time, Basil launched attacks beyond his borders: south to Syria and beyond; east all the way to Georgia and Armenia; southwest to southern Italy; and west to the Balkans, where he conquered the whole of the Bulgarian empire and reached the Adriatic coast. Basil's victory over the Bulgarians, celebrated on the psalter page shown in Plate 4.1, used to be considered his defining feat, and in the fourteenth century he was given the epithet "Bulgar-Slayer." But historians such as Michael Angold see Basil as an autocrat, ruling by whim and undermining hallowed Byzantine traditions. He never married or groomed a successor, which is one reason why Zoe and her sister could take the imperial throne after his death.

By the time of Basil's death in 1025, the Byzantine Empire was no longer the tight fist centered on Anatolia that it had been in the dark days of the eighth century. On the contrary, it was an open hand: sprawling, multi-ethnic, and multilingual. (See Map 4.2.) To the east it embraced Armenians, Syrians, and Arabs; to the north it included Slavs and Bulgarians (by now themselves Slavic speaking) as well as Pechenegs, a Turkic group that had served as allies of Bulgaria; to the west, in the Byzantine toe of Italy, it included

Lombards, Italians, and Greeks. There must have been Muslims right in the middle of Constantinople: a mosque there, built in the eighth century, was restored and reopened in the eleventh century. The Rus Varangian Guard served as the empire's elite troops, and by the mid-eleventh century, Byzantine mercenaries included "Franks" (mainly from Normandy), Arabs, and Bulgarians as well. In spite of ingrained prejudices, Byzantine princesses had occasionally been married to foreigners before the tenth century, but in Basil's reign this happened to a sister of the emperor himself.

All this openness went only so far, however. Toward the middle of the eleventh century, the Jews of Constantinople were expelled and resettled in a walled quarter in Pera, on the other side of the Golden Horn (see Map 4.1 on p. 114). Even though they did not expel Jews so dramatically, many other Byzantine cities forbade Jews from mixing with Christians. Around the same time, the rights of Jews as "Roman citizens" were denied; henceforth, in law at least, they had only servile status. The Jewish religion was condemned as a heresy.

Ethnic diversity and the emergence of the *dynatoi* were responsible for regional political movements that threatened centralized imperial control. In southern Italy, where the Byzantines ruled through an official called a catapan, Norman mercenaries hired themselves out to Lombard rebels, Muslim emirs, and others with local interests. In the second half of the eleventh century, the Normans began their own conquest of the region. On Byzantium's eastern flank, *dynatoi* families rose to high positions in government. The Dalasseni family was fairly typical of this group. Its founder, who took the family name from Dalassa, a city near Caesarea in Anatolia, was an army leader and governor of Antioch at the end of the tenth century. One of his sons, Theophylact, became governor of "Iberia"—not Spain but rather a theme on the very eastern edge of the empire. Another, Constantine, inherited his father's position at Antioch. With estates scattered throughout Anatolia and a network of connections to other powerful families, the Dalasseni sometimes defied the emperor and even coordinated rebellions against him. From the end of the tenth century, imperial control had to contend with the decentralizing forces of provincial *dynatoi* such as these. But the emperors were not dethroned, and Basil II triumphed over the families that challenged his reign to emerge even stronger than before.

The Formation of Rus'

Basil must have needed troops very badly to have married his sister to Vladimir (r.980–1015), ruler of Rus', in return for the Varangian Guard and Vladimir's conversion to Christianity. Known as Vikings in the West, the Rus originally came from Scandinavia. Well before the ninth century they had traveled eastward, to the regions of Lake Ladoga and Lake Ilmen (see Map 4.3 on p. 120). Mainly interested in trapping animals for furs and capturing people as slaves, they took advantage of river networks and other trade routes that led as far south as Iraq and as far west as Austria, exchanging their human and animal cargos for silks and silver. Other long-distance traders in the region were the Khazars, a Turkic-speaking people, whose powerful state, straddling the Black and Caspian Seas, dominated

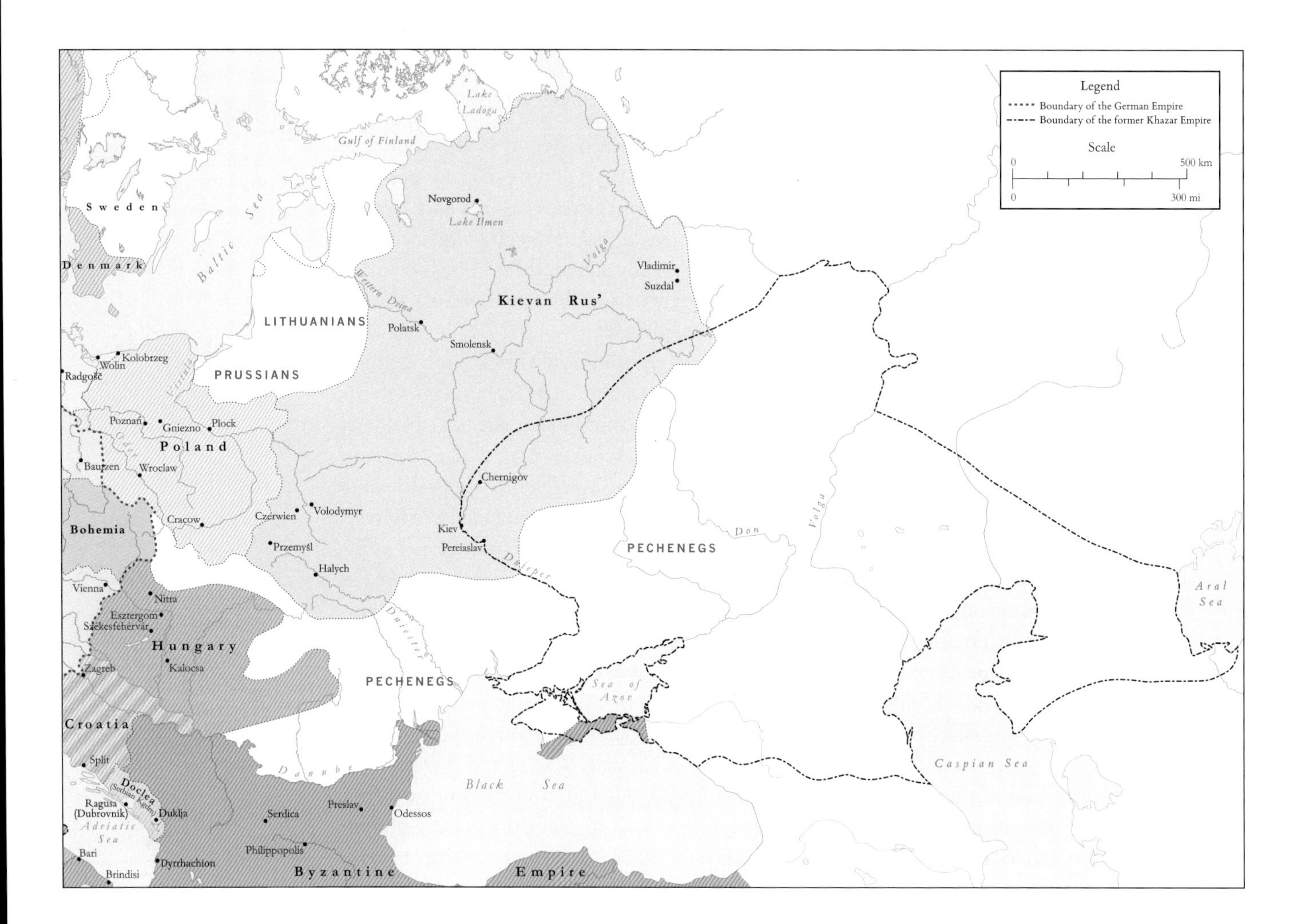

Map 4.3 Kievan Rus', *c.*1050

part of the silk road in the ninth century. The Khazars were ruled by a khagan (meaning khan of khans), much like the Avars, and, like other nomads of the Eurasian steppes, they were tempted and courted by the religions of neighboring states. Unusually, their elites opted for Judaism. The Rus were influenced enough by Khazar culture to adopt the title of khagan for the ruler of their own fledgling ninth-century state at Novgorod, the first Rus polity, but they did not embrace Judaism.

Soon northern Rus' had an affiliate in the south—in the region of Kiev. This was very close to the Khazars, to whom it is likely that the Kievan Rus at first paid tribute. While on occasion attacking both Khazars and Byzantines, Rus rulers saw their greatest advantage in good relations with the Byzantines, who wanted their fine furs, wax, honey, and—especially—slaves. In the course of the tenth century, with the blessing of the Byzantines, the Rus brought the Khazar Empire to its knees.

Nurtured through trade and military agreements, good relations between Rus' and Byzantium were sealed through religious conversion. In the mid-tenth century, quite a few Christians lived in Rus'. But the official conversion of the Rus to Christianity came under Vladimir. Ruler of Rus' by force of conquest (though from a princely family), Vladimir was anxious to court the elites of both Novgorod and Kiev. He did so through wars with surrounding peoples that brought him and his troops plunder and tribute. Strengthening his position still further, in 988 he adopted the Byzantine form of Christianity, took the name "Basil" in honor of Emperor Basil II, and married Anna, the emperor's sister. Christianization of the general population seems to have followed quickly. In any event, the *Russian Primary Chronicle*, a twelfth-century text based in part on earlier materials, reported that under Vladimir's son Yaroslav the Wise (r. 1019–1054), "the Christian faith was fruitful and multiplied, while the number of monks increased, and new monasteries came into being."[4]

Vladimir's conversion was part of a larger process of state formation and Christianization taking place around the year 1000. In Scandinavia and the new states of East Central Europe, as we shall see, the process resulted in Catholic kingships rather than the Orthodox principality that Rus' became. Given its geographic location, it was anyone's guess how Rus' would go: it might have converted to the Roman form of Christianity of its western neighbors. Or it might have turned to Judaism under the influence of the Khazars. Or, indeed, it might have adopted Islam, given that the Volga Bulgars had converted to Islam in the early tenth century. It is likely that Vladimir chose the Byzantine form of Christianity because of the prestige of the empire under Basil.

That momentary decision, it used to be argued, left lasting consequences: Rus', ancestor of Russia, became the heir of Byzantium and its many tensions with the West. Recently, however, some historians—Christian Raffensperger is one—have stressed the many interrelationships between Rus' and Europe. All shared the Christian religion, albeit in different forms; all were interconnected via traders and trade routes; and all were literally bound together through marriages. In that last sense, in particular, women were the bearers of cultural integration as they moved from one court to another.

DIVISION AND DEVELOPMENT IN THE ISLAMIC WORLD

While at Byzantium the forces of decentralization were relatively feeble, they carried the day in the Islamic world. Where once the caliph at Baghdad or Samarra could boast collecting taxes from Kabul (today in Afghanistan) to Benghazi (today in Libya), in the eleventh century a bewildering profusion of regional groups and dynasties divided the Islamic world. Yet this was in general a period of prosperity and intellectual blossoming.

The Emergence of Regional Powers

The Muslim conquest had not eliminated, but rather papered over, local powers and regional affiliations. While the Umayyad and Abbasid caliphates remained strong, they imposed their rule through their governors and army. But when the caliphate became weak, as it did in the tenth and eleventh centuries, old and new regional interests came to the fore.

A glance at a map of the Islamic world *c.*1000 (Map 4.4) shows, from east to west, the main new groups that emerged: the Samanids, Buyids, Hamdanids, Fatimids, and Zirids. But the map hides the many territories dominated by smaller independent rulers. North of the Fatimid Caliphate, al-Andalus had a parallel history. Its Umayyad ruler took the title of caliph in 929, but in the eleventh century he too was unable to stave off political fragmentation.

The key cause of the weakness of the Abbasid caliphate was lack of revenue. When landowners, governors, or recalcitrant military leaders in the various regions of the Islamic world refused to pay taxes into the treasury, the caliphs had to rely on the rich farmland of Iraq, long a stable source of income. But a deadly revolt lasting from 869 to 883 by the Zanj—black slaves from sub-Saharan Africa who had been put to work to turn marshes into farmland—devastated the Iraqi economy. Although the revolt was put down and the head of its leader was "displayed on a spear mounted in front of [the winning general] on a barge," there was no chance for the caliphate to recover.[5] In the tenth century the Qaramita (sometimes called "Carmathians"), a sect of Shiʿites based in Arabia, found Iraq easy prey. The result was decisive: the caliphs could not pay their troops. New men—military leaders with their own armies and titles like "commander of commanders"—took the reins of power. They preserved the Abbasid line, but they reduced the caliph's political authority to nothing.

Plate 4.2 Golden Jug (985–998). Four ribbons of angular kufic script praise the emir, probably the jug's owner. Complementing them are two large bands of interlaced medallions; those on the neck enclose what are probably griffons, while those on the body boast birds, perhaps peacocks.

The new rulers represented groups that had long awaited their ascendency. The Buyids, for example, belonged to ancient warrior tribes from the mountains of Iran. Even in the tenth century, most were relatively new converts to Islam. Bolstered by long-festering local discontent, one of them became "commander of commanders" in 945. Thereafter, the Buyids, with help from their own Turkish mercenaries, dominated the region south of the Caspian Sea, including Baghdad. For a time they presided over a glittering culture that supported (and was in turn celebrated by) scholars, poets, artists, and craftsman. Small wonder that the inscription decorating the golden jug in Plate 4.2 praises Emir Samsam al-Dawla (r.985–998) as "the image of the full moon at night, the first gleam of sun on the horizon of the morning."[6] Yet already in al-Dawla's day, other local men were challenging Buyid rule in a political process—the progressive regionalization and fragmentation of power—echoed elsewhere in the Islamic world and in much of Western Europe as well.

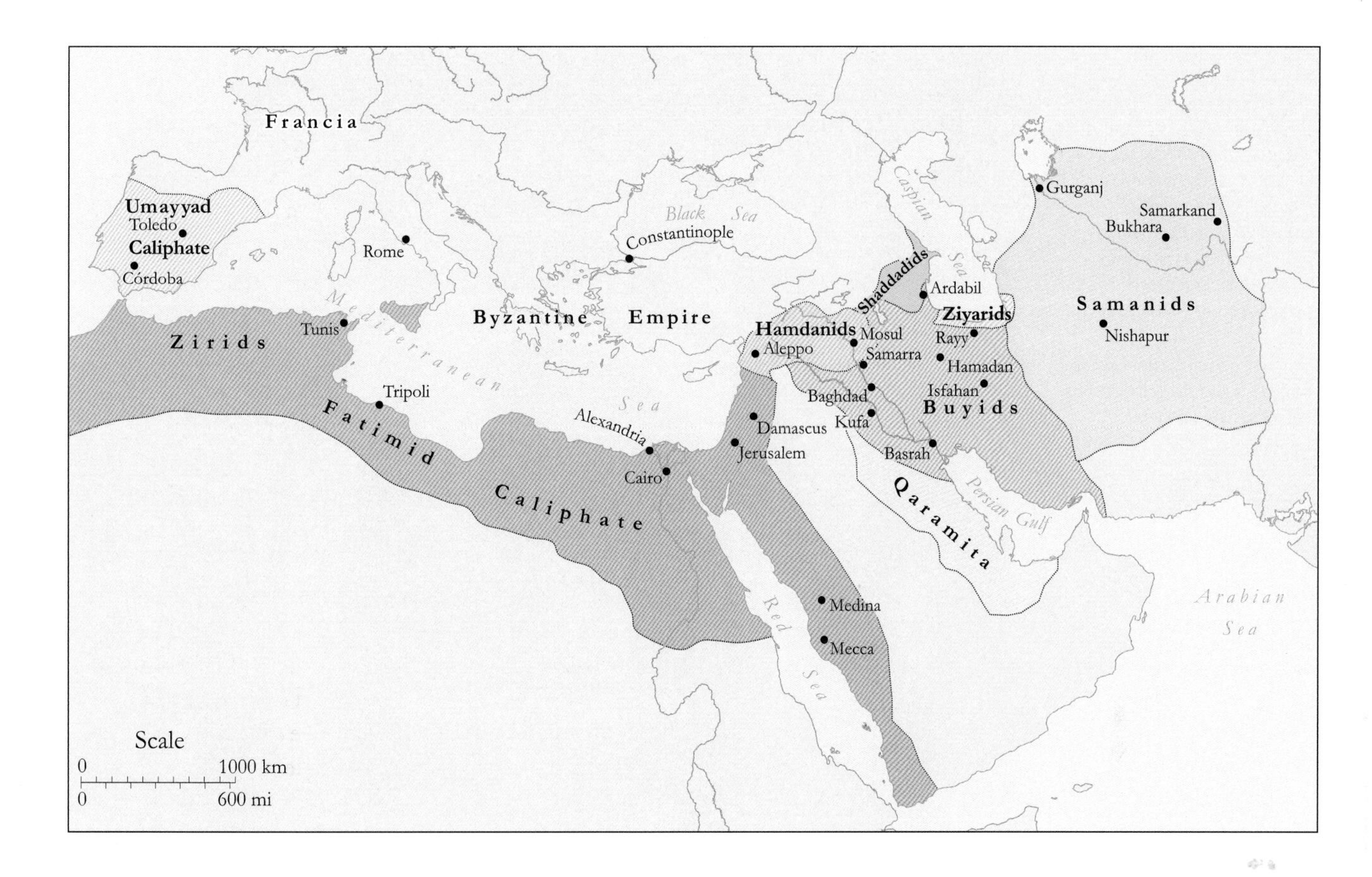

Map 4.4 Fragmentation of the Islamic World, *c.* 1000

The most important of the new regional rulers were the Fatimids. They, like the Qaramita (and, increasingly in the course of time, the Buyids), were Shi'ites, taking their name from Muhammad's daughter Fatimah, wife of Ali. The Fatimids professed a particular form of Shi'ism called Isma'ilism. The Fatimid leader claimed not only to be the true *imam*, descendant of Ali, but also the *mahdi*, the "divinely guided" messiah, come to bring justice on earth. Because of this, the Fatimids were proclaimed "caliphs" by their followers—the true "successors" of the Prophet. Allying with the Berbers in North Africa, by 910 the Fatimids had established themselves as rulers in what is today Tunisia and Libya. Within a half-century they had moved eastward (largely abandoning the Maghreb to the Zirids), to rule Egypt, southern Syria, and the western edge of the Arabian Peninsula. They cultivated contacts far beyond their borders: across the Mediterranean to Europe and Byzantium and beyond, to India and China. Jewish traders often served as the human links among these regions, as did Islamic religious scholars, who financed their many voyages to noted centers of learning by acting as merchants or mercantile agents. A flourishing textile industry kept Egypt's economy buoyant: farmers produced flax (not only for Egypt but for Tunisia and Sicily as well); industrial laborers turned the flax into linen; tailors cut and sewed garments; and traders exported the products of each phase or sold them at home. Public and private investment in both the agricultural and industrial side of this product guaranteed its success.

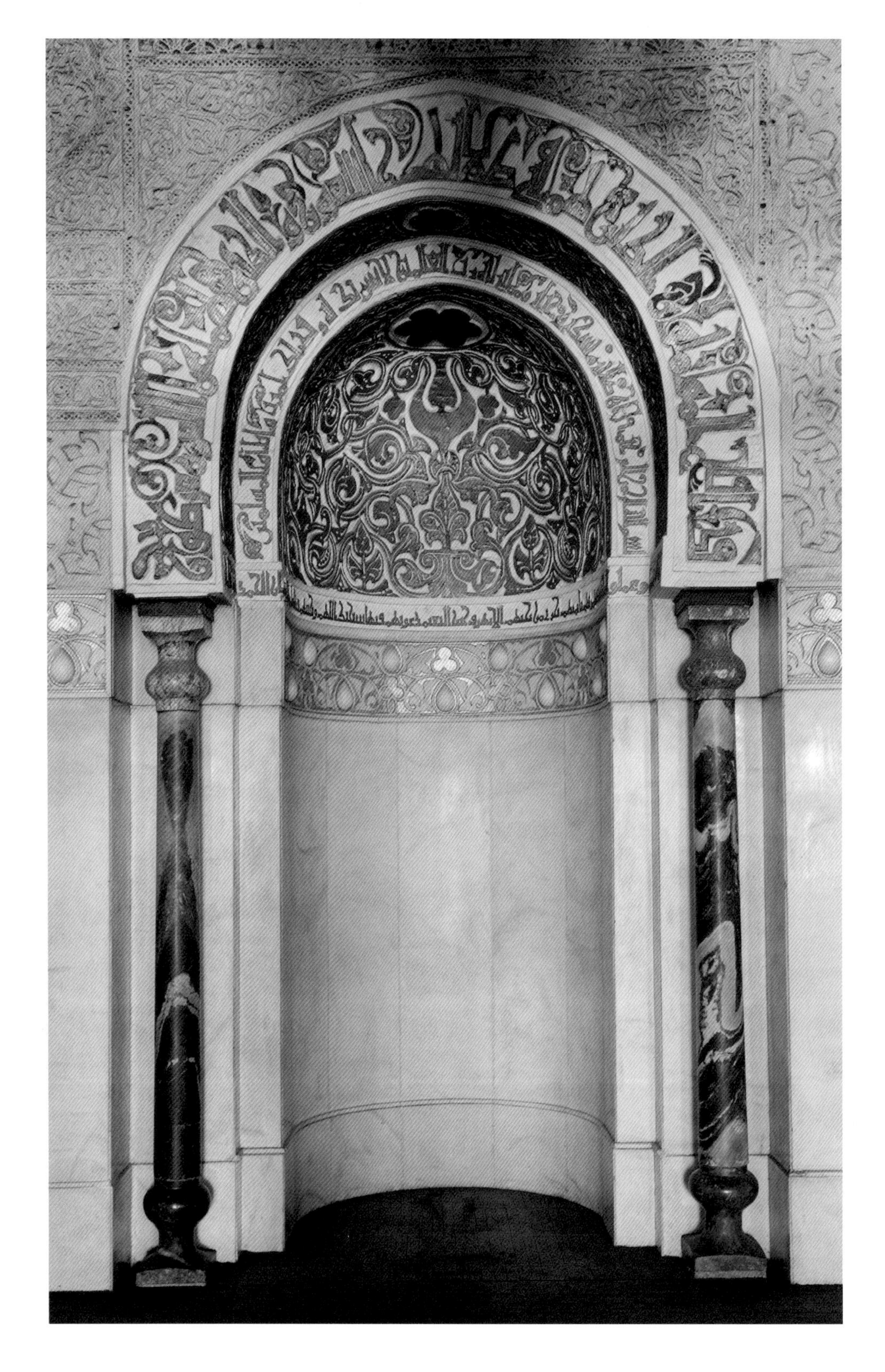

Plate 4.3 The *mihrab* of al-Azhar Mosque, Cairo (969/973). Two marble columns taken from older buildings frame the *mihrab*, which is decorated with carved stucco. As befits the purpose of the *mihrab*, the inscription quotes the Qur'an on prayer and the relationship between man and God.

Wealthy and cosmopolitan, the Fatimids created a new capital city, Cairo, filling it with palaces, libraries, shops, pavilions, gardens, private houses, and mosques. The al-Azhar mosque was built right after they conquered Egypt as a major gathering place and school. In its original form, it had a five-aisle prayer hall and a courtyard probably surrounded by arcades. Built in brick, its walls were covered with stucco carved with vegetal forms outlined by bands of Qur'anic inscriptions. The decoration was probably painted in bright colors. The *mihrab* (the niche pointing in the direction of Mecca) at al-Azhar was topped by a dome. (See Plate 4.3.) But the building had no minaret, following the Shi'ite practice of calling the congregation to prayer from the mosque door or roof.

The Shi'ites also emphasized commemoration of the dead (though Sunni Muslims often did so as well); a Fatimid cemetery at Aswan (see Plate 4.4) is filled with mudbrick tombs and mausolea (buildings for burials), each one originally containing one or more tombstones. Muhammad had prohibited ostentatious burials, but this ban was skirted as long as the tombs were open to the elements. That explains the many windows in the mausolea at Aswan.

The Fatimids achieved the height of their power before the mid-eleventh century. But during the rule of al-Mustansir (1036–1094), economic and climatic woes, factional fighting within the army, and a rebellion by Turkish troops weakened the regime, and by the 1070s, the Fatimid caliphate had lost most of Syria and North Africa to other rulers.

The Umayyad rulers at Córdoba experienced a similar rise and fall. Abd al-Rahman III (r.912–961) took the title caliph in 929 to rival the Fatimids and to assume the luster of the ruler of Baghdad. "He bore [signs of] piety on his forehead and religious and secular authority upon his right hand," wrote a court poet of the new caliph.[7] An active military man backed by an army made up mainly of Slavic slaves, Abd al-Rahman defeated his rivals and imposed his rule on all of al-Andalus. Under the new caliph and his immediate successors, Islamic Iberia became a powerful centralized state. Even so, regional elites sought to carve out their own polities. Between 1009 and 1031 bitter civil war undid the dynasty's power. After 1031, al-Andalus was split into small emirates called *taifas*, ruled by local strongmen.

Thus, in the Islamic world, far more decisively than at Byzantium, newly powerful regional rulers came to the fore. Nor did the fragmentation of power end at the regional level. To pay their armies, Islamic rulers often resorted to granting their commanders *iqta*—lands and villages—from which the *iqta*-holder was expected to gather revenues and pay their troops. As we shall see, this was a bit like the Western European institution of the fief. It meant that even minor commanders could act as local governors, tax-collectors, and military leaders. But there was a major difference between this institution and the system of fiefs and vassals in the West: while vassals were generally tied to one region and one lord, the troops under Islamic local commanders were often foreigners and former slaves, unconnected to any particular place and easily wooed by rival commanders.

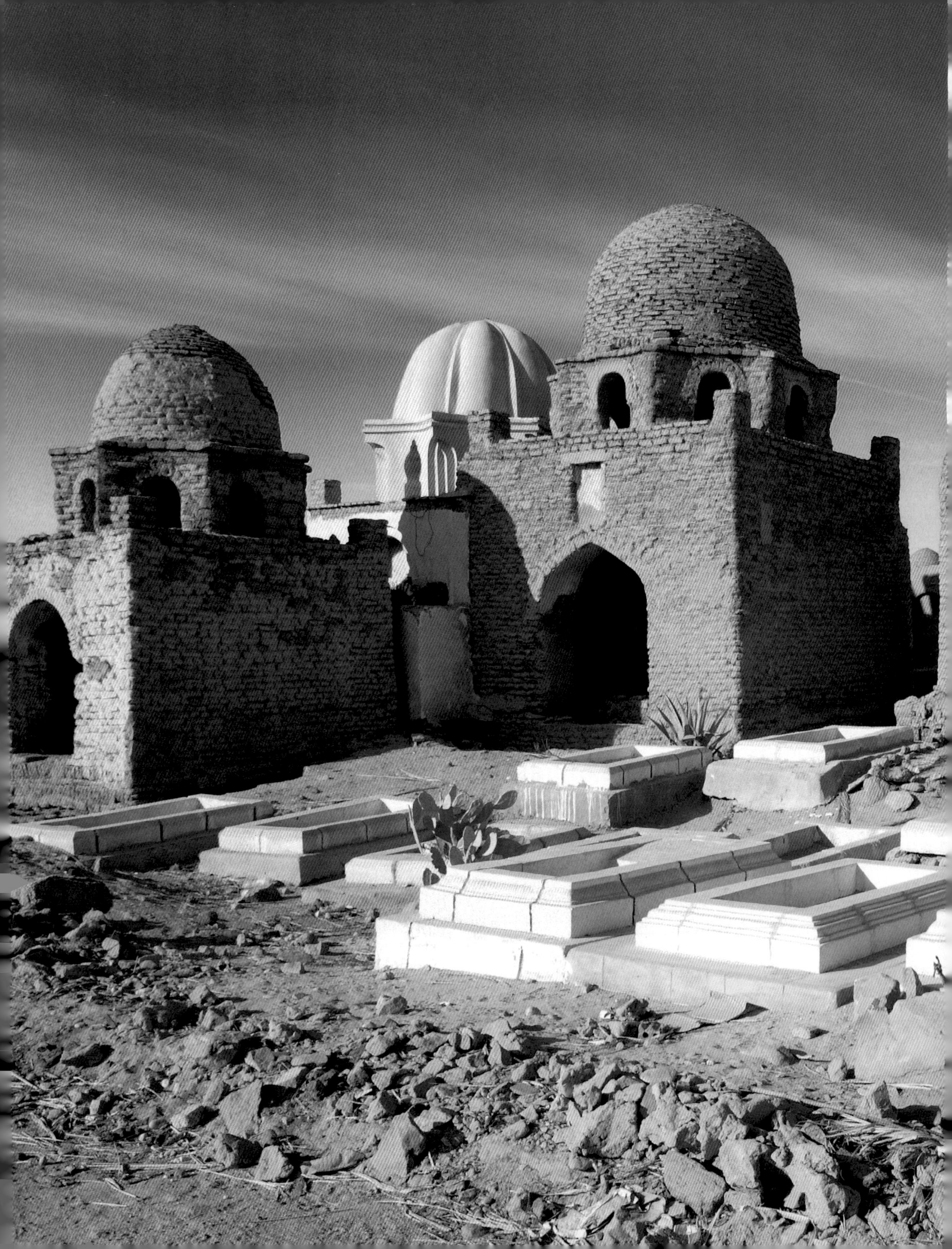

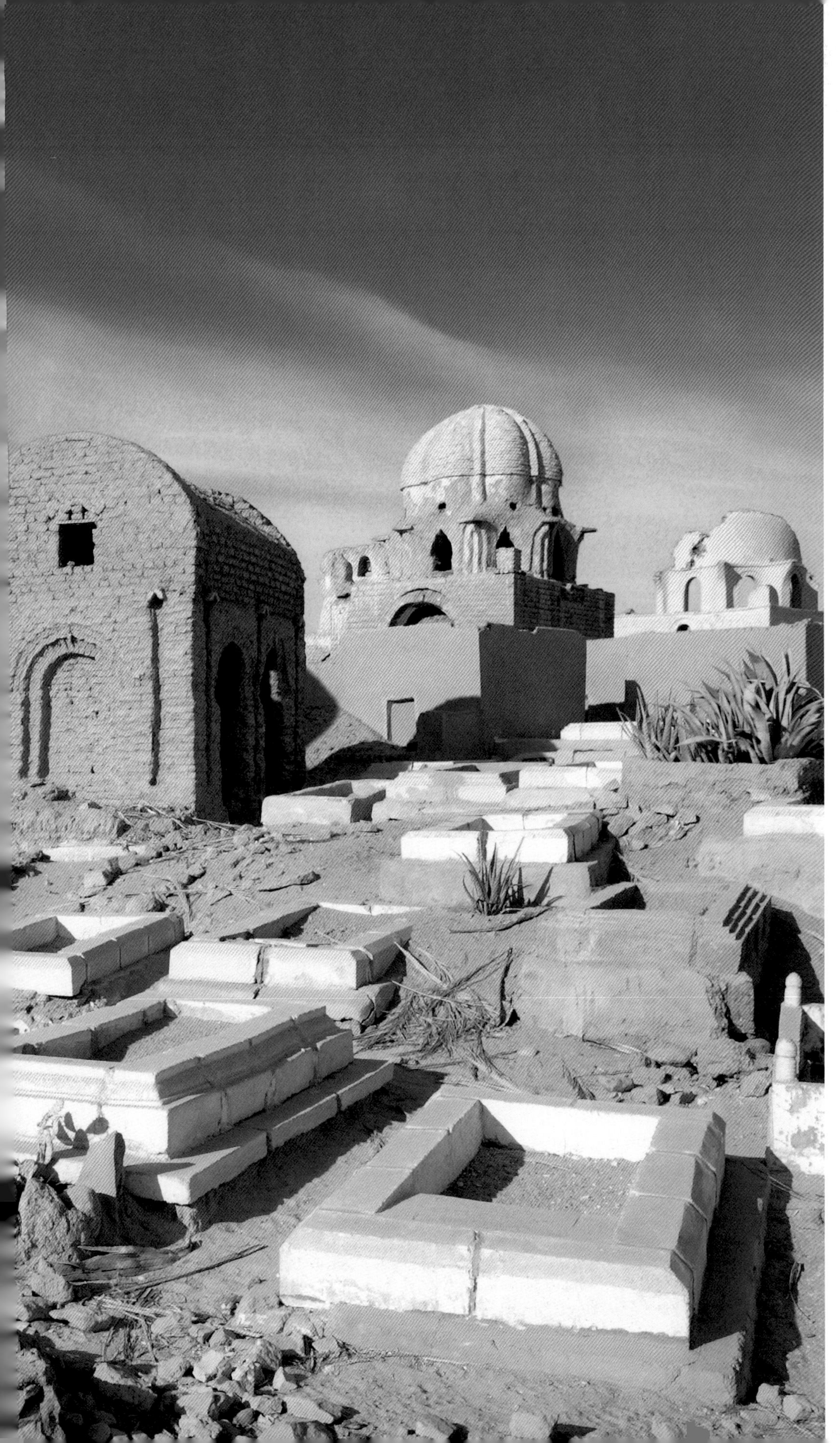

Plate 4.4 Fatimid Cemetery at Aswan (11th cent.). Outside of Cairo, an exuberant architectural imagination held sway. In this cemetery at Aswan, a series of mausolea with cubic bases topped by domes are particularly inventive in composing the zone that bridges dome and base: note here the octagonal structures with wing-like projections.

Cultural Unity, Religious Polarization

The emergence of local strongmen meant not the end of Arab court culture but a multiplicity of courts, each attempting to out-do one another in brilliant artistic, scientific, theological, and literary productions. We have already seen what the Fatimids achieved in Egypt. Even more impressive was the Umayyad court at Córdoba, the wealthiest and showiest city of the West. It boasted seventy public libraries in addition to the caliph's private library of perhaps 400,000 books. The Córdoban Great Mosque was a center for scholars from the rest of the Islamic world (the caliphs paid their salaries), while nearly thirty free schools were set up throughout the city.

Córdoba was noteworthy not only because of the brilliance of its intellectual life but also because of the role women played in it. Elsewhere in the Islamic world there were certainly a few unusual women associated with cultural and scholarly life. But at Córdoba this was a general phenomenon: women were not only doctors, teachers, and librarians but also worked as copyists for the many books widely in demand.

Male scholars were, however, everywhere the norm. They moved easily from court to court. The Fatimid scholar-merchants are barely known, but Ibn Sina (980–1037), who began his career serving the ruler at Bukhara in Central Asia, is famous. In the West, his name was Latinized as Avicenna. From Bukhara he traveled westward to Gurganj, Rayy, and Hamadan before ending up for thirteen years at the court of Isfahan in Iran. Sometimes in favor and sometimes decidedly not so (he was even briefly imprisoned), he nevertheless managed to study and practice medicine and to write numerous books on the natural sciences and philosophy. His pioneering systematization of Aristotle laid the foundations of future philosophical thought in the field of logic.

Despite its political disunity, then, the Islamic world of the tenth and eleventh centuries remained in many ways an integrated culture. This was partly due to the model of intellectual life fostered by the Abbasids, which even in decline was copied by the new regional rulers. It was also due to the common Arabic language, the glue that bound the astronomer at Córdoba to the merchant at Cairo.

Writing in Arabic, Islamic authors could count on a large reading public. Manuscripts were churned out quickly via a well-honed division of labor: scribes, illustrators, page cutters, and book-binders specialized in each task. Children were sent to school to learn the Qur'an; listening, reciting, reading, and writing were taught in elementary schools along with good manners and religious obligations. Although a conservative like al-Qabisi (d. 1012) warned that "[a girl] being taught letter-writing or poetry is a cause for fear," he also insisted that parents send their children to school to learn "vocalization, spelling, good handwriting, [and] good reading." He even admitted that learning about "famous men and of chivalrous knights" might be acceptable.[8]

Educated in similar texts across the whole Islamic world, speaking a common language, Muslims could easily communicate, and this facilitated open networks of trade. With no national barriers to commerce and few regulations, merchants regularly moved from one region to another. Consider paper. The sheets manufactured in Baghdad and Damascus were in demand across the entire Islamic world and beyond. Though scorned in Byzantium, paper was appreciated in peripheral regions of the Empire such as Armenia and Georgia. Indeed, Islamic merchants dealt in far-flung, various, and sometimes exotic goods. From England came tin, while salt, ivory, and gold were imported from Timbuktu in west-central Africa. From Russia came amber, gold, and copper; slaves were wrested from sub-Saharan Africa, the Eurasian steppes, and Slavic regions. Arab merchants set up permanent headquarters in China and South-East Asia, where traders brought wares from the Islamic world: flax and linen from Egypt (as we have seen), pearls from the Persian Gulf, ceramics from Iraq. Much of this trade was financed by enterprising government officials and other elites, whose investments in land at home paid off handsomely.

Although Muslims dominated these trade networks, other groups were involved in commerce as well. Thanks to the abundance of paper for everyday transactions, we know a good deal about one Jewish community living at Fustat, about two miles south of Cairo. It observed the then-common custom of depositing for eventual ritual burial all worn-out papers containing the name of God. For good measure, the Jews in this community included everything written in Hebrew letters: legal documents, fragments of sacred works, marriage contracts, doctors' prescriptions, and so on. By chance, the materials that they left in their *geniza* (depository) at Fustat were preserved rather than buried. They reveal a cosmopolitan, middle-class society. Many were traders, for Fustat was the center of a vast and predominately Jewish trade network that stretched from al-Andalus to India.

The Tustari brothers, Jewish merchants from southern Iran, offer a telling example. By the early eleventh century, the brothers had established a flourishing business in Egypt. Informal family networks offered them many of the same advantages as branch offices: friends and family in Iran shipped the Tustaris's fine textiles to sell in Egypt, while they exported Egyptian fabrics back to Iran.

Only Islam itself, ironically, pulled Islamic culture apart. In the tenth century the split between the Sunnis and Shi'ites widened to a chasm. At Baghdad, al-Mufid (d.1022) and others turned Shi'ism into a partisan ideology that insisted on publicly cursing the first two caliphs, turning the tombs of Ali and his family into objects of veneration, and creating an Alid caliph. Small wonder that the Abbasid caliphs soon became ardent spokesmen for Sunni Islam, which developed in turn its own public symbols. Many of the new dynasties—the Fatimids and the Qaramita especially—took advantage of the newly polarized faith to bolster their power.

THE WEST: FRAGMENTATION AND RESILIENCE

Fragmentation was the watchword in Western Europe in many parts of the shattered Carolingian Empire. Historians speak of "France," "Germany," and "Italy" in this period as a shorthand for designating broad geographical areas (as will be the case in this book). But there were no national states, only regions with more or less clear borders and rulers

Map 4.5 (facing page)
Viking, Muslim, and Hungarian Invasions, 9th and 10th cent.

with more or less authority. In some places—in parts of "France," for example—regions as small as a few square miles were under the control of different lords who acted, in effect, as independent rulers. Yet this same period saw consolidated European kingdoms beginning to emerge. To the north were England, Scotland, and two relatively unified Scandinavian states—Denmark and Norway; toward the east Bohemia, Poland, and Hungary. In the center of Europe, a powerful royal dynasty from Saxony, the Ottonians, came to rule an empire stretching from the North Sea to Rome.

The Last Invaders of the West

Three groups invaded Western Europe during the ninth and tenth centuries: the Vikings, the Muslims, and the Magyars (called Hungarians by the rest of Europe). (See Map 4.5.) In the short run, they wreaked havoc on land and people. In the long run, they were absorbed into the European population and became constituents of a newly prosperous and aggressive European civilization.

VIKINGS

Around the same time as they made forays eastward toward Novgorod, some Scandinavians were traveling to western shores. Their peregrinations were largely the result of the competition for power and wealth by kings and chieftains back home. In *Egil's Saga*, the core of which was composed in the Viking age though it was given written form only in the thirteenth century, King Harald Fairhair gave the chieftains "the options of entering his service or leaving the country, or a third choice of suffering hardship or paying with their lives."[9] Egil's family eventually fled to Iceland.

Wealth was obtained through plunder and gifts. The most precious and sought-after gifts were beautifully crafted and decorated jewelry made of gold and silver; weapons, too, well forged and ornamented, were highly prized (see Material Culture: Forging Medieval Swords, pp. 74–77). Chieftains fed their warrior followers' hunger for gifts by controlling nearby agricultural production, indigenous crafts, and long-distance trade. Some left home to fight for foreign kings; for example, Egil and his brother worked for English King Æthelstan (r.924–939) and shared in the fruits of his victories. Others raided under Viking leaders. This was the background to the "Viking invasions of Europe." Traveling in long, narrow, and shallow ships powered by wind and sails (see Plate 4.5 on pp. 132–33), the Vikings sailed down the coasts and rivers of France, England, Scotland, and Ireland, terrorizing not only the inhabitants but also the armies mustered to fight them: "Many a time an army was assembled to oppose them, but as soon as they were to join battle, always for some cause it was agreed to disperse, and always in the end [the Vikings] had the victory," wrote a chronicler in southern England.[10]

Some Vikings, like Egil's family, crossed the Atlantic, making themselves at home in Iceland or continuing on to Greenland or, in about 1000, touching on the coast of the North

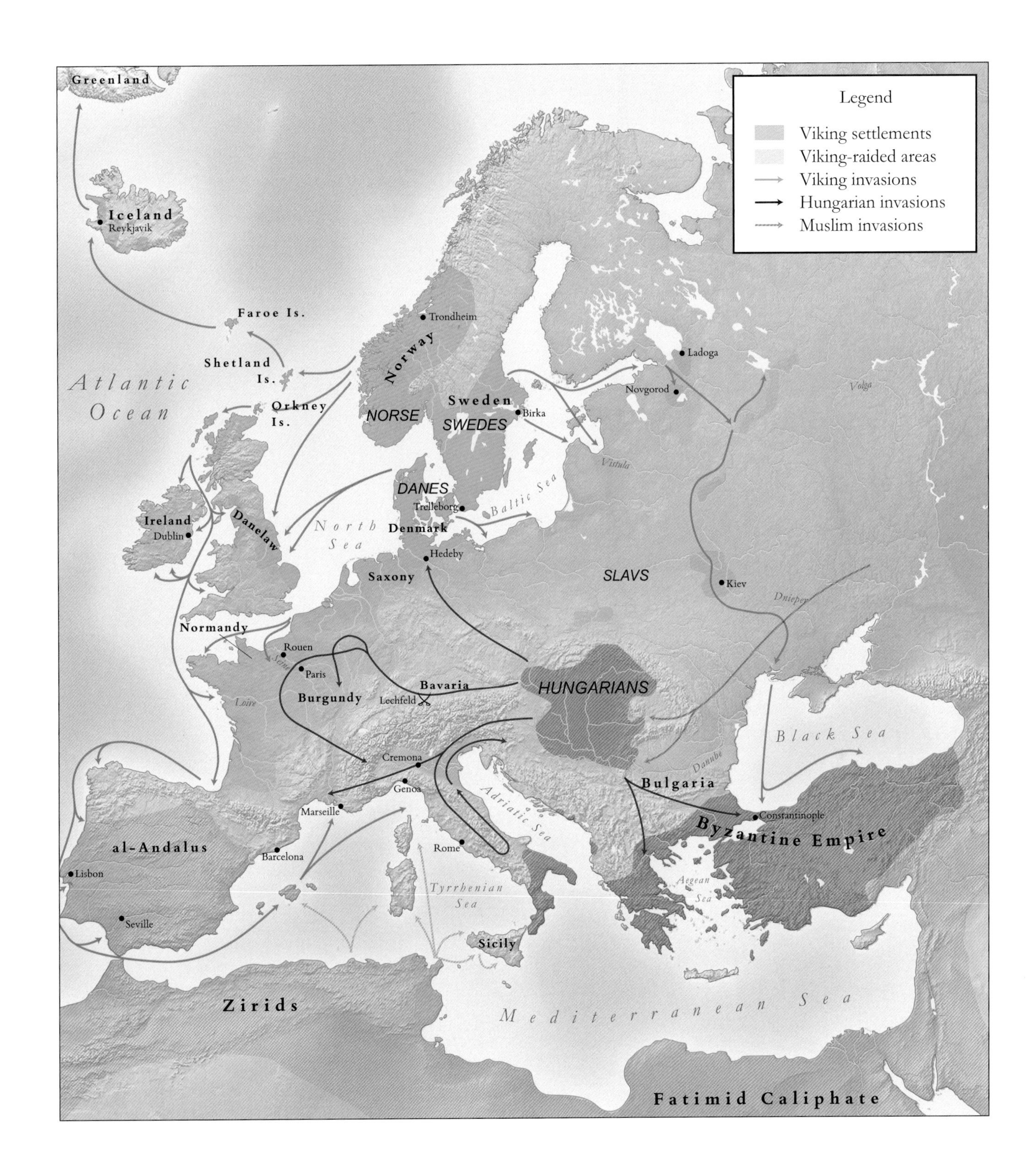
Legend
Viking settlements
Viking-raided areas
Viking invasions
Hungarian invasions
Muslim invasions
Greenland
Iceland
Reykjavik
Faroe Is.
Shetland Is.
Orkney Is.
Atlantic Ocean
Trondheim
Norway
NORSE
Sweden
SWEDES
Birka
Ladoga
Novgorod
Volga
Vistula
DANES
Trelleborg
Baltic Sea
North Sea
Denmark
Hedeby
Saxony
Ireland
Dublin
Danelaw
SLAVS
Kiev
Dnieper
Normandy
Rouen
Seine
Paris
Loire
Bavaria
Burgundy
Lechfeld
HUNGARIANS
Cremona
Genoa
Marseille
Barcelona
Rome
Adriatic Sea
Danube
Bulgaria
Black Sea
Constantinople
Byzantine Empire
al-Andalus
Lisbon
Seville
Tyrrhenian Sea
Aegean Sea
Sicily
Zirids
Mediterranean Sea
Fatimid Caliphate

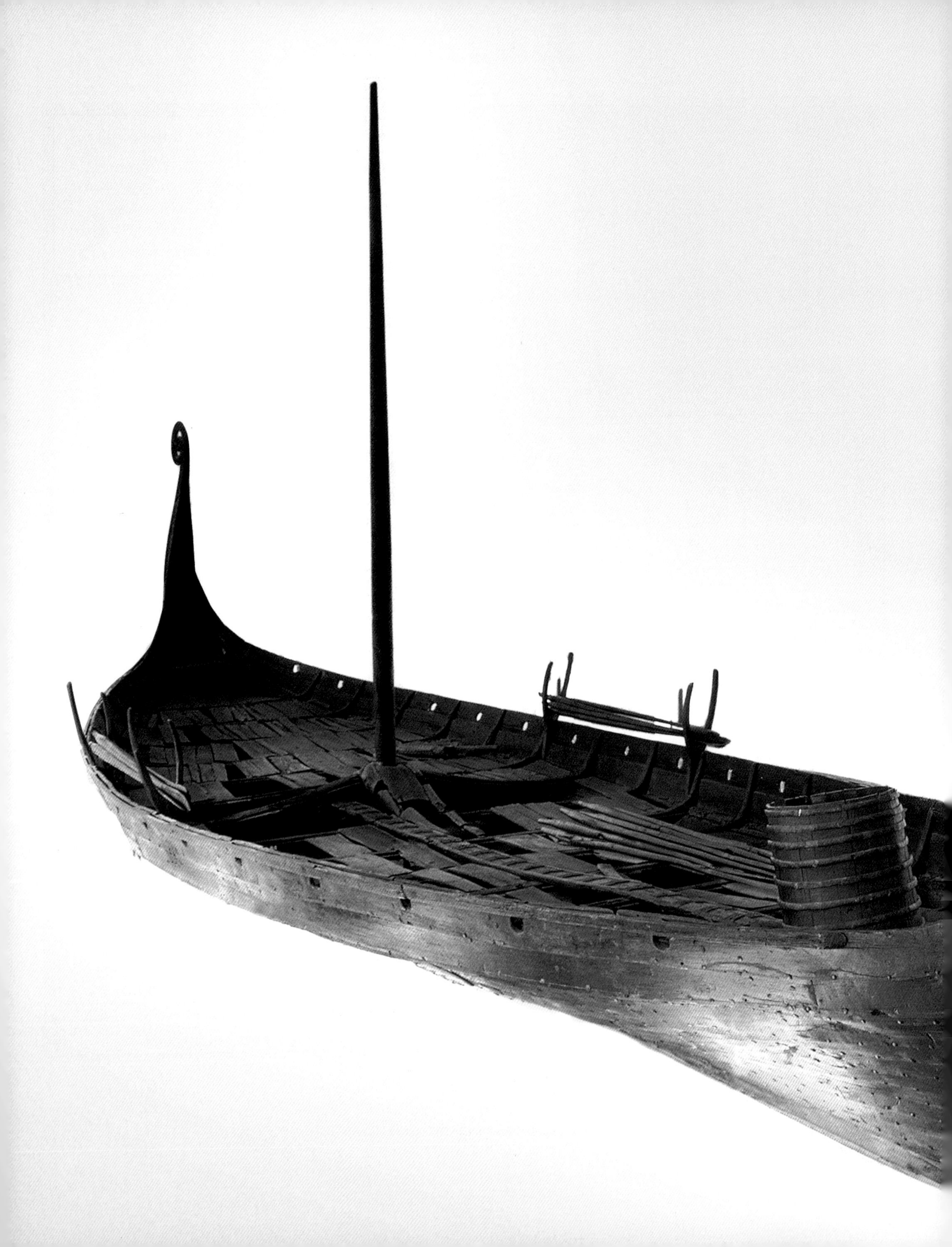

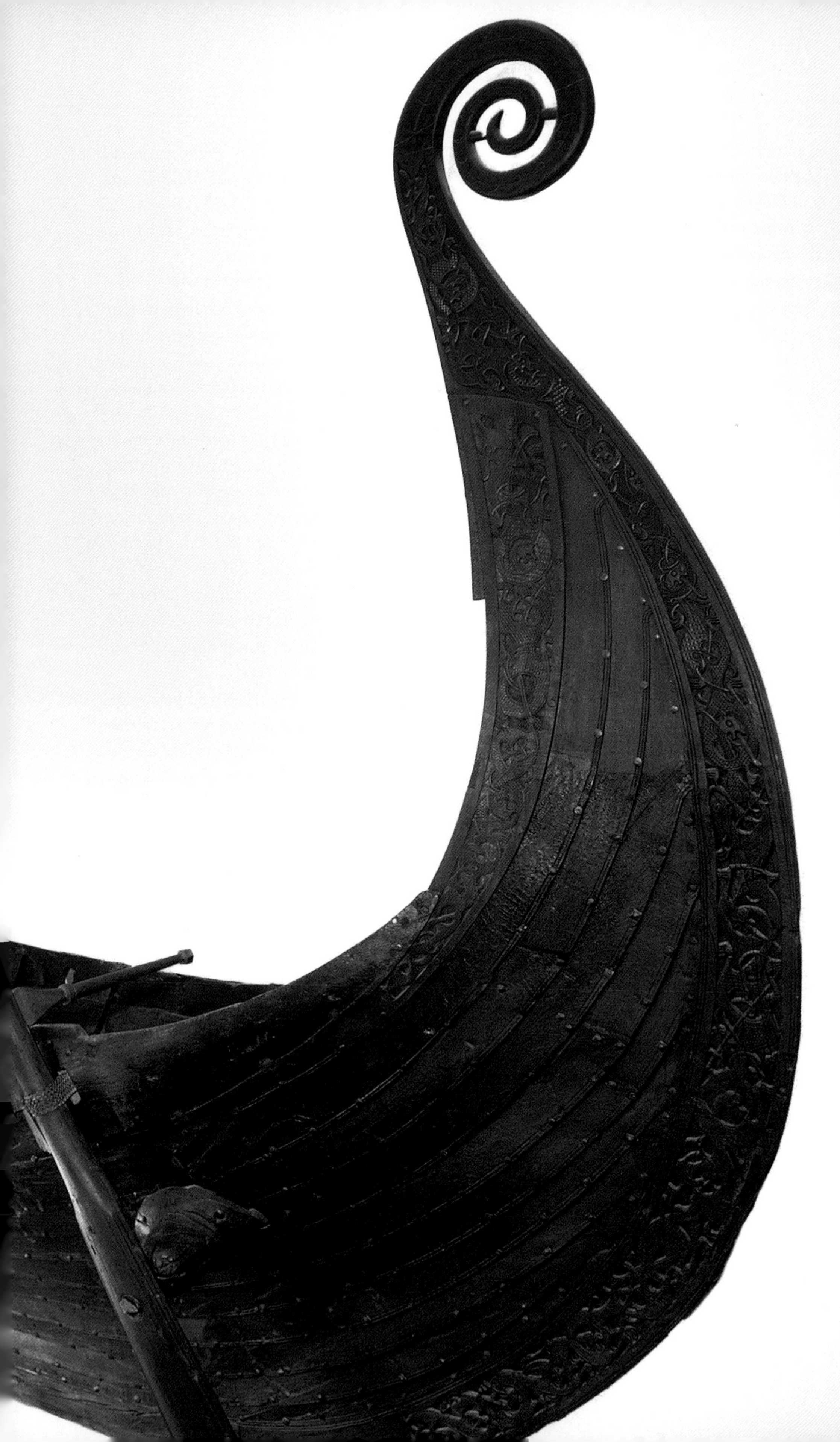

Plate 4.5 Oseberg Ship (834). This large ceremonial ship was found buried in a grave mound near the Oslo fjord in 1904. Within were the skeletons of two women, one more than eighty years old, the other in her early fifties. They were accompanied by high-quality artifacts, delicate foods (such as fruits, berries, and walnuts), and many animals and birds. Wooden carvings, including those of the ship's prow and stern-post, attest to the intricacy and finesse of Viking workmanship, characterized by interlaced animal motifs. Compare this interlace with the more abstract forms of the Lindisfarne Gospels in Plates 2.5, 2.6, and 2.7.

American mainland. While the elites came largely for booty, lesser men, eager for land, traveled with their wives and children to live after conquests in Ireland, Scotland, England, and Normandy (giving their name to the region: Norman = Northman, or Viking).

In Ireland, where their settlements were in the east and south, the newcomers added their own claims to rule an island already fragmented among several competing dynasties. In Scotland, however, in the face of Norse settlements in the north and west, the natives drew together under kings who allied themselves with churchmen and other powerful local leaders. Cináed mac Ailpín (Kenneth I MacAlpin) (d.858) established a hereditary dynasty of kings that ruled over two hitherto independent native peoples. By *c*.900, the separate identities were gone, and most people in *Alba*, the nucleus of the future Scotland, shared a common sense of being Scottish.

England underwent a similar process of unification. Initially divided into small competing kingdoms, it was weak prey in the face of invasion. By the end of the ninth century, the Vikings were plowing fields in northeastern England and living in accordance with their own laws, giving the region the name Danelaw. In Wessex, the southernmost English kingdom, King Alfred the Great (r.871–899) bought time and peace by paying tribute to the invaders with the income from a new tax, later called the Danegeld. (It eventually became the basis of a relatively lucrative taxation system in England.) In 878 he led a series of raids against the Vikings settled in his kingdom, inspired the previously cowed Anglo-Saxons to follow him, and camped outside the Viking stronghold until their leaders surrendered and accepted baptism. Soon the Vikings left Wessex.

Thereafter the pressure of invasion eased somewhat as Alfred reorganized his army, set up strongholds of his own (called *burhs*), and created a fleet of ships—a real navy. An uneasy stability was achieved, with the Vikings dominating the east of England and Alfred and his successors gaining control over most of the rest. Even so, the impact of the Vikings on the formation of Anglo-Saxon England has recently been downplayed, and Alfred's role has been somewhat minimized by historians such as George Molyneaux, who sees the real unification of England taking place via the administrative structures put into place in the second half of the tenth century.

On the Continent, the invaders were absorbed above all in Normandy, where in 911 their leader Rollo converted to Christianity and received Normandy as a duchy from the Frankish king Charles the Simple. Although many of the Normans adopted sedentary ways, some of their descendants in the early eleventh century ventured to the Mediterranean, where they established themselves as rulers of petty principalities in southern Italy. From there, in 1061, the Normans began the conquest of Sicily.

MUSLIMS

Sicily, once Byzantine, was the rich and fertile plum of the conquests achieved by the Muslim invaders of the ninth and tenth centuries. That they took the island attests to the power of a new Muslim navy developed by the dynasty that preceded the Fatimids in Ifriqiya. Briefly held by the Fatimids, by mid-century Sicily was under the control of independent Islamic princes, and Muslim immigrants were swelling the population.

Elsewhere the Muslim presence in Western Europe was more ephemeral. In the first half of the tenth century, Muslim raiders pillaged southern France, northern Italy, and the Alpine passes. But these were quick expeditions, largely attacks on churches and monasteries. Some Muslims established themselves at La Garde-Freinet, in Provence, becoming landowners in the region and lords of Christian serfs. They even hired themselves out as occasional fighters for the wars that local Christian aristocrats were waging against one another. But they made the mistake of capturing for ransom the holiest man of his era, Abbot Majolus of Cluny (*c.*906–994). Outraged, the local aristocracy finally came together and ousted the Muslims from their midst.

MAGYARS (HUNGARIANS)

By contrast, the Magyars remained. "Magyar" was and remains their name for themselves, though the rest of Europe called them "Hungarians," from the Slavonic for "Onogurs," a people already settled in the Danube basin in the eighth and ninth centuries. Originally nomads who raised (and rode) horses, the Magyars spoke a language unrelated to any other in Europe (except Finnish). Known as effective warriors, they were employed by Arnulf, king of the East Franks (r.887–899), when he fought the Moravians and by the Byzantine emperor Leo VI (r.886–912) during his struggle against the Bulgars. In 894, taking advantage of their position, the Hungarians, as we may now call them, conquered much of the Danube basin for themselves.

From there, for over fifty years, they raided into Germany, Italy, and even southern France. At the same time, however, the Hungarians worked for various western rulers. Until 937 they spared Bavaria, for example, because they were allies of its duke. Gradually they made the transition from nomads to farmers, and their polity coalesced into the Kingdom of Hungary. This is no doubt a major reason for the end of their attacks. At the time, however, the cessation of their raids was widely credited to the German king Otto I (r.936–973), who won a major victory over a Hungarian marauding party at the battle of Lechfeld in 955.

Public Power and Private Relationships

The invasions left new political arrangements in their wake. Unlike the Byzantines and Muslims, European rulers had no mercenaries and no salaried officials. They commanded others by ensuring personal loyalty. The Carolingian kings had had their *fideles*—their faithful men. Tenth-century rulers were even more dependent on ties of dependency: they needed their "men" (*homines*), their "vassals" (*vassalli*). Whatever the term, all were armed retainers who fought for a lord. Sometimes these subordinates held land from their lord, either as a reward for their military service or as an inheritance for which services were due. The term for such an estate, fief (*feodum*), gave historians the word "feudalism" to describe the social and economic system created by the relationships among lords, vassals, and fiefs. During the last forty years or so, however, the term has provoked great controversy. Some historians argue that it has been used in too many different and contradictory ways to mean anything at all. Was it a mode of exploiting the land that involved lords and serfs? A condition of anarchy and lawlessness? Or a political system of ordered gradations of power, from the king on down? Historians have used all of these definitions. Another area of contention is the date for the emergence of feudal institutions. At the beginning of the 1970s, the French historian Georges Duby assigned an early date: around the year 1000. His view prevailed for two decades, but in the 1990s it was forcefully challenged by Dominique Barthélemy, who argued that the major transformation took place in the twelfth century. In this book the *word* feudalism is avoided, but the institutions that historians associate with that term cannot be ignored. Their origins (where they took hold) are to be found in the break-up of the Carolingian order—the tenth and eleventh centuries.

LORDS AND VASSALS

The key to tenth- and eleventh-century society was personal dependency. This took many forms. Of the three traditional "orders" recognized by writers in the ninth through eleventh centuries—those who pray (the *oratores*), those who fight (the *bellatores*), and those who work (the *laboratores*)—the top two were free. The pray-ers (the monks) and the fighters (the nobles and their lower-class counterparts, the knights) participated in prestigious kinds of subordination, whether as vassals, lords, or both. Indeed, they were usually both: a typical warrior was lord of several vassals and the vassal of another lord. Monasteries normally had vassals to fight for them, while their abbots in turn were vassals of a king or other lord. At the low end of the social scale, poor vassals looked to their lords to feed, clothe, house, and arm them. At the upper end, vassals looked to their lords to enrich them with still more fiefs.

Some women were vassals, and some were lords (or, rather, "ladies," the female version). Many upper-class laywomen participated in the society of warriors and monks as wives and mothers of vassals and lords and as landowners in their own right. Others entered convents and became *oratores* themselves. Through its abbess or a man standing in for her, a convent was itself often the "lord" of vassals.

Vassalage was voluntary and public. The personal fidelity that the Carolingian kings required of the Frankish elites became more general, as all lords wanted the same assurance. Over time a ceremony of deference came increasingly to mark the occasion: a man kneeled and placed his hands together (in a position we associate with prayer) within the hands of another who stood: this was the act of homage. It generally included an oath: "I promise to be your man." The vassal-to-be then rose and promised "fealty"—fidelity, trust, and service—which he swore with his hand on relics or a Bible. Then the vassal and the lord kissed. In an age when many people could not read, a public moment such as this represented a visual and verbal contract, binding the vassal and lord together with mutual obligations to help each other. On the other hand, these obligations were rarely spelled out, and a lord with many vassals, or a vassal with many lords, needed to satisfy numerous conflicting claims. "I am a loser only because of my loyalty to you," Hugh of Lusignan told his lord, William of Aquitaine, after his expectations for reward were continually disappointed.[11]

LORDS AND PEASANTS

At the lowest end of the social scale were those who worked: the peasants. In many regions of Europe, as power fell into the hands of local rulers, the distinction between "free" and "unfree" peasants began to blur; many peasants simply became "serfs," dependents of lords. This was a heavy dependency, without prestige or honor. It was hereditary rather than voluntary: no serf did homage or fealty to his lord; no serf and lord kissed each other.

Indeed, the upper classes barely noticed the peasants—except as sources of labor and revenue. In the tenth century, the three-field system became more prevalent, and the heavy moldboard plows that could turn wet, clayey northern soils came into wider use. Such plows could not work around fences, and they were hard to turn: thus was produced the characteristic "look" of medieval agriculture—long, furrowed strips in broad, open fields. Peasants knew very well which strips were "theirs" and which belonged to their neighbors. A team of oxen was normally used to pull the plow, but horses (more efficient than oxen) were sometimes substituted. The result was surplus food and a better standard of living for nearly everyone.

In search of still greater profits, some lords lightened the dues and services of peasants temporarily to allow them to open up new lands by draining marshes and cutting down forests. Other lords converted dues and labor services into money payments, providing themselves with ready cash. Peasants, too, benefited from these rents because their payments were fixed despite inflation. As the prices of agricultural products went up, peasants became small-scale entrepreneurs, selling their chickens and eggs at local markets and reaping a profit.

In the eleventh century, and increasingly so in the twelfth, peasant settlements gained boundaries and focus: they became real villages. The parish church often formed the center, next to which was the cemetery. Then, normally crowded right onto the cemetery itself, were the houses, barns, animals, and tools of the living peasants. Boundary markers—sometimes simple stones, at other times real fortifications—announced not only the physical limit of the village but also its sense of community. This derived from very practical concerns: peasants needed to share oxen or horses to pull their plows; they were all dependent on the village craftsmen to fix their wheels or shoe their horses.

Variety was the hallmark of peasant society. In Saxony and other parts of Germany free peasants prevailed. In France and England most were serfs. In Italy peasants ranged from small independent landowners to leaseholders; most were both, owning a parcel in one place and leasing another nearby.

Where the power of kings was weak, peasant obligations became part of a larger system of local rule. As landlords consolidated their power over their manors, they collected not only dues and services but also fees for the use of their flour mills, bake houses, and breweries. In some regions—parts of France and in Catalonia, for example—some lords built castles and exercised the power of the "ban": the right to collect taxes, hear court cases, levy fines, and muster men for defense. These lords were "castellans."

WARRIORS AND BISHOPS

Although the developments described here did not occur everywhere simultaneously (and in some places hardly at all), in the end the social, political, and cultural life of the West came to be dominated by landowners who styled themselves both military men and regional leaders. These men and their armed retainers shared a common lifestyle, living together, eating in the lord's great hall, listening to bards sing of military exploits, hunting for recreation, competing with one another in military games. They fought in groups as well—as cavalry. In the month of May, when the grasses were high enough for their horses to forage, the war season began. To be sure, there were powerful vassals who lived on their own fiefs and hardly ever saw their lord—except for perhaps forty days out of the year, when they owed him military service. But they themselves were lords of knightly vassals who were not married and who lived and ate and hunted with them.

The marriage bed, so important to the medieval aristocracy from the start, now took on new meaning. In the seventh and eighth centuries, aristocratic families had thought of themselves as large and loosely organized kin groups. They were not tied to any particular estate, for they had numerous estates, scattered all about. With wealth enough to go around, the rich practiced partible inheritance, giving land (though not in equal amounts) to all of their sons and daughters. The Carolingians "politicized" these family relations. As some men were elevated to positions of dazzling power, they took the opportunity to pick and choose their "family members," narrowing the family circle. They also became more conscious of their male line, favoring sons over daughters. In the eleventh century, family definitions tightened even further. The claims of one son, often the eldest, overrode all else; to him went the family inheritance. (This is called "primogeniture"; but there were regions in which the youngest son was privileged, and there were also areas in which more equitable inheritance practices continued in place.) The heir in the new system traced his lineage only through the male line, backward through his father and forward through his own eldest son.

What happened to the other sons? Some of them became knights, others monks. Nor should we forget that many became bishops. In many ways, the interests of bishops and lay nobles were similar: bishops were men of property, lords of vassals, and faithful to patrons, such as kings, who often were the ones to appoint them to their posts. In some places, bishops wielded the powers of a count or duke. Some bishops ruled cities. Nevertheless, bishops were also "pastors," spiritual leaders charged with shepherding their flock, which included the laity, priests, and monks in their diocese (a district that gained clear definition in the eleventh century).

As episcopal power expanded and was clarified in the course of the tenth and eleventh centuries, some bishops in southern France, joined by the upper crust of the aristocracy, sought to control the behavior of the lesser knights through a movement called the "Peace of God." They were not satisfied with the current practices of peace-making, in which enemies, pressured by their peers, negotiated an end to—or at least a cessation of—hostilities. (Behind the negotiation was the threat of an ordeal—for instance a trial by battle whose outcome was in the hands of God—if the two sides did not come to terms.) This system of arbitration was not always satisfactory. Hugh of Lusignan, a discontented vassal, complained that his lord "[did not] broker a good agreement." The Peace movement began in 989 and grew apace, its forum the regional church council, where bishops galvanized popular opinion, attracting both grand aristocrats and peasants to their gatherings. There, drawing upon bits and pieces of defunct Carolingian legislation, the bishops declared the Peace, and knights took oaths to observe it. At Bourges a particularly enthusiastic archbishop took the oath himself: "I Aimon ... will wholeheartedly attack those who steal ecclesiastical property, those who provoke pillage, those who oppress monks, nuns, and clerics."[12] In the Truce of God, which by the 1040s was declared alongside the Peace, warfare between armed men was prohibited from Lent to Easter, while at other times of the year it was forbidden on Sunday (because that was the Lord's Day), on Saturday (because that was a reminder of Holy Saturday), on Friday (because it symbolized Good Friday), and on Thursday (because it stood for Holy Thursday).

To the bishops who promulgated the Peace, warriors fell conceptually into two groups: the sinful ones who broke the Peace, and the righteous ones who upheld church law. Although the Peace and Truce were taken up by powerful lay rulers, eager to sanctify their own warfare and control that of others, the major initiative for the movement came from churchmen eager to draw clear boundaries between the realms of the sacred and the profane.

CITIES AND MERCHANTS

These clerics were, in part, reacting to new developments in the secular realm: the growing importance of urban institutions and professions. Though much of Europe was rural, there were important exceptions. Italy was one place where urban life, though dramatically reduced in size and population, persisted. In Italy, the power structure still reflected, if feebly, the political organization of ancient Rome. Whereas in northern France great lords built their castles in the countryside, in Italy they often constructed their family seats within the walls of cities. From these perches the nobles, both lay and religious, dominated the *contado*, the rural area around the city.

In Italy, most peasants were renters, paying cash to urban landowners. Peasants depended on city markets to sell their surplus goods; their customers included bishops,

Map 4.6 (facing page) Europe, *c.*1050

nobles, and middle-class shopkeepers, artisans, and merchants. At Milan, for example, the merchants were prosperous enough to own houses in both the city center and the *contado*.

Rome, although exceptional in size, was in some ways a typical Italian city. Large and powerful families built their castles within its walls and controlled the churches and monasteries in the vicinity. The population depended on local producers for their food, and merchants brought their wares to sell within its walls. Yet Rome was special apart from its size: it was the "see"—the seat—of the pope, the most important bishop in the West. In the tenth and early eleventh centuries, the papacy did not control the church, but it had great prestige, and powerful families at Rome fought to place one of their sons at its head.

Outside Italy cities were less prevalent. Yet even so we can see the rise of a new mercantile class. This was true less in the heartland of the old Carolingian Empire than on its fringes. In the north, England, northern Germany, Denmark, and the Low Countries bathed in a sea of silver coins; commercial centers such as Haithabu reached their grandest extent in the mid-tenth century. Here merchants bought and sold slaves, honey, furs, wax, and pirates' plunder. Haithabu was a city of wood, but a very rich one indeed.

In the south of Europe, beyond the Pyrenees, Catalonia was equally commercialized, but in a different way. It imitated the Islamic world of al-Andalus (which was, in effect, in its backyard). The counts of Barcelona minted gold coins just like those at Córdoba. The villagers around Barcelona soon got used to selling their wares for money, and some of them became prosperous. They married into the aristocracy, moved to Barcelona to become city leaders, and lent money to ransom prisoners of the many wars waged to their south.

Kingship in an Age of Fragmentation

In such a world, what did kings do? At the least, they stood for tradition, serving as symbols of legitimacy. At the most, they united kingdoms and maintained a measure of law and order. (See Map 4.6.)

NORTHERN KINGDOMS

King Alfred of England was a king of the second sort. In the face of the Viking invasions, he developed new mechanisms of royal government, creating institutions that became the foundation of strong English kingship. We have already seen his military reforms: the system of *burhs* and the creation of a navy. Alfred was interested in religious and intellectual reforms as well. These were closely linked in his mind: the causes of England's troubles (in his view) were the sins of its people, brought on by their ignorance. Alfred intended to educate "all free-born men." He brought scholars to his court and embarked on an ambitious program to translate key religious works from Latin into Anglo-Saxon (or Old English). This was the vernacular, the spoken language of the people. Indeed, Anglo-Saxon was used in England not only for literature but for official administrative purposes as well:

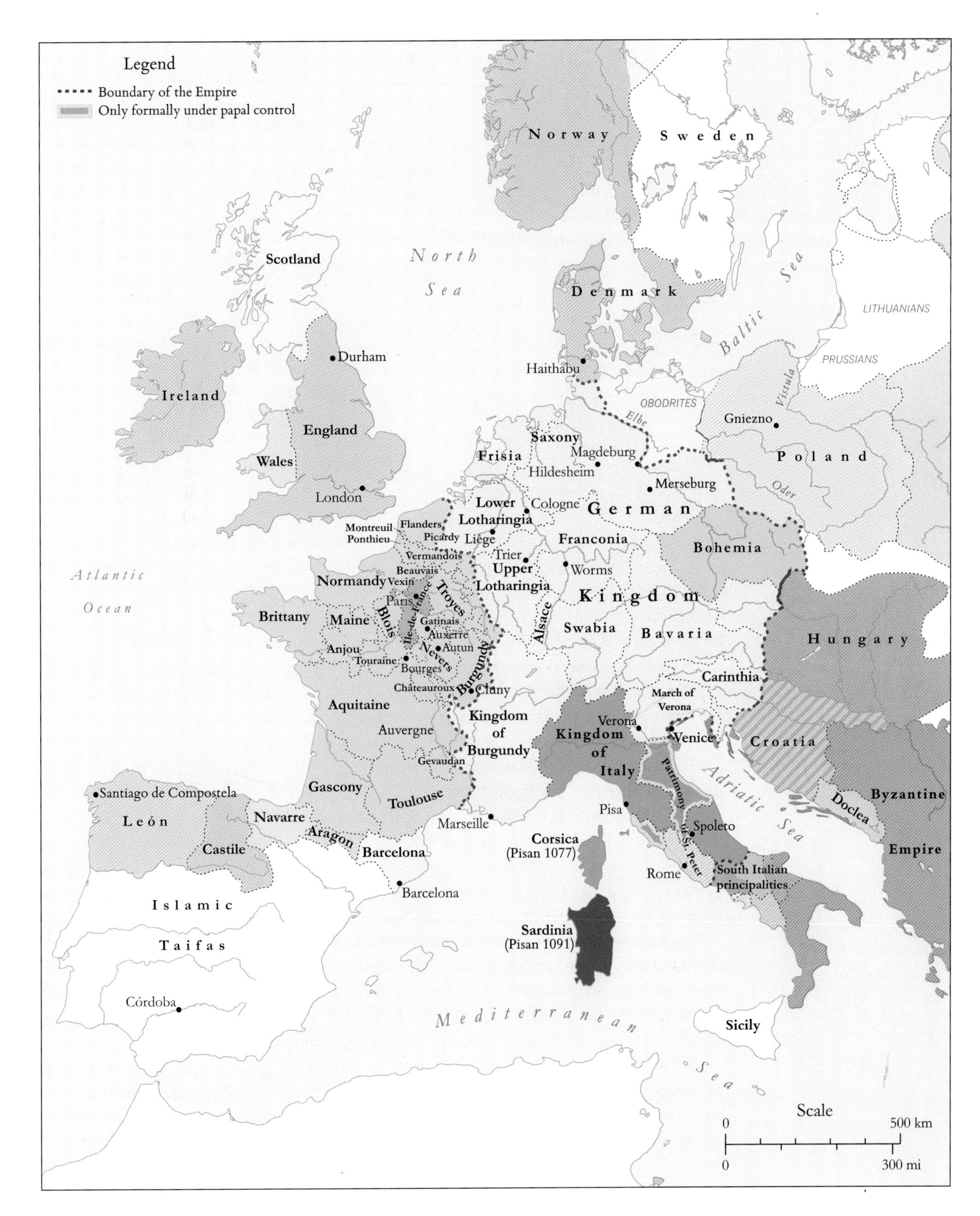
Legend
Boundary of the Empire
Only formally under papal control
Norway
Sweden
North Sea
Scotland
Denmark
Baltic Sea
LITHUANIANS
PRUSSIANS
Durham
Haithabu
Ireland
England
OBODRITES
Elbe
Vistula
Gniezno
Wales
Saxony
Frisia
Magdeburg
Hildesheim
Poland
Merseburg
Oder
London
Lower Lotharingia
Cologne
German Kingdom
Montreuil Ponthieu
Flanders
Picardy
Liège
Franconia
Bohemia
Vermandois
Trier
Upper Lotharingia
Worms
Atlantic Ocean
Beauvais
Normandy
Vexin
Paris
Troyes
Brittany
Maine
Blois
Île-de-France
Gatinais
Alsace
Swabia
Bavaria
Hungary
Auxerre
Autun
Anjou
Touraine
Nevers
Bourges
Burgundy
Carinthia
Châteauroux
Cluny
March of Verona
Aquitaine
Kingdom of Burgundy
Verona
Venice
Auvergne
Kingdom of Italy
Croatia
Gevaudan
Patrimony of St. Peter
Adriatic Sea
Santiago de Compostela
Gascony
Toulouse
Byzantine Empire
Doclea
León
Navarre
Pisa
Marseille
Spoleto
Aragon
Corsica (Pisan 1077)
Castile
Barcelona
Rome
South Italian principalities
Barcelona
Islamic Taifas
Sardinia (Pisan 1091)
Córdoba
Mediterranean Sea
Sicily
Scale
0
500 km
0
300 mi

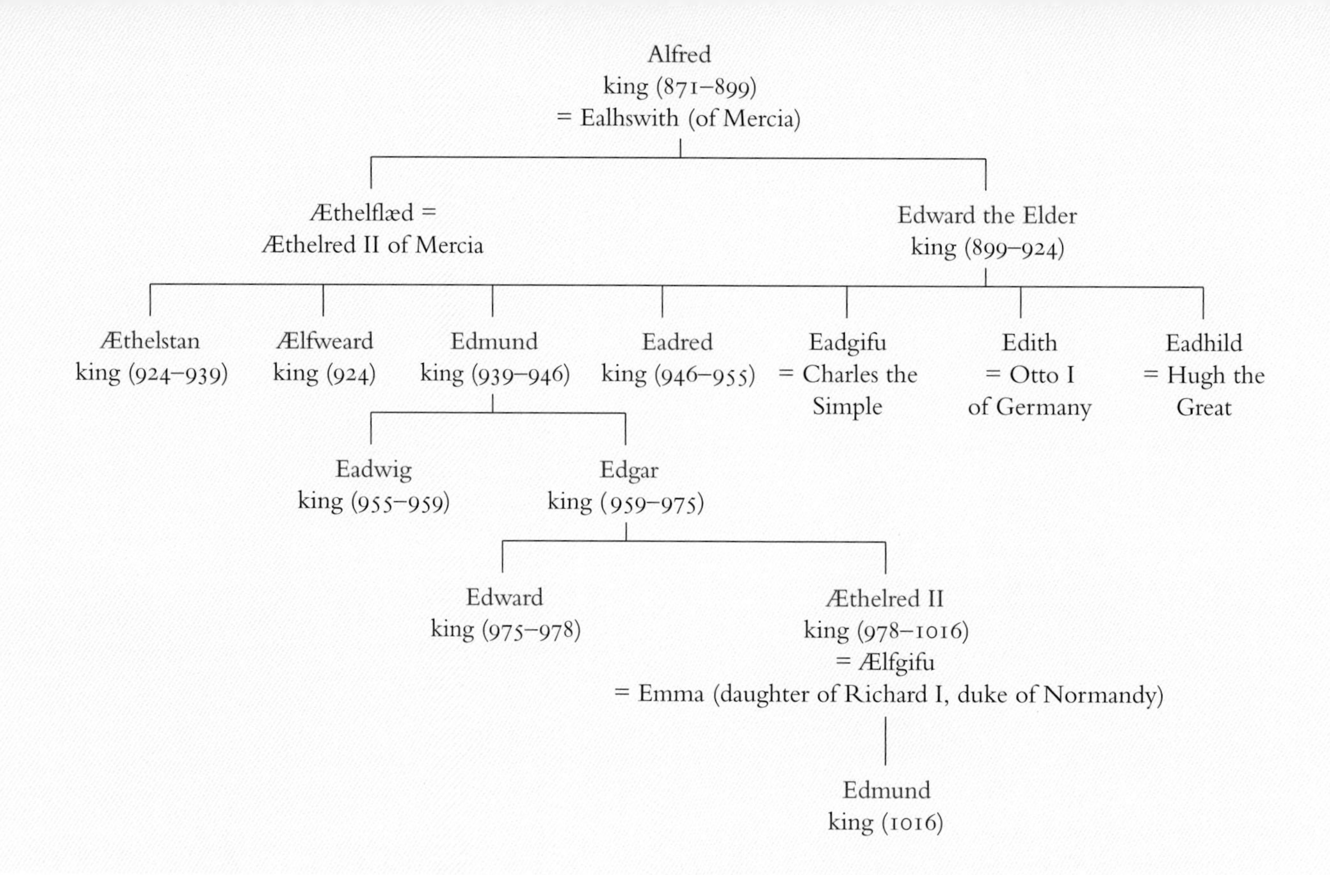

Genealogy 4.1 Alfred and His Progeny

for example, for royal "writs" that kings and queens directed to their officials and for law codes such as the one that Æthelred II the Unready (r.978–1016) issued in 1008.[13] England was not alone in its esteem of the vernacular: in Ireland, too, the vernacular language was a written one. But the British Isles *were* unusual by the standards of Continental Europe, where Latin alone was the language of scholarship and writing.

As Alfred harried the Danes who were pushing south and westward, he gained recognition as king of all the English not under Viking rule. His law code, issued in the late 880s or early 890s, was the first by an English king since 695. Unlike earlier codes, which had been drawn up for each separate kingdom, Alfred's contained laws from and for all the English kingdoms in common. The king's inspiration was the Mosaic law of the Bible. Alfred believed that God had made a new covenant with the victors over the Vikings; as leader of his people, Alfred, like the Old Testament patriarch Moses, issued a law for all.

His successors, beneficiaries of that covenant, rolled back the Viking rule in England. (See Genealogy 4.1.) Many Vikings fled back to Scandinavia, but others remained. Converted to Christianity, their great men joined Anglo-Saxons to attend the English king at court. The whole kingdom was divided into districts called "shires" and "hundreds," and in each shire, the king's reeve—the sheriff—oversaw royal administration.

Alfred's grandson Æthelstan (r.924–939) took advantage of all the institutions that early medieval kingship offered. The first king of all the Anglo-Saxon kingdoms, he was crowned in a new ritual created by the archbishop of Canterbury to emphasize harmony and unity. When Æthelstan toured his realm (as he did constantly), he was accompanied by a varied and impressive retinue: bishops, nobles, thegns (the English equivalent of high-status vassals), scholars, foreign dignitaries, and servants. Well known as an effective military leader who extended his realm northwards, he received oaths of loyalty from the rulers of other parts of Britain. Churchmen attended him at court, and he in turn chose bishops and other churchmen, often drawing on the priests in his household. Like Alfred, he issued laws and expected local authorities—the ealdormen and sheriffs—to carry them out.[14]

From the point of view of control, however, Æthelstan had nowhere near the power over England that, say, Basil II had over Byzantium at about the same time. The *dynatoi* might sometimes chafe at the emperor's directives and rebel, but the emperor had his Varangian Guard to put them down and an experienced, professional civil service to do his bidding. The king of England depended less on force and bureaucracy than on consensus. The great landowners adhered to the king because they found it in their interest to do so. When they ceased to do so, the kingdom easily fragmented, becoming prey to civil war. Disunity was exacerbated by new attacks from the Vikings. One Danish king, Cnut (or Canute), even became king of England for a time (r.1016–1035). Yet under Cnut, English kingship did not change much. He kept intact much of the administrative, ecclesiastical, and military apparatus already established. By Cnut's time, much of Scandinavia had been Christianized, and its traditions had largely merged with those of the rest of Europe.

In fact, two European-style kingdoms—Denmark and Norway—developed in Scandinavia around the year 1000, and Sweden followed thereafter. In effect, the Vikings took home with them not only Europe's plundered wealth but also its prestigious religion, with all its implications for royal power and state-building. (Consider how closely King Alfred linked God to royal authority, morality, and territorial expansion.) The impetus for conversion in Scandinavia came from two directions. From the south, missionaries such as the Frankish monk Ansgar (d.865) came to preach Christianity, while bishops in the north of Germany imposed what claims they could over the Scandinavian church. From within Scandinavia itself, kings found it worth their while to ally with the Christian world to enhance their own position.

Danish King Harald Bluetooth (r.*c*.958–*c*.986), much like Khan Boris-Michael of Bulgaria a century before (see p. 85), proclaimed his conversion through an artifact. Boris-Michael had used seals—items prestigious for their association with Byzantine imperial government. Before converting to Christianity, Harald buried his father in a mound—prestigious precisely for its non-Christian, pagan connotations. About a decade later, when he became Christian, he added a giant runestone to the burial place of his father, whose body he moved from the mound into a new church he built for the occasion. The runestone, which included an image of Christ, announced that Harald had "won for himself all of Denmark and Norway and made the Danes Christian."[15] Thus graphically turning a pagan site into a Christian one, Harald announced himself the ruler of a state that extended into what is today southern Sweden and parts of Norway. His successors turned their sights further outward, culminating in the conquest of England and Norway, but this grand empire ended with the death of Cnut in 1035.

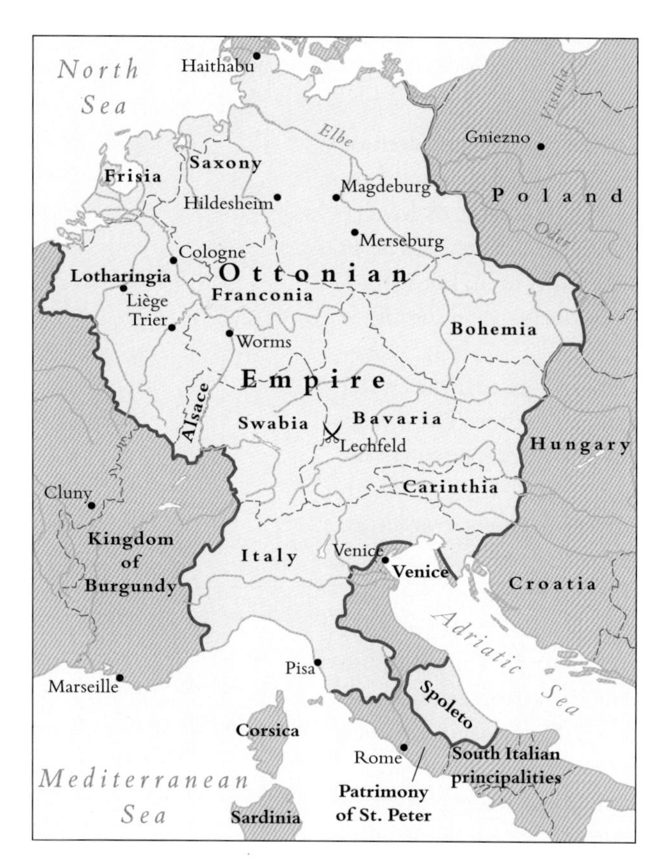

Map 4.7 Ottonian Empire, *c.*1000

The processes of conversion and the development of kingship in Norway are less easily traceable because there are few sources from the time. It is clear, however, that at the beginning of the eleventh century the baptism of Olav Haraldsson allowed him to ally with the English king ousted by the Danes. It also let Olav tie himself to his own men through the bonds of godparenthood. Building on the successes of Olav in opposing Danish King Cnut's hegemony in Norway, Magnus the Good (r.1035–1047) harnessed the Christian institutions already in place.

The story of Sweden was similar to that of Denmark and Norway, but delayed until the twelfth century. Before then, Sweden was divided among many competing rulers, most of them professing Christianity.

GERMANY

Just below Denmark was Germany. There the king was as effective and powerful as his English counterpart—and additionally worked with a much wider palette of territories, institutions, and possibilities. It is true that at first Germany seemed ready to disintegrate into duchies: five emerged in the late Carolingian period, each held by a military leader who exercised quasi-royal powers. But, in the face of their own quarrels and the threats of outside invaders, the dukes needed and wanted a strong king. With the death in 911 of the last Carolingian king in Germany, Louis the Child, they crowned one of themselves. Then, as attacks by the Hungarians increased, the dukes gave the royal title to their most powerful member, the duke of Saxony, Henry I (r.919–936), who proceeded to set up fortifications and reorganize his army, crowning his efforts with a major defeat of the Hungarians in 933.

Henry's son Otto I (r.936–973) defeated rival family members, rebellious dukes, and Slavic and Hungarian armies soon after coming to the throne. Through astute marriage alliances and appointments, he was eventually able to get his family members to head up all the duchies. In 951, Otto marched into Italy and took the Lombard crown. That gave him control, at least theoretically, of much of northern Italy (see Map 4.7). Soon (in 962) he received the imperial crown that recognized his far-flung power. Both to himself and to contemporaries he recalled the greatness of Charlemagne. Meanwhile, Otto's victory at Lechfeld in 955 (see p. 135) ended the Hungarian threat. In the same year, Otto defeated a Slavic group, the Obodrites, just east of the Elbe River and set up fortifications and bishoprics in the no-man's-land between the Elbe and the Oder Rivers.

Victories such as these brought tribute, plum positions to disburse, and lands to give away, ensuring Otto a following among the great men of the realm. His successors, Otto II (r.961–983), Otto III (r.983–1002)—hence the dynastic name "Ottonians"—and Henry II

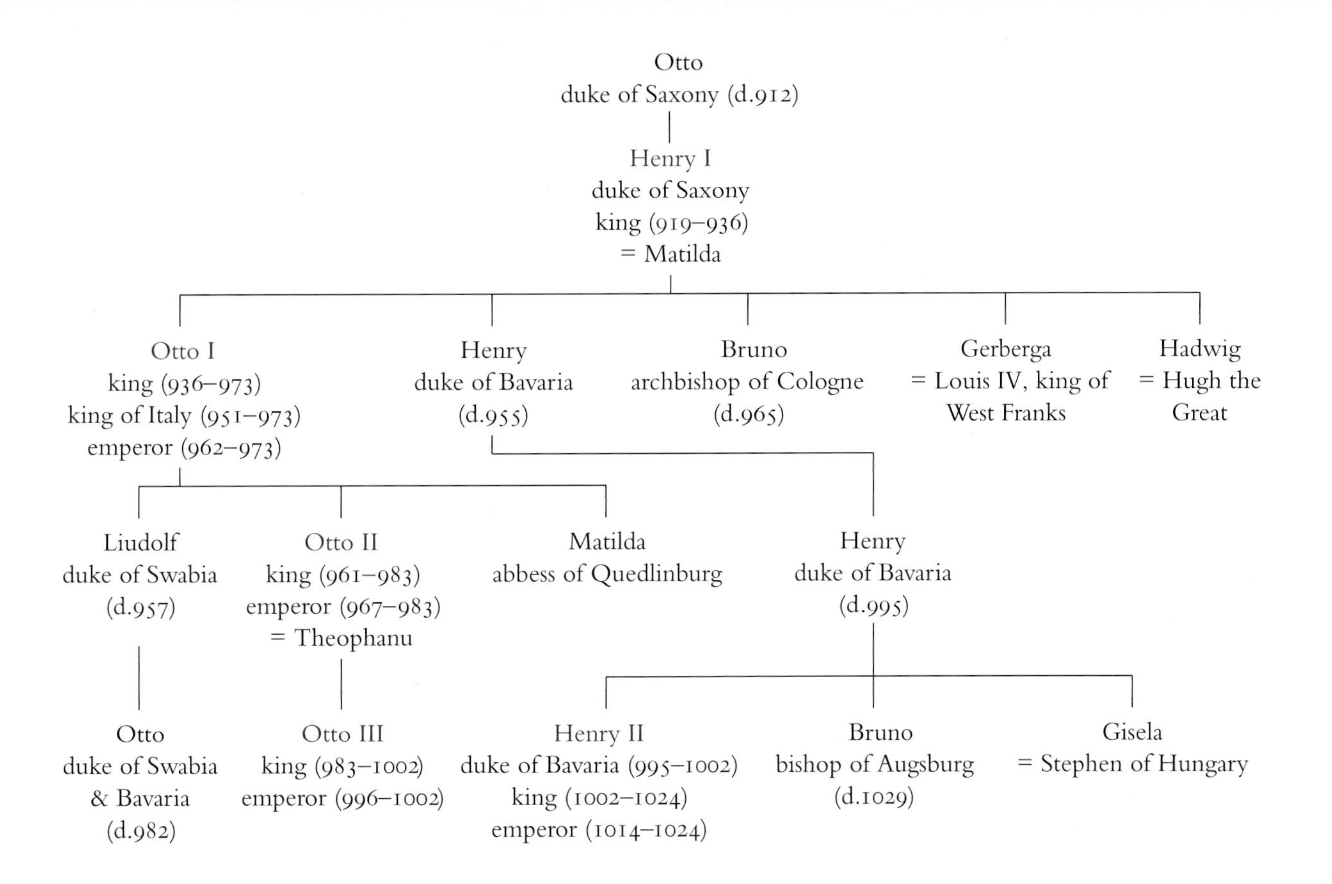

Genealogy 4.2 The Ottonians

(r.1002–1024), built on his achievements. (See Genealogy 4.2.) Granted power by the magnates, they gave back in turn: they distributed land and appointed their aristocratic supporters to duchies, counties, and bishoprics. Royal power was tempered by hereditary claims and plenty of lobbying by influential men at court and at the great assemblies that met with the king to hammer out policies. The role of kings in filling bishoprics and archbishoprics was particularly important to them because, unlike counties and duchies, those positions could not be inherited. Otto I created a ribbon of new bishoprics along his eastern border, endowing them with extensive lands and subjecting the local peasantry to episcopal overlordship. Throughout Germany bishops had the right to collect revenues and call men to arms.

Bishops and archbishops constituted the backbone of Ottonian rule. Once he had chosen the bishop (usually with the consent of the clergy of the cathedral over which the bishop was to preside), the king usually received a gift—a token of episcopal support—in return. Then the king "invested" the new prelate in his post by participating in the ceremony that installed him into office. Archbishop Bruno of Cologne is a good—if extreme—example of the symbiotic relations between church and state in the German realm. An ally of the king (as were almost all the bishops), he was also Otto I's brother. Right after he was invested as archbishop in 953, he was appointed by Otto to be duke of Lotharingia and to put down a local rebellion. Later Bruno's biographer, Ruotger, strove mightily to justify Bruno's role as a warrior-bishop:

Some people ignorant of divine will may object: why did a bishop assume public office and the dangers of war when he had undertaken only the care of souls? If they understand any sane matter, the result itself will easily satisfy them, when they see a great and very unaccustomed (especially in their homelands) gift of peace spread far and wide through this guardian and teacher of a faithful people.... Nor was governing this world new or unusual for rectors of the holy Church, previous examples of which, if someone needs them, are at hand.[16]

Ruotger was right: there *were* other examples near at hand, for the German kings found their most loyal administrators among their bishops. Consider the bishop of Liège; he held the rights and exercised the duties of several counts, had his own mints, and hunted and fished in a grand private forest granted to him in 1006.

Bruno was not only duke of Lotharingia, pastor of his flock at Cologne, and head (as archbishop of Cologne) of the bishops of his duchy. He was also a serious scholar. "There was nearly no type of liberal study in Greek or Latin," wrote the admiring Ruotger, "that escaped the vitality of his genius."[17] Bruno's interest in learning was part of a larger movement. With wealth coming in from their eastern tributaries, Italy, and the silver mines of Saxony (discovered in the time of Otto I), the Ottonians presided over a brilliant intellectual and artistic efflorescence. As in the Islamic world, much of this was dispersed; in Germany, the centers of culture included the royal court, the great cathedral schools, and women's convents.

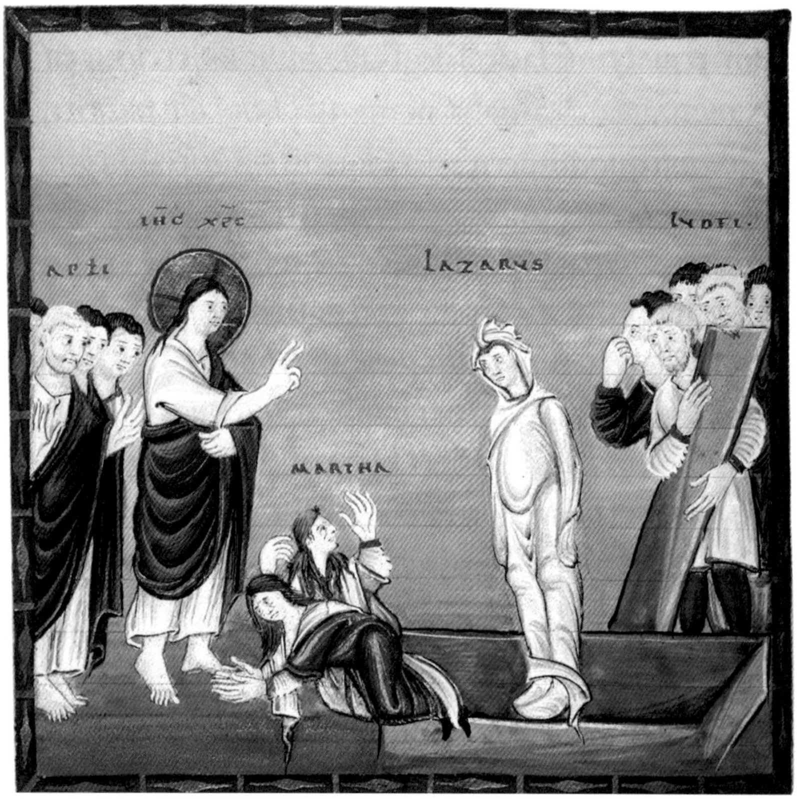

Plate 4.6 The Raising of Lazarus, Egbert Codex (985–990). This miniature is one of fifty-one illustrations in a Pericopes, a book of readings arranged for the liturgical year. The story of the Raising of Lazarus, which is recounted in John 11:1–45, is read during the week before Easter. Of the many elements of this story, the artist chose a few important moments, arranging them into a unified scene.

The most talented young men crowded the schools at the episcopal courts of Trier, Cologne, Magdeburg, Worms, and Hildesheim. Honing their Latin, they studied classical authors such as Cicero and Horace as well as Scripture, while their episcopal teachers wrote histories, saints' lives, and works on canon law. One such was the *Decretum* (1008/1012) by Burchard, bishop of Worms. This widely influential collection—much like the compilations of *hadith* produced about a century before in the Islamic world—winnowed out the least authoritative canons and systematized the contradictory ones. The men at the cathedral schools were largely in training to become courtiers, administrators, and bishops themselves.

Churchmen such as Egbert, archbishop of Trier (r.977–993), appreciated art as well as scholarship. Plate 4.6, an illustration of the Raising of Lazarus, from the Egbert Codex (named for its patron), is a good example of what is called the "Ottonian style." Drawing above all on the art of the late antique "renaissance" (see p. 20 and Plate 1.10), the Egbert Codex artists nevertheless achieved an effect all their own. Utterly unafraid of open space, which was rendered in otherworldly pastel colors, they focused on the figures, who gestured like actors on a stage. In Plate 4.6 the apostles are on the left-hand side, their arms raised and hands wide open with wonder at Christ. He has just raised the dead Lazarus from the tomb, and one of the Jews, on the right, holds his nose. Two women—Mary and Martha, the sisters of Lazarus—fall at Christ's feet, completing the dramatic tableau.

At around the same time, in convents that provided them with comfortable private apartments, noblewomen were writing books and supporting other artists and scholars. Plate 4.7 is from a manuscript made at Cologne between *c.*1000 and *c.*1020 for Abbess Hitda of Meschede. It draws on Byzantine and Carolingian models as well as the palette of the Egbert Codex to produce a calm Christ, asleep during a wild storm on the Sea of Galilee that ruffles the sails of the ship and seems to toss it into sheer air. The marriage of Otto II to a Byzantine princess, Theophanu, helps account for the Byzantine influence.

Among the most active patrons of the arts were the Ottonian kings themselves. In a Gospel book made for Otto III—a work fit for royal consumption—the full achievement of Ottonian culture is made clear. Plate 4.8 shows one of twenty-nine full-page miniatures in this manuscript, whose binding alone—set with countless gems around a Byzantine carved ivory—was worth a fortune. The figure of the evangelist Luke emerges from a pure gold-leaf background, while the purple of his dress and the columns that frame him recall imperial majesty. At the same time, Luke is clearly of another world, and his Gospels have here become a theological vision.

Following pages:

Plate 4.7 Christ Asleep, Hitda Gospels (*c.*1000–*c.*1020). The moral of the story (which is told in Matt. 8:23–26) is right in the picture: as the apostles look anxiously toward the mast to save them from the stormy sea, one (in the exact center) turns to rouse the sleeping Christ, the real Savior. The prow of this ship, in the shape of a beast, echoes the prow of Viking vessels.

Plate 4.8 Saint Luke, Gospel Book of Otto III (998–1001). St. Luke is like Atlas holding up the world, but in this case the "world" consists of Luke's symbol, the ox, surrounded by Old Testament prophets, each of whom is accompanied by an angel (King David, at the very top, is flanked by *two* angels). The artist was no doubt thinking of Heb.12:1 where Paul says that prophets are a "cloud of witnesses over our head." He also recalled Rev. 4:2–3, where Christ will be seated on a "throne set in heaven" with "a rainbow round about the throne." Here, Luke sits in the place of Christ.

FRANCE

By contrast with the English and German kings, those in France had a hard time coping with invasions. Unlike Alfred's dynasty, which started small and built slowly, the French kings had half an empire to defend. Unlike the Ottonians, who asserted their military prowess in decisive battles such as the one at Lechfeld, the French kings generally had to let local men both take the brunt of the attacks and reap the prestige and authority that came with military leadership. Nor did the French kings have the advantage of Germany's tributaries, silver mines, or Italian connections. Much like the Abbasid caliphs at Baghdad, the kings of France saw their power wane. During most of the tenth century, Carolingian kings alternated on the throne with kings from a family that would later be called the "Capetians." At the end of that century the most powerful men of the realm, seeking to stave off civil war, elected Hugh Capet (r.987–996) as their king. The Carolingians were displaced, and the Capetians continued on the throne until the fourteenth century. (See Genealogy 5.5 on p. 189.)

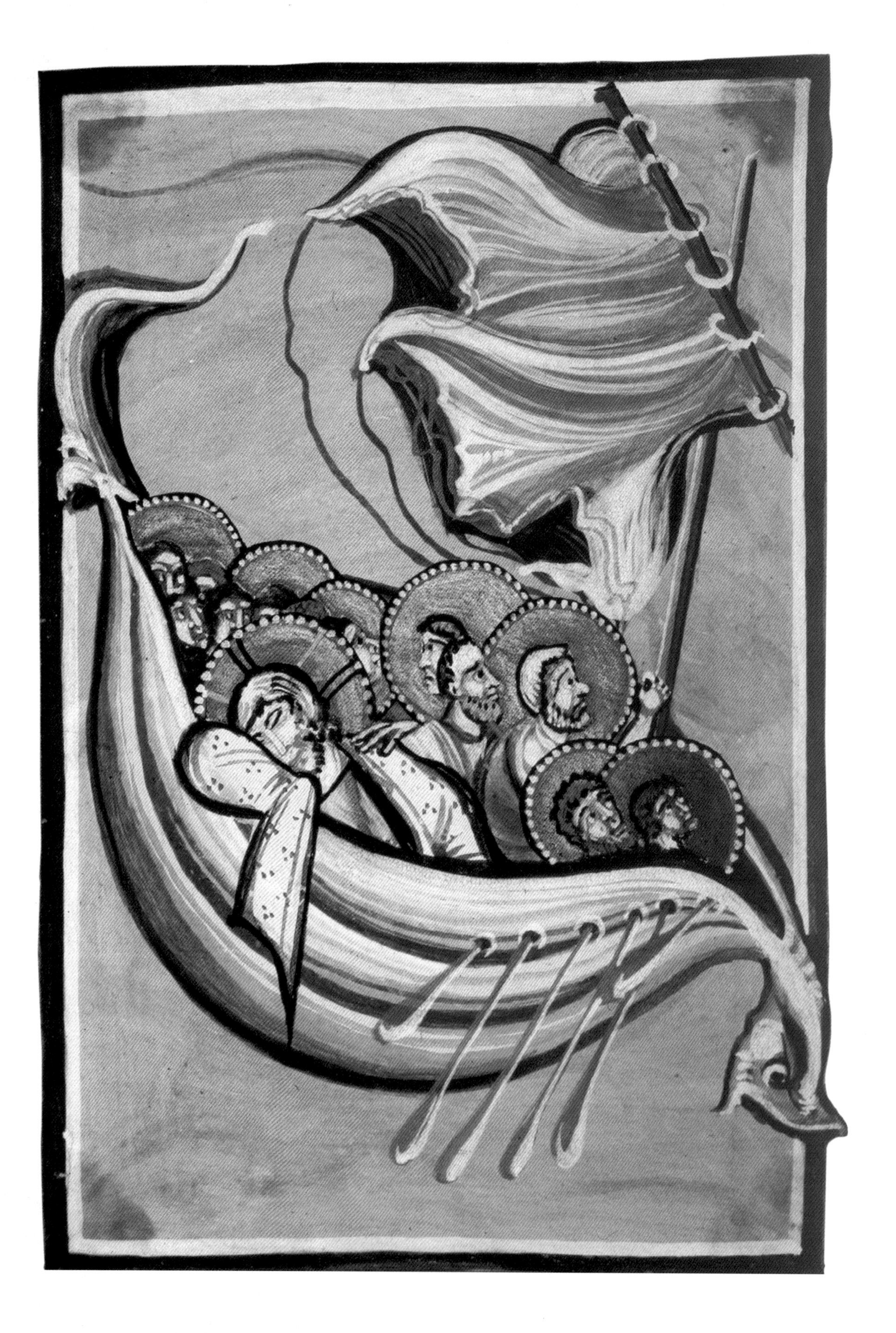

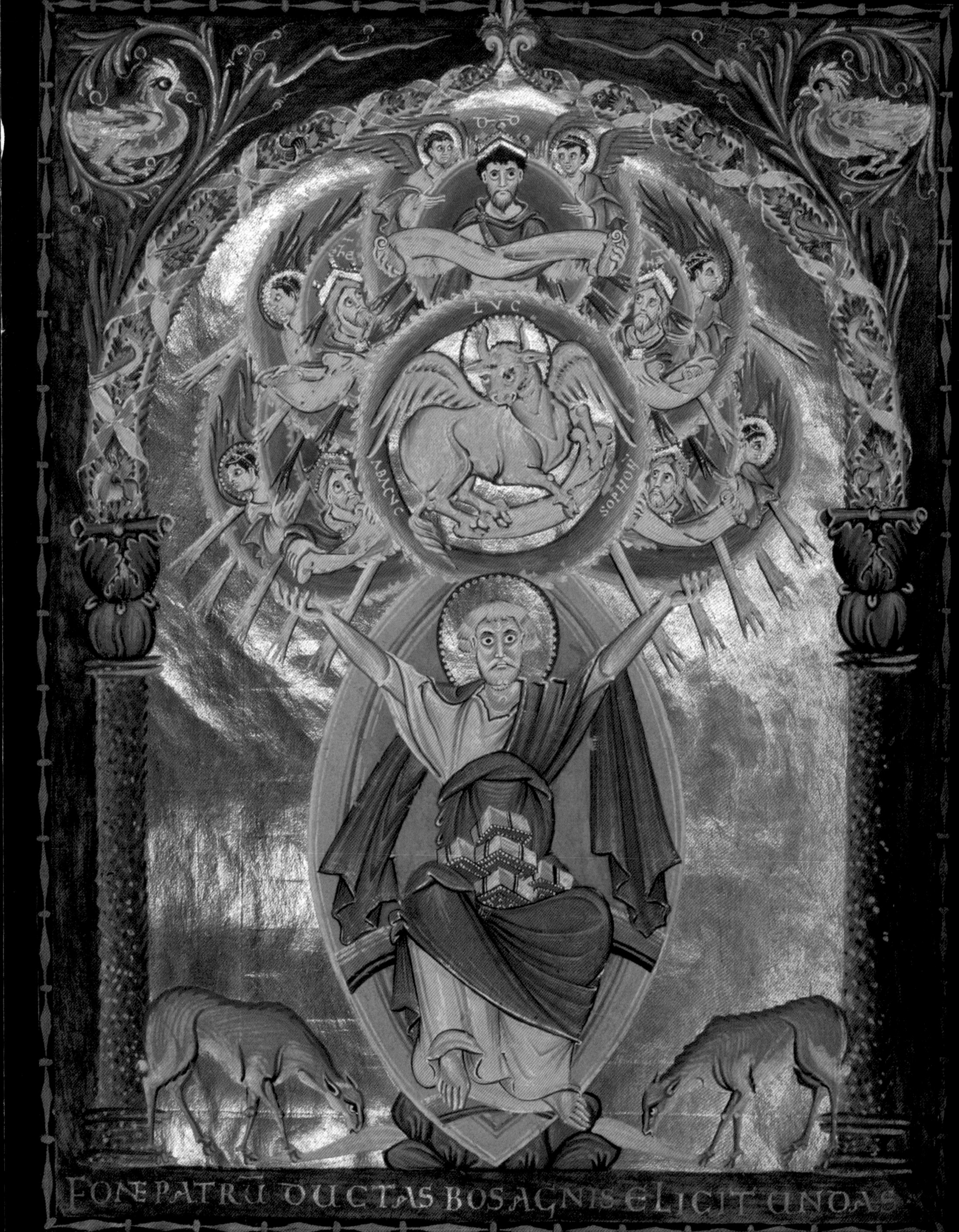
LUC
ABACUC
SOPHON
FONTE PATRŪ DUCTAS BOS AGNIS ELICIT UNDAS

The Capetians' scattered but substantial estates lay in the north of France, in the region around Paris. Here the kings had their vassals and their castles. This "Ile-de-France" (which was all there was to "France" in the period; see Map 4.6 on p. 141) was indeed an "island,"—an île—surrounded by independent castellans. In the sense that he, too, had little more military power than other castellans, Hugh Capet and his eleventh-century successors were similar to local strongmen. But the Capetian kings had the prestige of their office. Anointed with holy oil, they represented the idea of unity and God-given rule inherited from Charlemagne. Most of the counts and dukes—at least those in the north of France—swore homage and fealty to the king, a gesture, however weak, of personal support. Unlike the German kings, the French could rely on vassalage to bind the great men of the realm to them.

New States in East Central Europe

Around the same time as Moravia and Bulgaria lost their independence to the Magyars and the Byzantines (respectively), three new polities—Bohemia, Poland, and Hungary—emerged in East Central Europe. In many ways, they formed an interconnected bloc, as their ruling houses intermarried with one another and with the great families of the Empire—the looming power to the west. Bohemia and Poland both were largely Slavic-speaking; linguistically Hungary was odd man out, but in almost every other way it was typical of the fledgling states in the region.

BOHEMIA AND POLAND

While the five German duchies were subsumed by the Ottonian state, Bohemia in effect became a separate duchy of the Ottonian Empire. (See Map 4.7 on p. 144.) Already Christianized, largely under the aegis of German bishops, Bohemia was unified in the course of the tenth century. (One of its early rulers was Wenceslas—the carol's "Good King Wenceslas"—who was to become a national saint after his assassination.) Its princes were supposed to be vassals of the emperor in Germany. Thus, when Bretislav I (d.1055) tried in 1038 to expand into what was by then Poland, laying waste the land all the way to Gniezno and kidnapping the body of the revered Saint Adalbert, Emperor Henry III (d.1056) declared war, forcing Bretislav to give up the captured territory and hostages. Although left to its own affairs internally, Bohemia was thereafter semi-dependent on the Empire.

What was this "Poland" of such interest to Bretislav and Henry? Like the Dane Harald Bluetooth, and around the same time, the ruler of the region that would become Poland, Mieszko I (r.*c.*960–992), became Christian. In 990/991 he put his realm under the protection of the pope, tying it closely to the power of Saint Peter. Mieszko built a network of defensive structures manned by knights, subjected the surrounding countryside to his rule, and expanded his realm in all directions. Mieszko's son Boleslaw the Brave (or, in

Polish, Chrobry) (r.992–1025), "with fox-like cunning" (as a hostile German observer put it), continued his father's expansion, for a short time even becoming duke of Bohemia.[18] Above all, Boleslaw made the Christian religion a centerpiece of his rule when Gniezno was declared an archbishopric. It was probably around that time that Boleslaw declared his alliance with Christ on a coin: on one side he portrayed himself as a sort of Roman emperor, while on the other he displayed a cross.[19] Soon the Polish rulers could count on a string of bishoprics—and the bishops who presided in them. A dynastic crisis in the 1030s gave Bretislav his opening, but, as we have seen, that was quickly ended by the German emperor. Poland persisted, although somewhat reduced in size.

HUNGARY

Polytheists at the time of their entry into the West, most Magyars were peasants, initially specializing in herding but soon busy cultivating vineyards, orchards, and grains. Above them was a warrior class, and above the warriors were the elites, whose richly furnished graves reveal the importance of weapons, jewelry, and horses to this society. Originally organized into tribes led by dukes, by the mid-tenth century the Hungarians recognized one ruling house—that of Prince Géza (r.972–997).

Like the ambitious kings of Scandinavia, Géza was determined to give his power new ballast via baptism. His son, Stephen I (r.997–1038), consolidated the change to Christianity: he built churches and monasteries, and required everyone to attend church on Sundays. Establishing his authority as sole ruler, Stephen had himself crowned king in the year 1000 (or possibly 1001). Around the same time, "governing our monarchy by the will of God and emulating both ancient and modern caesars [emperors]," he issued a code of law that brought his kingdom into step with other European powers.[20]

★ ★ ★ ★ ★

Political fragmentation did not mean chaos. It simply betokened a new order. At Byzantium, in any event, even the most centrifugal forces were focused on the center; the real trouble for Basil II, for example, came from *dynatoi* who wanted to be emperors, not from people who wanted to be independent regional rulers. In the Islamic world fragmentation largely meant replication, as courts patterned on or competitive with the Abbasid model were set up by Fatimid caliphs and other rulers. In Europe, the rise of local rulers was accompanied by the widespread adoption of forms of personal dependency—vassalage, serfdom—that could be (and were) manipulated even by kings, such as the Capetians, who seemed to have lost the most from the dispersal of power. Another institution that they could count on was the church. No wonder that in Rus', Scandinavia, and East Central Europe, state formation and Christianization went hand in hand. The *real* fragmentation was among the former heirs of the Roman Empire. They did not speak the same language, they were increasingly estranged by their religions, and they knew almost nothing about one another. In the next centuries, the gaps would only widen.

MATERIAL CULTURE: THE MAKING OF AN ILLUMINATED MANUSCRIPT

Before the use of paper became widespread in the West in the fourteenth century, European books were made of parchment, the product of animal skins. The most common parchment was made from goats and sheep, while calfskin was considered the finest sort (commonly known as vellum, from the Latin *vitulinum*, i.e., "of a calf"). All parchments were produced through an elaborate process by a *percamenarius*, a parchmenter.

To begin, the parchmenter cleaned the skin in fresh, running water—generally a river—for a day or two. Then he (almost never she) soaked it for many days in vats filled with a thick mixture of lime and water. Lime, composed mainly of calcium carbonate, helped to de-hair the skin, which the parchmenter then scraped off by means of a long, concave knife. Once meticulously and thoroughly de-haired, the skin was rinsed in fresh water. Still wet, it was stretched on a wooden frame for the second stage of the process. Now the parchmenter scraped both sides of the skin (known as the flesh and hair sides) with a *lunellum*, a special, half-moon-shaped knife that reduced the risk of scratches while smoothing and thinning the skin (Plate 4.9).

Even while he was scraping, the parchmenter was constantly stretching the skin by expertly tightening the pegs of the wooden frame. The parchment stretched even more as it dried. After the parchmenter did a final scraping and smoothing of the dried skin, it was removed from the frame, rolled up, and sold. Between the fifth and the twelfth centuries, the entire production of books was monopolized—*almost* exclusively—by monks. By the thirteenth century, some commercial manuscript makers opened shops in urban centers.

In a model book-production schedule, monks first cut the parchment to the desired size of the book that was to be made, folding the rectangular sheet in half to obtain two pages (a bifolium), each page (*folium* in Latin) with a recto and a verso (technical terms for the two sides of one page). They put together several folded sheets to form a quire (or gathering). The sheets in a quire were assembled so that two facing pages presented the same side of the parchment: two facing flesh sides followed by two facing hair sides. At this point, the scribes—monks charged with copying texts—further prepared each *folium* by rubbing it with a pumice stone, a procedure that made the surface receptive to inks and paints. The scribes then had to "rule" the pages—make the lines that would keep their writing even and straight—by joining up prick marks made through a closed quire along a measured grid. Then the scribes "drew" barely visible lines with a tool that had a hard metal point; by the twelfth century this was commonly made of lead and was called a plummet marker. Later, ruling was done also in ink or in pigment.

With everything set, the scribe was ready to write. He or she (for there were many female monasteries, and women, too, were trained as scribes) wrote the text with a quill pen made from a wing feather—usually a goose or a swan feather (*penna* in Latin, a word that has been passed down for centuries!). In their free hand, scribes held a knife (see Plate 4.10), which they used for several operations: to cut the parchment, keep the pages firm while writing, erase errors (which occurred quite frequently), and sharpen the quill pen itself. Because the writing was done by hand, the resulting book is called a manuscript (from the Latin *manus*, hand and *scriptus*, written).

If the manuscript was to be "illuminated"—illustrated—production continued with the participation of illuminators. Illustrations might be as simple as an ornamental letter or as elaborate as a full page, as in Plate 4.10. The illuminator first made a sketch, then began to apply gold leaf. But gold was very expensive and therefore used in only the most extravagant of books. Alternatives included tin leaf or even "poorer" natural substances such as saffron. The "gold" was applied to selected letters or figures, using gesso, in most cases, as a ground. Next, illuminators painted the rest of their sketch. Paints were made with coloring agents (pigments) obtained from vegetables, animals, and minerals and bound with glair (made from egg white), gum and/or glue, and water. Additives such as salt, stale urine, honey, and ear wax were also used to alter the shade and the consistency of the paints. Red and blue, followed by green, were the most common colors used in medieval manuscripts.

The final production stage was carried out by bookbinders. In monastic *scriptoria*, binding could be performed by any monk who knew the techniques. Later, when books were produced by commercial workshops, lay professionals or stationers became widespread. The binder's job was to put together a stack of loose quires in the correct order (according to the progressive folio numeration) and to sew them onto bands or thongs across the spine of the book. Two wooden boards served as front and back covers and were often covered with leather and reinforced with corner metal pieces. Luxury binding was typically reserved for whole Bibles or the four Gospels. Some bejeweled bindings remain today, attesting to the full artistry of medieval book-making (see Plate 4.11).

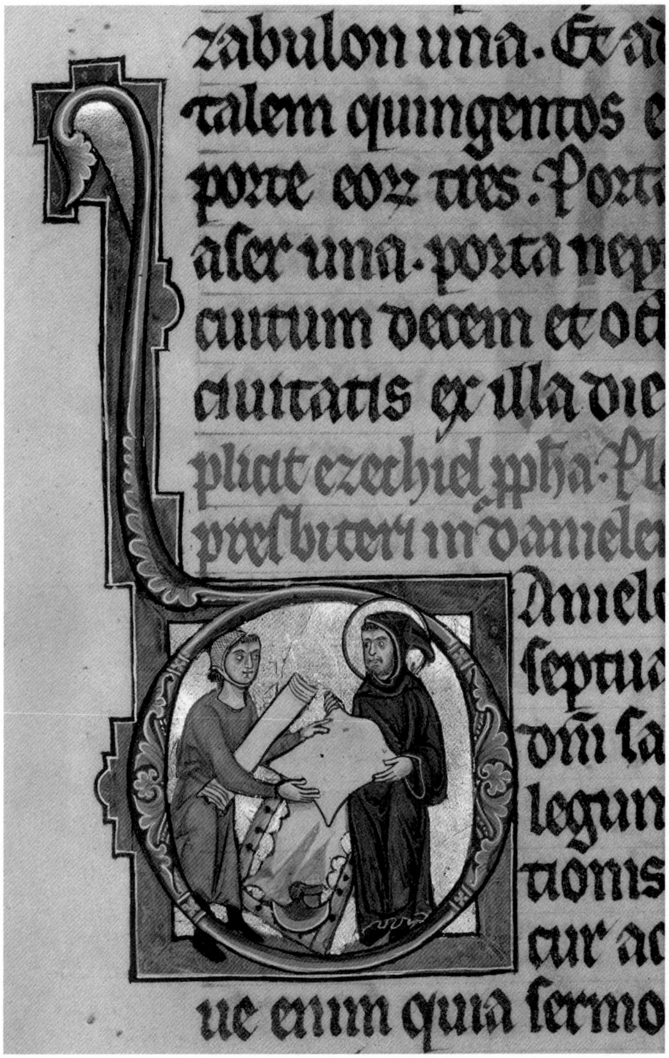

Plate 4.9 Hamburg Bible (1255). In this decorated initial letter (D for Daniel) of a Bible made at Hamburg's Cathedral canonry, a monk—possibly Saint Jerome (note the halo)—buys parchments from a lay craftsman. The parchmenter's wooden frame and scraping tool, the *lunellum*, are depicted in the lower half, between the two standing figures.

FURTHER READING

Clemens, Raymond and Timothy Graham. *Introduction to Manuscript Studies*. Ithaca: Cornell University Press, 2008.

De Hamel, Christopher. *Medieval Craftsmen. Scribes and Illuminators*. London: British Museum Press, 1992.

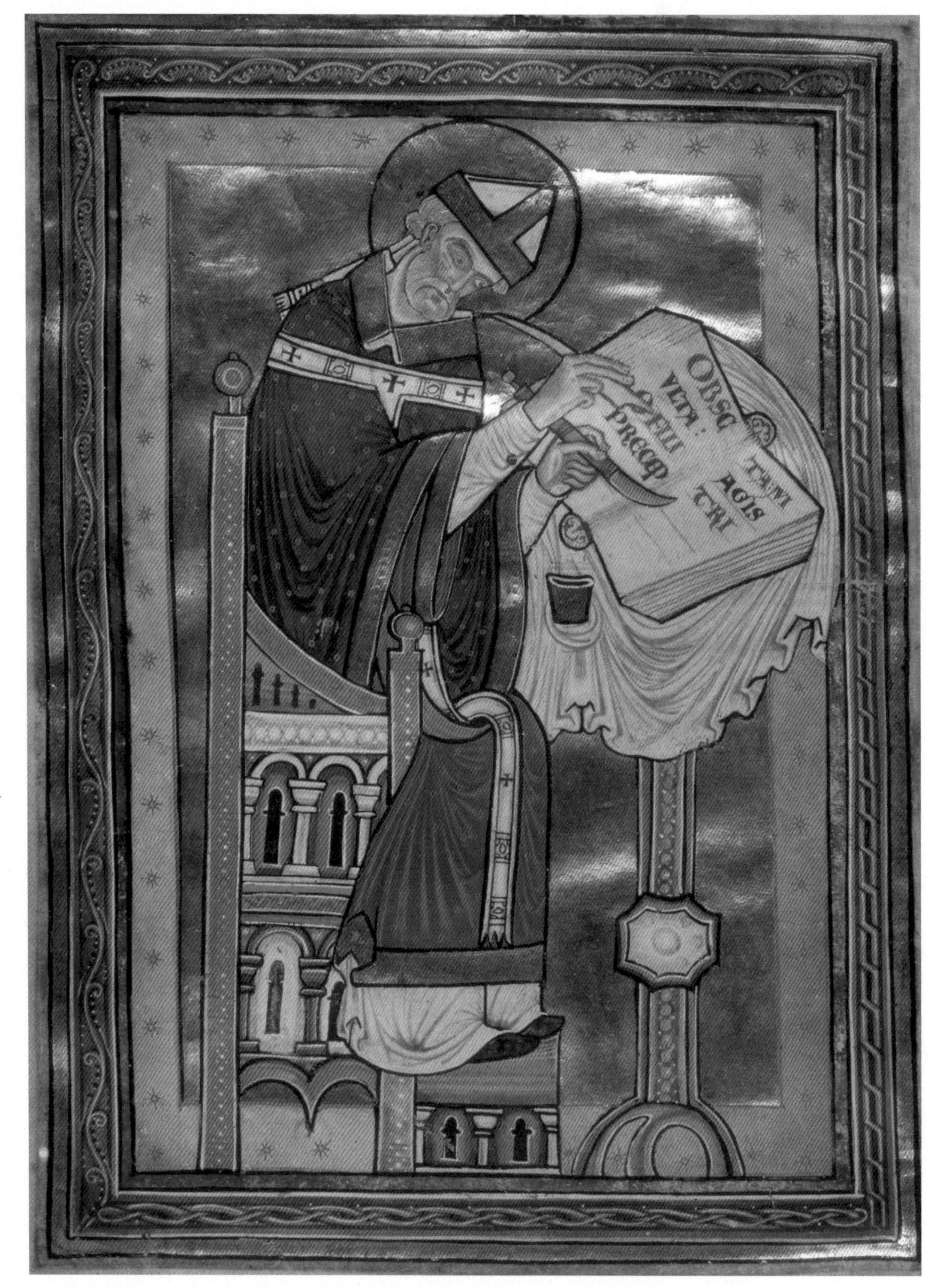

Plate 4.10 Miniature of Saint Dunstan (12th cent.). In this full-page miniature made between *c.*1170–*c.*1180 at the Benedictine cathedral priory of Holy Trinity or Christ Church, Canterbury, Saint Dunstan (d.988), former archbishop of Canterbury, is shown copying Smaragdus of Saint-Mihiel's *Commentary on the Rule of Saint Benedict*. The lavish image, embellished with gold leaf, shows the saint in full episcopal attire. With a quill pen in his right hand, a knife in his left, and a handy inkwell below, he writes by following the pale-gray lines that were drawn with a plummet.

Plate 4.11 (facing page) Codex Aureus (870). This so-called Golden book of Gospels received royal treatment with a bejeweled upper cover. It was most likely produced at the monastery of Saint-Denis, near Paris, by artists patronized by Emperor Charles the Bald, Charlemagne's grandson. At the center, Christ in Majesty is surrounded by the four evangelists and scenes from the life of Christ.

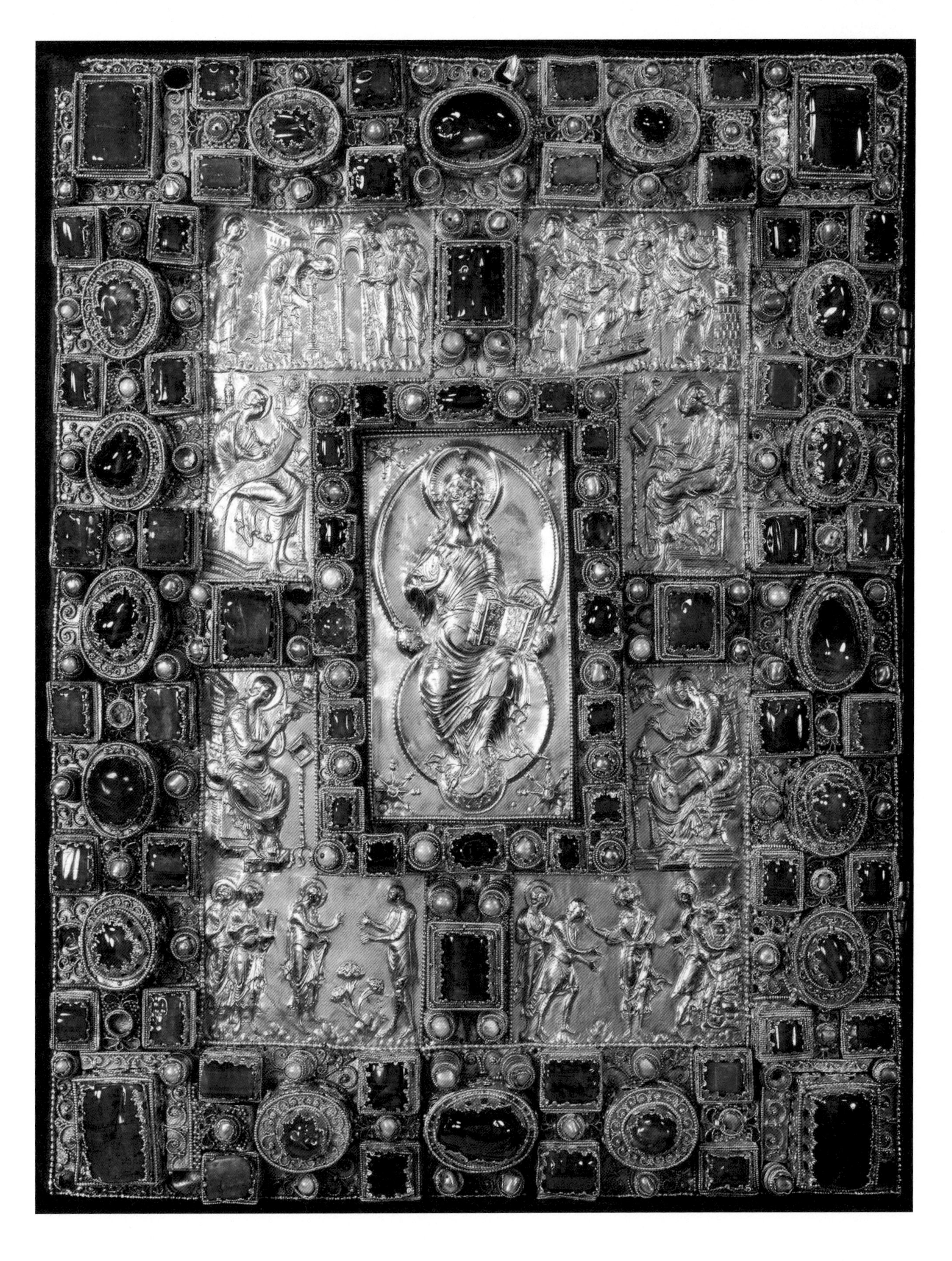

CHAPTER FOUR: ESSENTIAL DATES

910	Fatimids (in North Africa) establish themselves as caliphs
955	Victory of Otto I over Hungarians at Lechfeld
980–1037	Ibn Sina (Avicenna), scholar of medicine and philosophy
988	Conversion of Vladimir, ruler of Rus', to Byzantine Christianity
989	"Peace of God" movement begins
1000 (or 1001)	Stephen I crowned king of Hungary
1025	Death of Basil II the Bulgar Slayer
*c.*1031	Al-Andalus splits into *taifas*

NOTES

1 Michael Psellus, *Zoe and Theodora*, in *Reading the Middle Ages: Sources from Europe, Byzantium, and the Islamic World*, 3rd ed., ed. Barbara H. Rosenwein (Toronto: University of Toronto Press, 2018), p. 203.

2 *Epitaph of Basil II*, in *Reading the Middle Ages*, p. 200.

3 Romanus I Lecapenus, *Novel*, in *Reading the Middle Ages*, p. 178.

4 *The Russian Primary Chronicle*, in *Reading the Middle Ages*, p. 223.

5 Al-Tabari, *The Defeat of the Zanj Revolt*, in *Reading the Middle Ages*, p. 176.

6 Quoted in Elina Gertsman and Barbara H. Rosenwein, *The Middle Ages in 50 Objects* (Cambridge: Cambridge University Press, 2018), p. 122.

7 Ibn 'Abd Rabbihi, *Praise Be to Him*, in *Reading the Middle Ages*, p. 180.

8 Al-Qabisi, *A Treatise Detailing the Circumstances of Students and the Rules Governing Teachers and Students*, in *Reading the Middle Ages*, pp. 211–13.

9 *Egil's Saga*, in *Reading the Middle Ages*, p. 236.

10 *The Anglo-Saxon Chronicle*, in *Reading the Middle Ages*, p. 234.

11 *Agreement between Count William of the Aquitanians and Hugh IV of Lusignan*, in *Reading the Middle Ages*, p. 192.

12 Andrew of Fleury, *The Miracles of St. Benedict*, in *Reading the Middle Ages*, p. 196.

13 See King Æthelred II, *Law Code*, in *Reading the Middle Ages*, p. 228.

14 Both ealdormen and sherrifs (shire reeves) were powerful men, and sometimes their functions were the same. Originally the ealdorman was the equivalent of a count or duke who ruled a large region independently of any king. That changed with Alfred and his successors, and by the tenth century the term referred to a local ruler, generally of a shire, who, while certainly a nobleman, acted (or was expected to act) as an agent of the king. Reeves were of more variable status: they were administrators, whether for kings, bishops, towns, or estates. Royal sherrifs were responsible for (among other things) ensuring the peace and meetings of the local court.

15 For an image of this runestone, see *The Jelling Monument*, "Reading through Looking," in *Reading the Middle Ages*, p. IV.
16 Ruotger, *Life of Bruno, Archbishop of Cologne*, in *Reading the Middle Ages*, p. 227.
17 Ibid., p. 225.
18 See Thietmar of Merseburg, *Chronicle*, in *Reading the Middle Ages*, p. 220.
19 For an image of this coin, see Plate 2, "Reading through Looking," in *Reading the Middle Ages*, p. III.
20 King Stephen, *Laws*, in *Reading the Middle Ages*, p. 214.

FURTHER READING

Angold, Michael. *The Byzantine Empire, 1025–1204: A Political History*, 2nd ed. London, Longman, 1997.

Bagge, Sverre, Michael H. Gelting, and Thomas Lindkvist, eds. *Feudalism: New Landscapes of Debate*. Turnhout: Brepols, 2011.

Barthélemy, Dominique. "Revisiting the 'Feudal Revolution' of the Year 1000." In *The Serf, the Knight, and the Historian*, trans. Graham Robert Edwards, 1–11. Ithaca: Cornell University Press. 2009.

Berend, Nora, Przemysław Urbańczyk, and Przemysław Wiszewski. *Central Europe in the High Middle Ages: Bohemia, Hungary and Poland c. 900–c. 1300*. Cambridge: Cambridge University Press, 2013.

Berend, Nora, ed. *Christianization and the Rise of Christian Monarchy: Scandinavia, Central Europe, and Rus' c. 900–1200*. Cambridge: Cambridge University Press, 2007.

Bolton, Timothy. *Cnut the Great*. New Haven, CT: Yale University Press, 2017.

Bonfil, Robert, Oded Irshai, Guy G. Stoumsa, et al., eds. *Jews in Byzantium: Dialectics of Minority and Majority Cultures*. Leiden: Brill, 2012.

Brett, Michael. *The Fatimid Empire*. Edinburgh: Edinburgh University Press, 2017.

Bruce, Scott G. *Cluny and the Muslims of La Garde-Freinet: Hagiography and the Problem of Islam in Medieval Europe*. Ithaca, NY: Cornell University Press, 2015.

Cameron, Averil. *Byzantine Matters*. Princeton, NJ: Princeton University Press, 2014.

Chiarelli, Leonard C. *A History of Muslim Sicily*. Malta: Santa Venera, 2010.

Clemens, Raymond and Timothy Graham. *Introduction to Manuscript Studies*. Ithaca: Cornell University Press, 2008.

De Hamel, Christopher. *Medieval Craftsmen. Scribes and Illuminators*. London: British Museum Press, 1992.

Duby, Georges. "The Evolution of Judicial Institutions." In *The Chivalrous Society*, trans. Cynthia Postan, 15–58. London: Arnold, 1977.

Foot, Sarah. *Æthelstan: The First King of England*. New Haven, CT: Yale University Press, 2011.

Franklin, Simon, and Jonathan Shepard. *The Emergence of Rus, 750–1200*. London: Longman, 1996.

Harding, Stephen E., David Griffiths, and Elizabeth Royles, eds. *In Search of Vikings: Interdisciplinary Approaches to the Scandinavian Heritage of North-West England*. Boca Raton: CRC Press, 2015.

Jaritz, Gerhard. *Medieval East Central Europe in a Comparative Perspective: From Frontier Zones to Lands in Focus*. London: Routledge, 2016.

Kaldellis, Anthony. *The Byzantine Republic: People and Power in New Rome*. Cambridge, MA: Harvard University Press, 2015.

La Rocca, Cristina, ed. *Italy in the Early Middle Ages, 476–1000*. Oxford: Oxford University Press, 2002.

Magdalino, Paul. "Orthodoxy and Byzantine Cultural Identity." In *Orthodoxy and Heresy in Byzantium: The Definition and the Notion of Orthodoxy and Some Other Studies on the Heresies and the Non-Christian Religions*, ed. Antonio Rigo, 21–46. Rome: Università degli Studi di Roma Tor Vergata, 2010.

Michałowski, Roman. *The Gniezno Summit: The Religious Premises of the Founding of the Archbishopric of Gniezno*. Leiden: Brill, 2016.

Molyneaux, George. *The Formation of the English Kingdom in the Tenth Century*. Oxford: Oxford University Press, 2015.

Neville, Leonora. *Authority in Byzantine Provincial Society, 950–1100*. Cambridge: Cambridge University Press, 2004.

Raffensperger, Christian. *Reimagining Europe: Kievan Rus' in the Medieval World*. Cambridge, MA: Harvard University Press, 2012.

Romane, Julian. *Byzantium Triumphant: The Military History of the Byzantines, 959–1025*. Barnsley, South Yorkshire: Pen & Sword Military, 2015.

West, Charles. *Reframing the Feudal Revolution: Political and Social Transformation between Marne and Moselle, c. 800–c. 1100*. Cambridge: Cambridge University Press, 2013.

Wilson, Peter H. *Heart of Europe: A History of the Holy Roman Empire*. Cambridge, MA: Harvard University Press, 2016.

Winroth, Anders. *The Conversion of Scandinavia: Vikings, Merchants, and Missionaries in the Remaking of Northern Europe*. New Haven, CT: Yale University Press, 2012.

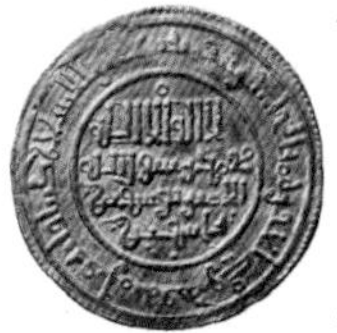

To test your knowledge of this chapter, please go to www.utphistorymatters.com for Study Questions.

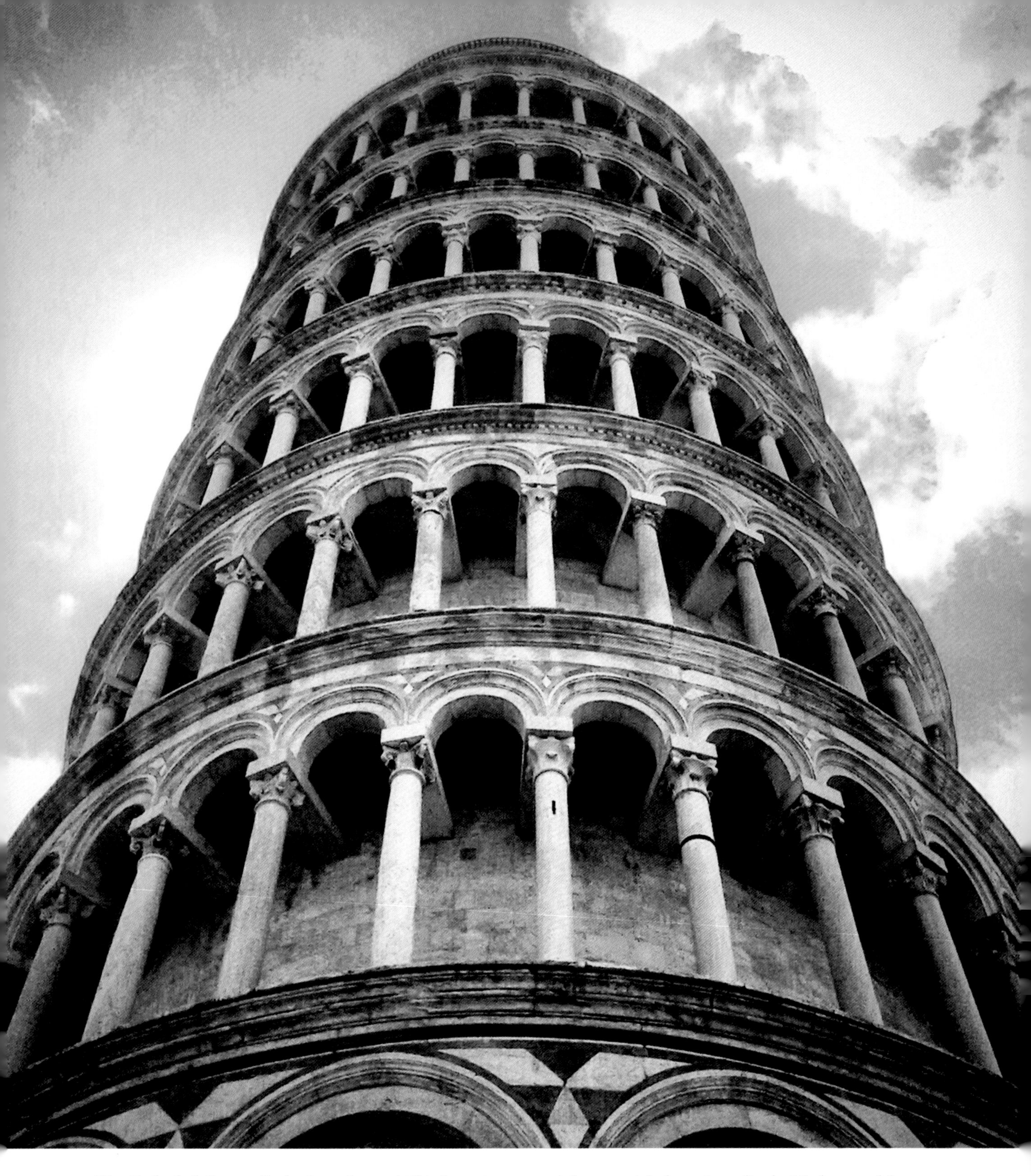

Pisa Cathedral Campanile (12th–14th cent.) This dramatic view of the belfry, or "leaning tower" of the Pisan cathedral complex (see Plate 5.8 on p. 196), emphasizes its sculptural depth. Its six "layers," all of which may be seen here, are composed of marble-paneled Romanesque arcades and colonnades that jut out from a central cylinder. Begun in 1173, it began to sink almost immediately. Work stopped for about a hundred years, picking up again in the late thirteenth century. Even when it was begun, its cylindrical style was old, modeled on the sorts of bell towers that Ravenna boasted. (A photograph of one of these, the Ravenna Cathedral campanile, is shown on p. 39.) (Image courtesy of Riccardo Cristiani.)

FIVE

NEW CONFIGURATIONS (*c.*1050–*c.*1150)

In the second half of the eleventh century, two powerful groups—Seljuk Turks from the east, Europeans from the west—entered the Byzantine and Islamic empires, changing the political, cultural, and religious configurations everywhere. Byzantium, though seemingly still a force to be reckoned with, lost ground. The Islamic world, tending toward Shiʻism with the Fatimids, now saw a revival of Sunnism. It elaborated new cultural forms to express its pride in its regained orthodoxy and to proclaim its cosmopolitanism. In Europe, a burgeoning population and vigorous new commercial economy helped fuel new forms of religious life and expand intellectual and territorial horizons.

THE SELJUKS AND THE ALMORAVIDS

In the eleventh century, the Seljuks, a new Turkic group from outside the Islamic world, entered and took over its eastern half. Eventually penetrating deep into Anatolia, they took a great bite out of Byzantium. Soon, however, the Seljuks themselves split apart, and eventually the Islamic world fragmented anew under the rule of dozens of rulers. Meanwhile, Berber tribespeople—the Almoravids—formed a new empire in the Islamic far West.

From Mercenaries to Imperialists

The Seljuk Turks were nomadic warriors from the Kazakh steppe—the extensive Eurasian grasslands of Kazakhstan. Some of them entered the region around the Caspian and Aral Seas at the end of the tenth century as mercenaries serving rival Muslim rulers. During

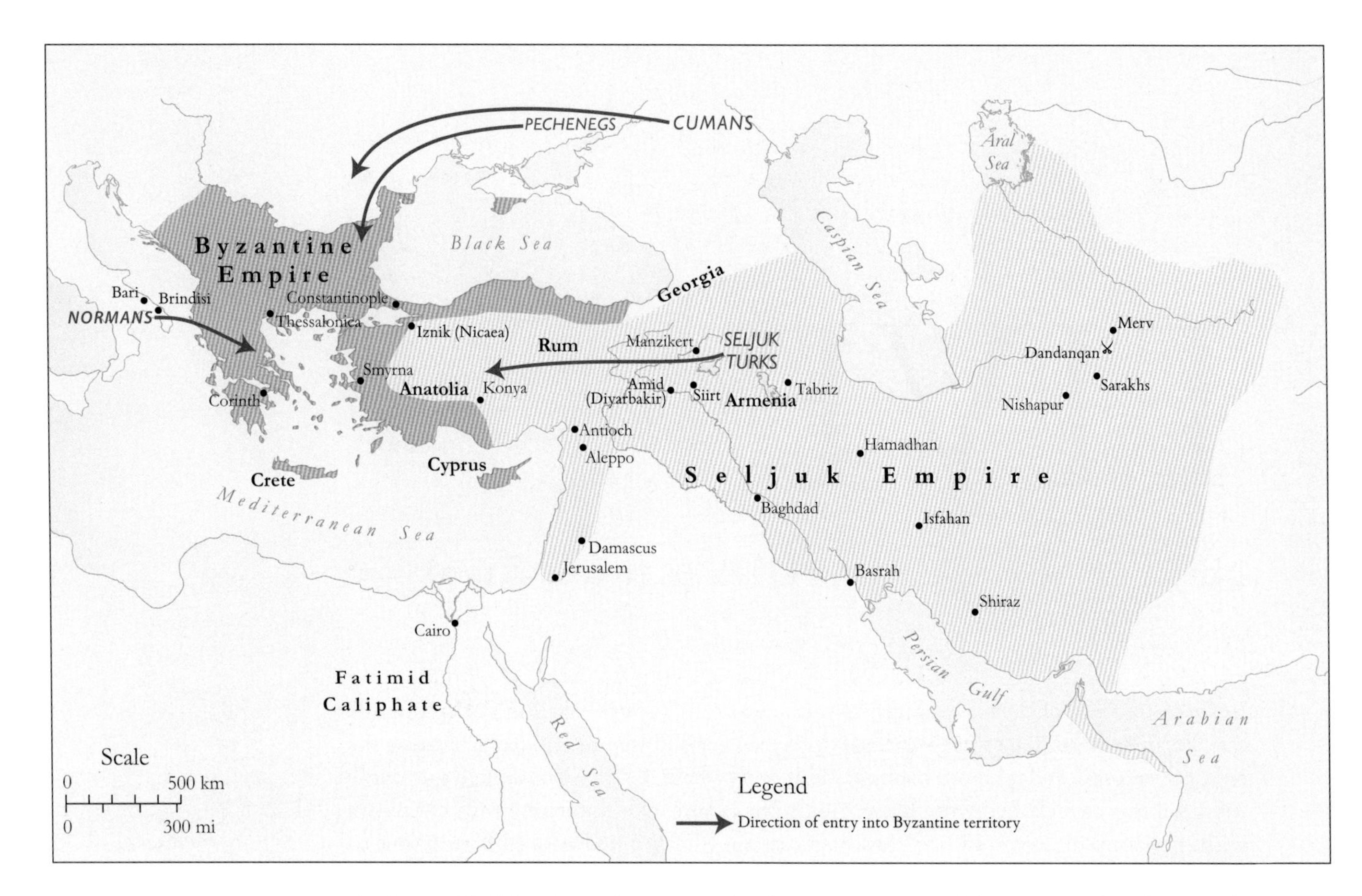

Map 5.1 The Byzantine and Seljuk Empires, *c.*1090

the first half of the eleventh century they began conquests of their own. The Ghaznavids, themselves Turks who had previously displaced the Buyids and Samanids, could perhaps have contained them, but Ghaznavid Sultan Mas'ud I (r.1030–1041) led an ill-prepared and demoralized army against the Seljuks and lost disastrously at the battle of Dandanqan (1040). Abu'l-Fazl Beyhaqi, who served as one of Sultan Mas'ud's secretaries and who witnessed the defeat, described what happened:

> The lack of water there [near Dandanqan] worried the [Ghaznavid] troops, and they became dismayed and disorderly. The enemy launched a fierce attack from all four sides.... We made strenuous attacks, and we thought that the compact formations of the right and left wings were still intact. We did not know that a detachment of the palace *gholams* [the elite body guards of the Sultan] mounted on camels had dismounted and were stealing the horses from anyone in sight so that they themselves might ride them into battle. This tussle over horses ... became so intense that [our men] started fighting among themselves.[1]

As Beyhaqi dryly observed, "the enemy exploited this opportunity," and the Ghaznavid troops were slaughtered. Thereafter the way to the west was open for the Seljuks, who conquered all the way to Anatolia. (See Map 5.1.)

From about the year 1000 to 1900, the Middle East was dominated by peoples of steppe origin, with the Seljuks among the first to arrive. They eventually formed two separate states. To the east, forming a crescent that embraced the southern halves of the Caspian and Aral Seas, was the Great Seljuk sultanate (*c.* 1040–1194). It encompassed the region now occupied by Uzbekistan, Turkmenistan, Iraq, and Iran. To the west, like a thumb stuck into what had been Byzantine Anatolia, was the Seljuk sultanate of Rum (*c.* 1081–1308). It took its name from those whom it vanquished: Rum means Rome. Although for the West the Seljuk army's humiliating defeat of the Byzantine emperor at Manzikert (today Malazgirt, in Turkey) in 1071 seemed to mark the conquest of Anatolia—and their occupation of Jerusalem (*c.* 1075) inspired the First Crusade—their real take-over of former Byzantine regions was effected by quieter methods, as Seljuk families moved in, seeking pastureland for their livestock. Like the Vikings, the Seljuks generally traveled as families.

The Seljuk sultanates were staunchly Sunni. They rolled back the Shi'ite wave that had engulfed the Islamic world since the decline of the Abbasids. Nizam al-Mulk (d. 1092), vizier for Alp Arslan and Malikshah I (see Genealogy 5.1) and in many ways *de facto* ruler himself for the last twenty years of his life, described Shi'ism as a fraud concocted out of pseudo-philosophy and mumbo-jumbo: "obscure words from the language of the imams, mixed up with sayings of the naturalists and utterances of the philosophers, and consisting largely of mention of The Prophet and the angels, the tablet and pen, and heaven and the throne."[2] It was a heresy and its followers were dangerous to the state. To counter its influence, he sponsored the foundation of numerous *madrasas*. As we have seen (see Chapter 4), the Islamic world had always supported elementary schools. The *madrasas*, normally attached to mosques, went beyond those schools by serving as centers of advanced scholarship. There young men attended lessons in religion, law, and literature. Sometimes visiting scholars arrived to debate in lively public displays of intellectual brilliance. More regularly, teachers and students carried on a quiet regimen of classes on the Qur'an and other texts. *Madrasas* had existed before the time of Nizam al-Mulk, but he gave them particular priority, hoping that they would fan new life into political, religious, and cultural Sunnism.

While allowing the Abbasid caliphs in Baghdad to maintain their religious role in a city still splendid in material and intellectual resources, the Seljuks shifted the cultural and political centers of the Islamic world to Iran and Anatolia. The strength and wealth of both the Great Seljuk sultanate (based in Iran) and the Seljuk sultanate of Rum (in Anatolia) were made particularly visible in their architecture. Consider the Friday mosque at Isfahan in Iran. First built in the tenth century, it received a major face-lift under Nizam al-Mulk, who focused his patronage on its courtyard, the heart of its many buildings. Nizam al-Mulk added four *iwans*—vaulted halls open to the courtyard—one at each wall. (See Plate 5.1.) The most important was the south *iwan*, for that was in the *qibla* wall—the wall facing Mecca. That *iwan* led in turn to a large square room housing the *mihrab* (the niche of the *qibla*), which was topped by a lofty dome. This, too, was built by Nizam al-Mulk. Competing for Nizam's al-Mulk's power, his rival Taj al-Mulk showed off his own importance by building another square domed room on the very same axis as the

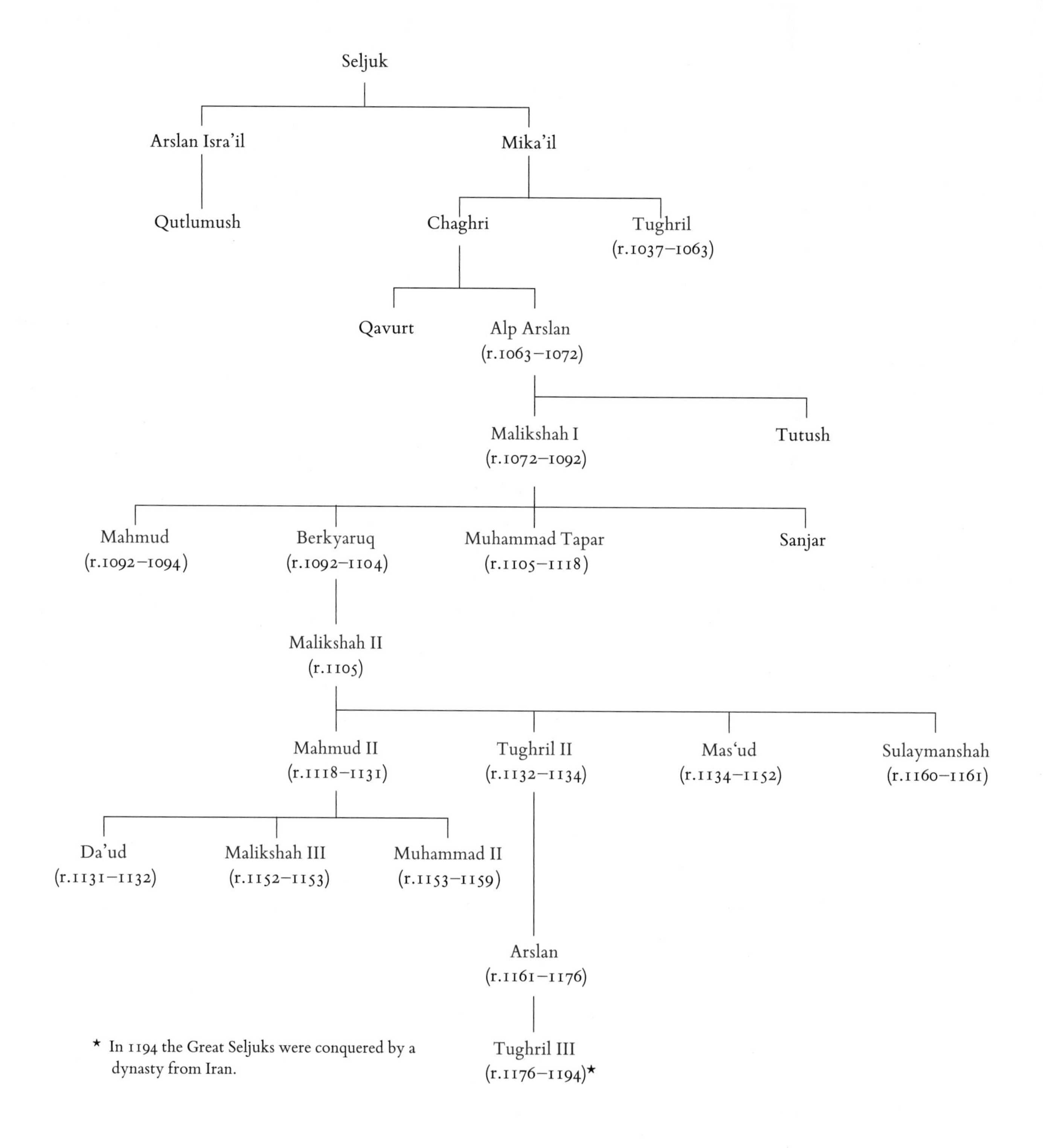

* In 1194 the Great Seljuks were conquered by a dynasty from Iran.

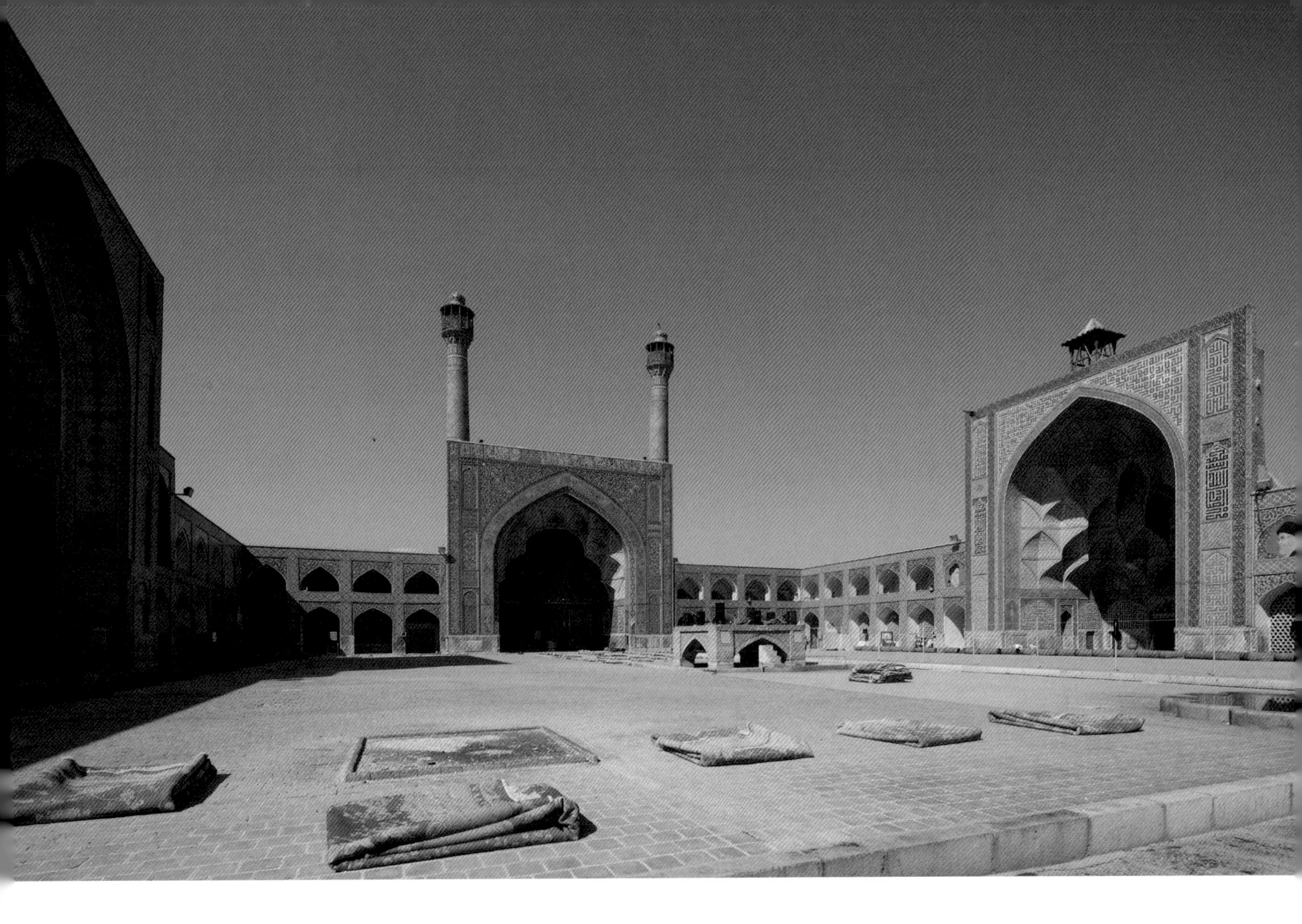

qibla dome, but in his case directly to the north of the courtyard. Less imposing, but more elegant than the southern dome, the northern dome included an inscription dating it to 1088 and named Taj al-Mulk as its donor. (See Plate 5.2.)

There was irony in such lavish expenditure on buildings in a culture originally nomadic. The ruling elite, in particular, was moving away from its roots. Malikshah made Isfahan his capital, far from the original centers of the Seljuk Empire such as Merv. For his part, Nizam al-Mulk cemented his position as virtual ruler by distributing not only money but also land to the army. Even before the time of the Seljuks, rulers had instituted the *iqta*: something like the European fief, it was a way to pay for military service by giving fighters the right to collect the revenues due from a particular piece of land. Under the Seljuks its use was greatly expanded to pay not only army leaders (emirs), but also bureaucrats and favored members of the dynasty. Like fiefs, *iqtas* were theoretically revocable by the ruler, and, again like fiefs, many *iqta* holders were able to make them hereditary.

Fortified by their revenues and land grants, the emirs of Iran and Iraq, originally appointed to represent the sultan's power at the local level, broke away from the centralized state. In the course of the twelfth century, in a process of fragmentation similar to the one that undermined the Abbasids, the Great Seljuk Empire fell apart. As under the

Plate 5.1 Isfahan Mosque Courtyard (11th–12th cent.). The courtyard is the heart of this huge and sprawling mosque. In this view to the west, three of the *iwans* built by Nizam al-Mulk are visible. The bulk of the courtyard is made up of double-decker walls. Each opening leads to an aisle topped by domes.

Genealogy 5.1 (facing page) The Great Seljuk Sultans

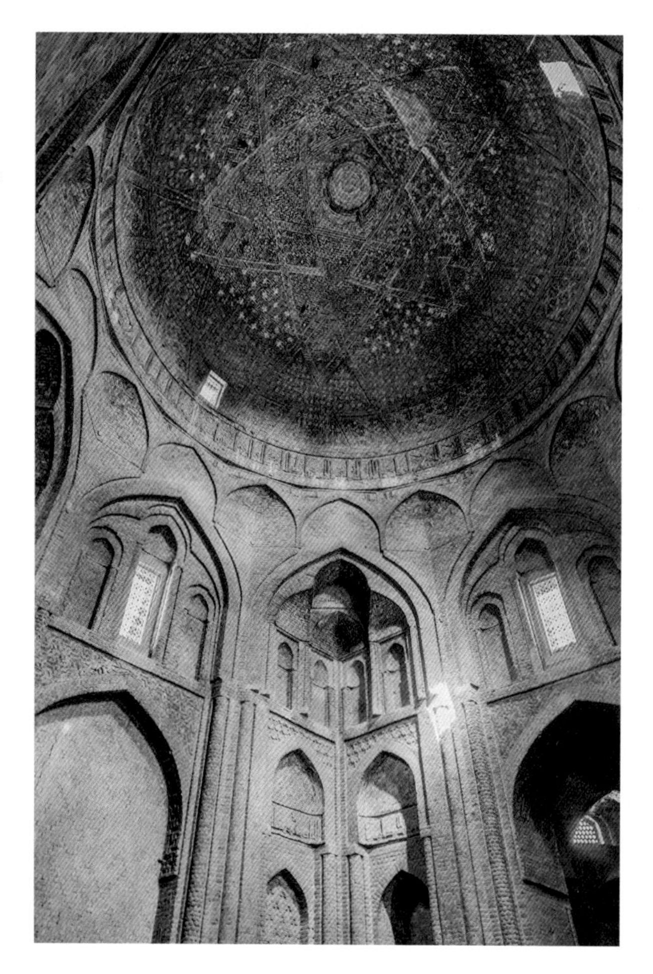

Plate 5.2 Isfahan Mosque North Dome (1088). Built according to a precise geometric design, the circular dome sits on a sixteen-sided polygon that rests in turn on an octagon perched on a square base. The design within the dome is equally mathematical, with an oculus in the mid-point of converging triangles. The perfection of this work demonstrates the skill of Seljuk architects.

Abbasids, this meant not the end of Seljuk culture and institutions but rather their replication in numerous smaller centers. The decline of the power of the Great Seljuk dynasty did not end the Great Seljuk era.

Meanwhile, the Anatolian branch of the dynasty prospered. It benefitted from the region's silver, copper, iron, and lapis lazuli mines and from the pastureland that supported animal products such as cashmere, highly prized as an export. The Anatolian sultans did not need to give out *iqtas*; they could pay their soldiers. Even so, Seljuk Anatolia was a sort of "wild west": most houses were made of mud, and the elites did not support the madrasas or the arts and literature as generously as did the rulers of most of the other centers of the Islamic world.

Unlike the Great Seljuk Sultanate, where the main "variety" was to be found in disputing versions of Islam, Anatolia had a significant Christian population. Because the region had been Byzantine before Manzikert, mosques had to be built quickly. (To be sure, the Anatolian Seljuks converted some churches into mosques as well.) At Siirt and elsewhere, the minaret loomed over the landscape (see Plate 5.3). The Shi'ite Fatimids had not built many minarets, but the Seljuks spent lavishly on such towers, asserting in concrete form their adherence to Sunni Islam. However, that adherence did not rule out

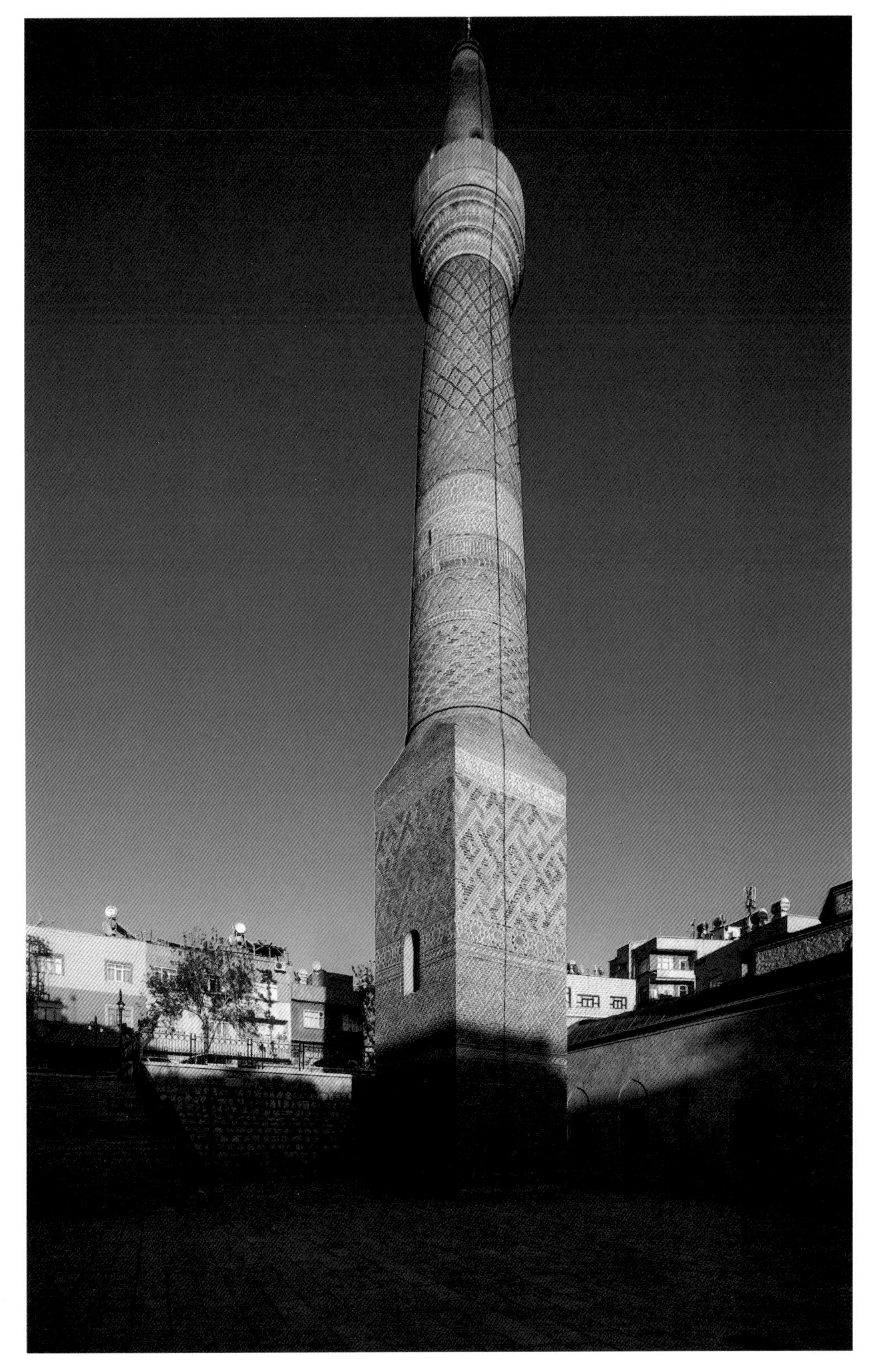

Plate 5.3 Great Mosque Minaret at Siirt (1128/1129?). The minaret has an inscription dating it to 1128/29, but some scholars think it was built a bit later. It is decorated with turquoise tile panels, tiles being a major crafts form of the Seljuks.

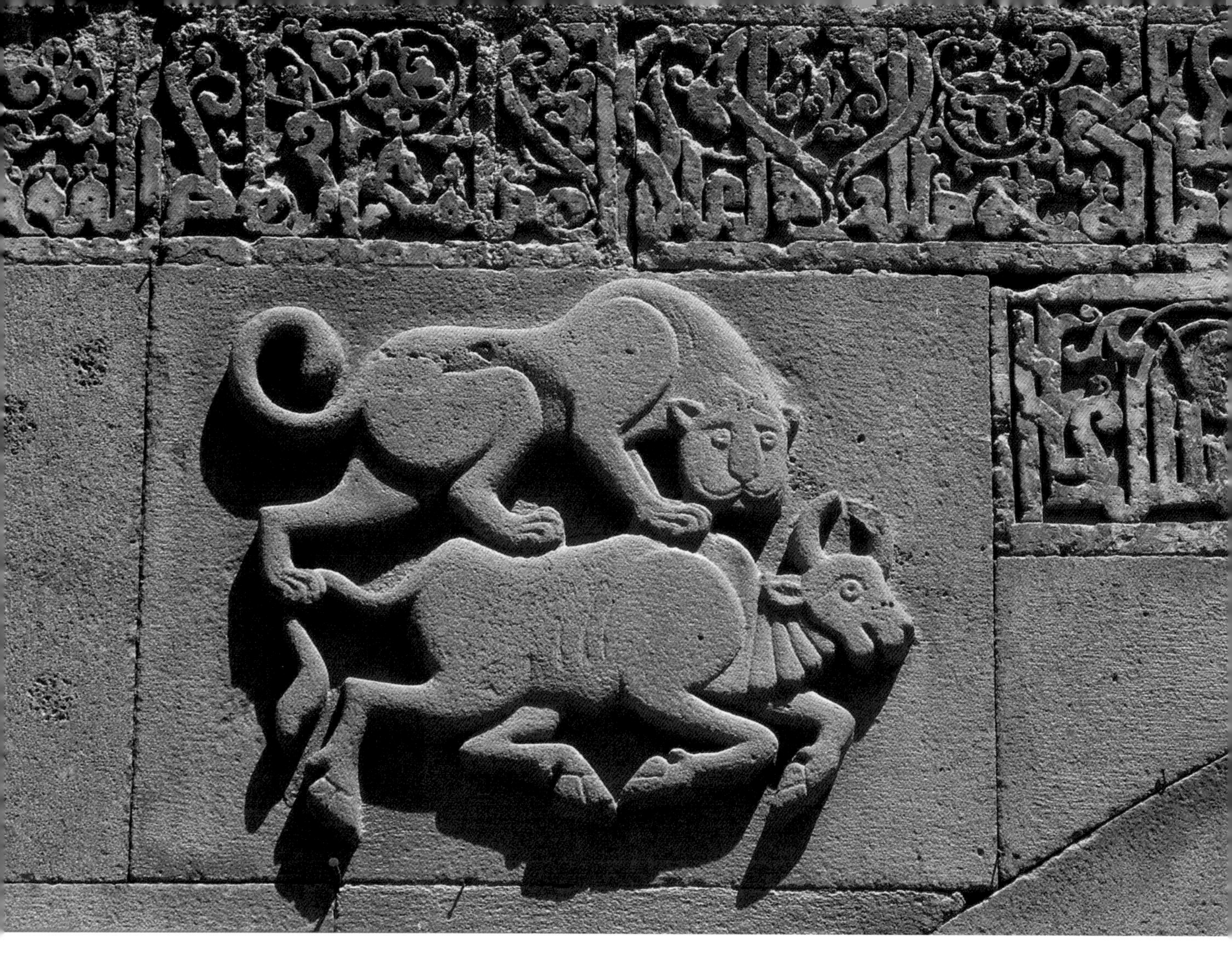

Plate 5.4 Great Mosque at Diyarbakir (1179/1180?). On one of two similar reliefs flanking the portal of the mosque, these fighting animals borrow from Christian church decoration. An inscription near the relief explains that the animals represent the superiority of one local elite dynasty over another.

borrowing from Christian motives. At the Great Mosque in Diyarbakir the unusual portal decoration of a fighting lion and bull betrays the influence of a similar motif on neighboring Georgian and Armenian churches. (See Plate 5.4.)

From Pastoralists to State-Builders

In the western half of the Islamic world, Berber Sanhaja tribesmen from the Sahara Desert forged a state similar to that of the Seljuks. Originally pastoralists who moved from one water source to another with their flocks and tents, they learned Islam from Muslim traders who needed guides and protectors to cross the Sahara. In the 1030s they were inspired by a tribal leader named Yahya ibn Ibrahim and his companions to follow a strict form of Sunni orthodoxy. In addition to adhering rigorously to Qur'anic injunctions, the men (along with the women) wore a veil over the lower part of their faces. Because of this, they were sometimes called *al-Mulaththamun*—The Veiled Ones. The earliest source for this practice did not connect it with Islam per se, but later sources claimed otherwise. They reported that the Sanhaja had originally lived in Yemen. In order to practice their fledgling monotheism, they were forced to flee to the Sahara with their men disguised as women. Their veils thus demonstrated their devotion to Islam.

Fired with zeal on behalf of their religious beliefs and also seeking economic opportunity, the Sanhaja formed a federation known as the Murabitun (Almoravids) and began conquering the (largely Shiʻite) regions to their north. Making common cause with local Sunni jurists and various tribal notables there, they took over cities bordering on the Sahara in the 1050s and soon had their eyes on the Maghreb. The foundation of their city at Marrakesh *c.*1070 marked the Almoravid transformation from nomadic tribespeople to settled state. Under their leader, Yusuf ibn Tashfin (d. 1106), and members of his clan, they subdued the Maghreb, taking Tangier in *c.*1078 and Ceuta in the 1080s.

Because their main goal was to control the African salt and gold trade, the Almoravids were at first not particularly interested in al-Andalus. But the Andalusian *taifa* rulers kept calling on them to help fight the Christian armies encroaching from the north of Spain. The chief nemesis of these rulers was Christian King Alfonso VI of León and Castile. (He was ruler of León 1065–1109 with a one-year interruption in 1071–72, when his older brother usurped the throne, and was king of Castile 1072–1109.) When Alfonso captured Toledo from its Muslim ruler in 1085, Yusuf ibn Tashfin at last took up the challenge. With Algeciras as the base of their operations, the Almoravids and their allies met Alfonso near Badajoz in 1086 and dealt him a stunning defeat. Dismayed by the *taifa* leaders' feuding and "lax" form of Islam (in their eyes) the Almoravids

Map 5.2 The Almoravid Empire, *c.*1115

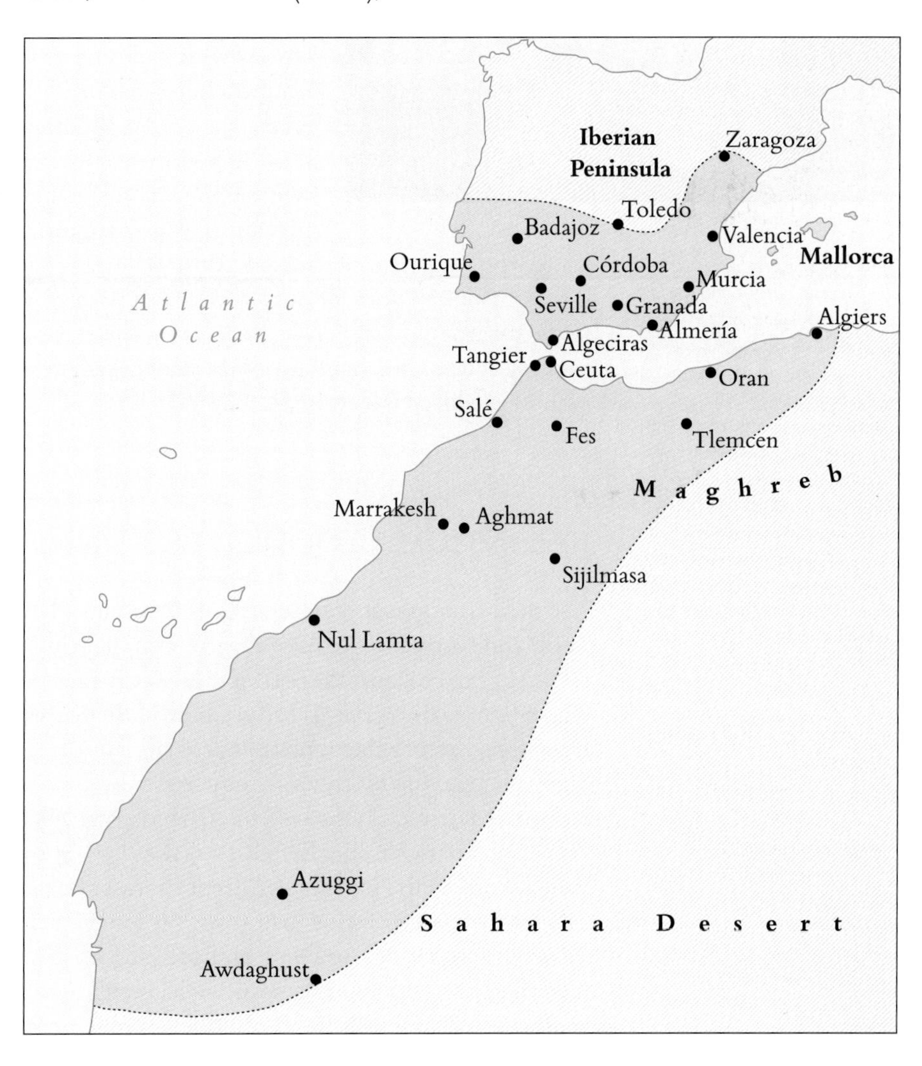

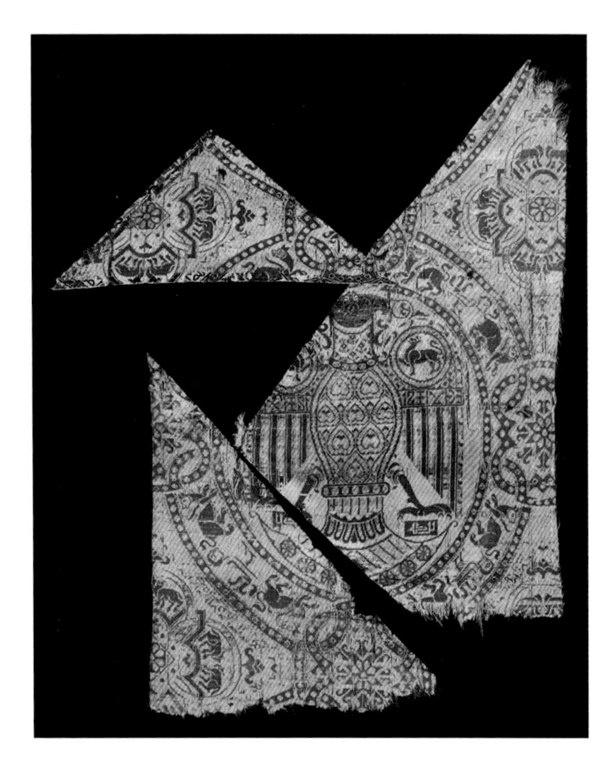

Plate 5.5 Almería Silk (first half of 12th cent.). Although made under the auspices of a Muslim ruler and containing Arabic writing, these silk fragments were used to cover relics of Saint Librada at Sigüenza. They were essential: relics were not ordinarily displayed "naked" but rather were wrapped in costly textiles, preferably made of silk. Every time a relic was moved from one place to another (an event called a "translation"), it had to be covered anew.

soon began to conquer the peninsula on their own behalf. By *c.*1115 all of al-Andalus not yet taken by Christian rulers was under Yusuf ibn Tashfin's control. The gold coin that forms the icon for accessing the Study Questions of this book was one of many gold dinars minted under his rule. The hegemony over the western Islamic world ended only in 1147, with the triumph of the Almohads, a rival Berber group.

The Almoravids thus came to control an empire stretching over 2,000 miles, from today's Ghana to much of Spain. Their wealth and power was mirrored in their crafts. Just as the cashmere of Anatolia had enough cachet to be popular in France, so fine textiles from places like Almoravid al-Andalus were widely distributed. A good example is shown in Plate 5.5. Thickly woven with stunning gold and silk threads, these fragments feature a huge eagle within a roundel interlaced with rosettes. Along the border are lithe catlike animals chasing their curvy tails. Across the eagle's wings are pseudo-Latin inscriptions, while under its talons are blessings in Arabic. The textile's preciousness was appreciated by Alfonso VII of Castile and León, who seized it when he took Almería in 1147 and held the city for ten years. Carrying it back to his kingdom, he cut it into pieces with which he covered relics that he donated to the cathedral of Sigüenza. Variants on this story could be multiplied. In addition to encasing relics, Christian Europeans used Islamic textiles for elegant garments, dined on Islamic-produced tableware, and decorated their churches with Islamic ceramics.

BYZANTIUM: BLOODIED BUT UNBOWED

The once triumphant empire of Basil II was unable to sustain its successes in the face of Turks and Normans. We have already seen the triumph of the Turks in Anatolia; meanwhile, in the Balkans, the Turkic Pechenegs raided with ease. The Normans, some of whom (as we saw on p. 134) had established themselves in southern Italy, began attacks on Byzantine territory there and conquered its last stronghold, Bari, in 1071. Entering Muslim Sicily in 1060, the Normans conquered it by 1093. Meanwhile, their knights attacked Byzantine territory in the Balkans. (See Map 5.3.) When Norman King Roger II (r.1130–1154) came to the throne, he ruled a realm that ran from southern Italy to Palermo—the Kingdom of Sicily. It was a persistent thorn in Byzantium's side.

Clearly the Byzantine army was no longer very effective. Few themes were still manned with citizen-soldiers, and the emperor's army was also largely composed of mercenaries—Turks and Russians, as had long been the case, and increasingly Normans and Franks as well. But the Byzantines were not entirely dependent on armed force; in

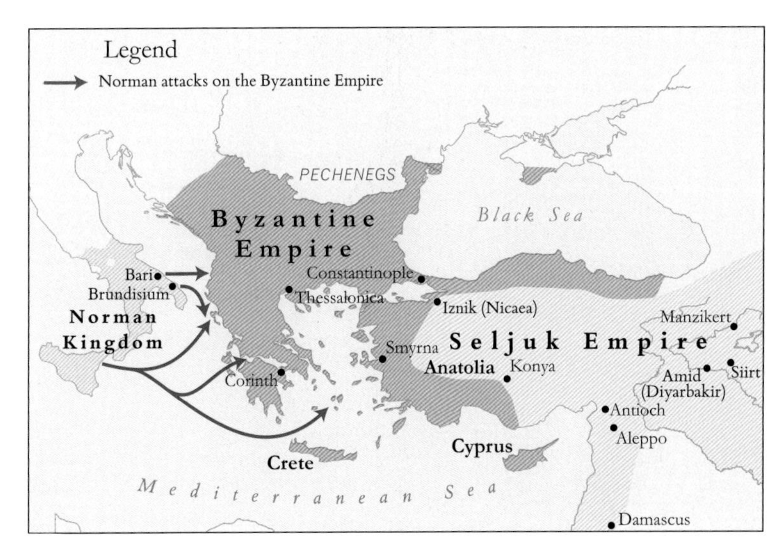

Map 5.3 Byzantium, 12th cent.

many instances they turned to diplomacy to confront the new invaders. When Emperor Constantine IX (r.1042–1055) was unable to prevent the Pechenegs from entering the Balkans, he shifted policy, welcoming them, administering baptism, conferring titles, and settling them in depopulated regions. Much the same process took place in Anatolia, where the emperors at times welcomed the Turks to help them fight rival *dynatoi*. Here the invaders were occasionally also welcomed by Christians who did not adhere to Byzantine orthodoxy; the Monophysites of Armenia were glad to have new Turkic overlords. The Byzantine grip on its territories loosened and its frontiers became nebulous, but Byzantium still stood.

There were changes at the imperial court as well. The model of the "public" emperor ruling alone with the aid of a civil service gave way to a less costly, more "familial" model of government. To be sure, for a time competing *dynatoi* families swapped the imperial throne. But Alexius I Comnenus (r.1081–1118), a Dalassenus on his mother's side, managed to bring most of the major families together through a series of marriage alliances. (The Comneni remained on the throne for about a century; see Genealogy 5.2.) Until her death in *c.*1102, Anna Dalassena, Alexius's mother, held the reins of government while Alexius occupied himself with military matters. At his revamped court, which he moved to the Blachernai palace, at the northwestern tip of the city (see Map 4.1 on p. 114), his relatives held the highest positions. Many of them received *pronoiai* (sing. *pronoia*), temporary grants of imperial lands that they administered and profited from. Just as the Seljuks turned to the *iqta* and the Europeans to the fief, so the Byzantines resorted to land grants rather than salaries.

Genealogy 5.2 The Comnenian Dynasty

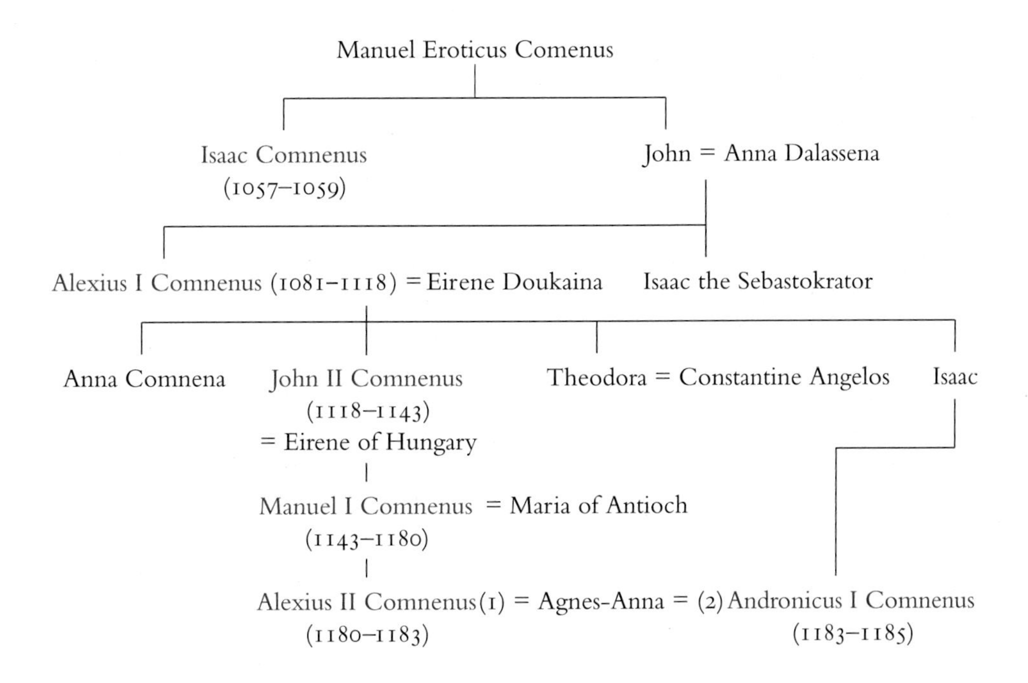

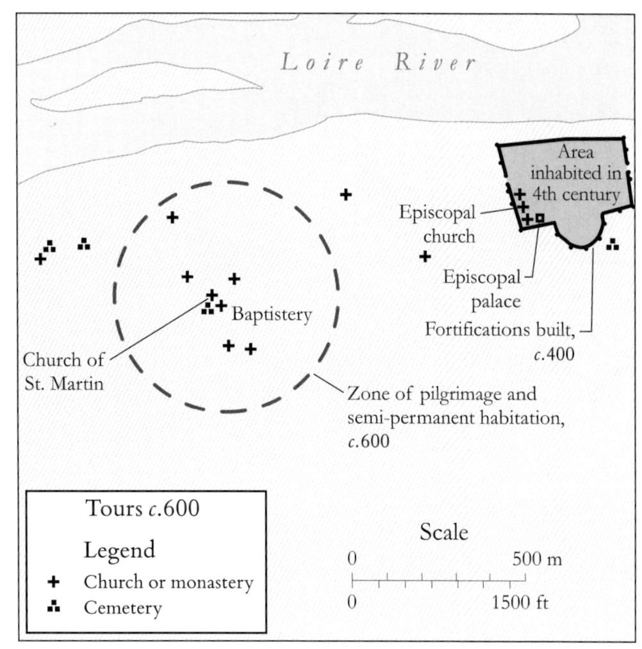

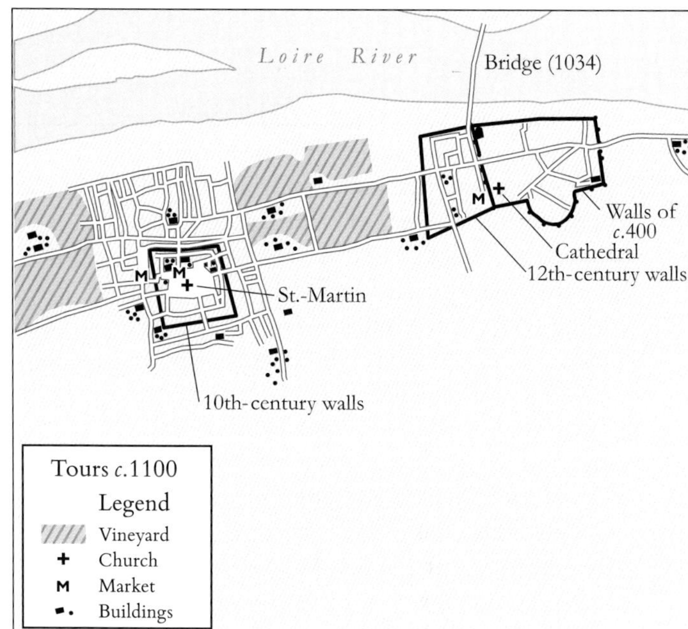

Map 5.4 Tours *c.*600 vs. Tours *c.*1100

In general, Byzantine rulers were becoming more like their European counterparts, holding a relatively small amount of territory, handing some of it out in grants, spending most of their time in battle to secure a stronghold here, a city there. Meanwhile, Western rulers were becoming less regional in focus, encroaching on Byzantine territory and (as we shall see) attacking the Islamic world as well.

THE QUICKENING OF THE EUROPEAN ECONOMY

The Norman take-over of Sicily and attacks on Byzantium were symptoms of European expansion, as were new economic developments. Draining marshes, felling trees, building dikes: this was the backbreaking work that brought new land into cultivation. With their heavy, horse-drawn plows, peasants were able to reap greater harvests; using the three-field system, they raised more varieties of crops. Great landowners, the same "oppressors" against whom the Peace of God fulminated (see p. 139), could also be efficient economic organizers. They set up mills to grind grain, forced their tenants to use them, and then charged a fee for the service. They wanted peasants to produce as much grain as possible. Some landlords gave peasants special privileges to settle on especially inhospitable land: the bishop of Hamburg was generous to those who came from Holland to work soil that was, as he admitted "uncultivated, marshy, and useless."[3]

As the countryside became more productive, people became healthier, their fertility increased, and there were more mouths to feed. Even so, surprising surpluses made possible the growth of old and the creation of new urban centers. Within a generation or two, city dwellers, intensely conscious of their common goals, elaborated new instruments of commerce, self-regulating organizations, and forms of self-government.

Towns and Cities

Around castles and monasteries in the countryside or at the walls of crumbling ancient towns, merchants came with their wares and artisans set up shop. At Bruges, it was the local lord's castle that served as a magnet. Churches and monasteries were the other centers of town growth. Recall Tours as it had looked in the early seventh century, with its semi-permanent settlements around the church of Saint-Martin, out in the cemetery, and its lonely cathedral nestling against one of the ancient walls. By the twelfth century, Saint-Martin was a monastery, the hub of a small town dense enough to boast eleven parish churches, merchant and artisan shops, private houses, and two markets. To the east, the episcopal complex was no longer alone: a market had sprung up outside the old western wall, and private houses lined the street leading to the bridge. Smaller than the town around Saint-Martin, the one at the foot of the old city had only two parish churches, but it was big and rich enough to warrant the construction of a new set of walls to protect it. (See Map 5.4.)

Early cities developed without prior planning, but some later ones were "chartered," that is, declared, surveyed, and plotted out. A marketplace and merchant settlement were already in place at Freiburg im Breisgau when the duke of Zähringen chartered it, promising each new settler there a house lot of 5,000 square feet for a very small yearly rent. The duke had fair hopes that commerce would flourish right at his back door and yield him rich revenues.

The look and feel of medieval cities varied immensely from place to place. Nearly all included a marketplace, a castle, and several churches. Most were ringed by walls. Within the walls lay a network of streets—narrow, dirty, dark, smelly, and winding—made of packed clay or gravel. Most cities were situated near waterways and had bridges; the bridge at Tours was built in the 1030s. Many had to adapt to increasingly crowded conditions. At the end of the eleventh century in Winchester, England, city plots were still large enough to accommodate houses parallel to the street; but soon those houses had to be torn down to make way for narrow ones, built at right angles to the roadway. The houses at Winchester were made of wattle and daub—twigs woven together and covered with clay. If they were like the stone houses built in the late twelfth century (about which we know a good deal), they had two stories: a shop or warehouse on the lower floor and living quarters above. Behind this main building were the kitchen, enclosures for livestock, and a garden. Even city dwellers clung to rural pursuits, raising much of their food themselves.

Although commercial centers developed throughout Western Europe, they grew fastest and most densely in regions along key waterways: the Mediterranean coasts of Italy, France, and Spain; northern Italy along the Po River; the river system of the Rhône-Saône-Meuse; the Rhineland; the English Channel; the shores of the Baltic Sea. During

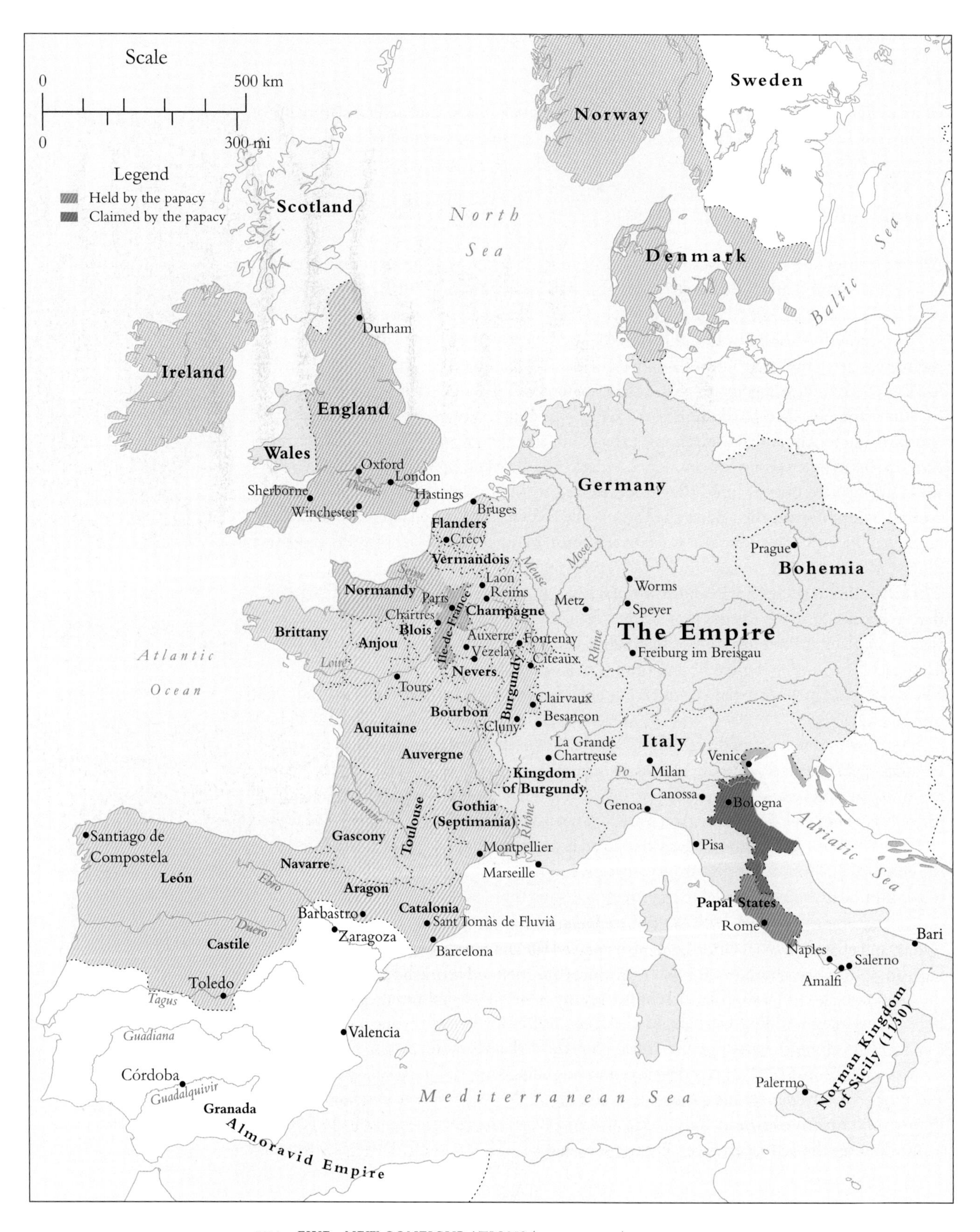
Scale
0
500 km
0
300 mi
Legend
Held by the papacy
Claimed by the papacy
Sweden
Norway
Scotland
North
Sea
Denmark
Baltic
Sea
Durham
Ireland
England
Wales
Oxford
London
Sherborne
Thames
Hastings
Winchester
Bruges
Flanders
Crécy
Vermandois
Germany
Prague
Bohemia
Laon
Reims
Worms
Normandy
Paris
Metz
Speyer
Champagne
Chartres
Brittany
Blois
Anjou
Ile-de-France
Auxerre
Fontenay
The Empire
Vézelay
Freiburg im Breisgau
Atlantic
Ocean
Loire
Nevers
Cîteaux
Tours
Burgundy
Clairvaux
Bourbon
Besançon
Cluny
Aquitaine
La Grande
Chartreuse
Italy
Auvergne
Venice
Milan
Kingdom
of Burgundy
Canossa
Gothia
(Septimania)
Genoa
Bologna
Garonne
Toulouse
Santiago de
Compostela
Gascony
Rhône
Adriatic
Sea
Pisa
Montpellier
Navarre
León
Marseille
Ebro
Aragon
Papal States
Catalonia
Barbastro
Sant Tomàs de Fluvià
Rome
Bari
Duero
Castile
Zaragoza
Naples
Barcelona
Salerno
Amalfi
Toledo
Tagus
Norman Kingdom
of Sicily (1130)
Valencia
Guadiana
Córdoba
Guadalquivir
Palermo
Mediterranean Sea
Granada
Almoravid Empire

the eleventh and twelfth centuries, these waterways became part of a single, interdependent economy. At the same time, new roads through the countryside linked urban centers to rural districts and stimulated the growth of fairs (regular, short-term, often lively markets). (See Map 5.5.)

Map 5.5 (facing page) Western Europe, *c.*1100

Business Arrangements

The revival of urban life and the expansion of trade, together dubbed the "commercial revolution" by historians, was sustained and invigorated by merchants. They were a varied lot. Some were local traders, such as one monk who supervised a manor twenty miles south of his monastery and sold its surplus horses and grain at a local market. Others—often Jews and Italians—were long-distance traders, much in demand because they supplied fine wines, spices, and fabrics to the aristocracy. Some Jews had long been involved at least part time in long-distance trade as vintners. In the eleventh century, more Jews swelled their ranks when lords reorganized the countryside and drove out the Jewish landowners, forcing them into commerce and urban trades full time.

Other long-distance traders came from Italy. The key players were from Genoa, Pisa, Amalfi, and Venice. Regular merchants at Constantinople, their settlements were strung like pearls along the Golden Horn (see Map 4.1 on p. 114). Italian traders found the Islamic world nearly as lucrative as the Byzantine. Establishing bases at ports such as Tunis, they imported Islamic wares—ceramics, textiles, metalwork—into Europe. In turn, Western traders exported wood, iron, and woolen cloth to the East.

Merchants invented new forms of collective enterprises to pool their resources and finance large undertakings. A cloth industry began, powered by water mills. New deep-mining technologies provided Europeans with hitherto untapped sources of metals. Forging techniques improved, and iron was for the first time regularly used for agricultural tools and plows, enhancing food production. Beer, a major source of nutrition in the north of Europe, moved from the domestic hearth and monastic estates to urban centers, where brewers gained special privileges to ply their trade.

Brewers, like other urban artisans, had their own guild. Whether driven by machines or handwork, the new economy was sustained by such guilds, which regulated and protected professionals ranging from merchants and financiers to shoemakers. In these social, religious, and economic associations, members prayed for and buried one another. Craft guilds agreed on quality standards for their products and defined work hours, materials, and prices. Merchant guilds regulated business arrangements, weights and measures, and (like the craft guilds) prices. Guilds guaranteed their members—mostly male, except in a few professions—a place in the market. They represented the social and economic counterpart to urban walls, giving their members protection, shared identity, and recognized status.

The political counterpart of the walls was the "commune"—town self-government. City dwellers—keenly aware of their special identity in a world dominated by knights and peasants—recognized their mutual interest in reliable coinage, laws to facilitate commerce, freedom from servile dues and services, and independence to buy and sell as the market dictated. They petitioned the political powers that ruled them—bishops, kings, counts, castellans, dukes—for the right to govern themselves.

Collective movements for urban self-government were especially prevalent in Italy, France, and Germany. Already Italy's political life was city-centered; communes there were attempts to substitute the power of one group (the citizens) for another (the nobles and bishops). At Milan in the second half of the eleventh century, for example, popular discontent with the archbishop, who effectively ruled the city, led to numerous armed clashes that ended, in 1097, with the transfer of power from the archbishop to a government of leading men of the city. Outside Italy movements for urban independence—sometimes violent, as at Milan, while at other times peaceful—often took place within a larger political framework. For example, King Henry I of England (r.1100–1135) freed the citizens of London from numerous customary taxes while granting them the right to "appoint as sheriff from themselves whomsoever they may choose, and [they] shall appoint from among themselves as justice whomsoever they choose to look after the pleas of my crown."[4] The king's law still stood, but it was to be carried out by the Londoners' officials.

CHURCH REFORM AND ITS AFTERMATH

Disillusioned citizens at Milan denounced their archbishop not only for his tyranny but also for his impurity; they wanted their pastors to be untainted by sex and money. In this they were supported by a new-style papacy, keen on reform in the church and society. The "Gregorian Reform," as modern historians call this movement, broke up clerical marriages, unleashed civil war in Germany, changed the procedure for episcopal elections, and transformed the papacy into a monarchy. It began as a way to free the church from the world, but in the end the church was deeply involved in the new world it had helped to create.

The Coming of Reform

Free the church from the world: what could that mean? In 910 the duke and duchess of Aquitaine founded the monastery of Cluny with some unusual stipulations. (For all the places involved here, see Map 5.5.) They endowed the monastery with property (normal and essential if it were to survive), but then they gave it and its worldly possessions to Saints Peter and Paul. In this way, they put control of the monastery into the hands of the two most powerful heavenly saints. They designated the pope, as the successor of Saint Peter, to be the monastery's worldly protector if anyone should bother or threaten it. But even the pope had no right to infringe on its freedom: "From this day," the duke wrote,

> those same monks there congregated shall be subject neither to our yoke, nor to that of our relatives, nor to the sway of any earthly power. And, through God and all his saints, and by the awful day of judgment, I warn and abjure that no one of the secular princes, no count, no bishop whatever, not the pontiff of the aforesaid Roman see, shall invade the property of these servants of God, or alienate it, or diminish it, or exchange it, or give it as a benefice to any one, or constitute any prelate over them against their will.[5]

Cluny's prestige was great because of the influence of its founders, the status of Saint Peter, and the fame of the monastery's elaborate round of prayers. The Cluniac monks fulfilled the role of "those who pray" in dazzling manner. Through their prayers, they seemed to guarantee the salvation of all Christians. Rulers, bishops, rich landowners, and even serfs (if they could) gave Cluny donations of land, joining their contributions to the land of Saint Peter. Powerful men and women called on the Cluniac abbots to reform new monasteries along the Cluniac model.

The abbots of Cluny came to see themselves as reformers of the world as well as the cloister. They believed in clerical celibacy, preaching against the prevailing norm in which parish priests and even bishops were married. They also thought that the laity could be reformed, become more virtuous, and cease its oppression of the poor. In the eleventh century, the Cluniacs began to link their program to the papacy. When they disputed with bishops or laypeople about lands and rights, they called on the popes to help them out.

The popes were ready to do so. A parallel movement for reform had entered papal circles via a small group of influential monks and clerics. Mining canon (church) law for their ammunition, these churchmen emphasized two abuses: nicolaitism (clerical marriage) and simony (buying church offices). Why were these two singled out? Married clerics were considered less "pure" than those who were celibate; furthermore, their heirs might claim church property. As for simony: the new profit economy sensitized reformers to the crass commercial meanings of gifts; in their eyes, gifts given or received by churchmen for their offices or clerical duties were attempts to purchase the Holy Spirit.

Initially, the reformers got imperial backing. German king and emperor Henry III (r.1039–1056) thought that, as the anointed of God, he was responsible for the well-being of the church in the empire. (For Henry and his dynasty, see Genealogy 5.3.) Henry denounced simony and personally refused to accept money or gifts when he appointed bishops to their posts. He presided over the Synod of Sutri (1046), which deposed three papal rivals and elected another. When that pope and his successor died, Henry appointed Bruno of Toul, a member of the royal family, seasoned courtier, and reforming bishop. Taking the name Leo IX (1049–1054), the new pope surprised his patron: he set out to reform the church under papal, not imperial, control.

Leo revolutionized the papacy. He had himself elected by the "clergy and people" to satisfy the demands of canon law. Unlike earlier popes, he often left Rome to preside over church councils and make the pope's influence felt outside Italy, especially in France and Germany. Leo brought to the papal curia the most zealous church reformers of his

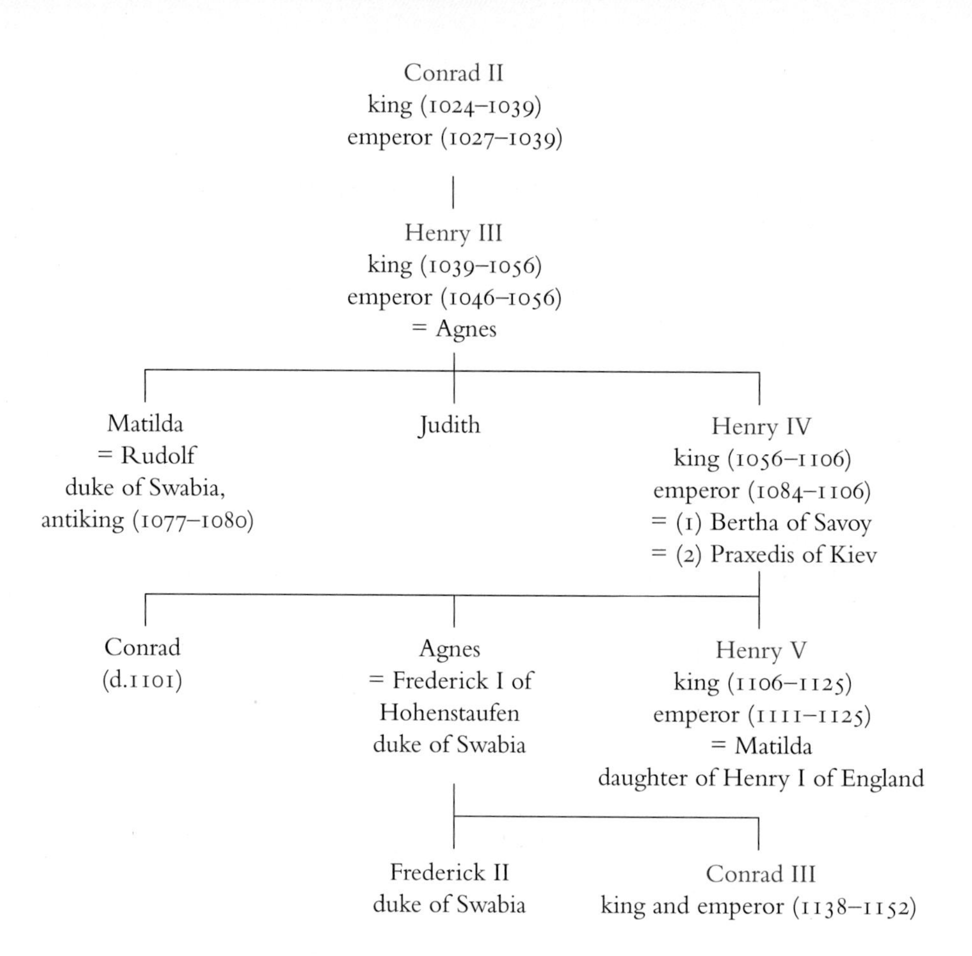

Genealogy 5.3 The Salian Kings and Emperors

day: Peter Damian, Hildebrand of Soana (later Pope Gregory VII), and Humbert of Silva Candida. They put new stress on the passage in Matthew's Gospel (Matt. 16:19) in which Christ tells Peter that he is the "rock" of the church, with the keys to heaven and the power to bind (impose penance) and loose (absolve from sins). As the successor to the special privileges of Saint Peter, the Roman church, headed by the pope, was said to be "head and mother of all churches." What historians call the doctrine of "papal supremacy" was thus announced.

Its impact was soon felt at Byzantium. On a mission at Constantinople in 1054 to forge an alliance with the emperor against the Normans and, at the same time, to "remind" the patriarch of his place in the church hierarchy, Humbert ended by excommunicating the patriarch and his followers. In retaliation, the patriarch excommunicated Humbert and his fellow legates. Clashes between the Roman and Byzantine churches had occurred before and had been patched up, but this one, though not recognized as such at the time, marked a permanent schism. After 1054, the Roman Catholic and Greek Orthodox churches largely went their separate ways.

More generally, the papacy began to wield new forms of power. It waged unsuccessful war against the Normans in southern Italy and then made the best of the situation by granting them parts of the region—and Sicily as well—as a fief, turning former enemies into vassals. It supported the Christian push into the *taifas* of al-Andalus, transforming the "*reconquista*"—the conquest of Islamic Spain—into a holy war: Pope Alexander II (1061–1073) forgave the sins of the Christians on their way to the battle of Barbastro (see Map 5.5 on p. 174).

The Investiture Conflict and Its Effects

The papal reform movement is associated particularly with Pope Gregory VII (1073–1085), hence the term "Gregorian Reform." A passionate advocate of papal primacy (the theory that the pope is the head of the church), Gregory was not afraid to clash directly with the king of Germany, Henry IV (r.1056–1106), over church leadership. In Gregory's view—an astonishing one at the time, given the religious and spiritual roles associated with rulers—kings and emperors were simple laymen who had no right to meddle in church affairs. Henry, on the other hand, brought up in the traditions of his father, Henry III, considered it part of his duty to appoint bishops and even popes to ensure the well-being of church and empire together.

The pope and the king first collided over the appointment of the archbishop of Milan. Gregory disputed Henry's right to "invest" the archbishop (i.e., put him into his office). In the investiture ritual, the emperor or his representative symbolically gave the church and the land that went with it to the bishop or archbishop chosen for the job. In the case of Milan, two rival candidates for archiepiscopal office (one supported by the pope, the other by the emperor) had been at loggerheads for several years when, in 1075, Henry invested his own candidate. Gregory immediately called on Henry to "give more respectful attention to the master of the Church," namely Peter and his living representative—Gregory himself.[6] In reply, Henry and the German bishops called on Gregory, that "false monk," to resign.[7] This was the beginning of what historians delicately call the "Investiture Conflict" or "Investiture Controversy." In fact it was war. In February 1076, Gregory called a synod that both excommunicated Henry and suspended him from office:

> I deprive King Henry [IV], son of the emperor Henry [III], who has rebelled against [God's] Church with unheard-of audacity, of the government over the whole kingdom of Germany and Italy, and I release all Christian men from the allegiance which they have sworn or may swear to him, and I forbid anyone to serve him as king.[8]

The last part of this decree gave it real punch: anyone in Henry's kingdom could rebel against him. The German "princes"—the aristocrats—seized the moment and threatened to elect another king. They were motivated partly by religious sentiments—many had established links with the papacy through their support of reformed monasteries—and partly by political opportunism, as they had chafed under strong German kings who had tried to keep their power in check. Some bishops, too, joined with Gregory's supporters, a major blow to Henry, who needed the troops that they supplied.

Attacked from all sides, Henry traveled in the winter of 1077 to intercept Gregory, barricaded in a fortress at Canossa, high in the Apennine Mountains. It was a refuge provided by the staunchest of papal supporters, Countess Matilda of Tuscany. In an astute and dramatic gesture, the king stood outside the castle (in cold and snow) for three days, barefoot, as a penitent. Gregory was forced, as a pastor, to lift his excommunication and to receive Henry back into the church, precisely as Henry intended. For his part, the pope had the satisfaction of seeing the king humiliate himself before the papal majesty. Although it made a great impression on contemporaries, the whole episode solved nothing. The princes elected an antiking, the emperor an antipope, and bloody civil war continued intermittently until 1122.

The Investiture Conflict ended with a compromise. The Concordat of Worms (1122) relied on a conceptual distinction between two parts of investiture—the spiritual (in which the bishop-to-be received the symbols of his office) and the secular (in which he received the symbols of the material goods that would allow him to function). Under the terms of the Concordat, the ring and staff, symbols of church office, would be given by a churchman in the first part of the ceremony. Then the emperor or his representative would touch the bishop with a scepter, signifying the land and other possessions that went with his office. Elections of bishops in Germany would take place "in the presence" of the emperor—that is, under his influence. In Italy, the pope would have a comparable role.

In the end, then, secular rulers continued to matter in the appointment of churchmen. But just as the new investiture ceremony broke the ritual into spiritual and secular halves, so too did it imply a new notion of kingship separate from the priesthood. The Investiture Conflict did not produce the modern distinction between church and state—that would develop only very slowly—but it set the wheels in motion. At the time, its most important consequence was to shatter the delicate balance between political and ecclesiastical powers in Germany and Italy. In Germany, the princes consolidated their lands and powers at the expense of the king. In Italy, the communes came closer to their goals: it was no accident that Milan gained its independence in 1097. And everywhere the papacy gained new authority: it had become a "papal monarchy."

Papal influence was felt at every level. At the general level of canon law, papal primacy was enhanced by the publication *c.*1140 of the *Decretum*, written by a teacher of canon law named Gratian. Collecting nearly two thousand passages from the decrees of popes and councils as well as the writings of the Church Fathers, Gratian set out to demonstrate their essential agreement. In fact, the book's original title was *Harmony of Discordant Canons*. If he found any "discord" in his sources, Gratian usually imposed the harmony himself by arguing that the conflicting passages dealt with different situations. A bit later another legal scholar revised and expanded the *Decretum*, adding Roman law to the mix. At a more local level, papal denunciations of married clergy made inroads on family life. At Verona, for example, "sons of priests" disappeared from the historical record in the twelfth century. At the mundane level of administration, the papal claim to head the church helped turn the curia at Rome into a kind of monarchy, complete with its own territory, bureaucracy, collection agencies, and law courts. It was the teeming port of call for litigious churchmen disputing appointments and for petitioners of every sort.

The First Crusade

On the military level, the papacy's proclamations of holy wars led to bloody slaughter, tragic loss, and tidy profit. We have already seen how Alexander II encouraged the *reconquista* in Spain; it was in the wake of his call that the *taifa* rulers implored the Almoravids for help. An oddly similar chain of events took place at the other end of the Islamic world. Ostensibly responding to a request from the Byzantine emperor Alexius for mercenaries to help retake Anatolia from the Seljuks, Pope Urban II (1088–1099) turned the enterprise into something new: a pious pilgrimage to the Holy Land to be undertaken by an armed militia—one commissioned like those of the Peace of God, but thousands of times larger—under the leadership of the papacy: "Let your quarrels end, let wars cease, and let all dissensions and controversies slumber. Enter upon the road to the Holy Sepulcher; wrest that land from the wicked race, and subject it to yourselves."[9]

The event that historians call the First Crusade (1096–1099) mobilized a force of some 100,000 people, including warriors, old men, bishops, priests, women, children, and hangers-on. The armies were organized not as one military force but rather as separate militias, each authorized by the pope and commanded by a different leader.

Several motley bands were not authorized by the pope. Though called collectively the "Peasants' (or People's) Crusade," these irregular armies included nobles. They were inspired by popular preachers, especially the eloquent Peter the Hermit, who was described by chroniclers as small, ugly, barefoot, and—partly because of those very characteristics—utterly captivating. Starting out before the other armies, the Peasants' Crusade took a route to the Holy Land through the Rhineland in Germany.

This indirect route was no mistake. The crusaders were looking for "wicked races" closer to home: the Jews. Under Henry IV many Jews had gained a stable place within the cities of Germany, particularly along the Rhine River. The Jews received protection from the local bishops (who were imperial appointees) in return for paying a tax. Living in their own neighborhoods, the Jews valued their tightly knit communities focused on the synagogue, which was a school and community center as well as a place of worship. Nevertheless, Jews also participated in the life of the larger Christian community. For example, Archbishop Anno of Cologne made use of the services of the Jewish moneylenders in his city, and other Jews in Cologne were allowed to trade their wares at the fairs there.

Although officials pronounced against the Jews from time to time, and although Jews were occasionally (temporarily) expelled from some Rhineland cities, they were not persecuted systematically until the First Crusade. Then the Peasants' Crusade, joined by some local nobles and militias from the region, threatened the Jews with forced conversion

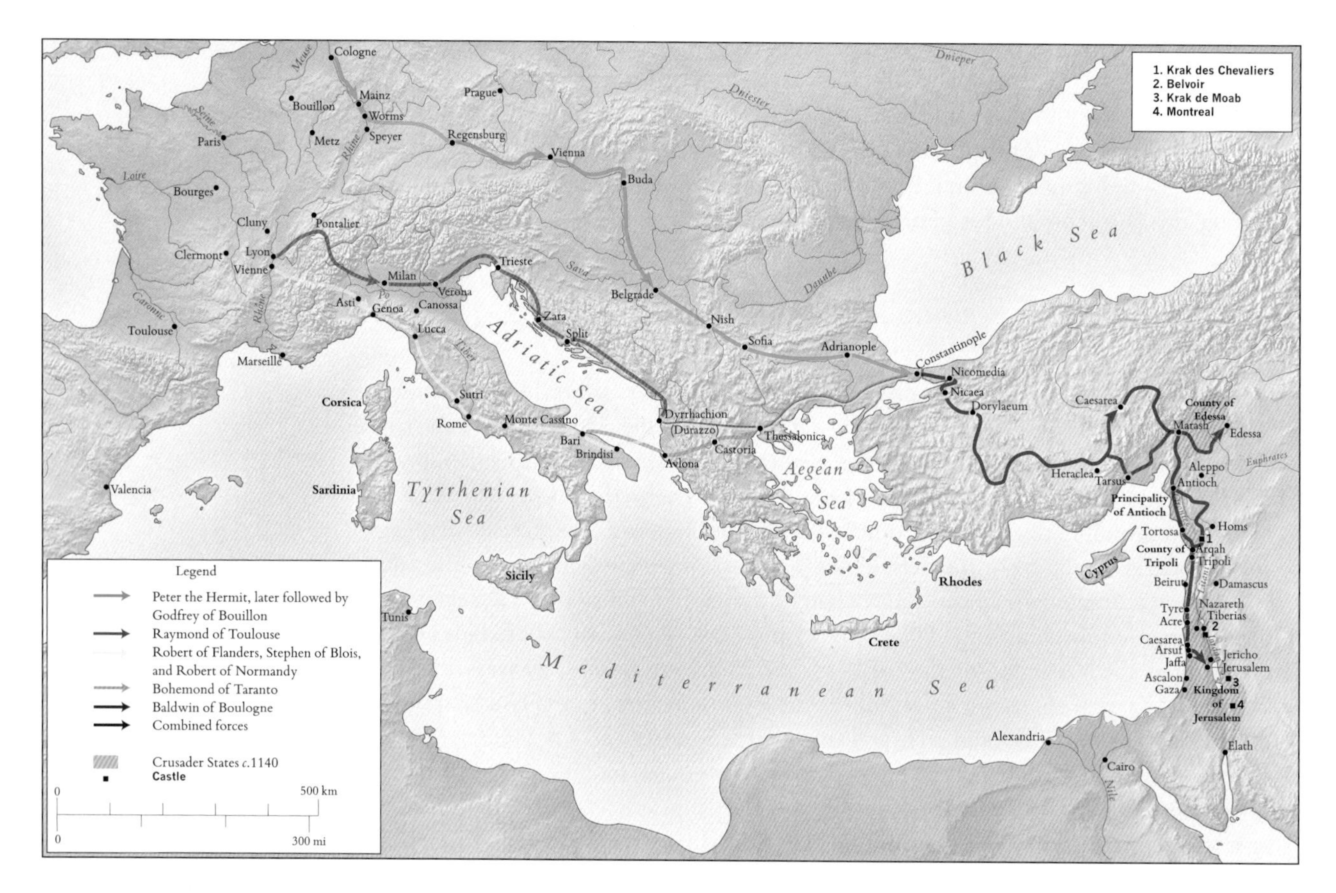

Map 5.6 The First Crusade and Early Crusader States

or death. Some relented when the Jews paid them money; others, however, attacked. Beleaguered Jews occasionally found refuge with bishops or in the houses of Christian friends, but in many cities—Metz, Speyer, Worms, Mainz, and Cologne—they were massacred. Leaving the Rhineland, some of the irregular militias disbanded, while others sought to gain the Holy Land via Hungary, at least one stopping off at Prague to massacre more Jews there. Only a handful of these armies continued on to Anatolia, where most of them were quickly slaughtered.

From the point of view of Emperor Alexius at Constantinople, even the "official" crusaders were problematic. One of the crusade's leaders, the Norman warrior Bohemond, had, a few years before, tried to conquer Byzantium itself. Alexius got most of the leaders to swear that if they conquered any land previously held by the Byzantines, they would restore them; and if they conquered new regions, they would hold them from Alexius as their overlord. Then he shipped the armies across the Bosporus. (For the various armies and their routes, see Map 5.6).

The main objective of the First Crusade—to conquer the Holy Land—was accomplished largely because of the disunity of the Islamic world and its failure to consider the crusade a serious military threat. Spared by the Turks when they first arrived in Anatolia, the crusaders' armies were initially uncoordinated and their food supplies uncertain, but soon they organized themselves, setting up a "council of princes" that included all the great crusade leaders, while the Byzantines supplied food at a nearby port. Surrounding

Iznik (Nicaea) and besieging it with catapults and other war machines, the crusaders, along with a small Byzantine contingent, took the city on June 19, 1097. The city surrendered directly to Alexius, who rewarded the crusaders amply but also insisted that any leader who had not yet taken the oath to him do so.

However, the crusaders soon forgot their promise to the Byzantines. While most went toward Antioch, which stood in the way of their conquest of Jerusalem, one leader went off to Edessa, where he took over the city and its outlying area, creating the first of the Crusader States: the County of Edessa. Meanwhile the other crusaders remained stymied before the thick and heavily fortified walls of Antioch for many months. Then, in a surprise turn-around, they entered the town but found themselves besieged by Muslim armies from the outside. Their mood grim, they rallied when a peasant named Peter Bartholomew reported that he had seen in many visions the Holy Lance that had pierced Christ's body—it was, he said, buried right in the main church in Antioch. (Antioch had a flourishing Christian population even under Muslim rule.) After a night of feverish digging, the crusaders believed that they had discovered the Holy Lance, and, fortified by this miracle, they defeated the besiegers. "[At Antioch,] the number of men, women, and children killed, taken prisoner, and enslaved from its population is beyond computation. About three thousand men fled to the citadel and fortified themselves in it, and some few escaped for whom God had decreed escape," wrote a Muslim chronicler looking back on the event some fifty years later.[10]

From Antioch, it was only a short march to Jerusalem, though disputes among the leaders delayed that next step for over a year. One leader claimed Antioch. Another eventually took charge—provisionally—of the expedition to Jerusalem. His way was eased by quarrels among Muslim rulers, and an alliance with one of them allowed free passage through what would have been enemy territory. In early June 1099, a large crusading force amassed before the walls of Jerusalem and set to work to build siege engines.[11] In mid-July they attacked, breaching the walls and entering the city. Jerusalem was now in the hands of the crusaders.

RULERS WITH CLOUT

While the papacy was turning into a monarchy, other rulers were beginning to turn their territories into states. They discovered ideologies to justify their hegemony, hired officials to work for them, and found vassals and churchmen to support them. Some of these rulers were women.

The Crusader States

In the Holy Land, the leaders of the crusade set up four tiny states, European colonies in the Levant. Two (Tripoli and Edessa) were counties, Antioch was a principality, Jerusalem a kingdom. (See Map 5.6 again.) The region was habituated to multi-ethnic and multi-religious territories ruled by a military elite; apart from the religion of that elite, the Crusader States were no exception. Yet, however much they engaged with their neighbors, the Europeans in the Levant saw themselves as a world apart, holding on to their western identity through their political institutions and the old vocabulary of homage, fealty, and Christianity.

The states won during the First Crusade lasted—tenuously—until 1291, though many new crusades had to be called in the interval to shore them up. Created by conquest, these states were treated as lordships. The new rulers carved out estates to give as fiefs to their vassals, who, in turn, gave portions of their holdings in fief to their own men. The peasants continued to work the land as before, and commerce boomed as the new rulers encouraged lively trade at their coastal ports. Italian merchants—the Genoese, Pisans, and Venetians—were the most active, but others—Byzantines and Muslim traders—participated as well. Enlightened lordship dictated that the mixed population of the states—Muslims, to be sure, but also Jews, Greek Orthodox Christians, Monophysite Christians, and others—be tolerated for the sake of production and trade. Most Europeans had gone home after the First Crusade; those left behind were obliged to coexist with the inhabitants that remained. Eastern and Western Christians learned to share shrines, priests, and favorite monastic charities, and when they came to blows, the violence tended to be local and sporadic.

The main concerns of the crusader states' rulers were military, and these could be guaranteed as well by a woman as by a man. Thus Melisende (r.1131–1152), oldest daughter of King Baldwin II of Jerusalem, was declared ruler along with her husband, Fulk, formerly count of Anjou, and their infant son. Taking the reins of government into her own hands after Fulk's death, she named a constable to lead her army and made sure that the greatest men in the kingdom sent her their vassals to do military service. Vigorously asserting her position as queen, she found supporters in the church, appointed at least one bishop to his see, and created her own chancery, where her royal acts were drawn up.

But vassals alone, however well commanded, were not sufficient to defend the fragile Crusader States, nor were the stone castles and towers that bristled in the countryside. Knights had to be recruited from Europe from time to time, and a new and militant kind of monasticism developed in the Levant: the Knights Templar. Vowed to poverty and chastity, the Templars devoted themselves to war at the same time. They defended the town garrisons of the Crusader States and ferried money from Europe to the Holy Land. Even so, they could not prevent Zangi, a Seljuk emir, from taking Edessa in 1144. The slow but steady shrinking of the Crusader States began at that moment. The Second Crusade (1147–1149), called in the wake of Zangi's victory, came to a disastrous end. After only four days of besieging the walls of Damascus, the crusaders, whose leaders could not keep the peace among themselves, gave up and went home.

England under Norman Rule

A more long-lasting conquest took place in England. England had been linked to the Continent by the Vikings, who settled in its eastern half, and in the eleventh century it had been further tied to Scandinavia under the rule of Cnut (see above, p. 143). Nevertheless, the country was drawn inextricably into the Continental orbit only with the conquest of Duke William of Normandy (d.1087). (See Map 5.7.)

When William left his duchy with a large army in the autumn of 1066 to dispute the crown of the childless King Edward the Confessor (r.1042–1066), who had died earlier that year, he carried a papal banner, symbol of the pope's support. Opposing his claim were Harald Hardrada, king of Norway, and Harold Godwineson, Edward's brother-in-law, earl of Wessex, and crowned king of England the day after Edward's death. At Stamford Bridge, Harold defeated the Norwegian king and then wheeled his army around to confront William at Hastings. That one-day battle was decisive, and William was crowned the first Norman king of England. (See Genealogy 5.4.) Treating his conquest like booty (as the crusader leaders would do a few decades later in the Levant), William kept about 20 per cent of the land for himself and divided the rest, distributing it in large but scattered fiefs to a relatively small number of his barons—his elite followers—and family members, lay and ecclesiastical, as well as to some lesser men, such as personal servants and soldiers. In turn, these men maintained their own vassals. They owed the king military service along with the service of a fixed number of their vassals; and they paid him certain dues, such as reliefs (money paid upon inheriting a fief) and aids (payments made on important occasions).

The king also collected land taxes. To know what was owed him, in 1086 William ordered a survey of the land and landholders of England. His officials consulted Anglo-Saxon tax lists and took testimony from local jurors, who were sworn to answer a series of formal questions truthfully. Compilers standardized the materials and organized them by county. Consider, by way of example, the entry for the manor of Diddington:

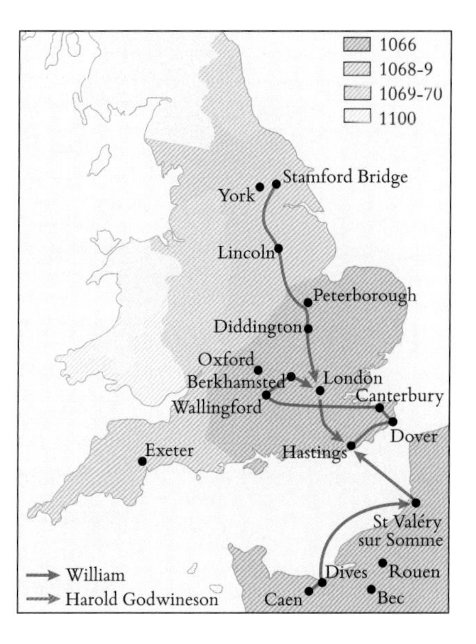

Map 5.7 The Norman Invasion of England, 1066–1100

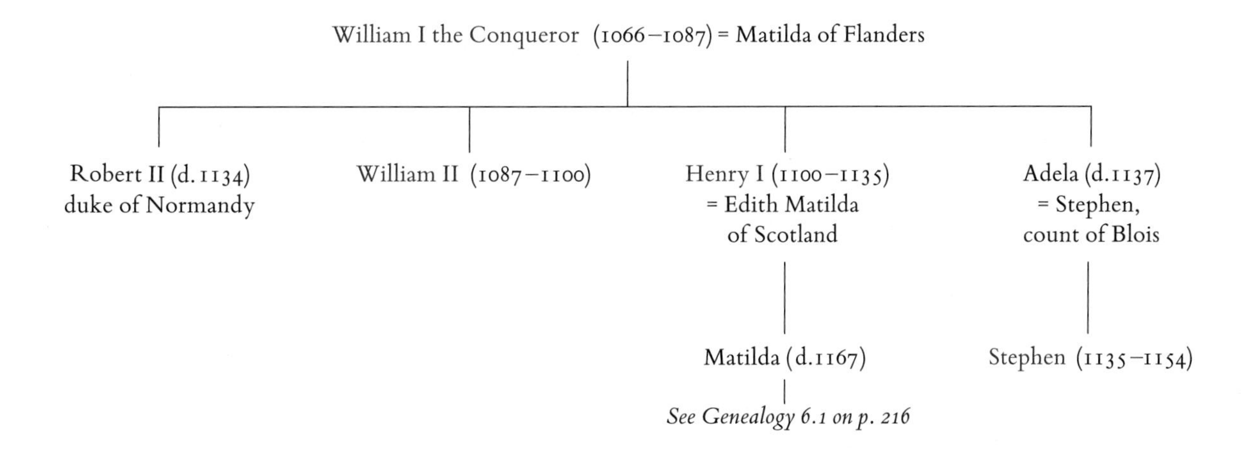

Genealogy 5.4 The Norman Kings of England

> the Bishop of Lincoln had 2½ hides to the geld. [There is] land for 2 ploughs. There are now 2 ploughs in demesne; and 5 villans having 2 ploughs. There is a church, and 18 acres of meadow, [and] woodland pasture half a league long and a half broad. TRE worth 60s; now 70s. William holds it of the bishop.[12]

The hides were units of tax assessment; the ploughs and acres were units of area, while the leagues were units of length; the villans were one type of peasant (there were many kinds); and the abbreviation TRE meant "in the time of King Edward." Anyone consulting the survey would know that the manor of Diddington was now worth more than it had been TRE. As for the William mentioned here: he was not William the Conqueror but rather a vassal of the bishop of Lincoln. No wonder the survey was soon dubbed "Domesday Book": like the records of people judged at doomsday, it provided facts that could not be appealed. Domesday was the most extensive inventory of land, livestock, taxes, and people that had as yet been compiled anywhere in medieval Europe.

Communication with the Continent was constant. The Norman barons spoke a brand of French; they talked more easily with the peasants of Normandy (if they bothered) than with those tilling the land in England. They maintained their estates on the Continent and their ties with its politics, institutions, and culture. English wool was sent to Flanders to be turned into cloth. The most brilliant intellect of his day, Saint Anselm of Bec (or Canterbury; 1033–1109), was born in Italy, became abbot of a Norman monastery, and was then appointed archbishop in England. English adolescent boys were sent to Paris and Chartres for schooling. The kings of England often spent more time on the Continent than they did on the island. When, on the death of William's son, King Henry I (r.1100–1135), no male descendent survived to take the throne, two counts from the Continent—Geoffrey of Anjou and Stephen of Blois—disputed it as their right through two rival females of the royal line. (See Genealogy 5.4 again.)

Christian Spain and Portugal

While initially the product of defeat, the Christian strip of northern Iberia in the eleventh and twelfth centuries turned the tables and became, in effect, the successful western counterpart of the Crusader States. The disintegration of al-Andalus into *taifas* opened up immense opportunities for the Spanish princes to the north. Wealth flowed into their coffers not only from plundering raids and the confiscation of lands and cities but also (until the Almoravids put an end to it) from tribute, paid in gold by *taifa* rulers—weak and disunited among themselves—to stave off attacks.

But it was not just the princes who were enriched. When Rodrigo Díaz de Vivar, the Cid (from the Arabic *sidi*, lord), fell out of favor with his lord, Alfonso VI, king of Castile and León, he and a band of followers found employment with al-Mutamin, ruler of Zaragoza. There he defended the city against Christian and Muslim invaders alike. In 1090, he struck out on his own, taking his chances in Valencia, conquering it in 1094 and ruling

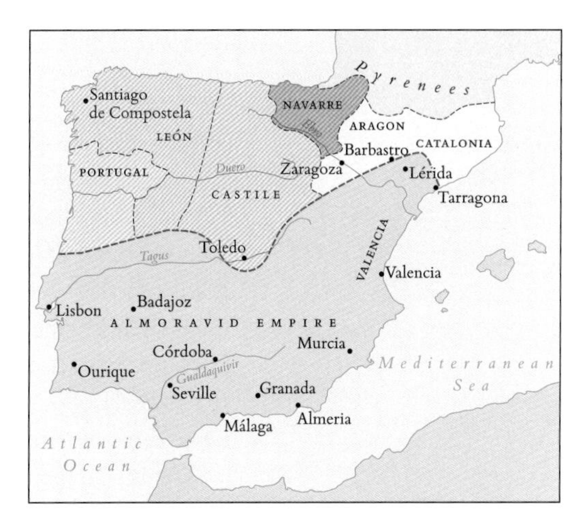

Map 5.8 The Iberian Peninsula, *c.*1140

there until his death in 1099. He was a Spaniard, but other opportunistic armies sometimes came from elsewhere. Pope Alexander II's call to besiege Barbastro in 1064 appealed to warriors from France.

The French connection was symptomatic of a wider process: the Europeanization of Spain. Initially the Christian kingdoms had been isolated islands of Visigothic culture. But already in the tenth century, pilgrims from France, England, Germany, and Italy were clogging the roads to the shrine of Saint James (Santiago de Compostela); in the eleventh century, monks from Cluny and other reformed monasteries arrived to colonize Spanish cloisters. Alfonso VI actively reached out beyond the Pyrenees, to Cluny—where he doubled the annual gift of 1,000 gold pieces that his father, Fernando I, had given in exchange for prayers for his soul—and to the papacy. He sought recognition from Pope Gregory VII as "king of Spain," and in return he imposed the Roman liturgy throughout his kingdom, stamping out the traditional Visigothic music and texts.

In 1085 Alfonso made good his claim to be more than the king of Castile and León by conquering Toledo. This was the original reason why the Almoravids came to Spain, as we saw on p. 169. After Alfonso's death, his daughter, Queen Urraca (r.1109–1126), ruled in her own right a realm larger than England. Her strength came from many of the usual sources: control over land, which, though granted out to counts and others, was at least in theory revocable; church appointments; a court of great men to offer advice and give their consent; and an army—everyone was liable to be called up once a year, even arms-bearing slaves.

In the wake of Almoravid victories, however, two new Christian states, Aragon-Catalonia and Portugal, began to challenge the supremacy of Castile and León. Aragon had always been a separate entity, but Portugal was the creation of Alfonso VI himself. As king of León, he ruled over the county of Portugal (the name came from Portucalia: land of ports) and in 1095 he granted his rights there to his illegitimate daughter Teresa and her husband, Henry of Burgundy, who then became the first count and countess of Portugal. They remained Alfonso's vassals, but their son, Count Afonso Henriques, rejected the domination of León, took the title of prince of Portugal in 1129, and began to encroach on Islamic territory to his south. In 1139 he defeated the Almoravids at the battle of Ourique and took the title of king of Portugal under the name of Afonso I, though it was not until 1179 that Pope Alexander III (1159–1181) acknowledged Portugal as an independent kingdom.

Reinforced with crusading warriors from France, the Christian half of Iberia vigorously defended its conquests. In the 1140s, they were ready for a new push southward, contributing to the fall of the Almoravid empire.

Genealogy 5.5 (facing page)
The Capetian Kings of France

Praising the King of France

Not all rulers had opportunities for grand conquest. How did they maintain themselves? The example of the kings of France reveals the possibilities. Reduced to battling a few castles in the vicinity of the Ile-de-France (see Map 5.5 on p. 174), the Capetian kings nevertheless wielded many of the same instruments of power as their conquering contemporaries: vassals, taxes, commercial revenues, military and religious reputations. Louis VI the Fat (r.1108–1137), so heavy that he had to be hoisted onto his horse by a crane, was nevertheless a tireless defender of royal power. (See Genealogy 5.5.)

Louis's virtues were amplified and broadcast by his biographer, Suger (1081–1151), the abbot of Saint-Denis, a monastery just outside Paris. A close associate of the king, Suger was his chronicler and propagandist. When Louis set himself the task of consolidating his rule in the Ile-de-France, Suger portrayed the king as a righteous hero. He was more than a lord with rights over the French nobles as his vassals; he was a peacekeeper with the God-given duty to fight unruly strongmen. Careful not to claim that Louis was head of the church, which would have scandalized the papacy and its supporters, Suger nevertheless emphasized Louis's role as vigorous protector of the faith and insisted on the sacred importance of the royal dignity. When Louis died in 1137, Suger's notion of the might and right of the king of France reflected reality in an extremely small area. Nevertheless, Louis laid the groundwork for the gradual extension of royal power. As the lord of vassals, the king could call upon his men to aid him in times of war (though the great ones could defy him). As king and landlord, he collected dues and taxes with the help of his officials, called *prévôts*. Revenues came from Paris as well, a thriving commercial and cultural center. With money and land, Louis could employ civil servants while dispensing the favors and giving the gifts that added to his prestige and power.

NEW FORMS OF LEARNING AND RELIGIOUS EXPRESSION

The commercial revolution and rise of urban centers, the newly reorganized church, close contact with the Islamic world, and the revived polities of the early twelfth century paved the way for the growth of urban schools and new forms of religious expression. Money, learning, and career opportunities attracted many to city schools. At the same time, some people rejected urbanism and the new-fangled scholarship it supported. They retreated from the world to seek poverty and solitude. Yet the new learning and the new money had a way of seeping into the cracks and crannies of even the most resolutely separate institutions.

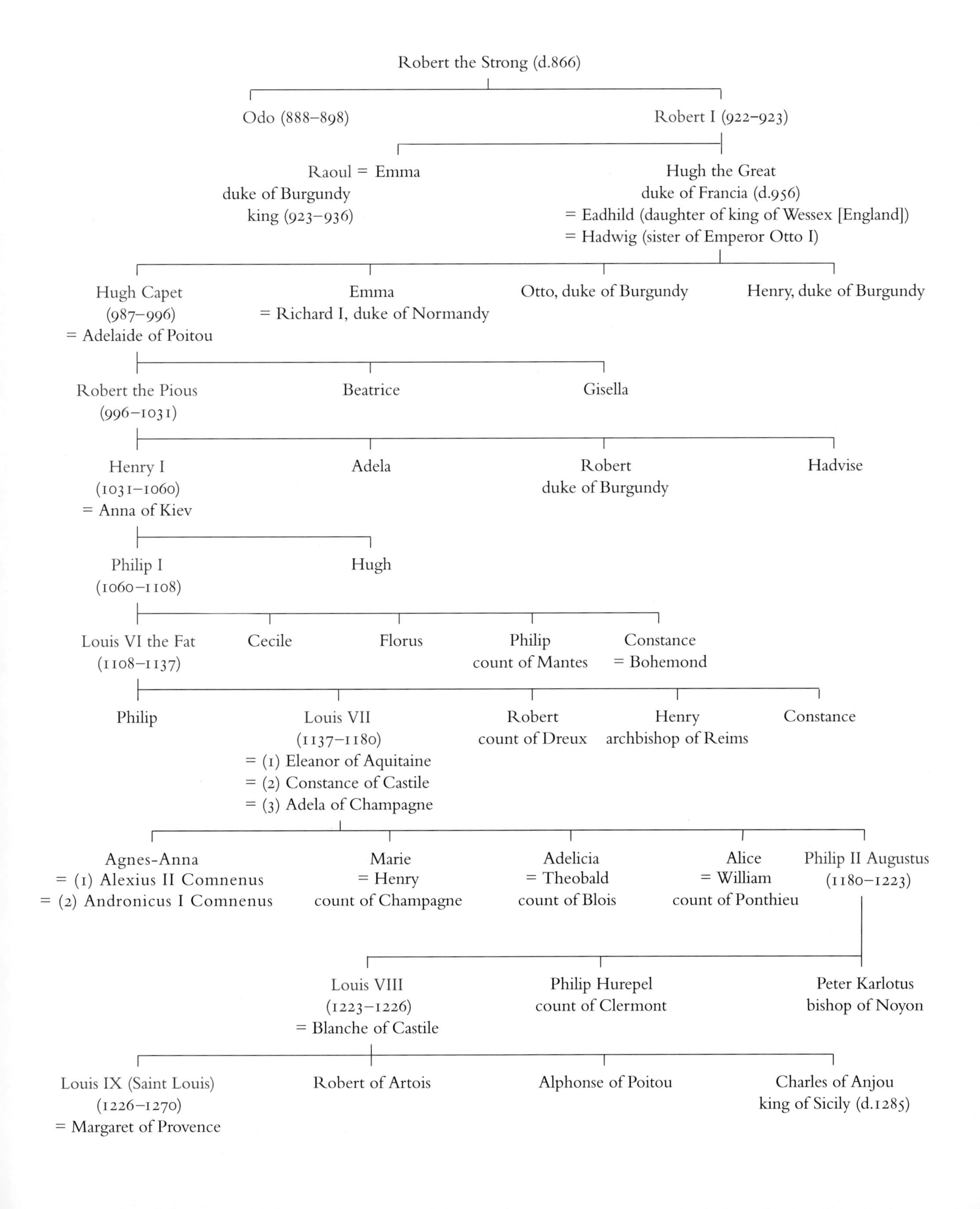

Robert the Strong (d.866)
Odo (888–898)
Robert I (922–923)
Raoul = Emma
duke of Burgundy
king (923–936)
Hugh the Great
duke of Francia (d.956)
= Eadhild (daughter of king of Wessex [England])
= Hadwig (sister of Emperor Otto I)
Hugh Capet
(987–996)
= Adelaide of Poitou
Emma
= Richard I, duke of Normandy
Otto, duke of Burgundy
Henry, duke of Burgundy
Robert the Pious
(996–1031)
Beatrice
Gisella
Henry I
(1031–1060)
= Anna of Kiev
Adela
Robert
duke of Burgundy
Hadvise
Philip I
(1060–1108)
Hugh
Louis VI the Fat
(1108–1137)
Cecile
Florus
Philip
count of Mantes
Constance
= Bohemond
Philip
Louis VII
(1137–1180)
= (1) Eleanor of Aquitaine
= (2) Constance of Castile
= (3) Adela of Champagne
Robert
count of Dreux
Henry
archbishop of Reims
Constance
Agnes-Anna
= (1) Alexius II Comnenus
= (2) Andronicus I Comnenus
Marie
= Henry
count of Champagne
Adelicia
= Theobald
count of Blois
Alice
= William
count of Ponthieu
Philip II Augustus
(1180–1223)
Louis VIII
(1223–1226)
= Blanche of Castile
Philip Hurepel
count of Clermont
Peter Karlotus
bishop of Noyon
Louis IX (Saint Louis)
(1226–1270)
= Margaret of Provence
Robert of Artois
Alphonse of Poitou
Charles of Anjou
king of Sicily (d.1285)

The New Schools and What They Taught

Connected to monasteries and cathedrals since the Carolingian period, traditional schools had trained young men to become monks or priests. Some were better endowed than others with books and teachers; a few developed reputations for particular expertise. By the end of the eleventh century, the best schools were generally connected to cathedrals in the larger cities: Reims, Paris, Bologna, Montpellier. But some teachers (or "masters," as they were called), such as the charismatic and brilliant Peter Abelard (1079–1142), simply set up shop by renting a room. Students flocked to his lectures.

What the students sought, in the first place, was knowledge of the seven liberal arts. Grammar, rhetoric, and logic (or dialectic) belonged to the "beginning" arts, the so-called trivium. Grammar and rhetoric focused on literature and writing. Logic—involving the technical analysis of texts as well as the application and manipulation of arguments—was a transitional subject leading to the second, higher part of the liberal arts, the quadrivium. This comprised four areas of study that would today be called theoretical math and science: arithmetic (number theory), geometry, music (theory rather than practice), and astronomy. Of these arts, logic had pride of place in the new schools, while masters and students who studied the quadrivium generally did so outside of the classroom.

Scholars looked to logic to clarify what they knew and lead them to further knowledge. That God existed, nearly everyone believed. But a scholar like Anselm of Bec (whom we met above, p. 186, as the archbishop of Canterbury) was not satisfied by belief alone. Anselm's faith, as he put it, "sought understanding." He emptied his mind of all concepts except that of God; then, using the tools of logic, he proved God's very existence in his *Monologion*. In Paris a bit later, Peter Abelard declared that "nothing can be believed unless it is first understood." He drew together conflicting authoritative texts on 158 key subjects in his *Sic et non* (*Yes and No*), including "That God is one and the contrary" and "That it is permitted to kill men and the contrary." Leaving the propositions unresolved, Abelard urged his students to discover the reasons behind the disagreements and find ways to reconcile them. Soon Peter Lombard (*c.*1100–1160) adopted Abelard's method of juxtaposing discordant viewpoints, but he supplied his own reasoned resolutions as well. His *Sententiae* was perhaps the most successful theology textbook of the entire Middle Ages.

One key logical issue for twelfth-century scholars involved the question of "universals": whether a universal—something that can be said of many—is real or simply a linguistic or mental entity. Abelard argued that "things either individually or collectively cannot be called universal, i.e., said to be predicated of many."[13] He was maintaining a position later called "nominalist." The other view was the "realist" position, which claimed that things "predicated of many" were universal and real. For example, when we look at diverse individuals of one kind, say Fluffy and Puffy, we say of each of them that they are members of the same species: cat. Realists argued that "cat" was real. Nominalists thought it a mere word.

Later in the twelfth century, scholars found precise tools in the works of Aristotle to resolve this and other logical questions. During Abelard's lifetime, very little of Aristotle's work was available in Europe because it had not been translated from Greek into Latin. By the end of the century, however, that lack had been filled by translators who traveled to Islamic or formerly Islamic cities—Toledo in Spain, Palermo in Sicily—where Aristotle had already been translated into Arabic and carefully commented on by Islamic scholars such as Ibn Sina (Avicenna; see p. 128 above) (980–1037) and Ibn Rushd (Averroes) (1126–1198). By the thirteenth century, Aristotle had become the primary philosopher for the scholastics (the scholars of medieval European universities).

The lofty subjects of the schools had down-to-earth, practical consequences in books for preachers, advice for rulers, manuals for priests, textbooks for students, and guides for living addressed to laypeople. Nor was mastery of the liberal arts the end of everyone's education. Many students went on to study theology (for which Paris was the center). Others studied law; at Bologna, for example, where Gratian worked on canon law, other jurists—such as the so-called Four Doctors—achieved fame by teaching and writing about Roman law. By the mid-twelfth century, scholars had made real progress toward a systematic understanding of Justinian's law codes (see above, p. 30). The lawyers who emerged from the school at Bologna went on to serve popes, bishops, kings, princes, or communes. In this way, the learning of the schools was used by the newly powerful twelfth-century states, preached in the churches, and consulted in the courts.

It found a place in the treatment of the ill as well. The greatest schools of medicine were at Salerno (in Italy) and at Montpellier (in France). In the course of the late eleventh and twelfth centuries, these schools' curricula began to draw on classical Greek medical texts, which had been translated into Arabic during the ninth century. Now the Arabic texts were turned into Latin. For example, Constantine the African, who was at Salerno before 1077, translated a key Arabic text based on Galen's *Art of Medicine*. He called it the *Isagoge* ("Introduction"), which indeed it was: "[The principal members of the body are] the brain, the heart, the liver, and the testicles. Other members serve the aforesaid principal members, such as the nerves, which minister to the brain, and the arteries which minister to the heart, and the veins, which minister to the liver, and the spermatic vessels, which convey sperm to the testicles."[14]

Soon the *Isagoge* was gathered together with other texts into the *Articella*, a major training manual for doctors throughout the Middle Ages.

Monastic Splendor and Poverty

To care for ill monks, monasteries had infirmaries—proto-hospitals that were generally built at a short distance from the monastic church and communal buildings (see Figure 5.3 on p. 199). The Benedictine Rule assumed that each religious community would carry out most of its tasks within an enclosed building complex. One Benedictine monastery that has been excavated particularly fully is Saint-Germain at Auxerre. In the twelfth century, it boasted a very large church with an elaborate narthex that served as a grand entranceway for liturgical processions (see Figure 5.1). Toward the east of the church,

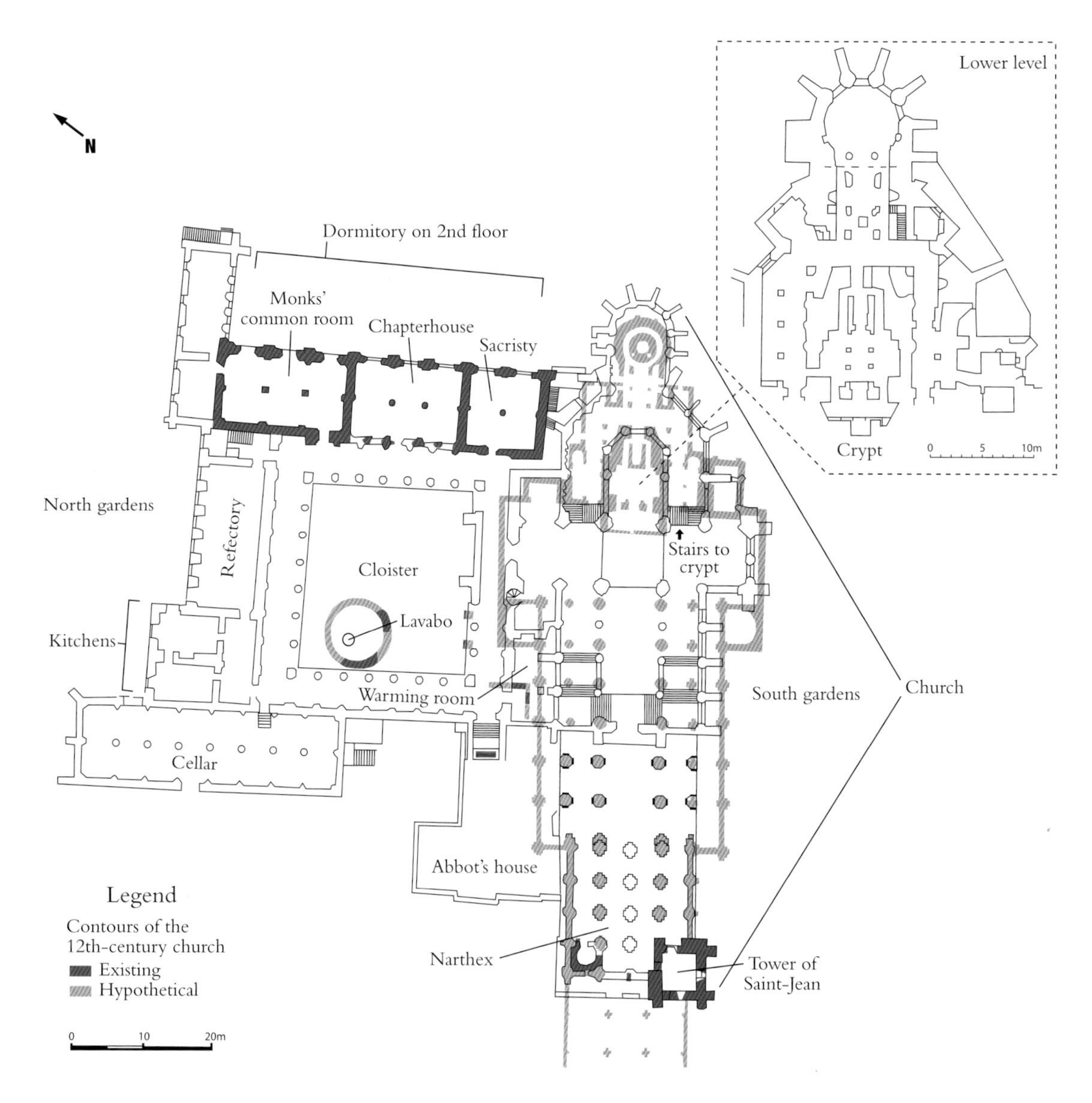

Figure 5.1 Saint-Germain of Auxerre (12th cent.)

Plate 5.6 (facing page) Durham Cathedral, Interior (1093–1133). Huge and imposing, Durham Cathedral is also inviting and welcoming, with its lively piers, warm colors, and harmonious spaces. Built by Norman bishops, it housed the relics of the Anglo-Saxon Saint Cuthbert; in just such ways did the Normans appropriate the power and prestige of English saints' cults.

where the altar stood and the monks sang the Offices, stairs led down to a crypt housing saintly relics constructed during the Carolingian period. To the north and south were the conventual buildings—the sacristy (which stored liturgical vessels and vestments), the "chapter house" (where the Benedictine Rule was read), the common room, dormitory (where the monks slept), refectory (dining hall), kitchens, and cellar. At the center of all was the cloister, entirely enclosed by graceful arcades. Beyond these buildings were undoubtedly others—not yet excavated—for the craftsmen and servants of the monastery, for the ill, for pilgrims and other guests. The whole purpose of this complex was to allow the monks to carry out a life of arduous and nearly continuous prayer. Every detail of their lives was ordered, every object splendid, every space adorned to render due honor to the Lord of heaven.

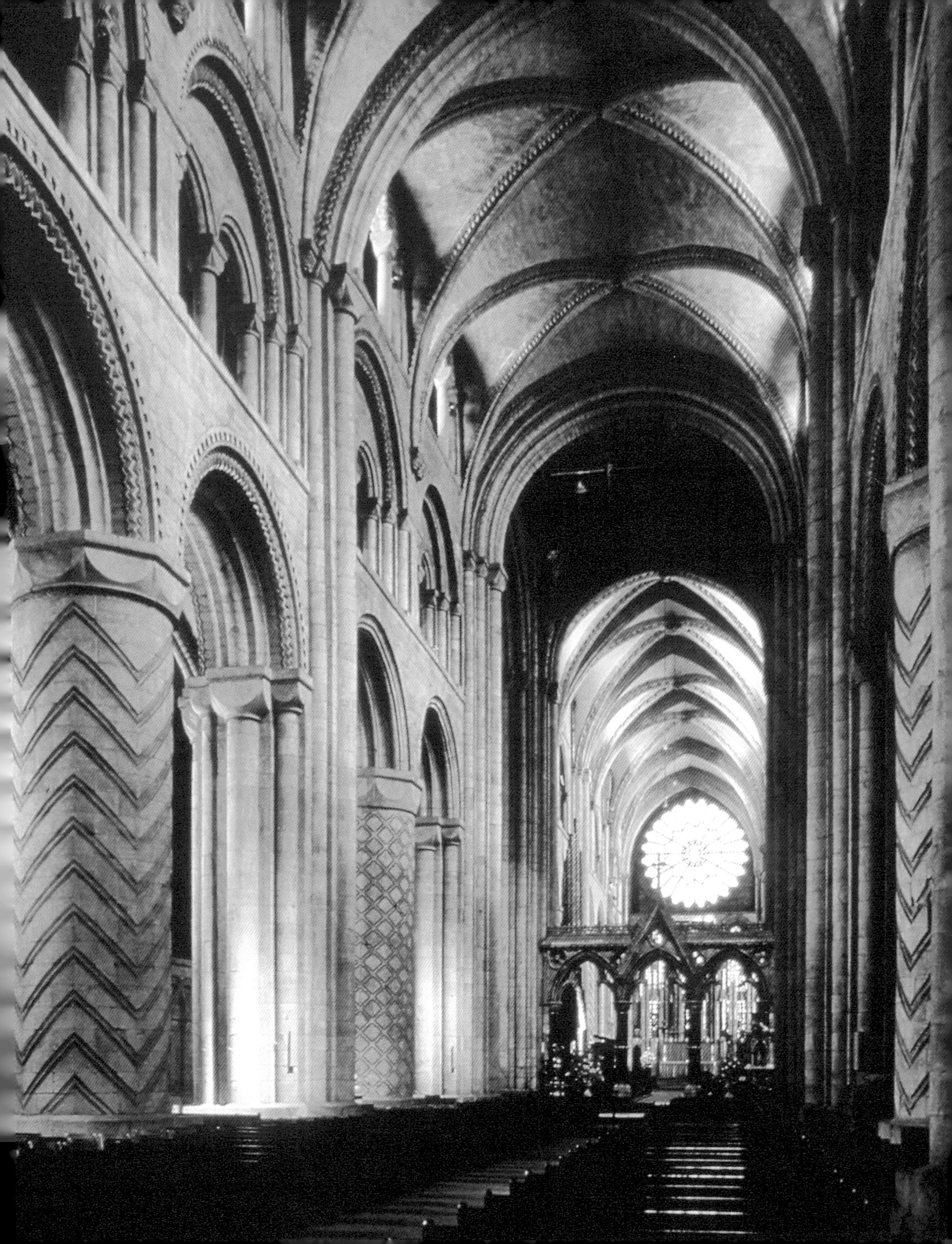

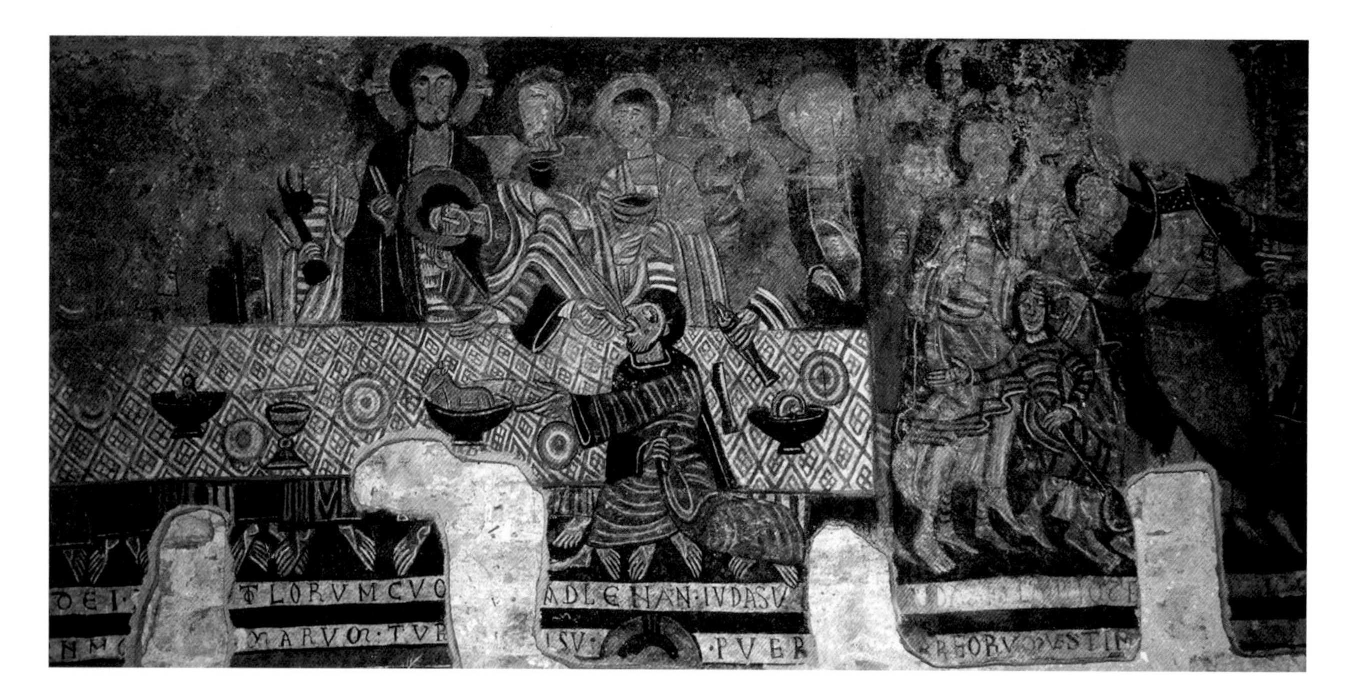

Plate 5.7 Sant Tomàs de Fluvià, The Last Supper, Painted Vault (early 12th cent.). Sant Tomàs was one of many monastic and parish churches in the County of Barcelona richly decorated with paintings in the twelfth century. Here Christ is at the Last Supper with his apostles. The depiction closely follows John 13:23 when Jesus announces that one of his disciples will betray him: "Now there was leaning on Jesus's bosom one of his disciples [John].... [John asked], 'Lord, who is it?' Jesus answered, 'He it is to whom I shall reach bread dipped.' And when he had dipped the bread, he gave it to Judas." To the right of the table a new scene begins: Jesus' disciple Peter cuts off the ear of the servant of the high priest who has come with Judas to betray him. Christ then utters the famous words from Matt. 26:52, "Put your sword back into its place; for all who take the sword will perish by the sword." Then, according to Luke 22:51, Jesus touched the servant's ear and healed him.

The architecture and sculpture of twelfth-century churches like Saint-Germain were suited to showcase both the solemn intoning of the chant and the honor due to God. The style, called Romanesque, represents the first wave of European monumental architecture. Built of stone, Romanesque churches are echo chambers for the sounds of the chant. Massive, weighty, and dignified, they are often enlivened by sculpture, wall paintings, or patterned textures. At Durham Cathedral (built between 1093 and 1133 in the north of England), the stone itself is a warm yellow/pink color, given added zest by piers incised with diamond or zig-zag patterns. (See Plate 5.6.) By contrast, the entire length of the vault of Sant Tomàs de Fluvià, a tiny monastic church in the County of Barcelona, was covered with paintings, a few of which remain today; Plate 5.7 shows the Last Supper. Pisa's famous leaning tower is in fact a Romanesque bell tower; here (Plate 5.8) the decoration is on the exterior, where the bright Italian sun heightens the play of light and shadow.

The church of Saint-Lazare of Autun (1120–1146) may serve as an example of a "typical" Romanesque church, though in fact the most typical aspect of that style is its extreme variety. Striking is the "barrel" or "tunnel" vault whose ribs, springing from the top of the piers, mark the long church into sections called bays. There are three levels. The first is created by the arches that open onto the side aisles of the church. The second is the gallery (or triforium), which consists of a decorative band of columns and arches. The third is the clerestory, where small windows puncture the walls. (See Plate 5.9 on p. 197.)

As at many Romanesque churches, the portals and the capitals (the "top hats" on the columns) at Autun were carved with complex scenes representing sacred stories. The story of the "Raising of Lazarus," patron saint of the church (Saint-Lazare = Lazarus), was once depicted on a tympanum (a half-circle) over the north transept door, the main entrance to the church. (For an Ottonian depiction of the scene, see Plate 4.6 on p. 146.) Other scenes were seemingly more fanciful. Like the fighting lion and bull at Diyarbakir in Seljuk Anatolia (see

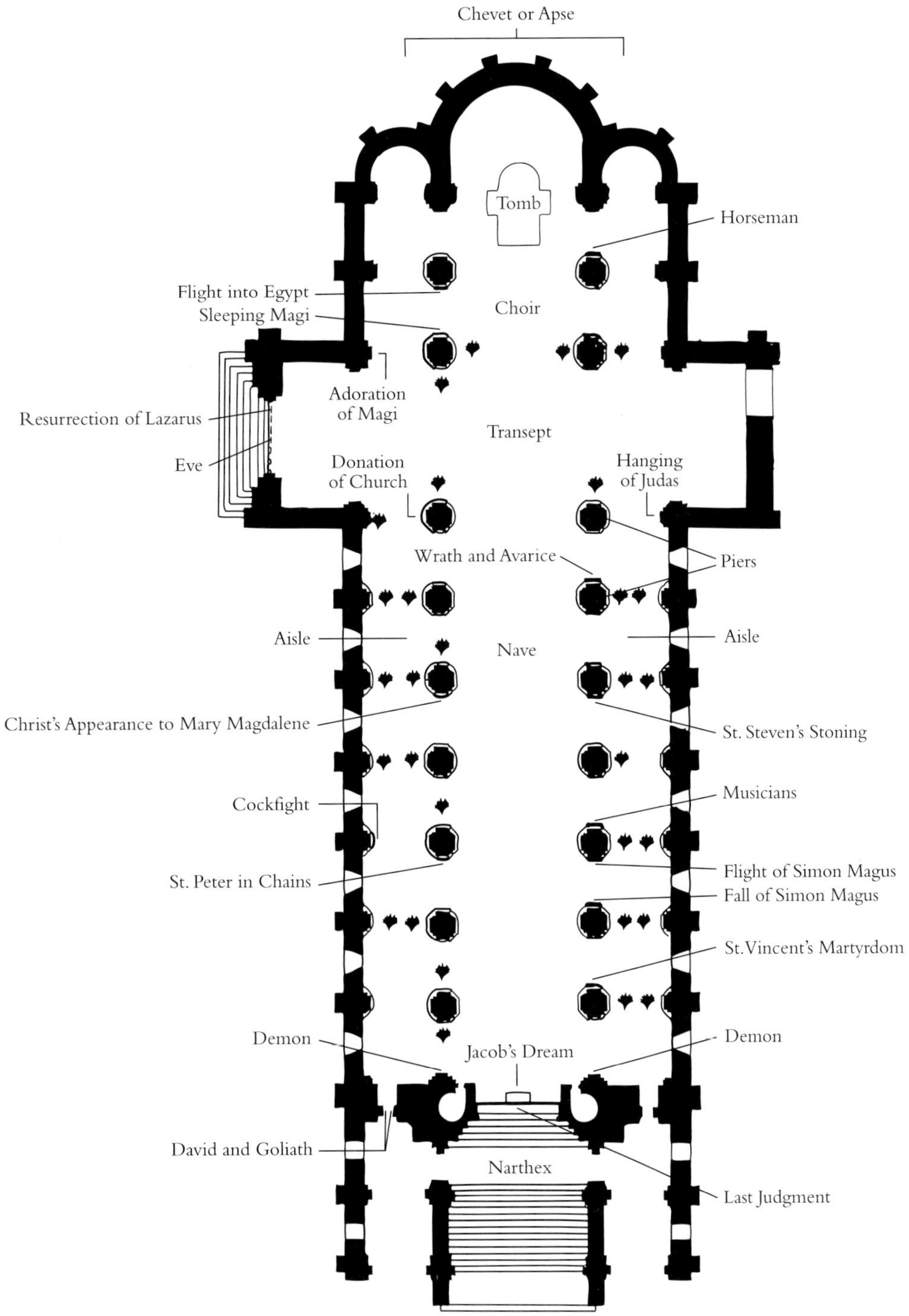

Chevet or Apse

Tomb

Horseman

Flight into Egypt

Sleeping Magi

Choir

Adoration of Magi

Resurrection of Lazarus

Transept

Eve

Donation of Church

Hanging of Judas

Wrath and Avarice

Piers

Aisle

Nave

Aisle

Christ's Appearance to Mary Magdalene

St. Steven's Stoning

Cockfight

Musicians

St. Peter in Chains

Flight of Simon Magus

Fall of Simon Magus

St. Vincent's Martyrdom

Demon

Demon

Jacob's Dream

David and Goliath

Narthex

Last Judgment

Figure 5.2 A Model Romanesque Church: Saint-Lazare of Autun

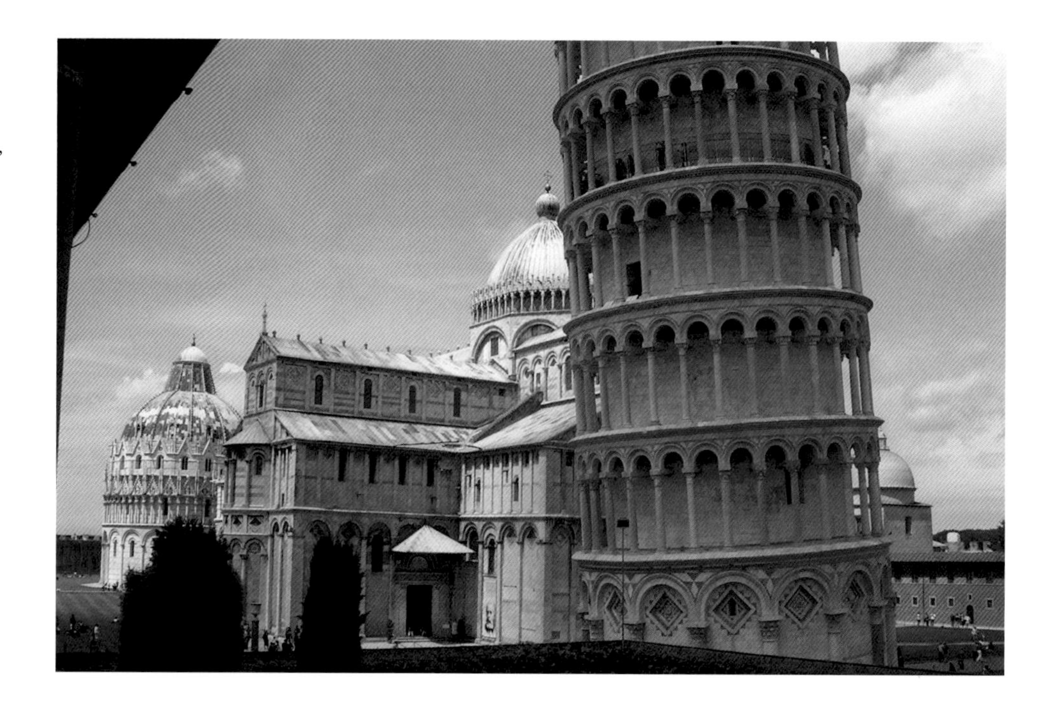

Plate 5.8 Cathedral Complex, Pisa (11th–12th cent.). The tower is part of a large complex that was meant to celebrate Pisa's emergence as a great political, economic, and military power. In this photograph, taken from the upper porch of the hospital (13th cent.), the cathedral (begun in 1064) is just behind and to the left of the tower (which started to lean in 1174, during construction). Behind that, and further to the left, is the baptistery (begun in 1152).

Plate 5.4 on p. 168), a cockfight decorates the capital of a pier right in the center of the nave (see Plate 5.10). But, also like the Seljuk motif, this one had a more profound meaning. The victorious cock is the one who has triumphed over death and symbolizes the hope of resurrection.

The plan of Autun shown in Figure 5.2 on p. 195 indicates the placement of many of the church's carvings, including the cockfight. It also shows that the church was in the form of a basilica (a long straight building) intersected, near the choir, by a transept. The chevet (or apse), the far eastern part of the church, had space for pilgrims to visit the tomb of Lazarus, which held the precious bones of the saint.

Not all medieval people agreed that such extravagant decoration pleased or praised God, however. At the end of the eleventh century, the new commercial economy and the profit motive that fueled it led many to reject wealth and to embrace poverty as a key element of the religious life. The Carthusian order, founded by Bruno of Cologne (d.1101; not the same person as the archbishop discussed on p. 145), represented one such movement. La Grande Chartreuse, the chief house of the order, was built in an Alpine valley, lonely and inaccessible. Each monk took a vow of silence and lived as a hermit in his own small hut. Only occasionally would the monks join the others for prayer in a common oratory. When not engaged in prayer or meditation, the Carthusians copied manuscripts: for them, scribal work was a way to preach God's word with the hands rather than the mouth. Slowly the Carthusian order grew, but each monastery was limited to only twelve monks, the number of Christ's Apostles.

And yet even the Carthusians dedicated their lives above all to prayer. By now new forms of musical notation had been elaborated to allow monks—and other musicians—to see graphically the melody of their chants. In Plate 5.11 on p. 200, a manuscript from a Carthusian monastery in Lyon, France, the scribe used a red line to show the pitch of F (you can see the letter F at the left of each red line) and a yellow line for the C above that.

The notes, square-headed and precisely placed, can easily be transcribed (by a musicologist who knows their conventions) onto a modern five-line staff.

Another new monastic order, the Cistercian, expanded rapidly. The first Cistercian house was Cîteaux (in Latin, *Cistercium*), founded in 1098 by Robert of Molesme (*c.*1027/1028–1111) and a few other monks seeking a more austere way of life. Austerity they found—and also success. With the arrival of Saint Bernard (*c.*1090–1153), who came to Cîteaux in 1112 along with about thirty friends and relatives, the original center sprouted a small congregation of houses in Burgundy. (Bernard became abbot of one of them, Clairvaux.) The order grew, often by reforming and incorporating existing monasteries. By the mid-twelfth century there were more than 300 monasteries—many in France, but some as well in Italy, Germany, England, Austria, and Spain—following what they took to be the customs of Cîteaux. By the end of the twelfth century, the Cistercians were an order: their member houses adhered to the decisions of a General Chapter; their liturgical practices and internal organization were standardized. Many nuns, too, as eager as monks to live the life of simplicity and poverty that the Apostles had endured and enjoyed, adopted Cîteaux's customs; some convents later became members of the order.

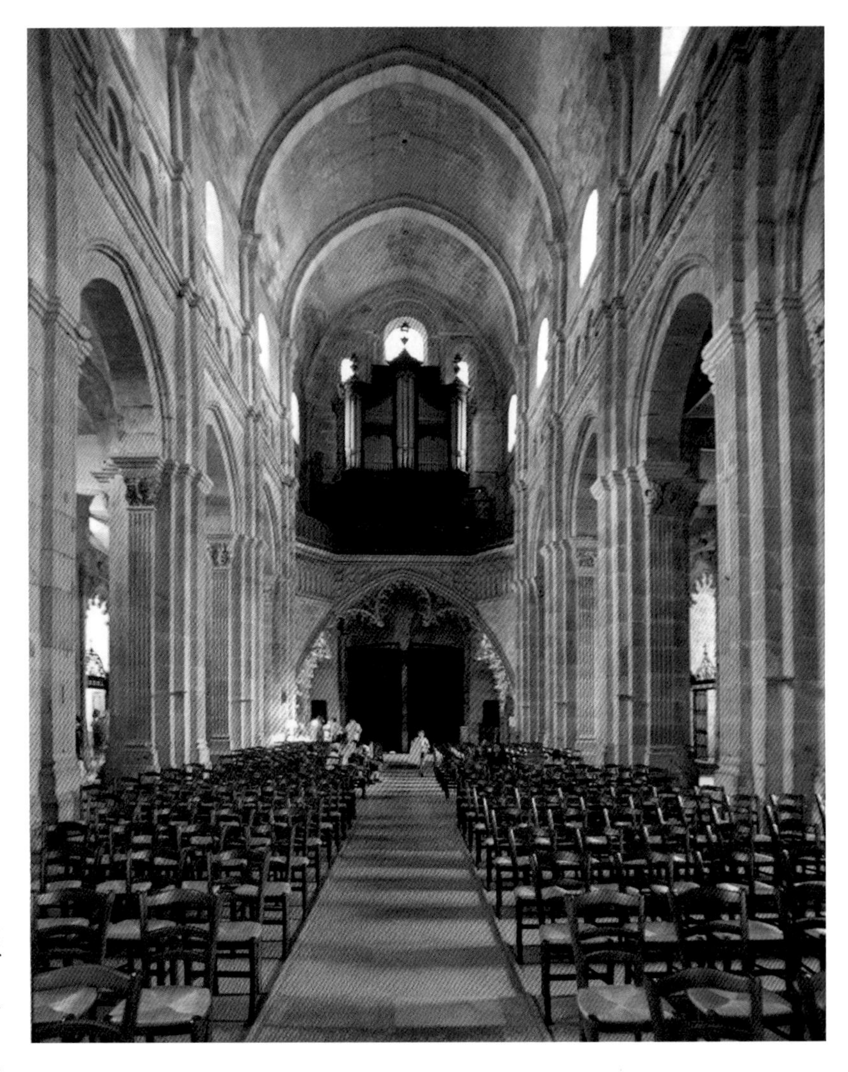

Plate 5.9 Saint-Lazare of Autun, Nave (1120–1146). In this view down the nave to the west entrance, a great organ obscures the windows that once allowed in the light of the setting sun.

Although the Cistercians claimed the Benedictine Rule as the foundation of their customs, they elaborated a style of life and an aesthetic all their own, largely governed by the goal of simplicity. They even rejected the conceit of dyeing their robes—hence their nickname, the "white monks." White, too, were their houses. Despite regional variations and considerable latitude in interpreting the meaning of "simplicity," Cistercian buildings had a different feel than the great Romanesque churches and Benedictine monasteries of black monks. Foursquare and regular, Cistercian churches and other buildings conformed to a fairly standard plan, typified by a monastery like Fountains (see Figure 5.3 on p. 199). The churches tended to be small, made of smooth-cut, undecorated stone. Wall and vault paintings were eschewed, and any sculpture was modest at best. Indeed, Saint Bernard

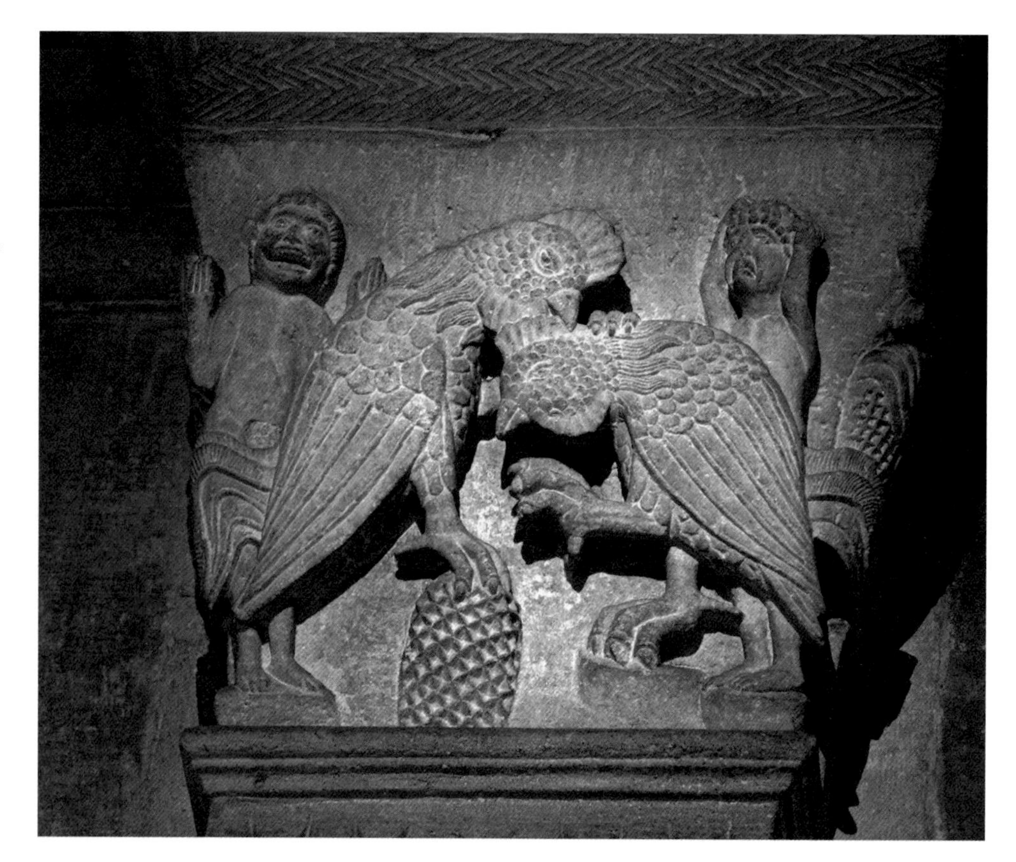

Plate 5.10 Autun, Cockfight (12th cent.). This relief, one of many carvings that decorate the capitals at Autun, shows the conclusion of a cockfight. In the twelfth century, cockfighting was among the favorite sports of young boys. At Autun, the cock's victorious trainer grins and throws up his arms as his winning animal puts its foot on the loser's head. The losing cock bows, waiting for the final blow, while his trainer grimaces and clenches his fists in despair. But why depict a youthful sport in the solemn space of a monastic church? In fact, cocks had significance in Christian thought: they recalled the cry that awakened the sleeper, foretelling the Day of Judgment. They were compared to priests, whose better selves did daily battle with their sinful tendencies. The fighting cocks reminded the monks of their own moral battles even as they recalled a frivolous pastime. Note how the sculptor made even this dramatic scene fit the shape of the lintel.

wrote a scathing attack on Romanesque sculpture in which, ironically, he admitted its sensuous allure:

> But what can justify that array of grotesques in the cloister where the brothers do their reading...? What place have obscene monkeys, savage lions, unnatural centaurs, manticores, striped tigers, battling knights or hunters sounding their horns? You can see a head with many bodies and a multi-bodied head.... With such a bewildering array of shapes and forms on show, one would sooner read the sculptures than the books.[15]

The Cistercians had few such diversions, but the very simplicity of their buildings and of their clothing also had beauty. Illuminated by the pure white light that came through clear glass windows, Cistercian churches were luminous, cool, and serene. Plate 5.12 on p. 201 shows the nave of Sénanque, begun in 1139. There are no wall paintings, carvings, or incised pillars. Yet the very articulation of the pillars and arches and the stone molding that gently breaks the vertical thrust of the vault lend the church a sober charm.

True to their emphasis on purity, the Cistercians simplified their communal liturgy, pruning the many additions that had been tacked on in the houses of the black monks. Only the liturgy as prescribed in the Benedictine Rule and one daily Mass were allowed. Even the music for the chant was modified: the Cistercians rigorously suppressed the

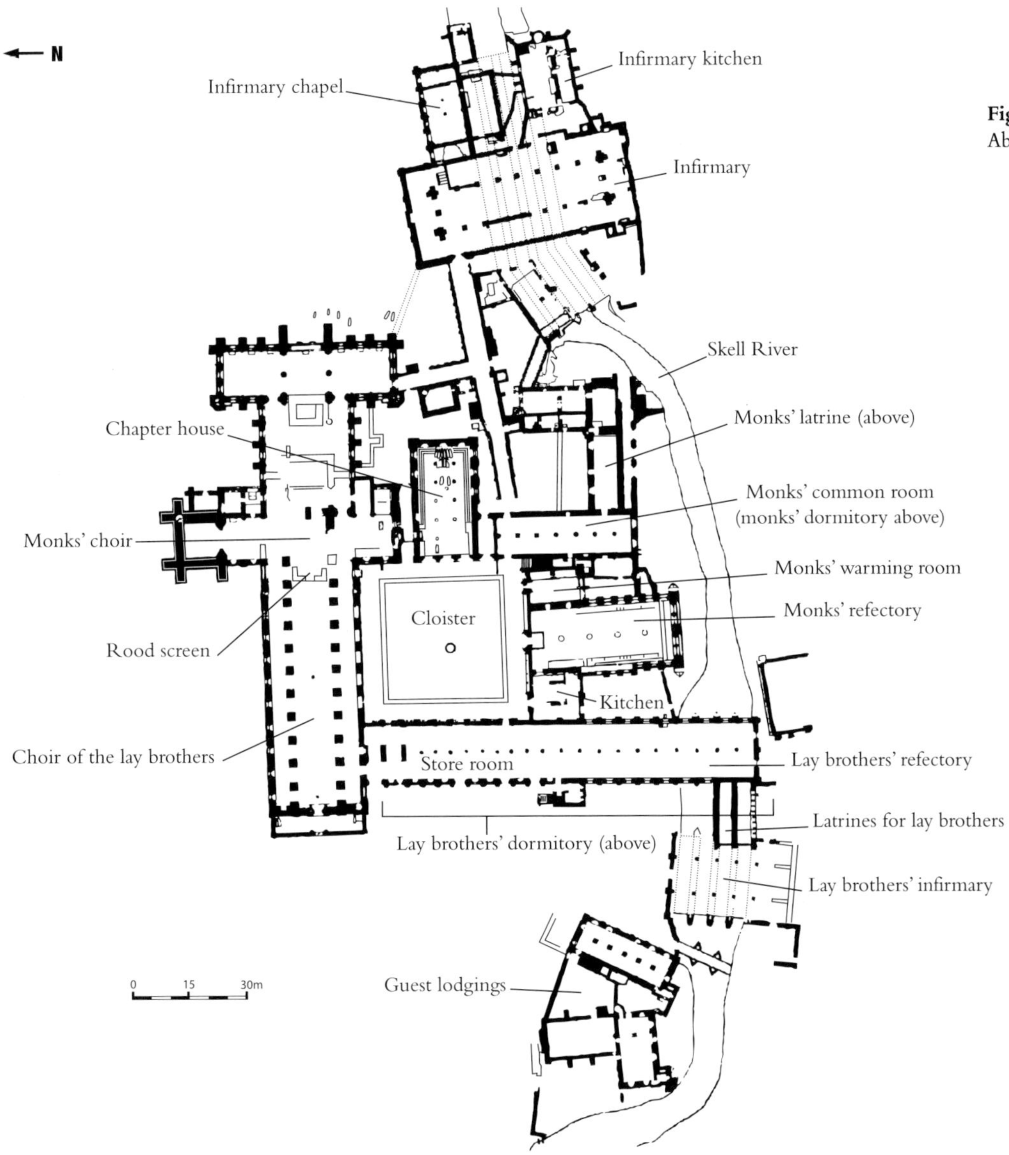

Figure 5.3 Plan of Fountains Abbey (founded 1132)

B flat, even though doing so made the melody discordant, because of their insistence on strict simplicity.

On the other hand, the Benedictine Rule did not prevent the Cistercians from creating a new class of monks—the lay brothers—who were illiterate and unable to participate in the liturgy. These men did the necessary labor—field work, stock raising—to support the community at large. Compare Figure 5.3 with Figure 5.1 on p. 192: the Cistercian monastery was in fact a house divided. The eastern half was for the "choir" monks, the western half for the lay brethren. Each half had its own dining room, latrines, dormitories, and

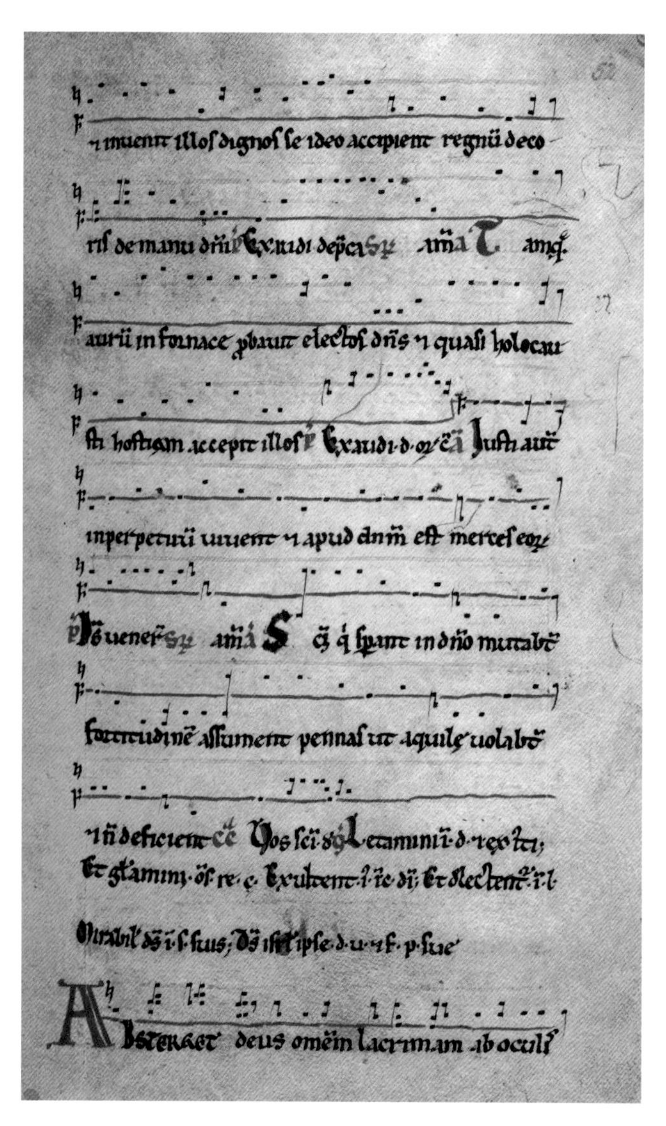

Plate 5.11 Carthusian Diurnal from Lyon (12th cent.). A Diurnal contains daytime monastic chants. On this page, the scribe has indicated (just beneath each yellow line) the placement of the B natural. Although (or perhaps because) Carthusian monks rarely came together to pray, they, like other sorts of monks, wanted clear guidance for their chants.

infirmaries. The monks were strictly segregated, even in the church, where a rood screen kept them apart.

The choir monks dedicated themselves to private prayer and contemplation and to monastic administration. The Cistercian *Charter of Charity*, in effect a constitution of the order, provided for a closely monitored network of houses, and each year the Cistercian abbots met to hammer out legislation for all of them. Cistercian monasteries held large and highly organized farms and grazing lands called "granges," and the monks spent much of their time managing their estates and flocks of sheep, both of which yielded handsome profits by the end of the twelfth century. Clearly part of the agricultural and commercial revolutions of the Middle Ages, the Cistercian order made managerial expertise a part of the monastic life.

Yet the Cistercians also elaborated a spirituality of intense personal emotion. Their writings were filled with talk of love—love of self, of neighbor, and of God. They were devoted to the humanity of Christ and to his mother, Mary. While pilgrims continued to stream to the tombs and reliquaries of saints, the Cistercians dedicated all their churches to the Virgin Mary (for whom they had no relics) because for them she signified the model of a loving mother. Indeed, the Cistercians regularly used maternal imagery to describe the nurturing care provided to humans by Jesus himself. The Cistercian God was approachable, human, protective, even mothering.

Were women simply metaphors for pious male monks? Or did they too partake in the new religious fervor of the twelfth century? The answer is that women's reformed monasteries proliferated at the same time as men's. Furthermore, monks and priests undertook to teach and guide religious women far more fully than they had done before. In the *Speculum Virginum (Mirror of Virgins)*, written in the form of a dialogue between a male religious advisor (Peregrinus) and a "virgin of Christ" (Theodora), exhortations to virtue were complemented by images. Some presented, as if in a "mirror," vices that should be avoided. Others gave examples of female heroines to be admired and imitated. In Plate 5.13 on p. 202, three tall and triumphant women stand on dead or defeated enemies. On the left is Jael, who killed the Israelites' enemy leader, and on the right is Judith, who did the same. In the middle, the model for both, is Humility striking Pride in the breast. Clearly the cloistered twelfth-century virgin was justified in considering herself, as Peregrinus said, "an example of disdain for the present life and a model of desire for heavenly things."[16]

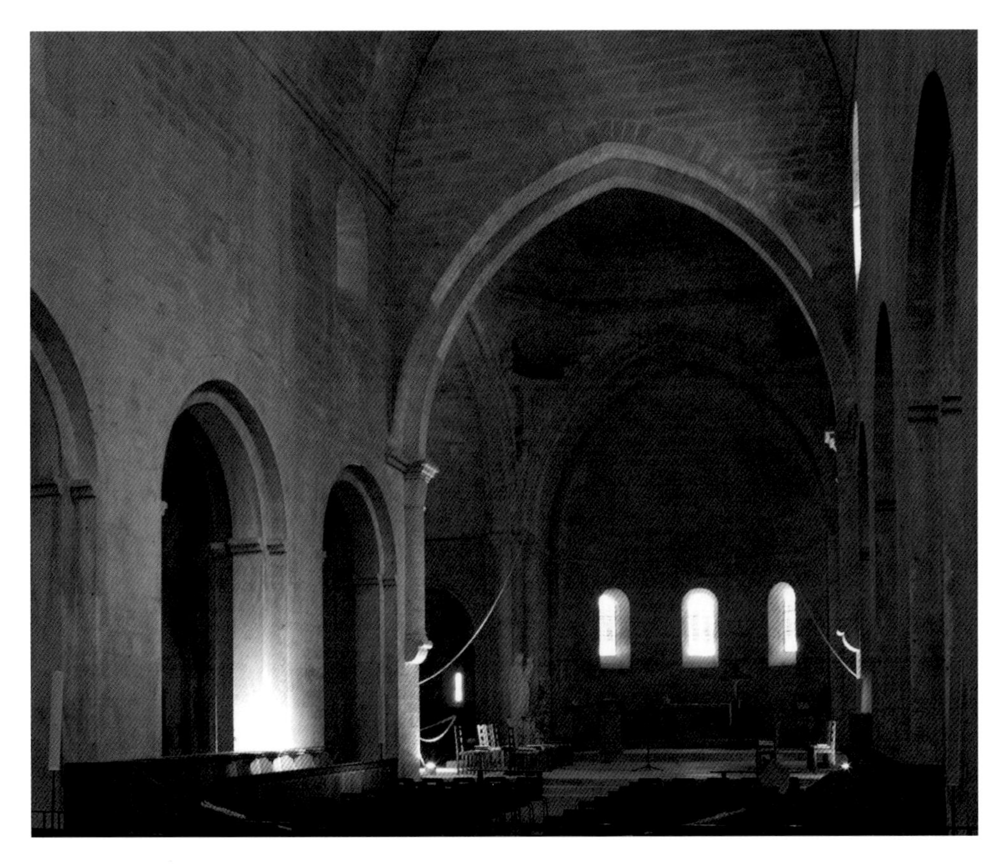

Plate 5.12 Sénanque Monastery Church, Interior (*c.*1160). Because of the geography of the valley where the monastery was constructed, the church is oriented so that the "north" end takes the usual place of the "east." In this view to the north, the bare walls reveal religious and artistic sensibilities completely different from those of the creators of Sant Tomàs de Fluvià (Plate 5.7).

* * * * *

In the eleventh and twelfth centuries, the Seljuk Turks reconfigured the geography of the Islamic world and put their stamp on religion by affirming Sunnism. Byzantium, badly maimed by the Seljuks on its eastern flank, nevertheless expected to recoup its losses, calling on the papacy to help man its army. The papacy, however, had its own agenda. Invigorated by the Investiture Conflict, it called for an armed pilgrimage to the east that would both ensure peace in Europe and control over regions that suddenly did not seem so far away. For, as the papacy recognized, Europe was burgeoning. Growing population and the profitable organization of the countryside promoted cities, trade, and wealth. Townspeople created new institutions of self-regulation and self-government. Kings and popes found new ways to exert their authority and test its limits. Scholars mastered the knowledge of the past and put it to use in classrooms, royal courts, papal offices, and the homes of the sick. Monks who fled the world ended up in positions of leadership: the great entrepreneurs of the twelfth century were the Cistercians; Saint Bernard was the most effective preacher of the Second Crusade.

Both Seljuk sultans and Byzantine emperors had to recognize the demands of elites. European rulers had, in addition, to reckon with the power of communities. They confronted and sometimes welcomed guilds and communes. The new theology of the time reinforced the importance of community by putting less emphasis on hierarchy and

Plate 5.13 Jael, Humility, and Judith (*c.*1140). In this early manuscript of the extremely popular *Mirror of Virgins*, exemplary women triumph over evil. Humility (in Latin, *humilitas*, a feminine noun) was the key virtue of the monastic life. Before she killed Holofernes, enemy of the Israelites, Judith prayed to God, reminding him that "the prayer of the humble and the meek hath always pleased thee" (Judith 9:16).

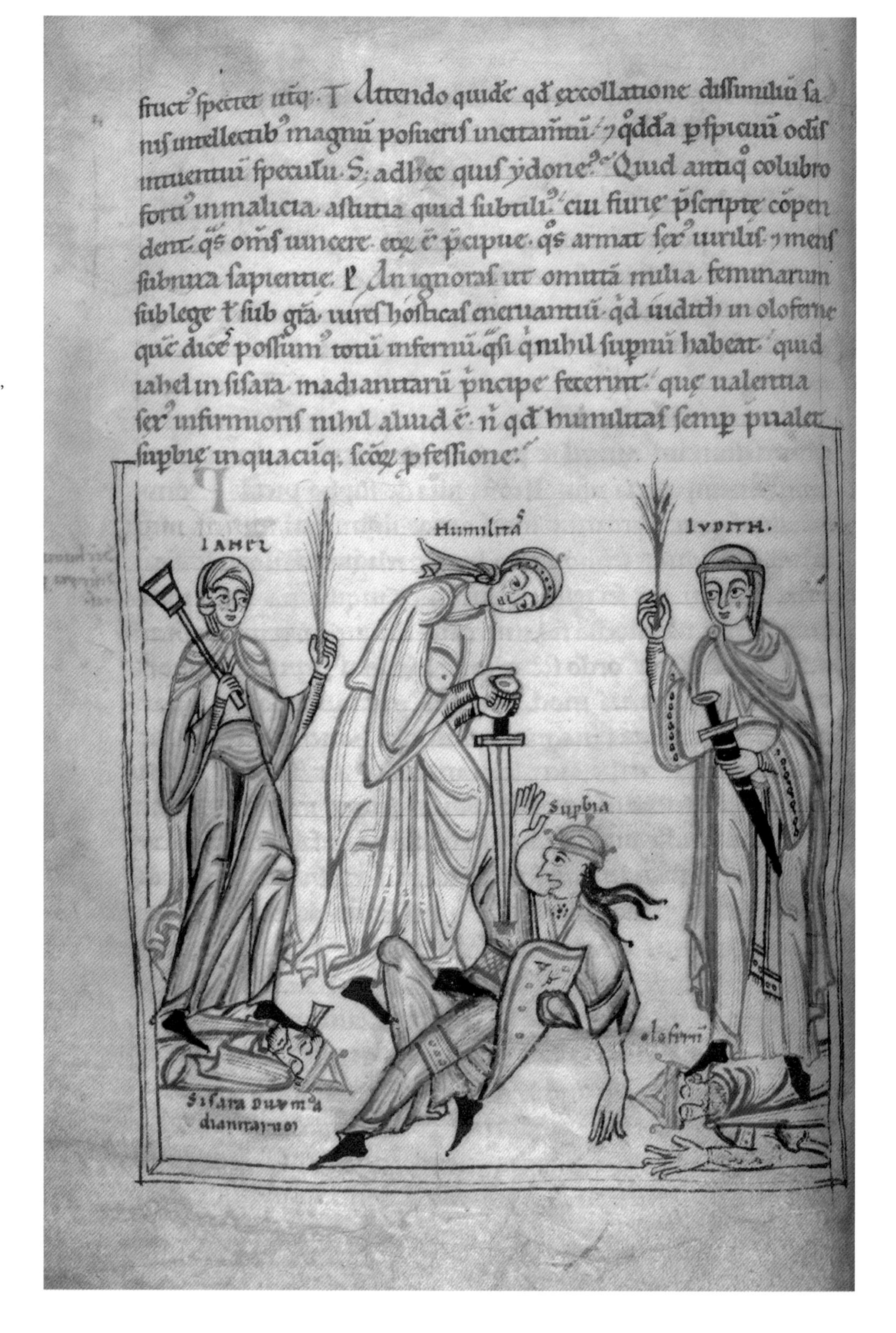

more on the dignity of each human being, the splendor of the natural world, and the nobility of reason. Historians speak of this development as "medieval humanism." In his theological treatise *Why God Became Man*, Anselm of Bec stressed Christ's humanity: Christ's sacrifice was that of one human being for another. The Cistercians spoke of God's mothering. Yet the stress on the loving bonds that tied Christians together also led to the persecution of others, like Jews and Muslims, who lived outside the Christian community. In the next century, Mongols from East Asia would move westward, changing yet again the configuration of the Islamic world, while Europeans moved eastward, taking over Constantinople itself.

CHAPTER FIVE: ESSENTIAL DATES

1066	Norman Conquest of England by William of Normandy
1071	Battle of Manzikert; Seljuk Turks defeat Byzantines
1075–1122	Investiture Conflict
1085	Conquest of Toledo by Alfonso VI
1094	Al-Andalus under Almoravid (Berber) control
1096–1099	The First Crusade; establishment of Crusader States
1122	Concordat of Worms; end of the Investiture Conflict
1147–1149	The Second Crusade

NOTES

1 Abu'l-Fazl Beyhaqi, *The Battle of Dandanqan*, in *Reading the Middle Ages: Sources from Europe, Byzantium, and the Islamic World*, 3rd ed., ed. Barbara H. Rosenwein (Toronto: University of Toronto Press, 2018), p. 243.

2 Nizam al-Mulk, *The Book of Policy*, in *Reading the Middle Ages*, p. 244.

3 *Frederick of Hamburg's Agreement with Colonists from Holland*, in *Reading the Middle Ages*, p. 246.

4 Henry I, *Privileges for the Citizens of London*, in *Reading the Middle Ages*, p. 250.

5 Cluny's *Foundation Charter*, in *Reading the Middle Ages*, p. 186.

6 Gregory VII, *Admonition to Henry IV*, in *Reading the Middle Ages*, p. 252.

7 Henry IV, *Letter to Gregory VII*, in *Reading the Middle Ages*, p. 254.

8 *Roman Lenten Synod*, in *The Correspondence of Pope Gregory VII: Selected Letters from the Registrum*, ed. and trans. Ephraim Emerton (New York: Columbia University Press, 1969), p. 91.

9 Robert the Monk, *Urban II Preaches the First Crusade*, in *Reading the Middle Ages*, pp. 262–63.

10 Ibn al-Qalanisi, *The Damascus Chronicle of the Crusades*, in *Reading the Middle Ages*, p. 270.

11 For siege engines, see "Reading through Looking," in *Reading the Middle Ages*, pp. XII–XIII, esp. Plate 8.

12 *Domesday Book*, in *Reading the Middle Ages*, p. 277.
13 Abelard, *Glosses on Porphyry*, in *Reading the Middle Ages*, p. 280.
14 Constantine the African's Translation of Johannitius's *Isagoge*, in *Reading the Middle Ages*, p. 281.
15 St. Bernard, *Apologia*, in *Reading the Middle Ages*, p. 288.
16 *Speculum Virginum*, trans. Barbara Newman, in *Listen, Daughter: The* Speculum Virginum *and the Formation of Religious Women in the Middle Ages*, ed. Constant J. Mews (New York: Palgrave Macmillan, 2001), p. 270.

FURTHER READING

Andrea, Alfred J., and Andrew Holt, eds. *Seven Myths of the Crusades*. Indianapolis: Hackett, 2015.
Barber, Malcolm. *Crusader States*. New Haven, CT: Yale University Press, 2012.
Bell, Nicholas. *Music in Medieval Manuscripts*. Toronto: University of Toronto Press, 2001.
Bruce, Scott G. *Cluny and the Muslims of La Garde-Freinet. Hagiography and the Problem of Islam in Medieval Europe*. Ithaca, NY: Cornell University Press, 2015.
Burton, Janet, and Julie Kerr. *The Cistercians in the Middle Ages*. Woodbridge: Boydell, 2011.
Catlos, Brian A. *Muslims of Medieval Latin Christendom, c. 1050–1614*. Cambridge: Cambridge University Press, 2014.
Christie, Niall. *Muslims and Crusaders: Christianity's Wars in the Middle East, 1095–1382, from the Islamic Sources*. London: Routledge, 2014.
Cobb, Paul M. *The Race for Paradise: An Islamic History of the Crusades*. Oxford: Oxford University Press, 2014.
El-Azhari, Taef. *Zengi and the Muslim Response to the Crusades: The Politics of Jihad*. London: Routledge, 2016.
Fromherz, Allen James. *The Near West: Medieval North Africa, Latin Europe and the Mediterranean in the Second Axial Age*. Edinburgh: Edinburgh University Press, 2016.
Hamilton, Louis I. *A Sacred City: Consecrating Churches and Reforming Society in Eleventh-Century Italy*. Manchester: Manchester University Press, 2010.
Harvey, Sally. *Domesday: Book of Judgement*. Oxford: Oxford University Press, 2014.
Little, Lester K. *Religious Poverty and the Profit Economy in Medieval Europe*. Ithaca, NY: Cornell University Press, 1978.
Messier, Ronald A. *The Almoravids and the Meanings of Jihad*. Santa Barbara, CA: Praeger, 2010.
Miller, Maureen C., ed. *Power and the Holy in the Age of the Investiture Conflict: A Brief History with Documents*. Boston: Bedford, 2005.
Morton, Nicholas Edward. *Encountering Islam on the First Crusade*. Cambridge: Cambridge University Press, 2016.
Peacock, A.C.S. *The Great Seljuk Empire*. Edinburgh: Edinburgh University Press, 2015.
Robinson, Ian S. *Henry IV of Germany*. Cambridge: Cambridge University Press, 2000.
Rubenstein, Jay. *The First Crusade: A Brief History with Documents*. Boston: Bedford/St. Martin's, 2015.
Thibodeaux, Jennifer D. *The Manly Priest: Clerical Celibacy, Masculinity, and Reform in England and Normandy, 1066–1300*. Philadelphia: University of Pennsylvania Press, 2015.

Toman, Rolf, ed. *Romanesque: Architecture, Sculpture, Painting*. Cologne: Könemann, 2010.

Yamroziak, Emilia. *The Cistercian Order in Medieval Europe, 1090–1500*. Abingdon: Routledge, 2013.

Yavari, Neguin. *The Future of Iran's Past: Nizam al-Mulk Remembered*. Oxford: Oxford University Press, 2018.

Yildiz, Sara Nur. *The Seljuk Empire of Anatolia*. Edinburgh: Edinburgh University Press, 2016.

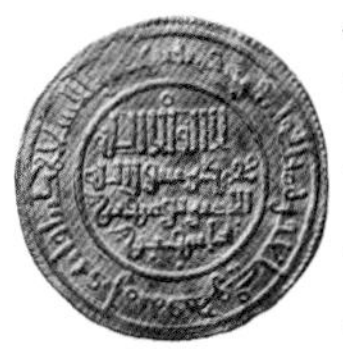

To test your knowledge of this chapter, please go to www.utphistorymatters.com for Study Questions.

SOURCES

PLATES

1.1 Scala/Art Resource, NY.
1.2 Jebulon/CC0 1.0.
1.3 Scala/Art Resource, NY.
1.4 © Vanni Archive/Art Resource, NY.
1.5 © Tyne & Wear Archives & Museums/Bridgeman Images.
1.6 Limestone stela with flat top and relief; Ghorfa; Carthage. © The Trustees of the British Museum. All rights reserved.
1.7 Scala/Art Resource, NY.
1.8 SEF/Art Resource, NY.
1.9 "Orant" Fresco, SS. Giovanni e Paolo, Rome, view of confessio (late 4th cent.). Reprinted by permission of the Ministero dell'Interno–Dipartimento per le Libertà civili e l'Immigrazione–Direzione Centrale per l'Amministrazione del Fondo Edifici di Culto.
1.10 Scala/Art Resource, NY.
1.11 Erich Lessing/Art Resource, NY.
1.12 Mihai Barbat/Alamy Stock Photo.
2.1 Cross from South Tympanum, Hagia Sophia. The Courtauld Institute of Art, London. Photograph by Ernest Hawkins. Reproduced by permission.
2.2 Islamic Arabic 1572a fol. 2r. Cadbury Research Library: Special Collections, University of Birmingham. Reproduced by permission.
2.3 © Andrea Jemolo: www.jemolo.com.
2.4 Square-headed brooch, Early Anglo-Saxon, Chessell Down. © The Trustees of the British Museum. All rights reserved.
2.5 Cotton Nero D.IV fol. 137v. Copyright © The British Library Board. All Rights Reserved.
2.6 Cotton Nero D.IV fol. 138v. Copyright © The British Library Board. All Rights Reserved.
2.7 Cotton Nero D.IV fol. 139. Copyright © The British Library Board. All Rights Reserved.
2.8 Scala/Art Resource, NY.
2.9 Cameraphoto Arte, Venice/Art Resource, NY.
2.10 Janzig/Europe/Alamy Stock Photo.
2.11 *Spatha* (FG2187). Photograph © Germanisches Nationalmuseum. Reproduced by permission.
2.12 MS 32, fol. 35v. Courtesy of Utrecht University Library.
3.1 Werner Forman Archive/Bridgeman Images.
3.2 MS gr. 510, fol. 78r. Reproduced by permission of the Bibliothèque nationale de France.
3.3 180 AH/796-797 Aquamanile in the Form of an Eagle; The State Hermitage Museum, St. Petersburg. Photograph © The State Hermitage Museum/photo by Vladimir Terebenin, Leonard Kheifets, Yuri Molodkovets.
3.4 Panel (lid from a chest?), second half 8th century, wood (fig); mosaic with bone and four different types of wood, Samuel D. Lee Fund, 1937. Image courtesy of the Metropolitan Museum of Art/CC0 1.0.
3.5 Scala/Art Resource, NY.
3.6 MS lat. 2291, fol. 14v. Reproduced by permission of the Bibliothèque nationale de France.
3.7 MS Voss. lat. Q. 79, fol. 30v. Leiden University Library. Reproduced by permission.

3.8 bpk, Berlin/Staatsbibliothek zu Berlin/Art Resource, NY.

3.9 MS lat. 257, fol. 147v. Reproduced by permission of the Bibliothèque nationale de France.

4.1 Erich Lessing/Art Resource, NY.

4.2 *Jug*, 900s. Iran or Iraq, Baghdad, Buyid Period, reign of Samsam al-Dawla (985–998 AD). Gold with repoussé and chased and engraved decoration; overall: 12.5 x 10.2 cm (4 ⅞ x 4 in.); diameter of base: w. 7 cm (2 ¾ in.). The Cleveland Museum of Art, purchase from the J.H. Wade Fund 1966.22. © The Cleveland Museum of Art.

4.3 travelpixs/Alamy Stock Photo.

4.4 Ivan Vdovin/Alamy Stock Photo.

4.5 akg-images/De Agostini Picture Library.

4.6 MS 24, fol. 52v. Photograph by Anja Runkel. Reproduced by permission of Stadtbibliothek/Stadtarchiv Trier.

4.7 MS 1640, fol. 117r. Hessische Landes- und Hochschulbibliothek Darmstadt. Reproduced by permission of Universitäts- und Landesbibliothek Darmstadt.

4.8 Bayerische Staatsbibliothek München, Clm 4453, fol. 139v. CC-BY-NC-SA 4.0.

4.9 By permission of Det Kongelige Bibliotek.

4.10 Royal MS 10 A XIII, f. 2v. British Library/ Granger, NYC—All Rights Reserved.

4.11 Bayerische Staatsbibliothek München, Clm 14000. CC-BY-NC-SA 4.0.

5.1 B. O'Kane/Alamy Stock Photo.

5.2 JTB Photo/Universal Images Group/Getty Images.

5.3 B. O'Kane/Alamy Stock Photo.

5.4 akg-images/Gerard Degeorge.

5.5 Inv. no. 9/2001, The David Collection. Photograph by Pernille Klemp. Reproduced by permission.

5.6 Anthony Scibilia/Art Resource, NY.

5.7 Sant Tomàs de Fluvià (Toroella). Photograph by Heinz Hebeisen. Reproduced by permission of Iberimage.

5.8 Photograph by Barbara H. Rosenwein.

5.9 © Emmanuel PIERRE/Romanes.com. Reproduced by permission.

5.10 Allie_Caulfield/CC-BY-SA 2.0.

5.11 Add 17302, fol. 52r. British Library/ Granger, NYC—All Rights Reserved.

5.12 Reproduced by permission of Stan Parry.

5.13 Arundel 44, fol. 34v. British Library/ Granger, NYC—All Rights Reserved.

FIGURES

1.1 From Deborah Mauskopf Deliyannis, *Ravenna in Late Antiquity* (Cambridge: Cambridge University Press, 2010), Fig. 78, p. 227. Courtesy of Cambridge University Press.

2.1 Adapted from Stefan Karwiese, *Gros is die Artemis von Ephesos* (Vienna: Phoibos Verlag, 1995), Maps 5 and 6. Courtesy of Österreichisches Archäologisches Institut.

2.2 Reconstruction drawing of Saxon Yeavering AD 627, by Peter Dunn (English Heritage Graphics Team). Historic England/Mary Evans. Reproduced by permission.

3.1 Adapted from J.J. Norwich, ed., *Great Architecture of the World* (DeCapo, 2001), p. 133.

5.1 Adapted from Christian Sapin (dir.), *Archéologie et architecture d'un site monastique: 10 ans de recherche à l'abbaye Saint-Germain d'Auxerre* (Auxerre: Centre d'etudes medievales; Paris: CTHS, 2000), Figs. 3 and 371.

5.2 Adapted from Linda Seidel, *Legends in Limestone: Lazarus, Gislebertus, and the Cathedral of Autun* (Chicago: University of Chicago Press, 1999), p. 120, original drawing attributed to Anthony Titus.

5.3 Adapted from Wolfgang Braunfels, *Monasteries of Western Europe: The Architecture of the Orders* (Princeton: Princeton University Press, 1972), p. 84.

MAPS

1.7 © Henri Galinie.

3.1 "Imperial Territory and the Themes, c. 917," from Mark Whittow, *The Making of Orthodox Byzantium, 600–1025* (Berkeley: University of California Press, 1996), p. 166. Reproduced with permission of Palgrave Macmillan.

4.1 Adapted from Linda Safran, *Heaven on Earth: Art and the Church in Byzantium* (University Park, PA: Penn State UP, 1998), Images 1.7 and 1.9.

5.1 "Byzantium and the Islamic World, c. 1090," from Christophe Picard, *Le monde musulman du XIe du XVe au siecle*. Copyright © Armand Colin, 2000. Reproduced by permission.

INDEX

Page numbers for illustrations appear in italics.